the sociology of urban regions

sociology series

John F. Cuber, *editor*
Alfred C. Clarke, *associate editor*

the sociology of urban regions

alvin boskoff
emory university

second edition

APPLETON-CENTURY-CROFTS
Educational Division

New York   MEREDITH CORPORATION

to katie, andy, and alex

contents

List of Tables ix

List of Illustrations xi

Preface to the Second Edition xiii

Preface to the First Edition xv

I

orientation to human communities

1. The Sociological Approach to the Community and Region 3
2. The City as an Emergent Type of Community 11
3. The Problem of Classifying Urban Regions 28

II

the interplay of demographic, ecological, and cultural themes

4. The Peopling of Urban Regions: Basic Population Characteristics and Trends 41
5. Ecological Organization: Understanding the Sociogeographic Differentiation of Urban Communities 77
6. The Dynamics of Urban Ecological Patterns 94
7. Emergence and Structure of the Urban Region: Suburb, Satellite, and Fringe 106
8. The Urban Regional System: A Theoretical Approach to Urban Specialization and Imperfect Coordination 131

III

social organization and cultural foci of the urban region

9. Primary Groups 153
10. Voluntary Groups and Formal Associations 172

11. Social Class Divisions in Urban Regions   190
12. Urban Power Structure: Decision Making on Public Issues   219
13. Major Urban Institutions: The Political Economy   236
14. Major Urban Institutions: Religion, Education, and Welfare   270
15. Mass Communications and Urban Leisure: A New Urban Ethic   292

V
urban planning and social problems

16. Social Problems and the Urban Region   313
17. Planning as an Urban Institution   324
18. Corrective Planning   338
19. Creative Planning: An Application of Urban Sociology?   360
Index   379

tables

Table 1. Typology of Cities by Profile of Occupational Distributions, as Expressed in Occupational Scores   30

Table 2. Urbanized Population, by Size Category and Continent, 1960   43

Table 3. Urban and Rural Population of the U.S. for Selected Decades   43

Table 4. Growth of Population in Standard Metropolitan Statistical Areas, by Central City and Ring Areas, and by Effect of Annexation, 1950 to 1960   44

Table 5. U.S. Population in Groups of Places Classified by Size, 1950 and 1960   45

Table 6. Age Distribution by Type of Urban and Rural Residence, 1960   47

Table 7. Age Distribution in Japan, by Size of Commune, 1930 and 1950   47

Table 8. Sex Ratio of Urban and Rural Areas of the U.S., by Race, 1960   49

Table 9. Sex Ratio of Urban and Rural Population: India, 1891–1941   50

Table 10. Sex Ratios in Japan, by Types of Area, 1920–1955   51

Table 11. Males Per 100 Females in the Civilian Population, by Type of Residence, April, 1959 and 1950   52

Table 12. Median Age at First Marriage, by Sex, 1920–1965   53

Table 13. Median Age at First Marriage, by Color and Sex, by Urban and Rural Areas, 1960   54

Table 14. Median Age at First Marriage for Those Married in 1891 to 1960, by Sex and Urban and Rural Residence   54

Table 15. Median Years Difference in Age Between Mates for First Marriages, by Rural and Urban Residence, 1960   55

Table 16. Marital Status of United States Population Over 14 Years, by Sex and Urban and Rural Residence, 1960   56

Table 17. Households, Families, and Subfamilies in the United States, by Residence, March, 1967   57

Table 18. Selected Educational Attainments of Persons 25 Years and Older in the United States, March, 1967, by Race and Place of Residence   58

Table 19. Composition of the Employed Male Labor Force by Major Occupational Group and Urban and Rural Residence   59

Table 20. Percent Distribution of Income Among Families in the United States, 1959, by Area and Size of Place   61

Table 21. Family Income by Race and Urban and Rural Residence, 1965   62

Table 22. Median Family Income by Age of Head and Residence, 1959   63

Table 23. Median Family Income by Size of Family and Residence, 1959   63

Table 24. Median Family Income by Number of Earners and Residence, 1959   63

Table 25. Racial Distribution of the U.S. Population by Urban and Rural Residence, 1950 and 1960   64

Table 26. Percent Distribution of the U.S. Population by Race and Nativity for Central Cities and Suburbs of Urbanized Areas, 1950   65

Table 27. Percent Distribution of Religious Affiliations in the United States Civilian Population, by Residence, March 1957   66

Table 28. Children Born Per Thousand Women Aged 15–44 Years, and 45 and Over, by Urban and Rural Residence, 1960–1964   67

Table 29. Child-Woman Ratios by Urban and Rural Areas, Gross Reproduction Rates, and Net Reproduction Rates for Selected Nations, 1959–1962   68

Table 30. Age-Adjusted Mortality Rates, by Color and Residence, United States, 1940 and 1950   69

Table 31. Components of Population Change for Metropolitan and Non-metropolitan Population Areas, 1960–1965 and 1950–1960   69

Table 32. Migration Patterns Among Males in the U.S., 1949, by Community of Origin and Destination   72

Table 33. Percentage of Ethnic Distribution of Population in Durban According to Sociographic Zones, 1951   101

Table 34. Differential Membership in Formal Organizations, by Residential Category and Population Type, 1953   178

Table 35. Differences of Formal Group Participation for Selected Status Characteristics in the Detroit Area   180

Table 36. Life-Styles in a National Sample of Housewives, 1960   199

Table 37. Occupational Distribution of Employed Civilian Workers in the U.S., 1940–1960 (Selected Characteristics) and Projections to 1975   240

Table 38. Local Government Revenue in the United States, by Source, 1962   254

Table 39. Social Class Composition of Major Religious Groups in the U.S., 1945–1946   273

Table 40. Forms of Specialization in Social Welfare in Modern Urban Regions   287

Table 41. Effects of Primary Group Pressures on the Voting Behavior of Different Categories of Voters   303

Table 42. Types of Societal Complexity and Responses to Problems   317

Table 43. A Comparison of Dominant Values in Planning, Political, and Economic Institutions of the Modern World   325

Table 44. Classification of Urban Planning Orientations   336

illustrations

Figure 1. Continuum of Community Types in Terms of Social and Cultural
    Complexity   12
Figure 2. Synoptic Classification of Urban Regions   36
Figure 3. Age Distribution in the Largest Cities of India as a Percentage of
    the All-India Distribution, 1931   48
Figure 4. Typology of Social Areas in Cities, by Social Rank and Degree of
    Urbanization   85
Figure 5. The Orthodox Ecological Structure of Cities   89
Figure 6. The Symbolic Ecological Structure of Cities   90
Figure 7. The Symbolic Ecology of New Orleans (*ca.* 1940)   92
Figure 8. A Simplified Ecological Diagram of the Urban Region   107
Figure 9. A Suggested Classification of Suburbs   114
Figure 10. Types of Integration   144
Figure 11. Types of Power Structure   145
Figure 12. A Schematic Version of the Structure of Urban Life-Styles   182
Figure 13. Major Urban Life-Styles and Related Strata   200
Figure 14. Types of Power Structure   224
Figure 15. Map of Seattle, Washington, Showing 17 Types of Governmental
    Jurisdiction   260
Figure 16. Basic Structure of Urban Mass Communication Systems   298
Figure 17. The Formal Structure of Urban Planning Organization in the So-
    viet Union   334
Figure 18. The Structure of the Finger Metropolis   376

preface to the second edition

Interest in urban affairs has become so widespread and strident in the last few years that a responsible and relevant treatment of urban features is more difficult than ever. The chaos of current disagreements, protests, indecision, and official inefficiency suggest to some that urbanism is either dying or has become so unstructured that sociological analysis is incapable of capturing the reality of the modern city and its harrowed residents. But legitimate concern for immediate and very disturbing urban problems should not dispel the perennial need for perspective and the continuing necessity of relating recent events to broader trends and processes in human association.

In preparing this second edition, I have had the benefit of constructive criticism and suggestions from many students and colleagues all over the nation, as well as gratifying encouragement on the general content and treatment of the first edition. Therefore, in deciding on the character of changes for this revision, it seemed wise to avoid merely updating material, or attempting a radical alteration in the design of discussions. Instead, I have made the following changes:

1. The materials on population (Chapter 4) have been compressed somewhat for more realistic use by the student. In addition, though the 1960 census data were the latest basic source, in many instances I was able to incorporate data from official sources for the latter part of the sixties.

2. Chapter 7 has been expanded to include a rather full discussion of different types of suburbs, as well as a discussion of phases of suburban growth. In addition, a study of different family types in an Atlanta suburban zone—completed just after the first edition was published—has been included to illustrate the subtle heterogeneity of suburban populations, which cannot be captured by occupational and income differences.

3. The earlier chapter "The Urban Regional System" has been completely revised to provide a more detailed theoretical orientation to the normal functioning and basic problems of complex urban areas. Specifically, the revised chapter focuses on eight general urban processes of development and four urban processes of coordination, all of which are used to suggest different kinds of interdependence in urban regions. For greater utility, this theoretical material has been moved from the earlier Chapter 14 to the current Chapter 8.

4. Chapter 11, "Social Class Divisions in Urban Regions," incorporates a greatly extended discussion of urban styles of life, and perhaps the only available analysis of phases in the process of social mobility in urban regions.

5. A new chapter on Urban Power Structure (Chapter 12) provides not only a comprehensive review of contemporary issues and investigations in this controversial field, but also (a) a pointed historical summary of trends in urban power systems, (b) a tentative distinction among contemporary forms of power structure, (c) a step-by-step analysis of urban decision making, and (d) a provisional theory of developments in current power structures.

6. The two chapters on urban institutions (now Chapters 13 and 14) have been considerably revised and somewhat expanded, though the richness of materials has only been sampled because of space limitations. The most significant change is an orientation to the political economy of urban regions, with emphasis on basic economic processes and mechanisms and an understanding of closely related aspects of political participation. Religion, education, and welfare have been reanalyzed and updated as a "cultural package." Essentially, discussions of these institutions are constructed around the pressure of lower class life-styles on traditional programs.

7. Finally, in Part IV, a great many minor changes were necessitated by the intervening alterations in events on the planning front. Greater attention is now given to housing and urban renewal and controversies about their effectiveness, to transportation problems and projects, and to the recent initiation of Model Cities programs. For other nations, planning developments in England, France, and the Netherlands are given somewhat more attention. As case studies of New Towns, I have added discussions of Reston, Virginia; Columbia, Maryland; and Ciudad Guyana, Venezuela.

I gratefully acknowledge permission to use various materials from the following sources: American Sociological Association, Jonathan Cape, McGraw-Hill, Frederick A. Praeger, Princeton University Press, Urban Land Institute, University of Michigan, University of California Press, John Wiley & Sons.

A. B.

Emory University

preface to the first edition

An understanding of modern man's increasingly typical habitat—the city and the urban region—is a practical necessity for almost everyone. But this is by no means a simple problem. Studies of virtually every aspect of city life, from a number of standpoints, are already overwhelming in quantity and quite confusing in their findings and implications. Sociologists are intensely interested in urban life and its extension for several reasons, but perhaps most significantly because so many sociological questions are increasingly (if not exclusively) matters of human behavior and relationships in an urban setting. Marriage and family problems, child rearing, crime, delinquency, migration, race relations, old age, mental health, social class, religion, education, and public opinion trends are only a sprinkling of the crucial problems that are found in, or derive from, an urbanized way of life.

In this work, I have tried to present an organized review and interpretation of the sociologist's work on the nature of contemporary urban regions as clusters of areas that seem to form a new kind of community. Specifically, considerable attention has been given to: (1) the unique features of urban communities; (2) the historical background of modern urbanism; (3) the continuous changes and adjustments in values and organization that accompany urban development; and (4) the rise of urban planning as an attempt to preserve the essence of urban life under conditions of rapid social and cultural change. Where possible, examples have been drawn from urban regions in various parts of the world; however, the primary focus is on the United States and modern European settings.

As indicated in numerous places throughout the book, I am indebted to many investigators of urban life for important information and helpful viewpoints. My students in classes on Urban Sociology through the years have also been unwitting but extremely necessary collaborators in discussions of many issues that await the reader. Also, I gratefully acknowledge permission to use various materials from the following publishers, periodicals, or individuals: The Free Press of Glencoe, Inc.; Princeton University Press; University of California Press; University of Michigan Press; University of Chicago Press; Jonathan Cape, Ltd.; King's Crown Press; Russell Sage Foundation; Twentieth Century Fund; The Macmillan Company; Harcourt, Brace &

World; Thomas Y. Crowell Company; *Social Forces;* American Sociological Association; International City Managers Association; John Wiley & Sons, Inc.; Morris Axelrod; Herbert H. Hyman; Wendell Bell; Morris Janowitz.

A. B.

Emory University

orientation to human communities

1

the sociological approach to the community and region

The human community, in its various forms, is one of man's most intriguing inventions. Since community is a hoary creation—so ancient that man without community is inconceivable—perhaps we might add that, throughout the long history of the human species, man has been changing the nature of his communities in a number of ways. These changes, which reflect the vicissitudes and achievements of human history, constitute a series of sociocultural experiments in providing a suitable context for the persistence of the species and a thrilling but checkered quest for the limits of man's potentialities.

No complexity of argument is needed to acknowledge not only the practical significance of community, but also its intellectual and emotional significance for humans. In their distinctive ways, religion, philosophy, art and literature, economics, geography, politics and political science, anthropology, and welfare movements have concerned themselves to some degree with the nature and problems of this constantly evolving invention. We owe a great deal to their respective insights and their efforts to focus man's attention on the community context. However, these contributions are understandably incidental to the more specialized objectives of each of these fields. From the very nature of human communities, the major (but not exclusive) responsibility for their analysis and understanding rests on the unique skills and viewpoint of sociology, which in the last 30 years has emphasized its obligation through a Himalayan mass of relevant researches and analyses. At the present time, therefore, we may justifiably conclude that a genuine, comprehensive study of community and the sociology of the community are virtually synonymous.

community and its dimensions

Since general usage of this important term is often vague and sometimes contradictory, we can best open the sociological approach by offering an initial, orienting definition of community and exploring the relations between community and region in complex societies. In the most general sense, we may define the community as a *relatively self-contained constellation of variably interdependent social groups within a definite, manageable geographic area, which, through their interrelated functioning, provide minimal satisfaction of the basic and acquired needs of their members.* However, a definition is an invitation, not a consummation; it requires elaboration, specification, and additional explanation.

Implicit in this definition is the conception of human communities as products of interacting parts, factors, or dimensions of human experience. First and most obvious is the character of the *population*—the socially relevant physical traits of the social aggregate (numbers, density, sex, age, etc.). Second, and likewise obvious, is the nature and extent of the *land area* (size, soil fertility, climate, resources, topography) occupied by a definite population. Third, we must recognize (*a*) a constant set of biological or basic needs or drives common to all normal human organisms, making proper allowances for age and sex differences, and (*b*) an infinitely variable set of learned needs (values, norms, goals, etc.—in short, *culture*), which serve to modify and often dominate the purely biological drives. Fourth, and closely related to (*b*), there is a more or less distinct distribution of specific technical skills, which are developed and employed to implement the satisfaction of biological and acquired needs. Finally, every community exhibits a typical *social organization*—composed of definite social groups and their interaction—which organizes and coordinates the potentialities of the previously mentioned factors and thus sustains an identity visible both to participants and observers.

community as a level of analysis

The detailed description of these dimensions and their empirical combinations in the urban community and region are focal and continuing objectives of this book. Therefore, we may now comfortably resist the temptation to anticipate discussions in later chapters. Instead, it may be helpful at this point to conceive of the community (defined in terms of these five dimensions) as a level of *social reality*. For those who might be perturbed by the epistemological implications of this term, let us therefore define "level of social reality" as the level or context of social *experience*—i.e., the level of meaningful stimuli, of the conscious or implicit projection of social behavior, and the level of consequences generated by such behavior. To develop perspective for analyzing the community (and particularly the urban community), let us consider the following simplified typology of social levels:

1. The *group* level. At this level, interest is focused on the structure and operation of analytically isolated sets of interaction—a family, a gang, an office clique, a governmental agency, etc. This is the realm in sociology and social psychology of group dynamics, small group research, formal organization, and socialization. On this level, groups are conceived as closed systems, legitimately abstracted from wider contexts.

2. The *community* level, as defined above.

3. The *regional* level.

4. The *societal* level.

5. Potentially, the level of *intraplanetary society*.

For present purposes, we may ignore levels 1, 4, and 5 and attempt to establish a crucial connection between the community and regional levels.

region as extension of community

Our earlier definition treated community as a "relatively self-contained constellation" of interrelated social groups. This was meant to be an orienting definition to community in general and therefore must be appropriately modified to take account of variations in types of community. Clearly, such a definition refers principally to small, agricultural communities in slowly changing societies, and in an overwhelming proportion of man's residence on this planet. However, the urban community type (and its subtypes) in antiquity, and with even more salience in modern society, is by its very nature an accessible and peculiarly dependent entity. As we shall see later in more detail (Chapter 7), the urban community characteristically stimulates the creation (or the modification) of surrounding communities in a network of interdependencies that constitute a complex innovation in human experience. This constellation of communities about a politically delimited urban center might be called a supercommunity, but we shall refer to it throughout this book as an *urban region*. Increasingly, study of human behavior in the urban center is inseparable from behavior and social organization in the urban region. Hence the title of this book: *The Sociology of Urban Regions*.

Indeed, the nature of the urban community type and its product—the urban region—subtly provides added significance to the community context of human experience. Whereas preurban community types functioned as rather isolated shells for their inhabitants—so that community and society were almost identical—the urban region now appears to be a two-way intermediary link between its component groups on the one hand and the environing society and the world on the other hand. As a consequence, the impact of changes within the urban region and in the broader social structures is quickly communicated to persons participating in both contexts. The urban region, therefore, becomes the crucial focus for understanding the complexities, the problems, the achievements, and the limitations of modern society.

understanding the community

Most readers are of course familiar with several concrete examples of the urban community and the urban region. They know its various parts through personal experience or through the media of magazines, films, and newspapers. Slum area, "Chinatown," "Beacon Hill," "the Gold Coast," downtown, suburbia, the freeway, "Wall Street," the university campus, mammoth shopping centers, the City Hall, hobohemia, the country club—these are not merely places, but symbols [1] of a wide range of activities and of the heterogeneous people who live, work, and expire in the urban region. But how do these interesting fragments unite to form the fascinating amalgam of communities called the urban region?

Essentially, this question simultaneously poses the underlying problem of this book and of the sociology of urban regions: understanding and explaining the peculiarities of the urban community and region in the modern world. This is obviously a large order, which can be filled most effectively with separable aspects of the basic problem. Indeed, research experience and serious thinking seem to distinguish four relevant foci of attention, investigation, and generalization. First, we may mention problems in the emergence and specific location of urban centers. This will be reviewed in Chapter 5. Second, there is the problem of analyzing the unfolding of community and regional development through the differentiation of their component parts in a complex sociogeographic division of labor. Chapters 5 and 6 are primarily concerned with this aspect. Third, an understanding of the urban region requires explicit and careful concern for the special mechanisms by which these component parts are organized and coordinated into a recognizable and unique entity. This is perhaps the most difficult and least understood facet of our larger problem; it will be given some discussion in Chapters 7 and 8. Finally, and perhaps most characteristically, there is the necessity of acquiring and deepening our understanding of social and cultural change in the urban region, of the practical difficulties and potentialities accompanying such changes, and of the typical readjustments which have either been devised or which can be reasonably predicted. To this important set of problems we devote all of Part IV.

[1] Kevin Lynch, *The Image of the City* (Cambridge, Mass., Harvard University Press, 1960).

a basic sociological approach

The sociological approach to these problems, which is basic to the discussions that follow, deals with the urban region as a relatively closed system
of structures and cultural patterns,[2] which operate to create and sustain the
identity of the region and likewise produce variations and changes in its
organization. This approach should be conceived as an attempt to provide a
useful, broad, orienting hypothesis—a reference point for investigation and
analysis—rather than a mental strait jacket. Because of the complexity of the
urban region, we would expect both a realm of organization and consistency,
and a puzzling component of unarticulated, nonconnectable activities and
values. We take the tentative position that an overwhelming proportion of
social behavior in urban regions is amenable to understanding, with proper
analysis, against the backdrop of the larger and more complex system. Pockets
of inconsistency, however, do exist and we shall take note of them whenever
necessary.

In considering the urban region as a sociological system, we shall find it
necessary to distinguish its parts and their interconnections (structure) in a
meaningful way. Familiar and indispensable sociological concepts—social
relations, social role, primary group, secondary group, status, class, elite,
ethnic category, etc.—are therefore important means of sifting and organizing
the multitudinous facts of urban life. But we must recognize that these facts
have both genesis and consequences, that persons and groups in the urban
system engage in social actions (behavior directed toward other persons and
groups) which exhibit developments and variations in specific time periods
and in definable units of space. Therefore, we shall use two kinds of sociological concepts to capture the dynamic elements in urban regional systems. On
the one hand, we shall have reference to *social processes* (such as cooperation,
conflict, accommodation) as relatively conscious and clear-cut means of im-
plementing values and pursuing social needs. To give proper prominence to
the unintended effects of social processes, on the other hand, we shall attempt
to analyze the *latent functional consequences* of urban behavior patterns—and
particularly as these consequences are embodied in *adaptive sociocultural
innovations*.[3] For example, the frequently studied ecological processes (competition, centralization, invasion, and succession) are best understood, from

[2] This viewpoint is persuasively discussed by Florian Znaniecki, *The Method of
Sociology* (New York, Rinehart & Co., 1934), Chap. I. See also Harry M. Johnson,
Sociology: A Systematic Introduction (New York, Harcourt, Brace, and World, 1960),
Chap. III.
[3] Robert K. Merton, *Social Theory and Social Structure*, revised and enlarged edi-
tion (New York, The Free Press of Glencoe, 1957), Chaps. I, IV, V.

the sociological standpoint, as latent consequences of numerous social action processes.[4]

A final sociological concept is imperative in the study of urban regions: social change. This term has suffered from so many abuses and permutations of meaning that consensus among sociologists is still difficult to achieve. However, since social organization is a dominating dimension of the urban region and since numerous variations in behavior and organization are repeatedly found by participants and observers, a concept of social change is required to aid in distinguishing and analyzing these phenomena. For reasons that are developed elsewhere,[5] social change will be used to refer to significant variations or alterations in the organization, functioning, and interrelations of social groups in a given community, region, or society. The study of social change in the urban region consequently demands attention to four related aspects: (a) the description of specific social change processes; (b) the search for explanatory factors in production of social changes; (c) the patterns of initial reactions to such changes—maladjustments, conflicts, etc.; and (d) the processes of adaptation and incorporation of social changes.

the need for auxiliary approaches

While the sociological orientation sketched in the preceding pages is conceived to be basic to the understanding of urban regions, the complexity of urban regions appears to justify the use of several auxiliary approaches. On hindsight, these are most profitably employed, not as alternatives or competitors, but as supplements to the sociological approach. Indeed, it is suggested that they be used whenever one or more of these supplementary viewpoints seems to be appropriate for specific problems in the study of urban regions. The most important auxiliary approaches are the following.

1. The *historical*. To provide perspective as well as rich comparative materials on earlier forms of the urban community, the historical approach has much to offer. Sociologists have often ignored historical materials in recent decades for several reasons; but it is becoming increasingly evident that this attitude closes off a broad avenue of information on processes of community and regional development.[6] Incidentally, the recent emergence of

---

[4] These processes are discussed by James A. Quinn, *Human Ecology* (Englewood Cliffs, N.J., Prentice-Hall, 1950), Part III; and Amos H. Hawley, *Human Ecology* (New York, Ronald Press, 1950), Parts III and V. See also Otis D. Duncan and Leo F. Schnore, "Cultural, Behavioral, and Ecological Perspectives in the Study of Social Organization," *American Journal of Sociology*, 65 (September, 1959), pp. 132–146.

[5] Alvin Boskoff, "Social Change: Major Problems in the Emergence of Theoretical and Research Foci," in Howard Becker and Alvin Boskoff, eds., *Modern Sociological Theory* (New York, Dryden Press, 1957), pp. 263–267.

[6] See especially Max Weber, *The City*, trans. by Don Martindale (New York, The Free Press of Glencoe, 1958); Carl Bridenbaugh, *Cities in the Wilderness* (New York, Ronald Press, 1938) and *Cities in Revolt* (New York, Alfred A. Knopf, 1945); Richard

an urban historical interest among many professional historians performs a distinctly useful service for the sociologist of urban regions.

2. The *demographic*. Since a community or region obviously is dependent on available personnel and their socially relevant physical characteristics, the demographic or population aspect must be given some attention by the sociologist. Population size, density, age and sex distribution, racial and ethnic composition, birth and death patterns, migration, etc., furnish specific clues to the human resources and deficiencies of given areas. Population trends may be viewed as consequences of social and valuational systems and likewise as conditions which affect the stability or variability of these systems.[7]

3. The *ecological*. There is some confusion about the meaning of the ecological approach in social phenomena. Much of the so-called ecological work by sociologists in recent decades seems to aim principally at discerning clear-cut *spatial distributions* of activities and population characteristics. However, while definitions and objectives are always somewhat arbitrary, this orientation seems unduly limited. In view of the history of the term and the special problems of sociology, it might be more useful to consider the ecological approach as generally concerned with the *mechanisms* by which human groups adjust to or modify the physical environment. To the extent that values can be even temporarily ignored in this approach, the human ecologist focuses on three related aspects: (*a*) the spatial distribution of groups and activities; (*b*) the conditions or factors in adjustment to subareas; and (*c*) the nature of the interrelations between and among subareas in an overall sociogeographic division of labor.[8] Since the community and region function with definable geographic bases, the ecological approach is one of the essential preparatory tools used by the urban sociologist.

4. The *cultural-valuational*. The temptation to explain human communities in mechanical, deterministic terms—as expressions of impersonal and irreversible forces—has a long and disastrous history. However, both historical perspective and the contemporary development of the social sciences

M. Morse, *From Community to Metropolis* (Gainesville, University of Florida Press, 1958); Richard C. Wade, *The Urban Frontier* (Cambridge, Mass., Harvard University Press, 1959); Eric F. Goldman, ed., *Historiography and Urbanization* (Baltimore, Johns Hopkins Press, 1941); Caroline F. Ware, ed., *The Cultural Approach to History* (New York, Columbia University Press, 1940); Henri Pirenne, *Les Villes et les institutions urbaines* (Paris, Alcan, 1939), 2 vols.; W. G. Hoskins, *Local History in England* (London, Longmans, Green, 1959); Asa Briggs, *Victorian Cities* (London, Odhams Books, 1963); Werner J. Cahnman, "The Historical Sociology of Cities: A Critical Review," *Social Forces*, 45 (December, 1966), pp. 155–161.

[7] Textbooks in population that emphasize this viewpoint to some degree include: Paul H. Landis and Paul K. Hatt, *Population Problems: A Cultural Interpretation*, 2nd ed. (New York, American Book Company, 1954); Warren S. Thompson, *Population Problems*, 4th ed. (New York, McGraw-Hill, 1953); Harold A. Phelps and David Henderson, *Population in its Human Aspects* (New York, Appleton-Century-Crofts, Inc., 1958); William Petersen, *Population Problems* (New York, Macmillan, 1961).

[8] Quinn, *op. cit.*, Parts I and IV; Hawley, *op. cit.*, Chaps. VI, XII–XIV.

furnish overwhelming evidence of human creativity and learning processes—values, ideas, desires, sentiments—in social phenomena. We shall, therefore, give considerable attention to cultural developments in the urban region. In particular, the economic aspect of culture—in which are located values of practical rationality, reduction of human efforts in specific enterprises, and standards of use and distribution of desired objects and services—requires appropriate study, without the easy but dangerous shift to economic determinism.[9]

5. The *psychological*. Increasingly, the understanding of complex human productions—especially the modern urban region—is enhanced at crucial points by exploring the psychological impact of typical experiences and situations on specific persons. Sociological analysis inevitably needs some psychological supplement, and vice versa. But the urban region is characteristically changeful and therefore always relatively new in some respects to its inhabitants. In general, we employ the psychological orientation to provide relevant analyses of variation in personality formation (for convenience, in the form of personality types). These variations may be considered responses to unique features of urban living and potentially, at least, as contributing factors in certain urban developments (e.g., the "picture window," the suburban movement, the "do it yourself" fad).[10]

[9] See Robert M. MacIver and Charles H. Page, *Society* (New York, Holt, Rinehart & Winston, 1949), Chaps. XXV, XXVI.

[10] See Gardner Murphy, *Personality* (New York, Harper & Brothers, 1947); S. Kirson Weinberg, *Society and Personality Disorders* (Englewood Cliffs, N.J., Prentice-Hall, 1952), Part I.

selected references

LYNCH, Kevin, *The Image of the City* (Cambridge, Mass., Harvard University Press, 1960).

NELSON, Lowry, RAMSEY, Charles E., and VERNER, Coolie, *Community Structure and Change* (New York, Macmillan, 1960).

SANDERS, Irwin T., *The Community: An Introduction to a Social System* (New York, Ronald Press, 1958), Chaps. I, VIII, XI.

ZIMMERMAN, Carle C., *The Changing Community* (New York, Harper & Brothers, 1938), Chaps. I–IV.

2

the city as an emergent type of community

Human society has been preeminently rural and localized throughout the approximately one million years of its development and for the larger part of the world's population in the modern era (1850 to date). Much of this rural experience is forever lost to us because a concern for posterity through record keeping (the stuff of history) is essentially alien to the uncontaminated rural life-style. Indeed, Spengler insists that rural peoples have no history, that history as we know it is a property of *developing* societies.[1]

But it is clear that some rural communities in antiquity were decidedly unlike their counterparts in other areas of the world; they were the scene of slowly cumulative cultural changes that eventually made possible a complex and inherently dynamic context for human existence: the urban community and its modern offspring, the urban region. Urbanization, the process of creating and developing urban communities, can be traced some 6500 years. However, urbanization until recently has been a relatively discontinuous process, with periods of attenuated growth, rapid and extensive expansion, and eras of stagnation and decline. This is a genuinely fascinating story—the tracing of modern community ancestry—but we are interested primarily in the basic threads of urbanism and their relevance to modern urban regions.

A matter of definition must be first on our agenda. What are the distinctive criteria of urban communities, wherever and whenever we find them?

In general, it will be helpful initially to conceive of a vast rural-urban continuum in terms of three interlocking dimensions: occupational dominance, division of labor, and density of population. The extremes of this continuum are points of reference, rather than reflections of concrete communities (see accompanying Fig. 1).

The urban community may be approached as a general type of community that occupies a roughly delimited portion of this continuum. Thus, it

[1] Oswald Spengler, *The Decline of the West* (New York, Alfred A. Knopf, 1937), Vol. 1, pp. 16–18.

figure 1

Continuum of Community Types in Terms of Social and Cultural Complexity

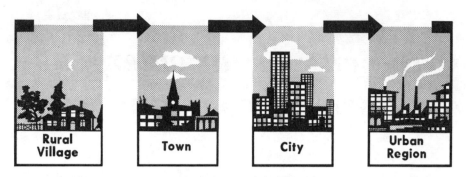

is clear that we may refer to different subtypes or varieties of urban community or, with the aid of the continuum idea, different degrees of urbanness. In this way, we avoid the temptation of assuming a unitary type of urban community, as well as an unnecessarily sharp distinction between the town and the full-blown city.[2]

the urban community defined

Recalling the definition of community in the previous chapter, we shall define the urban community type as a community (or complex of communities) characterized by a dominance of commercial, industrial, and service occupations; an extensive division of labor and its corresponding social complexity; an accompanying and underlying high density of population; and the development of coordination and social controls on a nonkinship basis. Urbanization is therefore a complex of social, ecological, and cultural trends which produce positive developments in any or all of these four aspects. Indeed, our discussions will implicitly combine the structural (organizational) with the dynamic (process) viewpoints, since the characteristic features of the urban community possess this dual significance.

[2] See discussions of the rural-urban continuum in Richard Dewey, "The Rural-Urban Continuum: Real But Relatively Unimportant," *American Journal of Sociology*, 66 (July, 1960), pp. 60–66; Stuart A. Queen and David B. Carpenter, *The American City* (New York, McGraw-Hill, 1953), Chap. III; Charles P. Loomis and J. Allan Beegle, *Rural Social Systems* (Englewood Cliffs, N.J., Prentice-Hall, 1950), Chap. I; Francisco Benet, "Sociology Uncertain: The Ideology of the Rural-Urban Continuum," *Comparative Studies in Society and History*, 6 (October, 1963), pp. 1–23.

prerequisites of urbanization

Urbanization ultimately originates from rural communities, but historical and archeological evidence seems to focus on relatively few rural communities possessing certain strategic features. These prerequisites of urbanization are largely obvious but nonetheless important social and cultural conditions, which link basic rurality with emerging urbanness.

1. agriculture and domestication of animals

A secure food supply and especially the ability to provide food surpluses are the most fundamental rural contributions to the urban community. It may be assumed that increasing efficiency in food production rests on some combination of favorable geographic conditions and a developed technical competence in raising crops and livestock. Whatever the reasons, food surplus constitutes one of the essential preconditions of the urban community. Surpluses enable a population to establish a permanent geographic base, in contrast to many contemporaneous nonliterate peoples, who are compelled to follow a shifting supply of game or to seek alternatives for "worked out" land. In general, over a substantial time period, food surpluses allow for larger population units—either by reducing the death rate or by accommodating the needs of migrants, captives, etc. Extremely significant is the fact that surpluses can either be stored or present possibilities for trade with other communities. Furthermore, surpluses permit reallocation of time, energy, and skills to other human pursuits and thus may result in greater specialization of roles and an expanded division of social labor. Indeed, increasing specialization (especially technical specialization) likewise increases production of articles suitable for trade.[3]

2. improvements in tools, weapons, and technical methods

Perhaps reciprocally related to surplus food production is the development of more efficient implements for a variety of practical purposes. Pottery making, weaving, the successive types of plow, the smelting of metals and their fabrication into reliable instruments, the sailboat, etc.—all create additional opportunities for specialization and/or extensions of commerce.

[3] V. Gordon Childe, *Man Makes Himself* (New York, New American Library, 1951), Chap. V; Leslie A. White, *The Evolution of Culture* (New York, McGraw-Hill, 1959), Chap. XII; Felix M. Keesing, *Cultural Anthropology* (New York, Holt, Rinehart and Winston, 1958), pp. 94–103; Robert J. Braidwood and Gordon R. Willey, eds., *Courses Toward Urban Life* (Chicago, Aldine, 1962), pp. 342–355; Carl H. Kraeling and Robert M. Adams, eds., *City Invincible: A Symposium on Urbanization and Cultural Development in the Ancient Near East* (Chicago, University of Chicago Press, 1960), p. 226.

Perfection of military weapons is particularly important, since defense of the community (and aggression against neighboring communities) was one of the dominant concerns in early urban experience.[4]

3. complex social organization

Two of the distinguishing features of genuinely rural communities are the intrusive factors of primary, personal relationships and powerful kinship loyalties. These are, of course, appropriate to rural community life. But urbanization inherently involves somewhat larger social aggregations, the development of minor and major cultural differences within populations, and the problems of coordinating a variety of activities and resolving inevitable disputes and controversies. The dominance of kinship ties perpetuates social fragmentation and a troublesome array of contending factions. Therefore, the urban community becomes an actuality (based on the potentialities of urbanization derived from previously discussed conditions) when kin or gentile organization is succeeded by civil organization.[5]

Civil organization provides for the first time a clear-cut public, community-wide form of coordination and control, in contrast to the narrow, particularized, and private organizations represented by leading clans. In place of status and opportunities associated with specific family connections (or the lack of such connections among newcomers to the community), civil organization is based on territorial and property criteria. Thus, residence within community boundaries and possession of land, livestock, money, and weapons become relatively rational determinants of citizenship-community membership rather than solely kin allegiance. Under these conditions, a central, universally applicable, and legitimate control system can develop; indeed, this corresponds to the creation of a separate political institution. At this point, specialization in the community is accompanied by class distinctions (in contrast to previously dominant lineage distinctions). Here the city and civilization become clearly visible on the canvas of history.

Historically, the urban community is the consequence of transformations in a limited number of rural communities, under the conditions we have outlined above. For the greater part of the urbanization process, however, cities have been numerically inferior to villages, and yet politically and economically dominant. The rise of cities, ultimately dependent on rural foundations, seems to have inevitable consequences for the larger and perhaps vaguer society in which they appear. In short, cities create civilizations—complex and subtly binding interdependencies among a considerable number of adjacent com-

---

[4] Childe, *op. cit.*, Chaps. VI, VII.

[5] White, *op. cit.*, pp. 294–314; Lewis H. Morgan, *Ancient Society* (New York, Henry Holt, 1877) ; Max Weber, *General Economic History* (New York, The Free Press of Glencoe, 1950), pp. 45–46; Werner J. Cahnman, "Religion and Nationality," *American Journal of Sociology*, 49 (May, 1944), pp. 524–529. See William Bascom, "Urbanism as a Traditional African Pattern," *Sociological Review*, 7 (July, 1959), pp. 29–43.

munities—which possess rather distinctive sociocultural features whenever and wherever they arise. Very briefly, these features are:

1. Cities tend to be few in number, but also tend to cluster near one another.

2. The countryside and its several types of rural community come to be economically dependent on the city.

3. Commerce and exchange become highly developed and diversified.

4. One or more cities attain dominant political positions in extensive geographic areas and often in a politically delimited society.

5. The city (or cities) becomes and remains the cultural center of a vast area; in particular, it tends to become the focus of change, innovation, creativity, and deviation in a variety of human pursuits.

urban waves and their significance

Extensive discussions of these characteristics in modern urban regions will be found in later sections of this work. However, it must be emphasized that any serious attempt to understand the nature of contemporary urbanism and its component parts must recognize the vast cumulative background of modern urban living. Indeed, the panorama of world history, when viewed from the special perspective of the urban sociologist, suggests a rough, discontinuous evolution of urban experience—an evolution which is not inevitable but rather a reflection of increasing social complexity that appears to be responsive to specific sociocultural conditions of given historical periods, and, to some extent, to peculiar geographic factors. To organize the rich storehouse of pertinent historical materials, we shall try to analyze it in terms of broad urban phases or waves, for which we can only hope to fix very approximate dates as boundary lines. More important, we shall try to summarize the unique social and cultural contributions of each wave to an evolving urbanization.

the first urban wave: 4500 B.C.–500 A.D.

Classical urbanism, which Gordon Childe refers to as the "urban revolution" following the Neolithic Revolution, was developed in a relatively long time span and in an extensive crescent-shaped slice of the Afro-Eurasian land mass.[6] In general, the earliest examples of classical urban centers appeared in the favorable environments of temperate or semitropical river valleys (Tigris,

[6] Childe, *op. cit.*, Chap. VII; Ralph Turner, *The Great Cultural Traditions* (New York, McGraw-Hill, 1941), Vol. I.

Euphrates, Nile, Ganges, Yangtze), where agricultural surplus was instrumental in transforming peasant villages into recognizable towns and cities. Undoubtedly, such phenomena as wars, migrations, and irregular commerce stimulated cultural contacts between distant urban centers (particularly after 2500 B.C.), which in some degree facilitated or accelerated the crystallization of urban features. However, the attempt to find a central radiation point of urbanization (e.g., the tortured theory of Egyptian diffusion to contemporary urban cultures—the "Heliocentric" theory)[7] contains too many pitfalls to warrant serious consideration by the sociologist. Let us instead focus on the general character of classical urbanization, without regard for its detailed, ultimate origins.

The most striking feature of this first urban wave is the foundation of cities on the triumvirate of *defense, worship,* and *commerce.* In Mesopotamia, Egypt, India, Crete, and later in Greece and Italy, these three activities were effectively coordinated on a constantly expanding scale. It must be remembered that agricultural surpluses were relatively new and precious, that the preexisting social fabric was largely a patchy confusion of localisms and errant bands, that newly affluent (in food and supplies) communities or areas were pioneers in a sociocultural wilderness. Consequently, cities were strategically located to draw upon nearby fields and orchards, and to take advantage of natural opportunities (e.g., hills) for defense against jealous marauders. It is not too farfetched to describe the classical city as the "fusion of fortress and market." [8] However, a great deal of evidence seems to underscore the importance of new religious forms in the transition from rural to genuinely urban organization, a topic to which we shall return.

With some variations in time and geography, urban communities in this general period embarked on relatively successful experiments in economic specialization. In addition to the central role of merchants (who were early differentiated but usually were accorded low social status), we can point to the development of such industries as textiles (based in part on advancements in preparation of dyes), pottery, metalworking and the production of alloys such as copper, the crafts of jewel working, furniture making, funerary skills, and construction (public buildings and temples). These specialties should be viewed as supplemental to, and perhaps dependent upon, the major technical and scientific innovations of classical cities: irrigation techniques, writing and the alphabet, geometry, astronomy, philosophy, and military science.

Commerce was surely the emerging center of urban interest and the raison d'être of many noneconomic innovations. One does not have to be an economic determinist to recognize this insistent pattern of dominance in classical antiquity. Indeed, the problems of disposing of agricultural surpluses

[7] W. J. Perry, *The Growth of Civilization* (New York, E. P. Dutton, 1923), pp. 32–35, 100–120.
    [8] Max Weber, *The City,* trans. by Don Martindale and Gertrud Neuwirth (New York, The Free Press of Glencoe, 1958), p. 78.

could only be dealt with in many cases by some form of intercommunity exchange, since neither long-term storage nor increased consumption was initially feasible. Furthermore, it must be presumed that successful trade experience came to be a desired end in itself. Thus, the Sumerians and their conquerors bartered or sold wheat, beer, and barley (temporarily storing surpluses in their temples); the Egyptian cities of Heliopolis, Coptos, and Abydos engaged in extensive trade in grains with North Africa and the Near East; Cretan-Minoan cities as early as 3000–2500 B.C. were already leading merchants of figs, barley, and olives; and Greek cities such as Athens and Corinth established commercial colonies on the Adriatic and in Italy.[9]

Though the earliest details are not always clear, it must not be forgotten that many classical cities were in part (at least) products of migration, warfare, and conquest. In practice, these developments involved increasing attention to the inadequacies of clan organization. The Greek evidence seems to show initial foundation of cities based on unions of leading families (confraternities or synoecism) for mutual defense, rather than for strictly commercial reasons. In Egypt, India, and China, irrigation problems faced by newly developed cities resulted in such political characteristics as a developed bureaucracy, compulsory labor for dependent groupings, a monopolization of military power by a single ruler, and a related opposition to family power. Returning to Greece, the continued predominance of leading families (aristoi) interfered with commercial developments and the aspirations of the urban masses. The famous tyrants of the fourth through the sixth centuries B.C. (Orthagoras, Cypselus, Periander, Pisistratus, Cleisthenes, Polycrates) seemed to be a favorite means of breaking the aristocratic vise and thereby prepared the transition to civil organization and "the public interest."[10]

As population movements, conquests, and aristocratic decline proceeded, the classical cities were faced with bothersome gaps in social control. The significance of property was changing; social relations, rights and duties between workers and possessors of surpluses required definition; the position of strangers and highly mobile merchants likewise needed clarification. Cities therefore constructed systems or codifications of previously discrete rules, which came to be written down and enforced by figures of authority. Here is the presumed origin of public law (criminal and civil types), for which we have such examples as Hammurabi's Code, the Law of the Twelve Tables, the constitutions of several Greek cities, and the complex legal developments of the Roman Empire.

As Max Weber has emphasized, the ancient city (particularly in the Greco-Roman world) was necessarily a military organization superimposed

---

[9] Michael Rostovtzeff, *A History of the Ancient World* (Oxford, The Clarendon Press, 1926), Vol. I; Turner, *op. cit.*

[10] Weber, *General Economic History*, pp. 320–331; Weber, *The City*, pp. 74–93; Karl Wittfogel, *Oriental Despotism* (New Haven, Yale University Press, 1957), Chaps. I, III, VIII.

on particularistic clan and religious organizations. According to this view, the understanding of military developments is a prerequisite to analysis of trends in classical urbanization. The essential facts seem to support this position, though it is probably misleading to explain city development primarily in military terms. Nevertheless, the representative classical cities were marked by a shift from individual combat to mass, disciplined formations (the hoplites, the phalanxes) for military efficiency. This not only established a firm basis for defensive operations, but made possible an extensive series of urban offensives and the famous urban empires (Egypt, Persia, Assyria, Athens, Sparta, Rome).[11] However, complex military organization also involved a diffusion of power from leading families to lower status groups (usually, moderately successful farmers financially able to equip themselves for battle). As dependence on broader groupings increased, the dominance of clans was weakened and the internal policies of the city (*polis*) gradually turned toward prevention of landlessness. The underlying aim of political leadership and the "reforms" of various tyrants seem to possess this unifying theme. Consequently, the development of classical democracy (which was philosophically and practically different from modern forms) and perhaps of the first demands for political freedom had their origins in the need for specialized military organizations.

It is perhaps paradoxical to our contemporaries that democratization in classical cities was accompanied by the emergence of a class system, which we can consider a characteristic feature of urbanization in general. Preurban stratification, as we have already suggested, was based on lineage and its dominance over economic, political, and religious spheres. This semicaste structure was inevitably modified by the significant institutional changes (political, economic, military) which are inseparable from the processes of urbanization. With considerable variations, the typical urban class system appeared to rest primarily on such status criteria as occupation and skill, rather than family and wealth. Normally, the leading groups consisted of the priesthood and military officials, though not without challenge from commercial groupings in the latter part of the classical period. The middle range of status levels (which should not be confused with modern middle classes) was composed of merchants and businessmen, whose position was exceedingly variable according to locality and time period. Finally, there were the lowest strata of peasants, artisans and craftsmen, and slaves (whose social and political status was sometimes greatly inferior to their financial position).[12]

We often forget one of the most important contributions of the first urban wave: complex, universal religions. The modern connotations of "urbanness" is overwhelmingly "secular," "rational," and even "antireligious." However, this is based on a misunderstanding both of the urban

---

[11] Weber, *General Economic History*, pp. 322–324.
[12] Rostovtzeff, *op. cit.*, Vol. I, pp. 216–223; Turner, *op. cit.*, pp. 454–473.

community and religion itself, a misconception we hope to remove in Chapter 14. As historical and literary sources rather well demonstrate, preurban and early urban communities were marked by a bewildering diversity of local (and sometimes ancestral) religious cults, "mysteries," and rituals.[13] Through the agency of leading clans (especially in Greece), towns and cities arose with a politically dominant public cult, supplemented by various tolerated or irrepressible private cults. Under these circumstances, leading families supplied both a religious and a political focus (the priest-kings). In general, each city was a religious island content in its splendid but limited isolation. The practical logic of urban trends, however, revolutionized religion in a direction from which it has not greatly deviated. While religious and political activities remained intertwined (political leaders were religious leaders and vice versa), the development of urban communities as partially democratized, politically expanding entities provoked persistent movements for national rather than local cults and simplification of the supernatural focus through monotheism.[14]

The Persians had been among the first to achieve religious unification (Zoroastrianism), while Hindu urbanism was exemplified in Brahminism. Under the influence of Ikhnaton, Egypt had likewise experimented with monotheism, however briefly. Hebrew monotheism, which was an essential ingredient of Christianity, was itself derived from the military campaigns against religiously diversified urban peoples. Military success and the adoption of urban living solidified a national religion, though frequent reinterpretations by the prophets indicate the Hebrew failure to integrate urbanism and religion. By contrast, the Greek cities continued to nurture local cults and polytheism (backed by the aristocratic families). The Athenian tyrant, Pisistratus, did encourage national cults, especially the cult of Athena and the famous Panathenaic festival, but with only temporary results. The imitative Romans generally followed Greek religious precedent; however, something akin to a national monotheism briefly developed under Augustus, who did more than any succeeding emperor in promoting urbanization in the Empire. Finally, we can only mention the rise of Christianity, at the end of the first urban wave, as essentially urban in derivation and organization (borrowing urban administrative forms from the Empire) and in appeal to new adherents during its infancy.[15]

A final contribution of this first urban wave is the emergence of complex,

---

[13] Fustel de Coulanges, *The Ancient City*, 10th ed. (Boston, Lee and Shepard, 1900), especially Book 3; Robert M. Adams, *The Evolution of Urban Society: Early Mesopotamia and Prehispanic Mexico* (Chicago, Aldine, 1966).

[14] See for example E. A. Wallis Budge, *From Fetish to God in Ancient Egypt* (London, Oxford University Press, 1934); H. A. R. Gibb, *Mohammedanism*, 2nd ed. (London, Oxford University Press, 1954).

[15] Lewis R. Farnell, *The Cults of the Greek States* (Oxford, The Clarendon Press, 1896–1907), 4 vols.; Gilbert Murray, *Five Stages of Greek Religion* (New York, Columbia University Press, 1925); Cyril Bailey, *Phases in the Religion of Ancient Rome* (Berkeley, University of California Press, 1932), Chap. V.

diversified arts—sculpture, architecture, painting and decoration, music, drama, the dance, and literary forms (the dialogue, satire, tragedy, comedy, verse). All the classical civilizations developed competence in at least several of the arts, creating and diffusing relatively distinctive styles over wide areas. Highly significant is the religious origin of the arts, but even more so is their tendency toward autonomous development. It is this typical artistic independence, it seems, that explains much of our continued appreciation of classical styles and art objects. The efflorescence of the arts, particularly in their increasingly independent forms, reflects a high point in social specialization, which is one of the hallmarks of genuine urbanization and civilization.

the second urban wave: 1000–1800 A.D.

Two generations of historical investigation have virtually destroyed any basis for viewing the medieval period as a Dark Age in which civilization was completely arrested and then scattered to the winds. On the contrary, much historical continuity was maintained—in agricultural and military techniques, in commerce, religion, and the major crafts.[16] However, if the barbarians did not embark on wholesale destruction of towns and cities in the fifth century and afterwards, it is certainly clear that urban communities were experiencing strongly regressive trends. As early as the third century A.D., urban areas were losing population, commerce and business enterprise suffered from perennial imperial restrictions, the middle class of officials was taxed to desperation, and the towns became festering sores rather than cases of responsible community life.[17] After the eighth century, rural feudalism, punctuated by short-lived military conquests, was incontrovertibly dominant. By the sixth century, towns were shadows of their former selves, often surviving as ecclesiastical bases for Catholicism. Significantly, *civitas*, which once meant "urban center," came to mean "episcopal city." [18]

A renewal of urbanization under these circumstances required a dramatic stimulus, one which could produce appropriate political and economic underpinnings for a second urban wave. This stimulus was probably the revival of extended commercial opportunities following the Crusades, though some

16 Alfons Dopsch, *The Economic and Social Foundations of European Civilization* (New York, Harcourt, Brace, 1937).

17 Arthur E. R. Boak, *Manpower Shortage and the Fall of the Roman Empire in the West* (Ann Arbor, Mich., University of Michigan Press, 1955), pp. 93–112; Michael Rostovtzeff, *Social and Economic History of the Roman Empire* (Oxford, The Clarendon Press, 1926), pp. 333, 358; Samuel Dill, *Roman Society in the Last Century of the Western Empire*, 2nd ed. (London, Macmillan, 1933), pp. 253–259.

18 Henri Pirenne, *Medieval Cities* (Princeton, Princeton University Press, 1925), Chap. III.

credit must be given to the relative stabilization of political order in Europe (dating from the tenth century) which unwittingly permitted these opportunities to be realized. Thus, from the latter part of the tenth century, itinerant merchants began to cluster in their slack season outside the walls of old fortress-towns—particularly those situated near main travel routes.[19] Originally, these merchant quarters were suburbs or faubourgs, but gradually they became the functional foci and then the geographic centers of a revived and vigorous urbanism.

The new city, which was primarily a European phenomenon, was principally organized in terms of six component structures.

1. economic features

The renewed dominance of commerce was allied to three significant economic developments. First, there was considerable improvement in agricultural methods and utilization of larger acreage for saleable crops (especially after the twelfth century). Second, expanded trade in manufactured goods (cloth, in particular) promoted the development of basic handicraft industries, normally located in the merchants' quarter. Finally, wide-ranging trade inevitably transformed restricted barter economies into money economies, so that a new and universal standard of value infiltrated both the city and the countryside.

2. the rise of the bourgeois

Since merchants were initially strangers and legally unassailable, their economic success was noted, but was also untranslatable into feudal terms. However, their peculiar status prompted the merchants to insure their favorable economic position by demanding (and receiving) political safeguards from feudal authorities (nobles and ecclesiastical lords). By the twelfth and thirteenth centuries, the merchants were becoming a respected and powerful middle class [20] (mediating between the semiskilled worker and the local

---

[19] Pirenne, *op. cit.*, Chaps. IV and V; Lewis Mumford, *The Culture of Cities* (New York: Harcourt, Brace & World, 1938), pp. 16–18; Henri Hauser, *Les débuts du capitalisme, 1223–1328* (Paris; Armand Colin, 1958), pp. 72–76; Henri Pirenne, *Les Villes et les institutions urbaines* (Paris, Alcan, 1939), 2 vols.; J. Lestocquoy, *Les Villes de Flandre et d'Italie* (Paris, Presses Universitaires de France, 1952) ; Weber, *The City*, pp. 95–110; John H. Mundy and Peter Riesenberg, eds., *The Medieval Town* (Princeton, Van Nostrand, 1958) ; M. Tikhomirov, *The Towns of Ancient Rus* (Moscow, Foreign Languages Publishing House, 1959), pp. 45–58.

[20] Pirenne, *Medieval Cities*, Chaps. VI and VII; Lestocquoy, *op. cit.*, pp. 17–41, 136–169; Sylvia L. Thrupp, *The Merchant Class of Medieval London, 1300–1500* (Chicago, University of Chicago Press, 1948), pp. 12–14, 282–285; Fritz Rörig, *The Medieval Town* (Berkeley, University of California Press, 1967; orig. ed., 1932), Chaps. 2 and 12; Gerald Strauss, *Nuremberg in the Sixteenth Century* (New York, Wiley, 1966).

nobility of the sword or cassock) and the essential unit in the urban social order.

3. urban legal innovations

The bourgeoisie as a political and social power (as distinct from its economic significance) was intimately connected with the legitimation of untrammeled commerce as the central concern of the community. As a result of organized merchant pressures, the city became independent of environing feudal regulations and restrictions. Eventually, freedom from these obligations became the basic legal status of all inhabitants; and residence in such communities for a year and a day guaranteed personal freedom ("Stadtluft macht frei"—city air [residence] extends freedom). From the merchants' standpoint, freedom to engage in trade was fundamental. Therefore, the right to own property and land, and the right to establish urban courts (for settling commercial disputes) was early achieved by the burghers or bourgeoisie. As civic responsibility became a problem, the merchants developed and legalized local police systems, excise and income taxes to pay for community services, and perhaps most important, a city council as the key administrative body armed with extensive powers.[21]

4. the university

Several cities, beginning in the twelfth and thirteenth centuries, unwittingly contributed the minimum essentials of higher, specialized education, which we now call the university. Originally a composite of trade union and fraternal lodge, the university or college was a semiformal organization of persons proficient in or prepared for the scholarly vocations of law, theology, and medicine. In Paris, masters and students banded together; in Bologna, the students developed their own organization and hired masters.[22] Learning was personal, barely dignified, and for many years an extremely mobile business. Ramshackle dwellings, suspicious landlords and neighbors, a few precious manuscripts owned by the masters, a motley assemblage of variously ill-prepared students, and the masters themselves—these were the initial ingredients. Gradually, despite numerous frictions, cities, princes, and the church came to accept (and even to subsidize) universities, whose products satisfied the increasing demand for civil professional services (especially law and medicine) in succeeding centuries of urban living.

21 Pirenne, *Medieval Cities*, Chap. VII; David Herlihy, *Medieval and Renaissance Pistoia* (New Haven, Yale University Press, 1967), pp. 184–200, 215–231.
22 Mumford, *op. cit.*, pp. 33–35; Nathan Schachner, *The Mediaeval Universities* (New York, Stokes, 1938), pp. 42–49; Hastings Rashdall, *The Universities of Europe in the Middle Ages* (Oxford, The Clarendon Press, 1936), 3 vols.

5. ecological structure

The fortress-like aspect of cities remained till the late fifteenth century, when gunpowder made ancient walls obsolete. Instead, cities resorted to intensive systems of ringed fortifications, manned by mercenaries, which inevitably limited city expansion. Consequently, population increase was followed by congestion and the genuine emergence of urban slums for most strata of urban communities.[23] At the same time, military needs were satisfied by radial, broad avenues, which facilitated deployment of troops at any point in the fortification system. Not till the rise of centralized national governments was this military strait jacket removed from the urban scene.

6. the stratification of art

In general, the arts of the first urban wave were public enterprises in which all or most of the citizens could participate. The arts often developed as expressions of dominant religious activities. Therefore, expansion of urban religions was accompanied by a relative democratization of such arts as the drama, sculpture, and architecture. But in the latter part of the second urban wave, the upper classes (the nobility, which had reestablished itself in cities, and also some of the long-established mercantile families) assumed a semimonopolistic responsibility for music, dancing, and the theater. The so-called patrons of the arts created private (and sometimes competing) artistic empires through subsidies to writers, musicians, and painters. Under this system, classical music, painting, drama, and literature attained great heights in, for example, Bach, Michelangelo, Shakespeare, and Racine. Yet it established a sharp cleavage between the bulk of the urban population and the cultivated arts ("culture"), which in some respects persists to the present time.[24] In short, the second urban wave emphasized the creation of art, rather than the appropriate conditions for its distribution and appreciation.

the third and current urban wave: 1800 to the present

The economic and political success of urban communities in the sixteenth through the eighteenth centuries led to further economic and social changes that clearly identify the emergence of the modern urban region. Since the

[23] Mumford, op. cit., pp. 83–86; Maurice Beresford, New Towns of the Middle Ages (London, Lutterworth Press, 1967); Harold Priestley, London: The Years of Change (London, Frederick Muller, 1966), pp. 30–49. Cf. Ira M. Lapidus, Muslim Cities in the Later Middle Ages (Cambridge, Harvard University Press, 1967), pp. 81–108, 190; Thomas Frederick Tout, "Medieval Town Planning," in The Collected Papers of Thomas Frederick Tout (Manchester, Manchester University Press, 1943), Vol. 3, pp. 59–91.
[24] Mumford, op. cit., pp. 111–113.

remainder of this work focuses on this phase of urbanism, at this point we shall merely outline a number of its most distinctive features as a prelude to the more detailed discussions in later chapters.

1. expansion and separation of industrial units

The rise of specialized work locations (mills, factories) near efficient sources of power was a response to the optimistic quest for mass production and the consequent invention of ever more complicated machines. Very rapidly, the handicraft and "putting out" systems of production became cumbersome and unprofitable; thus for the urbanite, the job and the home were irrevocably split and the journey to work was to take its place in the universal urban pattern.[25]

2. cooperative capital: the ubiquitous corporation

Expansion of enterprise and the intensification of mining ventures to provide metal for new and more complex machinery required more capital than a few entrepreneurs could muster. The joint stock company and its offspring, the corporation, provided additional capital and then specialized administration for a variety of industrial and maritime ventures. In time, the financier, the banker, and the investment organization played a silent but nonetheless powerful role in urban economic developments, functioning with increasing ease on regional, national, and international levels.

3. the urban-national axis

In the latter part of the second urban wave—and especially with the emergence of modern urban features—the city became the primary center of wealth in the Western world. During the bitter and prolonged struggles between the landed nobility and proponents of centralized government (the king), urban middle classes to a great extent subsidized the creation and maintenance of national states, to which they have been subsequently allied on most major issues. Basically, the city, through its characteristic operations, largely determines the overall functioning of the nation. However, it must be recognized that this "alliance" has been somewhat informal and indirect, especially in the United States. Yet there is growing evidence of closer and more formalized ties between urban areas and the national system (see Part IV). In any case, the city has become an arena of competitive power groups (with internal and external bases) and consequently the new locus of politics.

[25] Kate Liepmann, *The Journey to Work* (New York, Oxford University Press, 1944).

4. ecological complexities

As a consequence of technological and economic developments, the emergence of peculiarly modern urban class structures, and what we might call urbanized value systems, the urban community has experimentally (and often unconsciously) produced rather marked spatial divisions that reflect the intricate social and cultural specializations of this third urban wave. We shall analyze the nature and consequences of these ecological developments in some detail in Chapters 5 and 6. At this point, it is merely necessary to point to a highly differentiated central commercial-administrative area; the location of numerous retail areas; the relocation of industry in outlying zones; the meticulous diversification and grading of residential districts; the special separation of the arts, recreation, education, as well as deviant behavior (prostitution, gambling, crime, drug addiction, etc.); and finally, the specialization of dependent "urblets" as the urban region expands.

some trends in modern urbanism

Of course, many more features of modern urban organization might be listed here. As we shall have occasion to note many times, the numerous concrete patterns of the modern urban region are symptomatic reflections and illustrations of these few basic regularities. But it seems to be particularly important that we view modern urbanization as part of an understandable process that has been recorded in a series of relatively continuous changes in technique, values and objectives, social organization, achievements, and problems. Indeed, several major trends are more or less explicit in our review of the three urban waves.

First, though various forms of organized religion were inseparable from urban living during the first and second waves, modern urbanism appears to find preexisting organized religion somewhat incompatible with the other aims of community life. At this point, a widespread error must be corrected. Urbanization, as historical material clearly shows, is *not* basically antireligious. Religion in the formal sense was a basic ingredient in earlier stages of urbanism. It may well be that, for the modern urbanite, new forms of religious expression (not yet achieved or created) are needed to provide necessary spiritual support on his present sociocultural level.

Second, as we move from antiquity to the present, there is in urbanization a growing dominance of economic and technological values (profit, income, efficiency) in organizing and disorganizing clusters of social relationships in the community. However, each wave of urbanism likewise experienced serious challenges to rising economic groups by political and status groups (i.e., landed nobility, barbarian invaders, military cliques). The bourgeoisie of the second urban wave was able to conquer its enemies by encouraging centralized government and then acquiring control of major governmental organs.[26] In the current urban wave, and especially during the last generation or so, the yet dominant economic interests have again faced the necessity of resisting or diverting the resurgence of essentially non-economic demands. One such demand is extraurban and derives from the political necessity to be persistently prepared for war.[27] Thus, high taxation, various types of economic controls (price controls, rationing, etc.), and increasing production for a single customer—the government—rather than the market tend to interfere with the free development of economic incentives. The other type of demand is intraurban; it is variously reflected in the urbanite's desire for security and stable income, for costly but expected public services, for increasing stress on esthetic criteria in community developments,[28] and for a widespread sense of civic responsibility and accountability. Naked economic interest is therefore no longer fashionable, though it may still be pursued if publicity is avoided.

Finally, modern cities (and most obviously, the leading cities) have been increasingly expanding their radii of control over present and future behavior of populations. This is not basically political dominance—as in the first urban wave—or the limited economic supremacy of the second wave. The octopal growth of modern cities is instead proceeding on three inter-related levels. (a) Most obvious is *geographic expansion* into sprawling superurban units that ignore political and geographic obstacles—the metropolitan or urban region. Modern media of communication and rapid transportation are clearly basic to this growth. (b) Concentration of *economic functions*—the provision of jobs, desired services, capital and credit for business and consumption—inevitably attracts mobile individuals and families to aid in producing and/or consuming the fruits of metropolitan economic systems. Those who remain outside the geographic orbit find themselves increasingly willing captives in urban economic nets. Consequently, the often quoted desire of Americans to "live in a nice, quiet community—not too far from a big city" is symptomatic of the special magnetism of modern urbanism. (c) The spread of urbanism is, finally and most significantly, *cultural*. Urbanization in previous periods was largely reflected in extension of citizenship and legal rights. Modern urbanism is apparently exporting tastes, biases, fashions, aspirations, and even abstract values (e.g., education) to society at large.

Urban regions therefore seem to be gigantic functional empires in the

26 Harold J. Laski, *The Rise of Liberalism* (New York, Harper and Brothers, 1936).
27 J. Kenneth Galbraith, *The Affluent Society* (Boston, Houghton Mifflin, 1958), Chap. XVIII.
28 Edward L. Ullman, "Amenities as a Factor in Regional Growth," *The Geographical Review*, 44 (January, 1954), pp. 119–132.

vague political entities called national societies. Unlike classical empires, they remain more or less dependent on external but legitimate power units (state and/or national governments). As in previous urban waves, modern urban regions contain internal social divisions that are now rarely flagrant and dramatic, but nevertheless persist as latent deterrents to urban consensus and outright urban dominance. The key, sociologically speaking, to modern urbanism is perhaps the ambivalent status of urban regions; the political halter tends to limit the extraordinary potentialities for economic and cultural change that are synonymous with urbanism.[29] Cities of the second wave shattered feudal restrictions by supporting the national state. But what forms of alliance are available to modern urban regions?

[29] Gordon Baker, *Rural versus Urban Political Power* (Garden City, Doubleday, 1955); Scott Greer, *The Emerging City* (New York, The Free Press, 1962), pp. 33–49.

selected references

CHILDE, V. Gordon, *Man Makes Himself* (New York, New American Library, 1951).

GUTKIND, E. A., *Urban Development in Central Europe* (New York, The Free Press, 1964).

——, *Urban Development in Southern Europe: Spain and Portugal* (New York, The Free Press, 1967).

——, *Urban Development in the Alpine and Scandinavian Countries* (New York, The Free Press, 1965).

PIRENNE, Henri, *Medieval Cities* (Princeton, Princeton University Press, 1925).

WEBER, Adna F., *The Growth of Cities in the Nineteenth Century* (New York, Macmillan, 1899).

WEBER, Max, *The City*, trans. by Don Martindale and Gertrude Neuwirth (New York, The Free Press, 1958).

WHITE, Leslie A., *The Evolution of Culture* (New York, McGraw-Hill, 1959).

3

the problem of classifying urban regions

If modern cities—products of the third urban wave all over the world —share a number of distinctive features, it is likewise true that cities possess some uniqueness, divergences, and idiosyncrasies. The resulting variety, which should not be exaggerated, is obvious both to the intelligent traveler and the alert, wide-ranging reader, who thus sets forth on mental pilgrimages to distant urban regions. Therefore, it will be of some use to search for some order in this variety, through a meaningful classification of urban regions.

It should be stated at the outset that such a classification is quite difficult, and not at all an academic exercise. Basically, our quantitative knowledge of urban regions is highly compartmentalized: population data, occupational distributions, spatial location of various types of activities and functions, housing, traffic surveys, etc. Consequently, with few exceptions, any classification of urban regions according to *one* type of information is likely to be as significant as classifying human beings in terms of hair color.

The essential problem, in line with the sociological viewpoint presented in the first chapter, is to develop and apply a classification or typology that enables us to treat urban regions as relatively coherent systems of component parts, as functional wholes in which specific features (e.g., population facts, zonal developments) can be understood with reference to other components and to the structure of the region itself. This requires, it seems, both detailed cross-sectional information on various aspects of concrete urban regions and a creative, interpretative synthesis of these aspects to provide an intelligible, testable pattern of unity in urban regions. Significantly, though Chicago has been the most completely investigated of American urban regions,[1] we still lack anything resembling a comprehensive sociological picture of the Chicago region as an essential unit, despite the obvious contradictions of competing

---

[1] A sampling of these studies might include: Louis Wirth, *The Ghetto* (Chicago, University of Chicago Press, 1929); Harvey Zorbaugh, *The Gold Coast and the Slum* (Chicago, University of Chicago Press, 1929); Walter C. Reckless, *Vice in Chicago* (Chicago, University of Chicago Press, 1933); Ruth S. Cavan, *Suicide* (Chicago, University of Chicago Press, 1928).

jurisdictions. Even the sensitive novelist and short-story writer, who are often intuitive but effective sociological interpreters of contemporary life, fail to capture more than isolated fragments of urban regional life (i.e., the slum, Bohemia, and the middle-class suburb). Literature, which is said to be a creative reflection of its social environment, has yet to contribute a sure fictional treatment of the dominant locale in modern society—the urban region.

What, then, gives promise of supplying useful criteria for classifying urban regions? The answer must be tentative; it must be alternately cautious and audacious; and it must effectively provide continuity between past accomplishments and emerging ideas of verifiable intelligibility in sociological research. Such criteria, which have been chosen for their synthetic function (integrating several specific features) and their cross-cultural applicability, might well include: factors in the mature foundation of urban centers, relative stage of development in the urbanization process, and underlying cultural qualities derived from the larger society. Let us first examine these criteria separately, and then in their significant combinations.

1. mature foundations

Even a rapid survey of cities during the third urban wave indicates that urban centers tend to be distinguishable in terms of the reasons for specific locations and/or later, basic lines of development. One such factor, which is quite important though moderately rare as a dominant consideration, is the political-administrative type. Of the major world capitals, very few have appeared in recent years; London, Paris, Moscow, and others achieved recognizable maturity in the second urban wave. Modern examples of this type include Washington, D.C., New Delhi, Tel Aviv, Buenos Aires, and Brasilia.

The *economic* factor is an obvious and perhaps somewhat overworked criterion of distinction among urban regions. In general, we find three major subvarieties: (a) industrial regions, in which heavy industrial enterprises and/or light manufacturing and processing are significant; (b) commercial-financial regions—based on distribution functions, investment and credit activities, and such specialized commercial services as advertising, insurance, and stock exchanges; and (c) transportation and communication centers —strategic concentrations of air, rail, trucking, telephone and telegraph, shipping, publishing, radio, and television services. New York City, Chicago, London, and Paris are only a few random examples.

With the enormous economic successes of the past one hundred years, still a third factor is rising toward levels of importance—the matter of *desirable geographic features* (amenities).[2] The city of consequence that is principally (though not exclusively) attractive because of climate, scenery,

---

[2] Edward L. Ullman, "Amenities as a Factor in Regional Growth," *The Geographical Review*, 44 (January, 1954), pp. 119–132.

table 1

Typology of Cities by Profile of Occupational Distributions,
as Expressed in Occupational Scores

Basic Occupational Type of City*	Occupational Score Range
A	118 +
B	109–117
C	103–108
D	95–102
E	84–94
F	0–83

* Each type is based on predominance of high status, high income, high educational kinds of occupations, with decreasing occupational status from A to F.
Source: Paul G. Gillen, *The Distribution of Occupations as a City Yardstick*, p. 105.

and availability of water is largely a phenomenon of the United States. We distinguish here between the *resort* [3] (which tends to be comparatively small, highly seasonal in character, and with few permanent residents) and the *permanent urban playground* (whose development is marked by a steadily increasing, full-time population which seeks to combine economic and recreational pursuits in roughly equal proportions). Atlantic City, Las Vegas, Nice, and Bath are examples of the former, while Los Angeles, St. Petersburg, and Miami best represent the latter type.

However, political, economic, and recreational-geographic factors are rarely independent. Many major urban regions have developed several economic functions, as well as some emphasis on political, recreational, and artistic functions. A clear-cut functional classification of urban regions is therefore somewhat arbitrary, if unaccompanied by other considerations (to be discussed shortly). For example, Grace Kneedler worked out three classifications: one in terms of dominant *economic* activity (manufacturing, industrial, wholesale, retail, and diversified); another on the basis of *occcupation* (educational center, governmental center, mining, transportation, amusement-health resort); and a third in terms of *functional status* (independent city, central city, dormitory suburb, balanced suburb, and employing suburb). It should be noted that the third classification treats components of urban regions, not urban regions as units. Characteristically, most of the large cities (over 500,000 population) were economically diversified, while smaller urban centers showed a tendency to be specialized in economic and occupational

[3] J. Ellis Voss, *Summer Resort: An Ecological Analysis of a Satellite Community* (Philadelphia, University of Pennsylvania Press, 1941).

functions.[4] In the same vein, Paul Gillen classified 1,073 cities (10,000 population and over) by constructing for each a profile of occupational distribution and assigning weighted scores for each city.[5] The result is a typology that is quite arbitrary, the categories of which cannot be meaningfully described or labeled (see Table 1).

2. stage of development

If urban regions are to be distinguished in a sociologically useful manner, at least two additional problems must be considered. First, cities and their dependent areas are creative, historical, and constantly developing entities. World cities vary considerably in age, pace of development and growth, and range of community problems. Amsterdam and Cleveland, for example, are not easily comparable because of differing periods and patterns of growth. Indeed, staying within American society, New Orleans was ecologically quite different from Cincinnati—until about twenty-five years ago.[6] Consequently, it seems worthwhile to posit stages or phases in urban development as a means of comparing and differentiating specific urban centers. At least two attempts to discover processual stages have been made that deserve some attention.

Griffith Taylor, an urban geographer, focuses on *ecological* developments and changes in land use in the following series of stages: [7]

> *Infantile:* no clear distinction between residential, commercial, and industrial areas.
>
> *Juvenile:* fairly clear segregation of a commercial district near town or city center, but continuing mixture of shops, offices, and small industries.
>
> *Early mature:* definite differentiation of residential areas in terms of status, with movement of higher status areas toward the periphery.
>
> *Mature:* concentration of industrial areas along railways, with major community growth likewise following railway patterns; separation of industrial segment from residential segments.

In cities of over 50,000 population:

1. nearby villages are assimilated by growing city, while satellite villages (at some distance) become separate municipalities.
2. construction of highways, huge viaducts, and bridges to improve traffic between sections of the urban region.

[4] Grace Kneedler, "Functional Types of Cities," in Paul K. Hatt and Albert J. Reiss, Jr., eds., *Reader in Urban Sociology* (New York, The Free Press of Glencoe, 1951), pp. 49–57.

[5] Paul B. Gillen, *The Distribution of Occupations as a City Yardstick* (New York, King's Crown Press, 1951), p. 105.

[6] Harlan W. Gilmore, "The Old New Orleans and the New," *American Sociological Review*, IX (August, 1944), pp. 385–394.

[7] Griffith Taylor, *Urban Geography* (New York, E. P. Dutton and Company, 1946), pp. 76–81, 422–423.

3. satellite communities gradually become formally annexed to the city.
4. regional controls are exercised through zoning laws and their extension, county councils (as in London), metropolitan commissions, regional authorities (such as the Port of New York Authority).

This kind of classification presents a well-ordered succession of changes in the more tangible aspects of urban development. However, it seems to be most directly applicable to industrial regions and to diversified urban regions. Since these types are most frequently found in the Western world, and since the important cities of the East seem to be slowly developing toward these types, Taylor's classification is one valuable guide in urban analysis.

A classification that involves a more *sociocultural* approach to urban development has been offered by Patrick Geddes and modified somewhat by Lewis Mumford. As the titles of some of the stages indicate, this classification clearly contains personal judgments (as well as descriptions) of successive phases, which are of course interesting but not sociological. In the following summary of Mumford's stages, we shall ignore these valuations; the reader who wishes a lucid discussion and defense of such judgments is invited to consult Mumford's book.[8]

1. *Eopolis:* the preurban village community.
2. *Polis:* the protourban community, marked by partial division of labor in the economic sphere, the development of specialized crafts, sciences, and associations; the retention of such rural features as familism and ancestral religious types; a relatively undeveloped ecological organization; and close, interdependent ties with a narrow regional area.
3. *Metropolis:* the rise of a dominant polis, based on strategic location, secure food supply, and attractiveness to migrants; extensive trade with other regions and cultural interchange; development of heterogeneous population; highly developed division of labor and cultural specialization; decline of family influence and rise of individualism; fixation on money as material and symbol; centralized administration, public and private; social divisions into classes and minority groups.
4. *Megalopolis:* emphasis on bigness, expansion of space and scope of construction; the city comes to dominate the region by military or financial-commercial means; standardization, facilitated by money, of most activities (recreation, education, art, architecture, consumption); triumph of complex organization, bureaucratization, and impersonality; smaller cities are drawn into megalopolitan network.
5. *Tyrannopolis:* the city becomes extremely economically-oriented; the budget, taxation, expenditures are dominant mechanisms; politics as a struggle for control of public funds by special interest groups; white collar crime;

8 Lewis Mumford, *The Culture of Cities* (New York, Harcourt, Brace & World, 1938), pp. 285–292.

insufficient revenue prompts appeals for national aid and a consequent lessening of urban autonomy; population exodus to outskirts of the region as an escape from a variety of undesirable living conditions.

6. *Nekropolis:* the final logical (rather than actual) stage of disorganization; ghost cities and the resurgence of rural communities.

Mumford's approach to developmental stages has the advantage of emphasizing the broad cultural and organizational character of urban evolution. To a great extent, it complements Taylor's concern with the *ecological* and *physical* evolution of urban centers. But both classifications are couched in terms of Western civilization, which limits the present application of these types to the more familiar urban regions of Europe and North America. A distinct contribution of Mumford's basic scheme, however, is its regard for the changing *functional* nature of urban regions—as evolving constellations of interrelated groups, spatial units, and institutionalized activities. Stripped of its value judgments and prophecies, such a classification gives promise of definite sociological utility.

3. the cultural factor

Classifications of urban regions by dominant activities and/or developmental stages tend to assume a universal rationality and freedom of development in world cities. One finds in many discussions an implicit notion of an "urban dynamic" impelling cities toward economic complexity, physical and organizational expansiveness, and higher levels of functional unity (sometimes judged to be of a detrimental or irresponsible kind).[9] This view is understandably ethnocentric, based on our knowledge and underlying attachment to American urban processes. A wider comparative approach would indicate that several types of cultural differences help to account for peculiarities of urban regions that are otherwise not explainable. At least three forms of cultural differences may be considered relevant to the problem of classification.

the culture of racial attitudes

As centers of opportunity and varied experiences, urban areas have inevitably attracted or encouraged migration of distinctive racial, religious,

[9] See Howard W. Odum, *Understanding Society* (New York, Macmillan, 1947), Chaps. XVII, XVIII; Georg Simmel, *The Sociology of Georg Simmel*, trans. by Kurt H. Wolff (New York, The Free Press, 1950), pp. 409–424; John W. Bennett and Melvin M. Tumin, *Social Life* (New York, Alfred A. Knopf, 1948), Chaps. XXI–XXIII; J. Clyde Mitchell, "Theoretical Orientations in African Urban Studies," in Michael Banton, ed., *The Social Anthropology of Complex Societies* (London, Tavistock Publications, 1966), pp. 37–68.

and nationality groupings. The process of assimilating these minority groups into urban social and ecological organization is, however, dependent on the values held by the resident majority. In particular, urban regions may be distinguished to some extent in terms of their underlying attitudes toward racial minorities (especially Negroes). These attitudes are reflected in opportunities for freedom in residential selection, occupational mobility to higher status jobs, and participation in the civic affairs of the region. Perhaps three types may be noted here:

1. formal assimilation

In regions such as metropolitan New York, legal assurance of opportunities for racial groups has expanded the educational, occupational, and political scope of Negroes. Residential restrictions have in recent years been proscribed by law, though informal restrictions continue to operate in the outer edges of the region.

2. informal segregation

Many Southern urban regions—and Chicago as well—have effectively contained their respective Negro populations within one or two concentrated districts, largely through private restrictions supported by widespread public opinion and the acquiescence of local councils, commissions, officials, and courts. Under these circumstances, the segregated populations constitute relatively complete communities, whose members are linked with the larger community through employment and the provision of public services.

3. legal segregation

In such urban regions as Durban, South Africa,[10] where minority groups are numerically superior, segregation and apartheid are key values to the politically dominant European whites. Consequently, these cities are marked in varying degrees by legal restrictions on nonwhites with respect to voting, property holding, commercial activities, and residential location. In Durban, the situation is complicated by the existence of several nonwhite categories: Africans (Negroes); Coloreds (Negro mixtures); and Hindus. However, under these conditions, the orthodox structure of urban regions is greatly altered. For example, in Durban, the high status white population lives principally in a narrow, irregular band around the bay and along the

---

[10] Leo Kuper, *Durban: A Study in Racial Ecology* (London, Jonathan Cape, 1958); J. Denis, "Les Villes d'Afrique tropicale," *Civilisations*, 16 (1966), pp. 26–44; *The New York Times*, February 18, 1968.

Indian Ocean. Nonwhites, by contrast, are mainly located in a broad, outer crescent to the west.

political intervention of the state

We have become accustomed to emphasizing the functional autonomy of urban regions—that is, their relative freedom from larger political and administrative units in carrying out typical urban activities. Many cities in the Western world certainly fit this pattern and consequently are able to shape their own development. But some cities—notably Washington, D.C., and Paris—have been cultural wards of a national government; whether by positive consent, resignation, or acquiescence, these cities reflect in their structure and operation historic decisions made by extramunicipal or extra-regional authorities. Paris, for example, owes its current physical pattern (common to few major cities) to Napoleon III and his forceful Prefect of the Seine, Baron Haussmann.[11] Washington, D.C., on the other hand, is an urban anomaly in that its resident population is wholly dependent on a congressional committee, which is not at all answerable to the community it administers.

traditional and symbolic-sentimental values

If we continue to narrow our attention to American cities—most of which are no more than one hundred years old—the importance of tradition can be easily (and mistakenly) ignored. European and Asiatic cities have long histories as cities; often the values of the distant past intrude in contemporary urban centers and effectively restrict the development of modern urban features (such as zonal developments and relatively uncontrolled competition for space). Firey has shown,[12] for example, that Boston's deviation from typical urban development could be understood by the desire to preserve historic landmarks and high status residential areas and the extended refusal of successful immigrant groups (Italians) to leave their fellow countrymen for the unfamiliar suburbs. Rome, Tokyo, Amsterdam, Hong Kong, Edinburgh, Vienna, and other cities are still unmistakably attached to ancient traditions—in housing, street patterns, religion, etc.—which are difficult to root out, though they are being modified and, in part, replaced.

---

[11] Good accounts of both the man and his planning activities may be found in Brian Chapman, *The Life and Times of Baron Haussmann* (New York, Macmillan, 1957); David H. Pinckney, *Napoleon III and the Re-Building of Paris* (Princeton, Princeton University Press, 1958).

[12] Walter Firey, *Land Use in Central Boston* (Cambridge, Mass., Harvard University Press, 1947).

figure 2
Synoptic Classification of Urban Regions

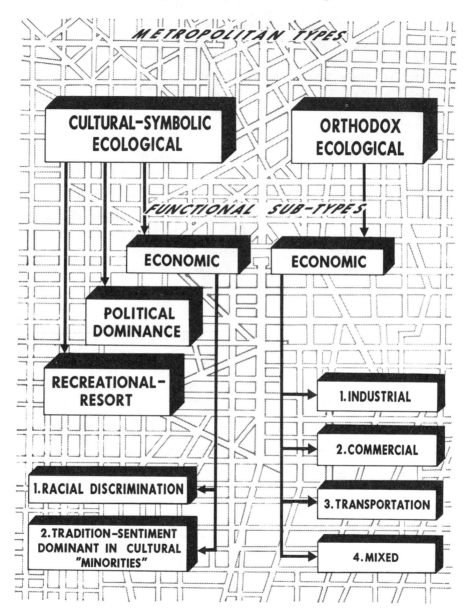

a suggested classification

How can these major dimensions or considerations be combined to provide a generally useful classification of urban regions—one that takes account of urban variety and basic, converging similarities? Figure 2 presents a tentative plan for incorporating the crucial features discussed in this chapter. Essentially, it distinguishes urban regions on the basis of ecological organization—which is analyzed in Part II—and dominant institutional function. Secondary attention is given to the cultural factor. Indeed, it may be useful to conceive of this factor in its various forms as a temporary deterrent to the development of more rationalized urban types. A great deal of historical material on world cities seems to indicate this fundamental direction in urban development.[13] Furthermore, this graphic classification explicitly excludes educational, religious, and artistic centers, since these are no longer dominant functions of modern urban regions.

Since urbanization seems to be concentrating toward the right side of the figure, most of our discussion in succeeding chapters will reflect this emphasis. However, it is important to approach the dominant types in this classification as parts of a larger picture of development. In the recent past, we have mainly contrasted urban regions with rural communities to sharpen our understanding of the former. It is also necessary to make comparisons, wherever possible, between types of urban regions, so that we can discover what is distinctive about urbanization in general, as well as about particular stages or types of urbanization.[14]

[13] William A. Robson, ed., *Great Cities of the World* (London, Allen and Unwin, 1954); Robert E. Dickinson, *The West European City* (London, Routledge and Kegan Paul, 1951); Horace Miner, *The Primitive City of Timbuctoo* (Princeton University Press, 1953); A. J. Youngson, *The Making of Classical Edinburgh 1750–1840* (Edinburgh, Edinburgh University Press, 1966).

[14] This view is well stated by Gideon Sjoberg, "Comparative Urban Sociology," in Robert K. Merton *et al.*, eds., *Sociology Today* (New York, Basic Books, 1959), pp. 334–359, and in his *The Pre-Industrial City* (New York, The Free Press of Glencoe, 1960).

selected references

MUMFORD, Lewis, *The Culture of Cities* (New York, Harcourt, Brace, and World, 1938), pp. 283–299.

SJOBERG, Gideon, *The Pre-Industrial City* (New York, The Free Press of Glencoe, 1960).

TAYLOR, Griffith, *Urban Geography* (New York, E. P. Dutton and Company, 1946).

ii

the interplay of demographic, ecological, and cultural themes

4

the peopling of urban regions: basic population characteristics and trends

Unfortunately, population statistics have little attraction for many students and laymen; this kind of information seems to be painfully dull, too often simply confusing, too technical, and only vaguely relevant to the social and cultural interests of the unwary consumer of reports and tables. But to the student of cities and urban regions, population facts provide an indispensable basis for analyzing organization and development. Let us briefly explore the reasons.

It is first important to recognize that population facts supply us with four types of information about a given area:

1. *Size:* the total number of persons in an area at a given time.
2. *Distribution* and *density:* the relative concentration or dispersal of persons within a land area.
3. *Composition:* the distribution of relevant physical and sociocultural characteristics among the members of a population (e.g., sex, age, race, occupation).
4. *Changes* in each of the preceding: the direction and degree of change in an area's population, with clues to the explanation of such changes.

Any single variety of population facts (e.g., size or density) is admittedly dry and potentially productive of yawns. However, if we consider these four types of population data in terms of their interrelationships, we may then find them extremely useful. Perhaps the attitude we should adopt is that population facts—studied as intertwined sets—serve as dual indicators of community and regional organization. Obviously, population statistics—especially those dealing with the composition or makeup of an area's population—give us vital information about the availability of persons for the area's functioning, and also its relative similarity to adjacent or distant areas. In short, patterns of social interaction and social distance can be clarified by knowledge of the socially pertinent characteristics of an area's population aggregate. In a recent study of Baltimore's population,[1] for example, delinquent behavior was found to be most concentrated in census tracts containing sizeable proportions of whites and nonwhites, rather than in predominantly white or predominantly Negro tracts—holding other population factors constant. The probable explanation for this finding is that areas with mixed population present greater opportunities for frustrating contacts, resultant personal tensions, and motivation for delinquent solutions.

Our major concern in this chapter is to present a simplified review of crucial population features and important trends in modern urban regions. At the present time, truly comparative statistics for the world's urban regions on many important aspects of population are not available. In fact, it is still difficult to obtain reasonably standardized definitions of urbanized population units, and therefore comparable figures on urban population size and composition, for most of the nations reporting. Consequently, we shall concentrate on data for the United States, with some attention to selected portions of world population data where these seem useful.[2]

recent growth of urban population

The revival of the city as an important type of population center can be approximately traced to the beginning of the nineteenth century for the Western nations and late nineteenth or early twentieth century for the rest of the world. In most cases, the development of numerous urban concentrations has been spurred by industrialization and/or the economic policies of newly created national entities. As Davis and Hertz indicate, the advance of world urbanization has been rapid—particularly since 1900.[3] It is equally clear that urbanites still constitute a minority of world population, though the proportions of urbanites vary considerably by continent and by nation (see Table 2).

For the U.S., the urban proportion of the population has been steadily increasing, particularly since 1940 (see Table 3). Virtually all size categories have increased their proportionate share of a growing national population. But the largest relative gains have been in the 500,000 to 1,000,000 category, particularly in the South and West (see Table 4).

Realistically, however, as we shall see in some detail in Chapter 7, the pattern of urban growth is somewhat obscured if we confine our analysis to

[1] Bernard Lander, *Towards an Understanding of Juvenile Delinquency* (New York, Columbia University Press, 1954), pp. 32–34.

[2] See the recent attempt to obtain comparable population figures by Kingsley Davis, *The World's Metropolitan Areas* (Berkeley, University of California Press, 1959).

[3] Kingsley Davis and Hilda Hertz, "The World Distribution of Urbanization," in Joseph J. Spengler and Otis D. Duncan, eds., *Demographic Analysis* (New York, The Free Press of Glencoe, 1956), p. 324.

table 2

Urbanized Population, by Size Category and Continent, 1960
(in percent)

CONTINENT	MILLION AND OVER	500,000– 1,000,000	300,000– 499,999	100,000– 299,999	100,000 AND OVER
North America	27.2	7.5	5.1	9.9	49.7
South America	14.7	3.8	3.4	5.6	27.4
Europe (including U.S.S.R.)	12.5	5.4	3.3	8.4	29.6
Asia	6.2	1.4	1.4	3.3	12.3
Africa	2.6	.9	1.4	3.2	8.1
Oceania	23.6	6.9	7.9	4.8	43.3
World	*9.6*	*3.0*	*2.2*	*5.1*	*19.9*

SOURCE: Homer Hoyt, *World Urbanization* (Washington, D.C., Urban Land Institute, Technical Bulletin #43, 1962), p. 26.

table 3

Urban and Rural Population of the U.S. for Selected Decades

		PERCENT URBAN	PERCENT RURAL
Current definition,	1960	69.9	30.1
	1950	64.0	36.0
Previous definition,	1960	63.0	37.0
	1950	59.6	40.4
	1940	56.5	43.5
	1930	56.1	43.9
	1920	51.2	48.8
	1910	45.7	54.3
	1900	39.7	60.3
	1890	35.1	64.9
	1860	19.8	80.2
	1830	8.8	91.2

SOURCE: U.S. Bureau of the Census, Supplementary Reports, PC (S1)–4, June 9, 1961, *Urban and Rural Population of the United States, By States, 1960 and 1950*, p. 3.

politically defined cities. Since 1950 the Census Bureau, urban demographers, and many users of population statistics have found it necessary to gather or apply urban population facts in terms of more comprehensive units such as "urbanized areas" and "standard metropolitan areas" (SMA). The latter unit, which is now widely used in the United States, deals mainly with the largest and economically most important urban areas. It is defined as con-

table 4

Growth of Population in Standard Metropolitan Statistical Areas, by Central City and Ring Areas, and by Effect of Annexation, 1950 to 1960
(in percent)

	CHANGE, 1950–60	CHANGE BASED ON 1950 LIMITS	CHANGE FROM ANNEXATION
United States	26.4	—	—
Central cities	10.8	1.5	9.3
Outside central cities	48.5	61.7	−13.1
Northeast region	13.0	13.0	—
Central cities	−3.1	−3.2	.1
Outside central cities	34.7	34.8	−.2
North central region	23.5	23.5	—
Central cities	4.3	−1.6	5.9
Outside central cities	56.4	66.5	−10.1
Southern Region	36.2	36.2	—
Central cities	28.5	5.3	23.3
Outside central cities	47.9	83.3	−35.4
Western region	48.5	48.5	—
Central cities	31.4	14.5	16.9
Outside central cities	66.4	84.1	−17.7
3 million and over	23.2	23.2	—
Central cities	1.0	.6	.4
Outside central cities	71.3	72.2	−.9
1 million–3 million	25.0	25.0	—
Central cities	5.6	−2.2	7.8
Outside central cities	44.8	52.7	−8.0
500,000–1 million	36.0	36.0	—
Central cities	21.4	4.8	16.7
Outside central cities	57.1	81.1	−24.0
250,000–500,000	25.6	25.6	—
Central cities	16.2	2.2	14.0
Outside central cities	36.2	51.9	−15.7
100,000–250,000	25.8	25.8	—
Central cities	24.4	4.8	19.6
Outside central cities	27.6	54.1	−26.5
Under 100,000	24.4	24.4	—
Central cities	29.2	8.6	20.1
Outside central cities	10.8	69.9	−59.6

SOURCE: U.S. Bureau of the Census, Supplementary Reports, PC (S1)-16, April 4, 1962, *Annexations and the Growth of Population in Standard Metropolitan Statistical Areas: 1950 to 1960*, p. 4.

table 5

U.S. Population in Groups of Places Classified by Size, 1950 and 1960

	1960		1950	
	PERCENT OF TOTAL POPULATION	PERCENT OF URBAN POPULATION	PERCENT OF TOTAL POPULATION	PERCENT OF URBAN POPULATION
Urban, total	*69.9*	*100*	*64.0*	*100*
Within urbanized areas	53.5	76.5	45.8	71.5
Central cities	32.3	46.5	32.0	50.0
1 million or more	9.8	14.0	11.5	18.0
500,000–1 million	6.2	8.9	6.1	9.5
250,000–500,000	6.0	8.6	5.3	8.3
100,000–250,000	5.5	7.9	5.4	8.5
50,000–100,000	4.4	6.3	3.4	5.3
under 50,000	.5	.7	.3	.4
Urban fringes	21.1	30.2	13.8	21.6
Outside urbanized areas	16.4	23.5	18.2	28.5
Rurals, total	*30.1*	*100*	*36.0*	*100*

SOURCE: U.S. Bureau of the Census, 1960 Census of Population, *Characteristics of the Population*, Part I: U.S. Summary (Washington, D.C., 1964), pp. 1–11.

taining one or more (but within 20 miles of one another) central cities of 50,000 or over, plus adjacent counties that exhibit arbitrarily defined urban characteristics. These include: either a minimum of 10,000 nonagricultural workers, or areas containing at least 10 percent of the SMA's nonagricultural worker supply, or at least half of county population living in clusters of 150 or more per square mile. The county's employed labor force must be at least two-thirds in nonagricultural occupations; at least 15 percent of county workers have employment in the central city; at least 25 percent of those working in the adjacent county live in the central city (or its county limits), or a monthly average of four or more telephone calls per subscriber from the adjacent county to the central city county.[4] This expanded unit seems to provide more valid measures of urbanization and, with increasing importance, it allows for more meaningful comparisons of trends in subareas of urban regions.

Clearly, suburbanization and related fringe developments are key factors in total urban growth. Currently, suburbs and urban fringe constitute over 30 percent of the urbanized population, 21 percent of the total U.S. population (Table 5). As Table 4 shows, in almost all size categories and regions,

[4] See Amos H. Hawley, *The Changing Shape of Metropolitan America* (New York, The Free Press of Glencoe, 1956), pp. 5–6.

peripheral growth far outweighs population increase in central cities. In fact, the relative growth of central cities would be substantially less than the table indicates without the increments provided by annexation of nearby populated areas.

population composition in urban regions

If urban patterns of growth are reasonably clear, the composition of urban populations presents several problems of analysis and understanding. Viewing the diversity of world urban areas, and also the changes in given cities over several generations, it is difficult to distinguish temporary or accidental trends from fundamental and characteristic population traits. The relative age of cities, their economic bases and broad cultural functions, geographic location, and the nature of specific urban historical events (e.g., diversion of railroad lines to other areas)—all of these subtly combine to create some diversity in population features. Essentially, urban populations are confluences of migration waves over several generations. Therefore, conditions both in cities and nations at large affect urban characteristics through the complex media of migration and social mobility. Let us try to be faithful to urban diversity and yet search for the most probable ingredients in the urban makeup. We may find that several widespread notions about cities require basic alteration, and even discard.

age distribution

Virtually all the available data for various nations, and for a period as long as 70 years, indicate that urban populations are relatively younger than rural categories. The materials for such a comparison are presented for the United States in Table 6, for Japan in Table 7, and for India in Figure 3. As we shall see later in more detail, this differential in age distribution is primarily a result of young urbanward migration from rural and small town areas; ruralward migration of older urban dwellers; and for the United States, the vast numbers of young European immigrants up to 1920. However, urban-rural age differences show some tendency to decrease, principally in the 20–29 category.

Nevertheless, the apparently typical concentration of urban populations in the productive age groups (20–44), compared with rural areas, exists in the United States in all major geographic regions. There is some tendency for southern urban areas to show a lower median age—28–30 years—as compared with 32–33 years for most of the other regions. This is perhaps due to the survival of rural population patterns in southern cities, e.g., a

table 6

Age Distribution by Type of Urban and Rural Residence, 1960

| | URBANIZED AREAS | | OTHER URBAN AREAS | | |
| | Central cities | Urban fringe | Places of 10,000 or more | Places of 2,500– 10,000 | RURAL |
AGE					
Under 5	10.7	12.1	11.3	11.2	11.6
5–9	9.3	11.2	10.1	10.3	11.3
10–14	8.2	9.5	9.0	9.4	10.6
15–19	6.8	6.6	7.9	7.6	8.3
20–24	6.6	5.3	7.0	5.9	5.7
25–29	6.4	6.3	6.2	5.8	5.6
30–34	6.7	7.6	6.5	6.3	6.1
35–39	7.0	8.1	6.7	6.5	6.4
40–44	6.6	7.2	6.2	6.2	6.1
45–49	6.4	6.2	5.8	5.9	5.8
50–54	5.8	5.2	5.2	5.2	5.1
55–59	5.3	4.2	4.6	4.6	4.5
60–64	4.5	3.5	3.9	4.0	3.8
65–69	3.9	2.8	3.5	3.8	3.4
70–74	2.9	2.1	2.8	3.1	2.6
75–79	1.8	1.3	1.9	2.2	1.8
80–84	.9	.7	1.0	1.2	.9

SOURCE: U.S. Bureau of the Census, 1960 Census of Population, *Characteristics of the Population*, Part I: U.S. Summary (Washington, D.C., 1964), p. 1–149.

table 7

Age Distribution in Japan, by Size of Commune, 1930 and 1950

AGE GROUP	ALL JAPAN	100,000 AND OVER	50,000– 99,999	10,000– 49,999	5,000– 9,999	UNDER 5,000
			1930			
0–5	16.5	14.4	15.8	16.8	17.3	17.1
6–14	20.1	16.4	18.2	20.0	21.3	21.4
15–19	10.2	13.1	12.3	10.8	9.5	8.5
20–64	48.5	53.4	50.7	48.5	46.8	46.9
65 and over	4.7	2.7	3.0	3.8	5.1	6.1
			1960			
0–4	13.5	13.0	13.5	14.0	13.7	13.3
5–14	21.9	19.7	21.2	22.5	23.1	22.9
15–19	10.3	10.3	10.5	10.4	10.4	10.0
20–64	49.4	53.4	50.6	48.5	47.3	47.4
65 and over	4.9	3.6	4.1	4.6	5.5	6.4

SOURCE: Irene B. Taeuber, *The Population of Japan* (Princeton, Princeton University Press, 1958), p. 77.

figure 3

Age Distribution in the Largest Cities of India as a Percentage of the All-India
Distribution, 1931

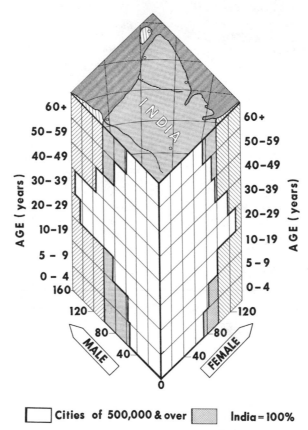

Cities of 500,000 & over   India = 100%

SOURCE: Kingsley Davis, *The Population of India and Pakistan* (Princeton, Princeton University Press, 1951), p. 141.

comparatively higher proportion in the 9–19 age group and a relatively lower proportion in the over 65 category.

In suburban or ring areas, the age composition differs somewhat from that of central cities. As an area typically settled by young families with children, suburban areas consequently have a lower median age than central cities.[5] There is, understandably, a substantially greater proportion in the 0–13 and 25–44 groups, and somewhat less in the 20–24 and 45 and over groups (Table 6). Whether this reflects the attractiveness of the suburb for

[5] Duncan and Reiss, *op. cit.*, pp. 120–121.

families with children or the encouragement of fertility among settled suburban families is not clear. In any case, the age distribution of suburban areas
is a product of selective migration of families with high urban birth rates.

sex ratio

The sex ratio (the number of males per 100 females) is one of the
most sensitive aspects of population composition, since it records the effects
of selective migration. (Differential death rates also affect sex ratios, of
course.) However, there has been a tendency to inflate the significance of
general sex ratios, particularly when ratios diverge from a presumably desirable standard of equality. From the urban sociologist's standpoint, sex ratios
not only reflect family structure and problems, but also economic conditions,
and the nature of available services in different parts of the community.

Urban sex ratios appear to be extremely varied, if we examine different
societies, different types and sizes of urban regions, specific segments of
urban regions, and different age categories.

Focusing on the United States, we find that urban areas tend to have
consistently lower sex ratios than rural areas. Indeed, the urban sex ratio
has declined in successive decades (see Table 8). If on the other hand,

table 8

Sex Ratio of Urban and Rural Areas of the U.S., by Race, 1960

	WHITE	NEGRO	TOTAL
Urban, total	94.4	90.4	94.1
Urbanized areas	94.5	90.6	94.2
Central cities	93.2	90.4	92.9
Urban fringe	96.3	92.2	96.2
Other urban	94.1	89.7	93.8
10,000 and over	94.4	89.9	94.1
2,500–10,000	93.8	89.1	93.5
Rural, total	104.5	101.9	104.3

SOURCE: U.S. Bureau of the Census, 1960 Census of Population, *Characteristics of the
Population*, Part I: U.S. Summary (Washington, D.C., 1964), p. 1–145.

non-Western urban regions are examined, the situation is quite different. In
India, urban sex ratios are higher than rural ratios, and also show a progressive *increase* from 1890 to 1940. Similarly, in Japan, urban sex ratios
show a surplus of males, but this seems to be declining. Nevertheless, Japa-

table 9

Sex Ratio of Urban and Rural Population: India, 1891–1941

DATE	URBAN	RURAL
1891	112.2	103.7
1901	111.9	103.0
1911	116.9	103.7
1921	120.9	104.3
1931	121.9	104.6
1941	122.8	104.8

SOURCE: Kingsley Davis, *The Population of India and Pakistan* (Princeton, Princeton University Press, 1951), p. 139.

nese cities also maintain a higher sex ratio than that of rural areas. We must conclude, then, that specific urban sex ratios reflect the larger society rather than a typical demographic pattern for urban communities.

Within the same society, urban sex ratios likewise fall into several types. Industrial cities and "military" cities, such as Norfolk, San Diego, Detroit, and San Francisco, have relatively high sex ratios. On the other extreme, commercial and administrative centers tend to have rather low sex ratios (between 80 and 90 males per 100 females). In general, the highest urban sex ratios can be found in the largest urban regions, perhaps because these cities furnish more balanced employment opportunities for both sexes. Smaller cities, on the other hand, seem to develop a wider range of sex ratios than other size categories; both rather high and rather low ratios are primarily found in this group.[6] It is likely that, since smaller cities are more specialized occupationally, they tend to be especially attractive to male rather than female migrants, or vice versa.

Since the urban region is a complex of communities, we would expect some variation in sex ratios in its different segments. White sex ratios are lowest in central cities and small urbanized areas; they show an approximately equal proportion of the sexes in suburban and urban fringe areas. Incidentally, all segments of American urban regions are developing lower sex ratios, which may be partially attributed to the decline in the foreign-born, and the increasing proportion of nonwhites (who tend to have comparatively lower sex ratios; see Table 8).

Another internal comparison deals with sex ratios by differentiated cultural areas of the central city. Adequate comparative material on this point

[6] *Ibid.*, p. 44; Joseph H. Greenberg, *Numerical Sex Disproportion* (Boulder, Colo., University of Colorado Press, 1950), pp. 21–23. Cf. C. N. Vakie and Krishna Roy, "Growth of Cities and Their Role in the Development of India," *Civilisations*, 15 (1965), pp. 326–352.

table 10

Sex Ratios in Japan, by Types of Area, 1920–1955

TYPE OF AREA AND AGE GROUP	MALES PER 1,000 FEMALES				
	1920	1930	1940	1950	1955
Metropolitan, total	1,103	1,107	1,061	1,001	1,022
0–4	1,016	1,023	1,027	1,048	1,060
5–14	1,063	1,048	1,042	1,031	1,039
15–19	1,239	1,191	1,194	1,073	1,179
20–34	1,189	1,189	1,040	952	1,052
35–49	1,142	1,197	1,171	1,005	911
50–64	1,006	998	1,004	1,072	1,044
65 and over	674	666	662	685	720
Other industrial, total	1,032	1,025	1,024	966	974
0–4	1,014	1,017	1,028	1,043	1,064
5–14	1,018	1,012	1,019	1,025	1,218
15–19	1,043	997	1,052	988	961
20–34	1,105	1,084	1,041	901	972
35–49	1,068	1,102	1,114	973	907
50–64	995	982	976	1,000	999
65 and over	764	736	717	726	722
Intermediate,* total	1,015	1,020	1,005	950	944
0–4	1,018	1,019	1,029	1,052	1,036
5–14	1,030	1,024	1,020	1,019	1,019
15–19	1,067	1,052	1,022	1,000	982
20–34	1,081	1,101	1,041	883	911
35–49	996	1,037	1,051	925	862
50–64	980	952	950	976	981
65 and over	795	775	744	723	771

* Areas with 40–49 percent of gainfully employed in agricultural work.
SOURCE: Taeuber, op. cit., p. 79.

is not available, but intensive studies of such cities as Chicago, Cincinnati, and Los Angeles enable us to discern rather sharp differences. In the innermost zones of Chicago and Cincinnati, the sex ratio is high, with an understandable preponderance of males in rooming-house districts near the central business area (a ratio of 900 or more). With increasing distance from the center, sex ratios tend to decline—first sharply from 800–900 to just over 100, then more gradually to the 90–95 range.[7] This rough gradient in urban sex ratios, however, is difficult to establish in many cities that do not approximate the concentric pattern of growth found in Chicago. Shevky and Williams have been able to distinguish for Los Angeles levels of sex ratios

[7] Hatt and Reiss, op. cit., p. 288; James A. Quinn, Human Ecology (Englewood Cliffs, N.J., Prentice-Hall, 1950), pp. 438–445.

table 11

Males Per 100 Females in the Civilian Population, by Type of Residence,
April, 1959 and 1950

RESIDENCE	1959	1950
Total	*95.2*	*97.3*
Standard metropolitan statistical areas	*93.5*	*94.9*
Urban	91.5	93.6
Rural nonfarm	100.7	102.1
Rural farm	106.4	109.3
Other territory	*97.6*	*100.4*
Urban	91.8	93.3
Rural nonfarm	97.8	100.6
Rural farm	105.7	108.2

SOURCE: *Civilian Population of the United States, by Type of Residence, April 1959 and 1950.* Bureau of the Census, Current Population Reports, Series P–20 (Washington, D.C., Feb. 25, 1960), p. 3.

related to cultural areas, regardless of their geographic location in the city.[8] These areas are categorized by *degree of urbanization* and *level of social rank* (based on occupation, education, and income). In general, sex ratios are low in areas of high social rank and highest degree of urbanization (as indicated by low fertility, low proportion of women working, and high proportion of multifamily dwellings). The highest sex ratios are in low social rank and high urbanization areas. From a geographic standpoint, Los Angeles' highest sex ratios are near the downtown area and in Long Beach, while the low sex ratios are in the inner ring of older, fashionable residential areas (Wilshire, Hollywood, and Westlake).

Finally, urban sex ratios may be analyzed for various age groups in the population. In the United States, high or moderate sex ratios occur in categories under 14 years of age, after which ratios decline progressively in the productive, mature, and old age groups—for all sizes of urban regions. This pattern is a consequence of young female migration to cities, and also of differential mortality rates. Incidentally, urban Negroes show a rise in sex ratio in the 40–60 age group, which may be an indication that the more stable families (with husband present) are clustered among Negroes in the over 40 age group. By contrast, Japan's urban sex ratios favor males at most age groups. The highest ratios have been the 15–19 category for at least forty years, while the lowest (91) is currently in the 35–49 age group.

[8] Eshref Shevky and Marilyn Williams, *The Social Areas of Los Angeles* (Berkeley, University of California Press, 1949), map facing p. 70, and p. 77.

marital status and household characteristics

The demographic character of urban families is especially confusing to the layman, and therefore open to many misconceptions and, sometimes, to forebodings about the instability of urban family life. What, then, are the special features of urban families, and what is the direction of their development?

1. age at marriage

The overall age for first marriages has been declining since about 1940 (Table 12). However, urban whites tend to marry six months to a year later than rural whites. Virtually the same difference can be found among non-whites in urban and rural areas (Table 13). Both male and female nonwhites

table 12

Median Age at First Marriage, by Sex, 1920–1965

Year	Male	Female
1920	24.6	21.2
1930	24.3	21.3
1940	24.3	21.5
1950	22.8	20.3
1955	22.6	20.2
1960	22.8	20.3
1961	22.8	20.3
1962	22.7	20.3
1963	22.8	20.5
1964	23.1	20.5
1965	22.8	20.6

SOURCE: *Statistical Abstract of the United States, 1966*, p. 63.

marry earlier than their white counterparts, probably in line with the earlier marriage age pattern of lower socioeconomic categories. Furthermore, in an era of considerable remarriage, it is interesting to note that males with multiple marriages tend to marry the first time at a younger age than those who only marry once—with the exception of males marrying during 1958–1960 (Table 14). Whether earlier marriage therefore signifies unwise or necessarily unsuccessful marriages, or not, is subject to further investigation. Females likewise marry earlier when they have more than one marriage,

table 13

Median Age at First Marriage, by Color and Sex, by Urban and Rural Areas, 1960

	WHITE MALES	NEGRO MALES	WHITE FEMALES	NEGRO FEMALES
Central cities	24.4	23.7	21.5	20.7
Urban fringe	24.2	23.6	21.5	20.5
Other urban	23.6	23.3	20.7	20.1
Rural nonfarm	23.3	22.9	20.2	19.8
Rural farm	23.8	22.6	20.4	19.6
United States	23.9	23.4	21.0	20.4

SOURCE: U.S. Bureau of the Census, Subject Reports, *Age at First Marriage,* Final Report, PC (2)–4D, 1966, Table 1.

table 14

Median Age at First Marriage for Those Married in 1891 to 1960, by Sex and Urban and Rural Residence

	U.S.	CENTRAL CITIES	URBAN FRINGE	OTHER URBAN	RURAL
1891–1960					
Males					
Married once	25.6	25.8	25.3	24.9	24.7
Married more than once	23.8	24.1	23.8	23.6	23.6
1958–1960					
Males					
Married once	24.8	25.5	25.1	24.1	24.0
Married more than once	29.1	29.9	28.9	29.4	27.8
1950–1954					
Males					
Married once	25.3	26.1	25.4	24.8	24.7
Married more than once	23.9	24.5	23.6	23.5	23.8
1891–1960					
Females					
Married once	22.5	23.1	22.8	22.2	21.6
Married more than once	20.7	21.0	20.7	20.5	20.5
1958–1960					
Females					
Married once	21.7	22.6	22.2	21.0	20.7
Married more than once	24.0	24.6	23.2	23.8	23.6
1950–1954					
Females					
Married once	22.4	23.2	22.7	21.9	21.4
Married more than once	21.0	21.5	20.7	20.6	20.6

SOURCE: U.S. Bureau of the Census, Subject Reports, *Marital Status,* Final Report PC (2)–4E, 1966, pp. 152–155.

table 15

Median Years Difference in Age Between Mates for First Marriages, by Rural and Urban Residence, 1960

	MEDIAN AGE DIFFERENCE BETWEEN MATES
Central cities of	
urbanized areas	2.7
Husband under 35 years	1.7
Husband 35–54 years	2.7
Husband 55 or over	4.2
Urban fringe	2.4
Husband under 35 years	1.7
Husband 35–54	2.5
Husband 55 or over	3.8
Rural nonfarm	2.9
Husband under 35 years	2.0
Husband 35–54	3.0
Husband 55 or over	4.5
Rural farm	3.2
Husband under 35 years	2.1
Husband 35–54	3.1
Husband 55 or over	4.2

SOURCE: U.S. Bureau of the Census, Subject Reports, *Marital Status*, Final Report PC (2)–4E, 1966, pp. 152–155.

except for 1958–1960. In addition, urbanites tend to marry persons closer to their own age than do rural people, perhaps because of greater availability of potential mates in the same or similar age categories (Table 15).

2. family-building

Perhaps the most controversial aspect of urban population composition is marital opportunities and marital status. In general, rural-urban differences are less marked than many suppose. For white males, the differences are slight, with a rate higher among urbanites. Nonwhite urban males seem to show marriage rates intermediate between those in farm and fringe areas. Among females, however, urban areas show somewhat lower rates than farm and fringe areas for whites, and more comparable rates for nonwhites. Indeed, 91–95 percent of the urban population (over 14 years of age) has been married at one time or another, compared with 91.8–97 percent of rural or fringe populations.

Yet the "currently single" present a problem. Apparently, urban males over 14 years of age are also more often single than urban females, but have a smaller proportion of currently unmarried than rural males. Single urban females are more often found in central cities than in the fringe or small urban areas outside metropolitan regions. Indeed, the difference between rural and urban unmarried females is basically one of the central city female and the rural female. Parenthetically, it is likely that the surplus of single urban males and females is a condition found largely in the biggest metropolitan centers, perhaps as a consequence of unfavorable age distributions. Finally, as expected, married males are relatively more numerous in suburban areas—and also in small urban areas. But a higher proportion of married females is in rural areas, followed closely by those in suburban areas (Table 16).

As a final demographic clue to family-building, let us explore the comparative distributions of types of family units. The Census Bureau distinguishes: *primary families*—related persons with a family head; *secondary families*—related persons without a recognized head of the household; and *subfamilies*—married couples (with or without children) living with in-laws. Further tabulations are available for family units containing one parent and children (*parent-child groups*) and *unattached individuals* who are either family heads or not (primary or secondary sub-types). The distributions are summarized in Table 17.

table 16

Marital Status of United States Population Over 14 Years, by Sex and Urban and Rural Residence, 1960

| | URBANIZED AREAS | | OTHER URBAN | | RURAL |
	Central city	Urban fringe	Places of 10,000 or more	Places of 2,500 to 10,000	
Males					
Single	25.5	21.3	24.6	22.3	26.2
Married	67.8	74.3	69.7	72.0	68.6
Separated	1.3	.8	1.0	.9	.8
Widowed	4.0	2.8	3.4	3.7	3.4
Divorced	2.7	1.7	2.3	2.0	1.8
Females					
Single	20.7	17.6	19.5	17.6	17.3
Married	61.4	69.6	64.0	65.7	71.0
Separated	1.7	1.1	1.4	1.2	.8
Widowed	14.0	10.2	13.3	14.1	10.2
Divorced	3.9	2.6	3.2	2.6	1.5

SOURCE: U.S. Bureau of the Census, 1960 Census of Population, *Characteristics of the Population*, Part I: U.S. Summary (Washington, D.C., 1966), p. 1–156.

table 17

Households, Families, and Subfamilies in the United States, by Residence,
March, 1967

HOUSEHOLD AND FAMILY TYPES	U.S.	NONFARM	FARM
Households	100.0	100.0	100.0
Head with no relatives in household	17.1	17.6	8.2
Head with relatives	82.9	82.4	91.8
Husband-wife households	72.2	71.6	84.1
Other households with male head	2.0	2.0	2.9
Households with female head	8.7	8.9	4.8
Families	100.0	100.0	100.0
Husband-wife families	87.0	86.7	91.5
Other families with male head	2.4	2.4	3.1
Families with female head	10.6	10.9	5.4
Primary Families	100.0	100.0	100.0
Husband-wife families	87.1	86.8	91.6
Other families with male head	2.4	2.4	3.1
Families with female head	10.5	10.8	5.3
Secondary Families	100.0	100.0	100.0
Husband-wife families	49.2	50.0	—
Other families with male head	9.2	9.5	—
Families with female head	41.5	40.5	—
Subfamilies	100.0	100.0	100.0
Husband-wife subfamilies	52.5	51.5	64.0
Other subfamilies with male head	7.1	7.4	4.5
Subfamilies with female head	40.5	41.1	31.5

SOURCE: U.S. Bureau of the Census, Current Population Reports, *Housing and Family Characteristics*, P-20, #173, June 25, 1968, p. 13.

Unfortunately, these distributions are not further broken down by such important categories as race and nationality, or occupation. However, it is clear that cities have somewhat smaller proportions of normal family units (with male heads, and only spouses and children present), larger proportions of families with female heads, as compared to farm and fringe areas.[9] This is undoubtedly due to the higher concentration in urban areas of groups with unconventional family structure (e.g., Negroes and certain foreign-born groups). Secondary families—those without a genuine household head—are principally an urban phenomenon, and a substantial part of this group seems to contain unmarried couples or wives without currently available spouses. Finally, subfamilies (families lodging with in-laws) seem to be proportionately similar for urban and rural areas, though the incidence of married

[9] Bogue, *op. cit.*, pp. 281–282.

couples living with in-laws is greater in farm and fringe areas. It may be concluded, therefore, that urban families are less likely to be conventionally constituted, but are more likely to achieve independent household status.

3. educational distribution

The increasingly widespread emphasis on more formal education for more young people (and for senior citizens as well) is a typical urban value, though the rural-urban differential is diminishing in the sixties (Table 18).

table 18

Selected Educational Attainments of Persons 25 Years and Older in the United States, March, 1967, by Race and Place of Residence

	MEDIAN SCHOOL YEARS COMPLETED	FOUR YEARS OF COLLEGE OR MORE
		(Percent)
Metropolitan—in central cities, total	*11.9*	*9.8*
White	12.1	10.7
Negro	10.2	4.2
Metropolitan—outside central cities, total	*12.3*	*12.9*
White	12.3	13.2
Negro	9.7	4.2
Nonmetropolitan, total	*11.0*	*7.6*
White	11.4	8.0
Negro	7.3	3.4

SOURCE: U.S. Bureau of the Census, Current Population Reports, *Educational Attainment: March 1967*, P-20 #169, February 9, 1968, p. 2.

The greatest difference is between white and Negro educational levels in rural areas. Significantly, the racial difference is smallest in central cities— though it still involves almost two years of schooling. But the rural-urban difference is especially sharp in college level work. Despite the recent swelling of college enrollments, suburban areas continue to send proportionately more young people to college than do rural and small town areas.

4. occupational distribution

Since urban regions are principally organized about economic activities, the degree and types of participation in economic functions provide impor-

table 19

Composition of the Employed Male Labor Force by Major Occupational Group
and Urban and Rural Residence, 1960

Occupational Group	U.S.	Urban	Rural Nonfarm	Rural Farm
Professional, technical, and kindred workers	10.3	12.0	7.8	1.7
Farmers and farm managers	5.5	.4	3.5	53.0
Managers, officials, and proprietors	10.7	11.9	9.7	2.7
Clerical and kindred workers	6.9	8.3	4.6	1.6
Sales workers	6.9	8.0	5.1	1.6
Craftsmen, foremen, and kindred workers	19.5	20.2	22.3	7.0
Operatives and kindred workers	19.9	19.7	24.5	10.1
Private household workers	.1	.1	.2	.1
Farm laborers and foremen	2.8	.6	5.1	15.1
Laborers, except farm and mine	6.9	6.6	9.2	3.9

Source: U.S. Bureau of the Census, 1960 Census of Population, *Characteristics of the Population*, Part I: U.S. Summary (Washington, D.C., 1966), p. 1–216.

tant clues about urbanites. In general, urban areas have a somewhat smaller proportion of their male residents in the labor force, either working or looking for some job. The reverse is true for females. In line with our expectations, labor force participation tends to rise as we turn from the larger to the smaller urban areas. This is probably due to the longer period of formal education found in larger cities.

The typical pattern of urban occupations can be approached either in terms of major occupational or skill groups, or by broad types of economic activities (see Table 19). It is clear from this table that urban areas are distinguishable by higher proportions in urban skill groups: professional, managerial, clerical, sales, and service workers. Craftsmen and skilled laborers form about equal proportions of urban and suburban categories, both of which are considerably higher than those in farm areas. Incidentally, the greatest percentage increase in urban occupations is in professional, managerial, and skilled worker categories, whereas suburban and fringe communities seem to be growing most noticeably in skilled workers and farm laborers.

A more simplified and perhaps more conspicuous picture can be found in a comparison of major types of work. Not surprisingly, urban areas are particularly concentrated in manufacturing and trade, while farm areas have less than 15 percent of their labor force in these activities. Urban areas also have higher concentrations in transportation, finance, personal services, entertainment, professional services, and public service. In many of these categories, suburban and fringe populations show considerable similarity to urban areas; likewise, rates of growth in these categories are highest for suburban and fringe areas—evidence that the latter are increasingly urban in character.[10]

5. income distribution

An interest in urban income patterns may have some mercenary implications to some, but the urban sociologist is primarily concerned with the cultural and organizational consequences of income distributions. For example, comparative income distributions inevitably reflect occupational differences. In addition, income statistics provide measures of comparative community resources (for taxation, private welfare funds, etc.) and clues to changing motives or habits in consumption of available goods and services.

As Table 20 demonstrates, urban populations have smaller proportionate shares of low income brackets (under $4000) and larger shares of higher incomes ($10,000 and over), compared to farm populations. The differential is greatest between urban and farm populations, as we would expect. Furthermore, the comparative rates of increase (from 1947 to 1959) indicate that suburban areas are narrowing their moderate differential, increasing by 94 percent while cities increased by 72 percent. Farm areas show only a 57 percent rise in median income.

Table 20 also indicates that median income is positively related to size of urban community. Suburban and fringe areas seem to be most similar to cities under 250,000 population, and to densely populated areas (25,000 and over) that are not included in urbanized areas as defined by the Census. An interesting income pattern is also apparent when comparing incomes by age of family heads. The highest median income for farm heads occurs in the 25–34 age group. Suburban and fringe median incomes are highest in the 35–44 group, while the highest median for urban heads is in the 45–54 age group.

As Table 21 indicates, in 1965 rural-urban income differences have been maintained, even though median incomes have risen sharply. But more clearly, the low income categories refer primarily to Negro families—and with particular concentration in rural areas.

Two additional aspects of income distribution have generally been neglected, though they are of some interest. All three population categories attain their highest median incomes in families composed of five persons (i.e., three children), even though the median size of family differs to some extent between farm and city populations. This may mean that these populations or community types are approaching convergence in desirable family size

[10] Duncan and Reiss, *op. cit.*, pp. 96, 129, 175.

table 20

Percent Distribution of Income Among Families in the United States, 1959, by Area and Size of Place

TOTAL MONEY INCOME FOR FAMILIES	Total	URBANIZED AREAS				PLACES NOT IN URBANIZED AREAS			
		Total	1,000,000 and over	250,000 to 1,000,000	Under 250,000	25,000 and over	Under 25,000	Rural nonfarm	Rural farm
Under $500	1.6	1.5	1.3	1.4	2.2	1.9	1.7	2.3	8.3
$500 to $999	1.7	1.5	1.0	1.8	2.2	2.0	2.6	3.0	8.7
$1,000 to $1,499	3.0	2.8	2.3	3.3	3.4	3.4	3.8	4.0	10.1
$1,500 to $1,999	3.7	3.5	3.0	4.0	4.0	3.6	4.7	4.2	8.9
$2,000 to $2,499	4.1	3.6	3.1	4.6	3.6	4.7	5.5	4.1	9.8
$2,500 to $2,999	4.4	3.9	3.0	4.9	4.9	6.0	5.4	4.6	7.0
$3,000 to $3,499	4.9	4.5	3.8	4.6	6.0	5.8	6.2	5.2	7.9
$3,500 to $3,999	4.6	4.2	3.6	4.2	5.7	5.2	5.7	5.1	5.9
$4,000 to $4,499	5.8	5.7	5.8	5.3	5.9	6.6	5.9	6.1	6.0
$4,500 to $4,999	5.8	5.8	5.5	5.0	7.3	6.7	5.7	6.3	3.9
$5,000 to $5,999	13.6	13.6	13.0	14.9	14.0	12.2	14.0	14.2	6.6
$6,000 to $6,999	11.9	11.8	12.0	11.5	11.8	12.9	11.7	10.9	5.1
$7,000 to $7,999	8.8	9.1	9.2	9.3	8.4	8.2	8.3	9.2	3.2
$8,000 to $9,999	11.9	12.7	13.8	12.1	10.6	11.4	9.3	10.1	3.4
$10,000 to $14,999	10.6	11.8	14.3	19.6	7.8	8.4	7.3	8.0	3.3
$15,000 to $24,999	2.7	3.2	4.0	2.5	1.9	0.9	1.7	2.1	1.6
$25,000 and over	0.8	1.0	1.1	1.1	0.5	0.3	0.6	0.6	0.2
Median income	$5,755	$5,956	$6,366	$5,732	$5,350	$5,348	$5,211	$5,361	$2,800

SOURCE: *Income of Families and Persons in the United States: 1959*, Bureau of the Census, Current Population Reports, Series P–60, No. 35 (Washington, D.C., Jan. 5, 1961), p. 23.

table 21

Family Income by Race and Urban and Rural Residence, 1965
(in percent)

INCOME CATEGORY	NONFARM		FARM	
	White	Nonwhite	White	Nonwhite
Under $1,000	2.2	5.9	6.6	28.9
$1,000–1,499	2.1	5.4	5.7	23.3
$1,500–1,999	2.7	6.7	6.6	15.4
$2,000–2,499	2.6	7.4	7.1	10.2
$2,500–2,999	2.8	7.1	6.6	6.8
$3,000–3,499	3.1	7.8	6.7	3.8
$3,500–3,999	3.3	7.4	5.1	3.8
$4,000–4,999	7.3	7.4	11.9	4.1
$5,000–5,999	9.3	11.2	9.6	1.1
$6,000–6,999	9.9	7.2	8.3	1.5
$7,000–7,999	10.4	6.8	5.6	—
$8,000–8,999	8.8	4.4	5.1	—
$9,000–9,999	7.0	3.3	2.9	—
$10,000–11,999	11.1	4.6	5.0	.8
$12,000–14,999	8.4	3.4	2.7	.4
$15,000–24,999	6.9	1.4	3.7	—
$25,000 and over	1.7	.2	.7	—
Median family income	$7,414	$4,212	$4,476	$1,456

SOURCE: U.S. Bureau of the Census, Current Population Reports, *Income in 1966 of Families and Persons in the United States*, P–60 #53, December 28, 1967, p. 19.

among the more successful families. A second point of interest concerns the consequences of multiple family earners for median income. In all three population categories, two or more earners are quite prominent. Indeed, for all three categories, families with only one earner show less than median incomes for their respective groups. Only with an additional earner do family incomes surpass the population medians. However, one sharp difference emerges from the statistics. Farm families with three or more earners have median incomes lower than those of farm families with two earners. City and suburban fringe families, on the other hand, show vastly increased median incomes when three or more earners are involved. It may well be that farm families with multiple earners are in the lowest income categories occupationally, while the individual incomes of multiple earner city families are reflections of higher educational and occupational status.

Apparently, there is some significance not only in urban-rural income distributions, but in variations among urban regions. Duncan and Reiss compared high and low income categories of urban population units on a

table 22

Median Family Income by Age of Head and Residence, 1959

TOTAL MONEY INCOME	14–24	25–34	AGE OF HEAD 35–44	45–54	55–64	65 and over
Urban	$4,075	$5,580	$6,366	$6,729	$6,150	$3,335
Rural nonfarm	$3,760	$5,664	$6,347	$5,802	$4,683	$2,195
Rural farm	—	$3,250	$3,196	$3,107	$2,356	$2,176

SOURCE: *Income of Families and Persons in the United States: 1959*, Bureau of the Census, Current Population Reports, Series P–60, No. 35 (Jan. 5, 1961), p. 25.

table 23

Median Family Income by Size of Family and Residence, 1959

TOTAL MONEY INCOME BY RESIDENCE	Total	FAMILIES HAVING SPECIFIED NUMBER OF PERSONS 2	3	4	5	6	7 or more
Urban	$5,755	$4,701	$5,963	$6,355	$6,439	$6,036	$5,945
Rural nonfarm	$5,361	$4,105	$5,136	$5,980	$6,042	$5,951	$5,173
Rural farm	$2,800	$2,049	$2,976	$3,329	$3,750	$3,514	$2,473

SOURCE: *Ibid.*, p. 26.

table 24

Median Family Income by Number of Earners and Residence, 1959

MEDIAN INCOME AND RESIDENCE	Total	FAMILIES HAVING SPECIFIED NUMBER OF EARNERS None	1	2	3 or more
Urban	$5,755	$1,773	$5,208	$6,676	$8,823
Rural nonfarm	$5,361	$1,476	$5,145	$5,960	$7,160
Rural farm	$2,800	—	$2,397	$3,459	$3,271

SOURCE: *Ibid.*, p. 27.

number of demographic and economic items. In general, they found high income areas tended to have more formal education, lower proportions of nonwhites, higher sex ratios, higher proportions in the productive age groups, and higher proportions in professional, managerial, and manufacturing categories.[11]

6. color, nationality, and religion

It is likely that the widest variation in urban population composition in the world today is in racial, religious, and nationality makeup. These factors are responsive to other features of urban regional operation (economic and political), but are more often reflections of policies in the larger society, opportunities for international migration, and historical idiosyncrasies of individual nations. In cities of India and Pakistan, for example, about two-thirds of the population is Hindu, almost 30 percent is Muslim, about 3 percent is Christian.[12] By contrast, cities in the United States are predominantly Christian, with few Muslims and perhaps 5 percent who are Jews. Similarly, racial and religious distributions in African and South

table 25

Racial Distribution of the U.S. Population by Urban and Rural Residence,
1950 and 1960

(in percent)

	TOTAL	WHITE	NONWHITE
1950			
Urban, total	64.0	64.3	61.7
Urbanized areas	45.8	45.8	45.3
Central cities	32.0	31.1	39.2
Urban fringe	13.8	14.7	6.1
Other urban	18.2	18.5	16.4
Rural	36.0	35.7	38.3
1960			
Urban, total	69.9	69.5	72.4
Urbanized areas	53.5	52.7	58.9
Central cities	32.3	30.3	50.5
Urban fringe	21.1	22.8	8.4
Other urban	16.4	16.8	13.5
Rural	30.1	30.5	27.6

SOURCE: *Statistical Abstract of the United States, 1966*, p. 25.

[11] *Ibid.*, pp. 351–365.
[12] Kingsley Davis, *The Population of India and Pakistan* (Princeton, Princeton University Press, 1951), p. 142.

American cities are clearly different from those in North America and the Far East.[13]

In view of this diversity, we can only make the generalization that urban regions tend to have more diversified mixtures of racial, religious, and nationality categories than rural areas. Let us focus on each of these three separately for the United States.

table 26

Percent Distribution of the United States Population by Race and Nativity for Central Cities and Suburbs of Urbanized Areas, 1950

RACE AND NATIVITY	TOTAL URBANIZED AREAS	CENTRAL CITIES	SUBURBS AND URBAN FRINGE
Native white	78.9	75.9	86.2
Foreign-born white	10.5	11.1	9.1
Negro	10.2	12.6	4.5
Other races	0.4	0.4	0.2

SOURCE: Duncan and Reiss, *op. cit.*, p. 122.

1. *Color.* The concentration of nonwhites, most of whom are Negroes, is generally greater in urban regions than in small towns and rural areas (except for the South). *Within* urban regions, on the other hand, central cities have higher proportions of nonwhites than do suburban and fringe areas. Likewise, as Table 25 indicates, Negroes have become even more urbanized since 1950, both in central cities and in suburban and fringe areas.

2. *Nationality.* Foreign-born persons constitute a larger portion of urban populations than of farm or small town categories. However, immigration restrictions since 1920 help to explain a decreasing proportion of the foreign-born in all urban size categories. As in the case of nonwhites, the foreign-born are primarily located in central cities, rather than in suburban or peripheral areas of urban regions. Yet Table 26 also shows considerable variation in proportions of the foreign-born (and of nonwhites) among central city categories and among suburban rings. Geographic location of cities and differentials in job opportunities in previous generations may account for these differences.

[13] See Leo Kuper, *Durban: A Study of Racial Ecology* (London, Jonathan Cape, 1958); Richard Morse, *From Community to Metropolis* (Gainesville, University of Florida Press, 1958); Horace Miner, *The Primitive City of Timbuctoo* (Princeton, Princeton University Press, 1953).

table 27

Percent Distribution of Religious Affiliations in the United States Civilian
Population, by Residence, March 1957

RELIGIOUS AFFILIATION	TOTAL	URBANIZED AREAS OF 250,000 OR MORE	OTHER URBAN	RURAL NONFARM	RURAL FARM
Percent by religion					
(14 years old and over)					
Protestant	58.6	49.1	71.3	77.8	83.2
White	49.5	38.4	64.4	70.8	72.3
Nonwhite	9.1	10.7	6.9	7.0	10.9
Roman Catholic	31.7	37.8	23.4	16.6	11.9
Jewish	4.9	7.7	1.0	0.5	0.1
Other religion	1.6	1.9	1.2	0.8	0.9
No religion	2.3	2.2	2.4	3.4	3.3
Religion not reported	1.0	1.3	0.6	0.9	0.7
Percent by residence					
(14 years old and over)					
Protestant	56.6	27.2	29.5	28.7	14.7
White	55.2	24.5	30.7	30.1	14.7
Nonwhite	66.1	44.6	21.6	19.3	14.5
Roman Catholic	78.8	53.9	24.9	15.8	5.4
Jewish	96.1	87.4	8.7	3.6	0.2
Other religion	77.4	52.9	24.5	14.9	7.7
No religion	54.2	29.5	24.7	31.3	14.5
Religion not reported	68.2	49.5	18.7	23.4	8.4

SOURCE: *Religion Reported by the Civilian Population of the United States: March, 1957,*
Bureau of the Census, Current Population Reports, Series P–20, No. 79 (Washington,
D.C., Feb. 2, 1958), p. 7.

3. *Religion.* Statistics on religion are notoriously limited in accuracy
and often well out-of-date. However, a sample survey taken by the Census
Bureau in 1957 is summarized in Table 27. Urban areas tend to have smaller
than national, farm, or suburban-fringe proportions of Protestants, higher
proportions of Catholics, and considerably higher proportions of Jews.

natural increase

A good deal of apprehension about the urban region's ability to survive
demographically was current in the thirties, when urban growth was primarily based on rural-urban migration and high birth rates of recent immi-

grant families. Clearly, urban birth rates in the United States and most parts of the world have for a long time been lower than rural birth rates. But what does this mean when a greater range of relevant population statistics is examined? How can we reasonably characterize urban vitality?

First, and still the outstanding generalization, is a prevailing difference between urban and rural fertility rates. In the United States, as well as in Japan and India, fertility ratios (the number of children under 5 years of age per 1000 women in childbearing age groups), or the number of children born, are lowest in the largest cities and generally increase in smaller population centers (Table 28).[14]

Second, it is sometimes forgotten that in non-Western cities, and more recently, in the highly industrialized urban regions of the West, urban fertility has been high enough to insure population replacement without migration. Evidence for this is of three sorts. Gross reproduction rates, which measure the supply of females for the next generation of childbearing, tend to be above normal replacement in Japanese cities, though the figures for 1955 indicate the first descent below replacement. In the United States, India, and other nations, urban areas likewise now show rates above normal replacement (Table 29).

Another trend that is extremely important is the relative course of urban mortality rates since 1900. For Japan, crude mortality rates have been lower for cities than for rural areas, though both show sharp declines during the last 15 years. In fact, urban mortality rates for females are lower than

table 28

Children Born Per Thousand Women Aged 15–44 Years, and 45 and Over, by Urban and Rural Residence, 1960–1964

	Women 15–44 Years			Women 45 Years and Over		
	1964	1962	1960	1964	1962	1960
Metropolitan areas	1,810	1,733	1,640	2,218	2,202	—
Central cities	1,759	—	1,549	2,136	—	2,091
Outside central cities	1,861	—	1,735	2,317	—	2,350
Nonfarm	1,790	1,851	—	2,285	—	—
Farm	2,031	—	—	3,194	—	—
Nonmetropolitan areas	2,168	2,062	2,008	3,037	2,936	3,012
Nonfarm	2,113	—	—	2,956	—	—
Farm	2,456	—	—	3,418	—	—

Source: U.S. Bureau of the Census, Current Population Reports, *Fertility of the Population: June 1964 and March 1962*, P–20 #147, January 5, 1966, p. 15.

14 Colin Clark, *Population Growth and Land Use* (New York, St. Martin's Press, 1967), pp. 215–220, shows very slight differences between rural and urban fertility.

table 29

Child-Woman Ratios by Urban and Rural Areas, Gross Reproduction Rates,
and Net Reproduction Rates for Selected Nations, 1959–1962

NATION AND YEAR	CHILD-WOMAN RATIO Rural	Urban	GROSS REPRODUCTION RATE	NET REPRODUCTION RATE
Honduras, 1961	923	674	2.77 (1957)	*
Mexico, 1960	797	511	3.1 (1960)	*
Netherlands, 1960	800	651	1.54 (1964)	1.5
United States, 1960	539	468	1.62 (1963)	1.5
Brazil, 1960	786	552	3.0 (1945)	*
Indonesia, 1961	611	675	2.8 (1956)	*
India, 1961	668	617	2.7 (1960)	*
Japan, 1960	365	283	.96 (1963)	.92
Pakistan, 1961	839	780	3.38 (1962)	*
Austria, 1961	820	462	1.35 (1964)	1.29
Czechoslovakia, 1961	403	315	1.21 (1963)	1.17
France, 1962	375	307	1.41 (1964)	1.37
Hungary, 1960	382	263	.87 (1964)	.81
Norway, 1960	438	327	1.41 (1963)	1.37
Sweden, 1960	404	274	1.12 (1963)	1.09
England and Wales, 1961	361	329	1.37 (1962)	1.33
Scotland, 1961	398	380	1.49 (1964)	1.44
U.S.S.R., 1959	820	576	1.37 (1961)	*

* Not available.
SOURCE: United Nations, *Demographic Yearbook, 1965*, pp. 234–240, 605–617.

rural rates, for the younger age groups (10–34 years), while urban mortality rates for males are higher than rural rates only in the 10–14 year group. Turning to the United States, while urban mortality is higher than rural rates, urban rates have dropped to a differential of about 1.5 deaths per thousand population. A substantial part of this decline in mortality is found among nonwhites in urban areas, somewhat less in rural areas.[15]

The composite effects of fertility and mortality on natural increase can be gauged by net reproduction rates, which take account of the supply of new females as adjusted by their probable reduction through mortality. This replacement rate is now available for a number of nations (see Table 29). However, few nations provide rural and urban replacement rates. Indeed, some demographers have cautioned against uncritical dependence on this measure, noting that predictions based on these replacement rates are particularly erratic in nations undergoing rapid demographic changes (e.g., an acceleration of marriages). Nevertheless, computations for cities in the U.S.

[15] Bogue, *op. cit.*, p. 195.

table 30

Age-Adjusted Mortality Rates, by Color and
Residence, United States, 1940 and 1950

RESIDENCE AND COLOR	DEATHS PER 1,000 POPULATION 1940	1950
Urban	11.4	8.9
Rural	9.8	7.4
White urban	10.8	8.5
Nonwhite urban	18.1	13.1
White rural	9.3	7.1
Nonwhite rural	14.4	10.9

SOURCE: C. Horace Hamilton, "A Study of Ecological and Social Factors in Mortality Variation," unpublished paper delivered to the American Sociological Society, 1955.

table 31

Components of Population Change for Metropolitan and Nonmetropolitan
Population Areas, 1960–1965 and 1950–1960

(in thousands)

	1960–1965 Natural increase	Net migration	1950–1960 Natural increase	Net migration
United States	12,626	1,846	25,337	2,660
Metropolitan counties	8,589	2,436	16,336	8,634
Central counties	6,620	740	12,910	4,131
Suburban counties	1,969	1,696	3,426	4,504
Nonmetropolitan counties	4,037	−590	9,002	−5,974

Contribution to population change
(percent)

United States	87.3	12.7	91.0	9.0
Metropolitan counties	77.2	22.8	65.4	34.6
Central counties	89.5	10.5	75.8	24.2
Suburban counties	53.7	46.3	43.2	56.8
Nonmetropolitan counties	100.0	0.0	100.0	0.0

SOURCE: U.S. Bureau of the Census, Current Population Reports, *Estimates of the Population of Standard Metropolitan Statistical Areas, July 1, 1965*, P–25, #371, August 14, 1967, p. 2.

now indicate that net reproduction rates have risen since World War II and that about 77 percent of urban population increase can be attributed to natural increase (the difference between birth and death rates).[16] Natural increase accounts for a much larger proportion of population growth in central cities than in suburban and fringe areas. However, since 1960, suburban growth itself has been due more to natural increase than to net migration (Table 31).

migration

As much of the preceding discussion in this chapter indicates, migration patterns affect virtually every sort of population statistics. In addition, migration provides an excellent source of information on the inherently dynamic nature of urban regions. Unfortunately, despite their incalculable importance, migration data of a widely comparable and detailed sort are not available for urban analysis. Only in recent years, in fact, have demographers in the United States been able to acquire reasonably adequate direct information on migration, and to discover recognizable (rather than probable or guessed) patterns in population movements related to the urban region.[17]

One genuinely useful discovery is the fact that several streams of migration coexist in modern urban regions, instead of the oversimplified notion of rural-urban migration. These are:

1. *Intracity migration:* changes of residence within municipal limits in a given time period.

2. *Intrametropolitan migration:* changes of residence from central city to suburb and fringe areas, or vice versa.

3. *Interurban migration:* migration between central cities.

4. *Intermetropolitan migration:* movements between suburban and fringe areas of different urban regions.

5. *Rural-urban migration:* movements from farms to central cities.

6. *Rural-metropolitan migration:* movements from farms to urban fringes or suburbs.

Urban regional migration, therefore, consists of two aspects: the population characteristics of *incoming* migrant categories; and the character of

[16] Cf. the pattern for Mexico City, where natural increase accounts for only 42 percent of population growth. Oliver Oldman *et al., Financing Urban Development in Mexico City* (Cambridge, Harvard University Press, 1967), p. 7.

[17] In the past, migration has been estimated by comparing an actual age distribution with one predicted on the basis of mortality rates for each age group. The difference between actual and predicted figures was then taken as a measure of migration.

migrant patterns among *existing* urban populations. In short, migration and mobility are distinguishable into *urban-building* and *urban-dispersion* types. But urban mobility is itself responsive to the particular nature of various urban (or urbanizing) nations. Such factors as the current proportions of rural and urban populations, the type and pace of economic growth, the amount and variety of demand for labor, the relative development of large, competitive urban centers—these and others help to account for a substantial diversity in urban migration throughout the world. However, several conclusions about urban migration seem tenable.

In early stages of urban growth, rural-urban migration is most important. This type of migration seems to attract relatively young, single (or married but migrating without family) persons—white and nonwhite—with limited skills and formal education. Sex ratios among migrants are variable, but tend to be selective of more males.[18] In general, long-distance migration to cities is higher among males, shorter distances among females. In addition, migrants in this stage tend to settle first in central cities and in the informally designated "migrant zones" (the zone of transition in Western cities, suburban slums in African and some Far Eastern cities). Some inter-urban migration occurs during this period, it is true; this usually consists of family units with young children.[19]

A later stage in urban migration patterns is reached when economic and residential opportunities have combined to convert the central city into the nucleus of an urban or metropolitan region. Since this has attained its most advanced stage in the United States, let us try to outline the composite of major ingredients of American urban migration and residential mobility as a potential direction for trends in other urban regions.

1. The suburban movement, which has a long history in American cities, began to assume a new level of importance by the late thirties. But the continuing migration to suburbs has changed both in character and in its demographic impact on central cities. During the forties—and presumably also in the fifties—suburban migrants came from two mobile sources, according to the calculations of Bogue. One source was a category of relatively long-term city residents, which accounts for only about ten percent of net suburban population increase. Even this loss by the cities was counterbalanced by urban migration from nonmetropolitan areas. The other source was migration from farms and population centers outside the SMAs.[20]

---

18 Taeuber, *op. cit.*, pp. 133, 156–159; Davis, *The Population of India and Pakistan*, pp. 134–136. See also Michael Banton, *White and Coloured* (London, Jonathan Cape, 1959); Sydney Collins, *Coloured Minorities in Britain* (London, Lutterworth Press, 1957); I. Schapera, *Migrant Labour and Tribal Life* (London, Oxford University Press, 1947); E. P. Hutchinson, *Immigrants and Their Children, 1850 to 1950* (New York, John Wiley and Sons, 1956).

19 Ronald Freedman, *Recent Migration to Chicago* (Chicago, University of Chicago Press, 1949), Chap. IV; Taeuber, *op. cit.*, p. 161.

20 Bogue, *op. cit.*, pp. 406–410.

table 32

Migration Patterns Among Males in the U.S., 1949, by Community of Origin
and Destination

Migration Category	Percent
Nonfarm to nonfarm	73.7
Farm to nonfarm	7.2
Farm to farm	7.8
Nonfarm to farm	4.5
Origin not known, to nonfarm	6.3
Origin not known, to farm	.5
Total	*100.0*

Source: Beyer, *Housing*, p. 29.

2. Suburban and similar peripheral movements were increasingly selective of higher status occupational and racial groups, though there is evidence of surprisingly high Negro migration to urban rings in two Southern areas.

3. Age groups among migrants to suburban areas tended to differ by racial group and by community of origin. Migrants from central cities were mainly children under nine years of age (40.7 percent); also city migrants were more concentrated in the 40 and over age category than those from nonmetropolitan areas. White migrants from nonmetropolitan areas were somewhat more likely to be older and married than their predecessors a few decades ago, or than nonwhite migrants from nonmetropolitan areas.

4. Though there have been occasional intimations of this tendency for some years, it is now quite clear that interurban (and to some extent intermetropolitan) migration is even more pronounced than rural-urban or other types. As early as the thirties, rural-urban migration accounted for only about 19 percent of total migration, while interurban and intermetropolitan types constituted almost half of the migration during 1935–1940.[21] If we focus on the migration of males during 1949, the results are equally striking.[22] This general pattern was previously suggested by a study of migration to Stockholm and in a careful analysis of migration to Chicago in the period 1935–1940. Apparently, most migrants to urban regions come from other urban areas (cities or urban fringe), or in stages of migration from farm to urban to metropolitan areas.[23]

5. If we compare rates of migration to any destination *from* cities with

[21] *Ibid.*, p. 104.
[22] Glenn H. Beyer, *Housing: A Factual Analysis* (New York, Macmillan, 1958), p. 29.
[23] Freedman, *loc. cit.;* Jane Moore, *Cityward Migration* (Chicago, University of Chicago Press, 1938).

those from rural areas, we find that the former are somewhat lower. This means that urban populations tend to be proportionately less mobile than ruralites or suburbanites. Furthermore, as Bogue has demonstrated, the velocity of migration, i.e. (the number of migrants in a given stream as a proportion of its home population, multiplied by the population in the specific destination area as a proportion of the population of all potential areas of destination) is lowest for urban to rural migration, rural to urban, and suburban to rural types. The highest velocity seems to be found among rural to rural and suburban to suburban streams. In short, urbanites are more stable than our folklore suggests, while the greatest proportionate movement is really among the suburbanites and ruralites.

6. Since 1940, however, rural-metropolitan migration has increased, probably as a result of World War II and postwar economic opportunities. Likewise, there is some evidence that an increasing part of urbanward migration comes from small towns and villages, rather than farm areas.[24]

Before we attempt to summarize and interpret the specific materials on urban populations that have been presented in this chapter, several limitations must be recognized. First and most important, population data for urban areas of the world are not comparable in definition of units, in accuracy of compilation, and in attention to statistical breakdowns useful for the urban sociologist. Consequently, our discussion has been confined to nations with the best record-keeping, and particularly, the United States.

Second, it is difficult to make more than tentative generalizations from population data of the past few decades, since population phenomena seem to show numerous short-term variations, in response to the rapid cultural and social changes of our times. For example, birth rates have been a constant source of difficulty to those who try to make population predictions or to explain rather sharp changes in fertility.

Finally, and this is related to the previous point, population data are products of an infinite number of events and decisions. But these events and the social actions associated with them are the meaningful core of processes that are largely removed from the simplified end-figures (e.g., birth rates). Therefore, analysis of population statistics requires persistent recourse to facets of social organization and attitudinal trends, some of which have not yet been adequately investigated (e.g., the relation of perceived status to fertility). With these limitations in mind, we may draw several plausible implications from urban population trends.

1. Urban population growth has been comparatively high for several generations in the Western world, for 20–50 years in Asia, Africa, and the Pacific region. Statistics show a continually high level of growth, not pri-

---

[24] Bogue, op. cit., p. 413; Henry S. Shryock, Jr., *Population Mobility Within the United States* (Chicago, Community and Family Study Center, University of Chicago, 1964), Chap. 10.

marily in central cities, but in regional patterns. Consequently, the old fear of urban decline is at least demographically unfounded.

2. Urban populations consistently show the fundamental urban attribute of heterogeneity. However, the nature of heterogeneity can and does undergo recognizable changes. In American urban regions, internal variations in nationality, occupation, and education have been reduced, but, on the other hand, there has been a notable increase in the proportion of nonwhites and a continuing broad range of income categories. In other urban regions of the world, particularly where nonwhites are relatively numerous, racial heterogeneity either remains a dominant feature, or is replaced in significance by occupational heterogeneity—when legal and social restrictions are loosened. Throughout the world, urban heterogeneity is patterned through specialization of function (occupation, education, income) and through the development of distinctive areas or segments in the urban region ("natural areas," suburbs, etc.).

3. Population composition in urban regions seems to be moving toward the more normal patterns of older communities. For example, the initially high proportion of young adults is being replaced by a somewhat older concentration in the more advanced urban regions. This is explained by such trends as reduced mortality rates, the decline in immigration, and the shift in economic opportunities toward persons with greater formal education.

Furthermore, the unusual sex ratios of early urban growth are no longer typical of regions that have advanced beyond the pioneer stage of demand for huge pools of unskilled labor. A rough sequence of stages may be posited. In the first phase, industrial needs attract high proportions of male migrants, though mill towns constitute a clear exception. The second phase involves commercial and clerical functions as supplements to, or competitors of, the industrial focus. Females are consequently attracted in this phase. A third phase accompanies a more balanced economic base and increased opportunities for family life in the city and in an expanding suburban fringe. At this point, sex ratios tend to move from the 80–90 range to the upper 90s—the continuing excess of females reflecting differential mortality rather than differential migration.

Another aspect of increasing normality is related to the growing proportion of married persons in urban regions. This is found both in resident groups and in recent migrant streams. Furthermore, the proportion of complete families (both mates present), of primary families, and of families with two or more children has recently increased in American urban regions.

4. A surprising trend in urban population is an apparent reversal in the role of natural increase in population growth. It is sometimes forgotten that early migrants to cities have moderately high fertility (though less than rural populations) and therefore contribute substantially to urban growth, quite apart from subsequent rural-urban migration. During the twenties and thirties, at least in the United States and Western Europe, any net increases

in urban population were primarily contributed by migration. In the thirties for example, urban net reproduction rates in the United States were about 76 percent, an indication that urban population would decline by 24 percent without the counterbalancing effect of migration. Since the midforties, however, American urban regions have become self-sufficient in population growth. We can only guess about the continuation of currently high urban birth rates, but it seems likely that they will persist throughout the early seventies.

5. Despite a good deal of grumbling and literary denunciation of urbanism, urban population statistics tends to support the conclusions that urban regions are here to stay (if humans are not obliterated by their own destructive abilities) and that people are increasingly satisfied with the urban regional life-style. Several kinds of evidence bear on this point. Throughout the world, wherever substantial rural populations exist, urbanward migration continues at a high rate. In highly urbanized societies, and in particular the United States in recent decades, urbanites show little tendency to move to farms or small towns; they move instead within cities, to suburban outposts, or to other cities. Urbanites with greater exposure to life in urban regions seem to be better adjusted to urban complexity than their predecessors (the rural-urban migrants in the nineties to the thirties), though there is some room for improvement in the mental health of contemporary urbanites. They seem to be giving more attention to family formation, to planning for larger families than the previous generation of urbanites.

A comparison of urban population statistics for various nations of the world, and for different time periods since 1870 or so, seems to lend support to the idea of stages in urban development, as we have suggested in this chapter in terms of demographic data, and in Chapters 2 and 3. In this sense, population data reflect the state of human resources as "inputs" into the community. These very same facts also represent the products of social and cultural organization and change in the urban region.

In particular, we can analyze urban population data for basic clues about specific facets of urban life. In Chapter 2 it was suggested that the distinctive characteristics of urbanism include: (a) extensive division of labor; (b) dominance of commercial, industrial, and service occupations; (c) high density of population; and (d) dominance of social control mechanisms on a nonkinship basis. The necessary evidence for (a) and (b) is provided by data on occupational and income distributions, educational levels, etc., while census enumerations of population size by well-defined census tracts enable us to measure (c). Only in the case of (d) do we find population data to be of limited utility.

But other important aspects of urbanism can be directly or indirectly analyzed through adequate population statistics. For example, the extent of social and cultural heterogeneity is largely found in such data as religious and racial distributions, nationality backgrounds, occupational distributions, and also by comparing subareas of the urban region on any population dimension of interest (e.g., sex ratio, nonwhites, median age). Likewise, the relative stability or change of urban regions can be measured and understood in some degree by analyzing data for trends in births, deaths, migration, and age distributions. In addition, the urbanite's opportunity (as distinct from motivation) for informal and formal associations with other residents can be estimated from analyses of the present chapter (see pp. 58–64). Perhaps most of our prevalent notions about urban life derive from information and experiences in the earlier and more chaotic phases of urbanism. It is therefore specially important to take account of the latest data and investigations, wherever possible, for clues to continued trends or significant shifts in composition and distribution of urban populations.

This chapter has generally concentrated on population composition and its changes, with only secondary attention to patterns of distribution. In the next three chapters, we shall give primary emphasis to (a) the typical ways in which urban populations and their dominant activities are arranged in urban areas; (b) the interrelations between these urban segments; and (c) changes in these patterns.

selected references

BOGUE, Donald J., *The Population of the United States* (New York, The Free Press of Glencoe, 1959).

DAVIS, Kingsley, *The Population of India and Pakistan* (Princeton, Princeton University Press, 1951).

————, *The World's Metropolitan Areas* (Berkeley, University of California Press, 1959).

DUNCAN, Otis D. and REISS, Albert J. Jr., *Social Characteristics of Urban and Rural Communities* (New York, John Wiley and Sons, 1956).

FREEDMAN, Ronald, *Recent Migration to Chicago* (Chicago, University of Chicago Press, 1949).

GOLDSTEIN, Sidney, *Patterns of Mobility 1910–1950* (Philadelphia, University of Pennsylvania Press, 1958).

HAWLEY, Amos H., *The Changing Shape of Metropolitan America* (New York, The Free Press of Glencoe, 1956).

NAM, Charles B., ed., *Population and Society* (Boston, Houghton Mifflin, 1968).

TAEUBER, Irene B., *The Population of Japan* (Princeton, Princeton University Press, 1958).

5

ecological organization: understanding the socio-geographic differentiation of urban communities

As we have seen in the preceding chapter, the nature of a given population (size, composition, growth pattern) furnishes valuable clues to the potentialities of community organization and functioning. In all communities, and particularly in urban communities, the population seems to distribute itself in recognizable patterns within the land area occupied by an identifiable community. These patterns may be conceived as reflecting a differentiation of land usage, as well as a division of social labor. In other words, it is possible to view the community as consisting of patterns of allocating population and human activities to subunits of a specific land area. However, it is extremely important to recognize that allocation and distribution are accompanied by some coordination and implicit or explicit regulation. Taken together, these patterns constitute the ecological organization of human communities, which we may define as the organization of population and land units, through processes of social interaction and the pursuit of values, into definable entities. It should be noted that ecological organization is not equivalent to community organization, but is rather a level or aspect of community organization.

Ecological organization may be profitably studied in two ways: (*a*) as a system or structure in its own right, whose component parts and processes require investigation; and (*b*) as a special component of the community, regarded as a system or structure. In this chapter and the next, emphasis will be given to the first type of analysis, while later chapters (notably Chapters 7 and 8) will be more concerned with ecological organization as a functional subsystem of the community. There are several compelling reasons for the sociologist's continued interest in the ecological organization of urban communities and urban regions.

1. To begin with, the sheer complexity of urban activities and social organizations demands orderly attempts to simplify this overwhelming mass of facts by the obvious expedient of classifying them in terms of their objective—e.g., economic, familial, etc. and spatial location. In this manner, the tendency to view social behavior too abstractly, in terms of implicit values and somewhat intangible regularities called social relations and social groups is corrected (but not replaced) by a recognition of the material setting in which human groups necessarily operate.

2. In addition, ecological analysis of urban communities provides a realistic approach to universal human problems of devising creative accommodations between a variety of social-cultural needs and a more or less differentiated physical environment. This is particularly evident in ecological studies of regularities in spacing and timing the cumulative stream of urban activities so that maximum use of limited units of land by dense populations can be successively approached.

3. Ecological analysis likewise depicts in graphic form an extensive division of labor among groups in complex communities, which supplements and perhaps deepens our understanding of the nature and functioning of numerous specialized groups. There has been a noticeable tendency in sociology toward studying social groups apart from larger social settings and the direct or indirect influences of competing groups. For example, we may mention the investigations of small groups, industrial organizations, modern families, and religious groups.[1] One of the contributions of ecological analysis is a necessary consideration of specific groups and activities in their role as segments of larger, more complex enterprises—communities. Indeed, one of the special features of the ecological approach is the search for patterns of organization that create and sustain some coordination above and beyond the more obvious facts of division and separation.

4. Finally, and perhaps most important, ecological analysis supplies clues to the nature and problems of social organization in the community. If ecological organization is a human product, imperceptibly constructed from antecedent social processes, it is also a set of conditions that affect in some manner the daily decisions of individuals and groups in the routines of community functioning. Thus, knowledge of ecological organization pro-

---

[1] See such compilations or summaries of these fields in Dorwin Cartwright and Alvin Zander, *Group Dynamics* (Evanston, Row, Peterson and Company, 1953); Michael S. Olmsted, *The Small Group* (New York, Random House, 1959); Allan W. Eister, "Basic Continuities in the Study of Small Groups," in Howard Becker and Alvin Boskoff, eds., *Modern Sociological Theory* (New York, Dryden Press, 1957), Chap. X; Delbert C. Miller and William H. Form, *Industry, Labor, and Community* (New York, Harper and Brothers, 1960); Marvin B. Sussman, ed., *Sourcebook in Marriage and the Family* (Boston, Houghton Mifflin, 1955).

vides an essential link among past, present, and probable future developments in the community. However, since communities are inherently dynamic and subject to external influences, complete consistency in community organization is ordinarily lacking. Ecological analysis therefore can indicate the points at which the community exhibits discontinuities or gaps in its organization, both as an explanation of current problems and as an omen of potential difficulties.

The ecological approach, in short, stresses the importance of relative *location* of groups and activities with respect to one another and to the units of land they respectively occupy. As Mukerjee has wisely suggested,[2] relative location or position in the ecological order is comparable (and perhaps somewhat equivalent) to relative *status* (i.e., differential opportunities, responsibilities, and rewards) in the social order. But it is unprofitable to ask which order has priority, or which causes the other. We may only conclude that ecological organization and social organization are related aspects of human communities.

location of urban communities

Obviously, ecological organization is in part dependent on the character of the urban site.[3] For over one hundred years, economists, historians and urban sociologists have analyzed the factors presumed to be basic in the location of cities. We have already discussed this problem for cities of the first and second waves (Chapter 2). At this point, we are concerned only with understanding modern cities. At least two cautions must be observed in our discussion.

1. The search for ultimate origins of urban location is inevitably a matter of considerable inference from fragmentary facts. Under these circumstances, it is easy to substitute our hindsight for the foresight of urban pioneers. We should always be wary of imputing "modern" motives and needs to our predecessors. Often we have only three sets of facts to work with: the geographic base (extent, topography, natural resources, etc.), the number and social characterisitcs of the initial population, and the recorded activities of this population.

2. In addition, we must recognize a distinction between initial location of a potential city and the location of a clearly realized urban community. In other words, the factors and motives connected with the earliest choice of

2 Radhakamal Mukerjee, *Social Ecology* (London, Longmans, Green, 1945).

3 For the most useful summary of theories and studies, see Harold M. Mayer and Clyde F. Kohn, eds., *Readings in Urban Geography* (Chicago, University of Chicago Press, 1959), Part VII; Edward L. Ullman, "A Theory of Location for Cities," *American Journal of Sociology*, 46 (May, 1941), pp. 853 864; Pierre George, *Précis de Géographie Urbaine* (Paris, Presses Universitaires de France, 1961); Harold Carter, *The Towns of Wales* (Cardiff, University of Wales Press, 1965), Chap. 2.

a site may be quite irrelevant to some subsequent change in the significance of that site for genuinely urban development. As we have already suggested in Chapter 3, the city may be properly conceived as a stage in community development, which requires careful analysis of cultural factors. For example, it is erroneous to explain the extraordinary development of Chicago as an illustration of its favorable location (at the base of Lake Michigan). This location was certainly not favorable in the 1840s and 1850s, when Chicago was merely a name for well-scattered clusters of shacks. Intensive political activity (which diverted the transcontinental railroads to Chicago), the favorable economic gains derived from the Civil War, an aggressive group of businessmen, and the massive financial support of bankers in New York City enabled Chicago to convert mere potentiality into well-defined actuality in a scant generation.[4] Communities within a 100-mile radius of Chicago (mostly south of Lake Michigan) were, from a purely geographic standpoint, as favorably located as Chicago. But they have become essentially minor cities, such as Rockford, Beloit, and Kankakee. With these cautions in mind, we may now consider the most useful attempts to explain urban location.

1. the theory of central place

In general, proponents of this theory seem to focus on those cities that may be called regional service centers. The urban community is viewed as a response to the economic needs of a fairly definite agricultural region: middleman services in buying and disposing of agricultural production, provision of technical and financial services, and availability of products from other regions. Consequently, the location of these cities tends to be at the most accessible (i.e., central) position in the service region. A corollary of this theory is the plausible hypothesis that the larger the service region (both in population and extent), the larger and more complex the central city.[5]

Several limitations seem to be generally recognized in this theory. First, it is primarily applicable to agricultural rather than highly industrialized areas. Second, its predicted patterns of urban location are quite distorted by developments in transportation, which change patterns of accessibility. Third,

[4] Bessie L. Pierce, *A History of Chicago* (New York, Alfred A. Knopf, 1937–1957), 3 vols.; Homer Hoyt, *One Hundred Years of Land Values in Chicago* (Chicago, University of Chicago Press, 1933); Wyatt W. Belcher, *The Economic Rivalry Between St. Louis and Chicago 1850–1880* (New York, Columbia University Press, 1947), pp. 114–116, 185. Cf. Richard M. Morse, "Some Characteristics of Latin American Urban History," *American Historical Review*, 67 (January, 1962), pp. 317–338.

[5] Ullman, *op. cit.*; James A. Quinn, *Human Ecology* (Englewood Cliffs, N.J., Prentice-Hall, 1950), pp. 86–96, 286–289; Brian J. L. Berry and Allen Pred, *Central Place Studies: A Bibliography of Theory and Applications* (Philadelphia, Regional Science Research Institute, 1961); Gunnar Olsson, *Distance and Human Interaction* (Philadelphia, Regional Science Research Institute, 1965); Forrest R. Pitts, ed., *Urban Systems and Economic Development* (Eugene, Ore., School of Business Administration, University of Oregon, June, 1962).

variations in fertility of soil, type of cultivation, and local administrative patterns tend to interfere with theoretically central locations.

2. the "break in transportation" theory

Urban location, according to this theory, is likewise understandable in terms of accessibility. However, instead of accessibility to a service area, we now shift our attention to the problem of accessibility with respect to differing but converging forms of transportation. The problem of storing and transferring commodities from one type of transportation to another is crucial in a commercial-industrial society. Therefore, cities tend to develop at these transfer points (or breaks) to coordinate needed transfers, maintain records of changes in ownership and responsibility, and to provide the normal range of services for the necessary personnel. The most frequent breaks in transportation are between water traffic (lake, river, and ocean) and railroads, railroad and truck, airplane and railroad, and intersecting railroad routes. Indeed, many of the most important world cities—often called *entrepôts* or gateway cities—can be basically understood as illustrations of this theory.[6] New York City, London, Chicago, Boston, Philadelphia, Stockholm, Amsterdam, and Calcutta are outstanding instances.

3. the theory of historical accidents

Both of the preceding explanations reflect the operation of rational motives in urban location, particularly with respect to facilitating economic processes (production, distribution). A few cities, however, seem to have been located as a result of such nonrational historic accidents as personal whims of powerful leaders and political deals. Washington, D.C., for example, was clearly a consequence of a power struggle between contending factions in the Constitutional Convention. St. Petersburg (now Leningrad) was located in part for military reasons, in part to satisfy the egotism of Peter the Great. Even Paris, the city of light, which was almost a forgotten, out-of-the-way village for centuries, was transformed into a major city when the Capetians assumed the French throne and willfully moved the capital from Aachen.[7]

These theories of urban location, which seem to be complementary rather than contradictory, aid in understanding several aspects of basic urban ecology. However, it is increasingly clear that these theories by themselves in many instances do not adequately explain the location of specific cities. Essentially, it is unwise to analyze the origins and development of cities without consideration of regional and sometimes national conditions. Indeed, the

[6] Mayer and Kohn, *op. cit.*, Sect. 12; Charles H. Cooley, "The Theory of Transportation," in *Sociological Theory and Social Research*, ed. by R. C. Angell (New York, Holt, Rinehart & Winston, 1930), pp. 75–83.

[7] See William A. Robson, ed., *Great Cities of the World* (London, Allen and Unwin, 1954), especially Chaps. VI, X, XII.

location of particular cities is often affected by the number and relative distance of preexisting cities. Furthermore, changes in transportation, technological advances, and political vicissitudes undoubtedly function to alter
the desirability of given sites for urban development.

We should not underestimate the great diversity of urban locations—
near oceans, rivers, lakes; on plains, plateaus, on mountainsides as well as
below sea level; in agricultural and industrial areas; as far as several hundred miles from other major cities or as close as thirty miles (e.g., Dallas
and Fort Worth); in extremely dry to rather humid climates. Perhaps it is
more fruitful to stress the distinctive ways in which cities generally make
use of their diversified locations in performing urban functions. Locational
factors, in other words, provide a base for the development of subsequent
ecological organization.

urban ecological units

Accurate and useful description of urban ecological organization—the
distribution and functional coordination of population, organized activities,
and material culture—ultimately rests on the way in which ecological parts
or units are selected. Ideally, these units should be both geographically limited
and socioculturally homogenous. In other words, they should be easy to
identify on a map (for convenience) and should represent relatively distinctive population features and cultural and social organization (as functional
units). In practice, however, this dual aim is difficult to achieve because the
actual distributions reflect considerable mixture of activities and populations;
and processes of mobility and social change alter the significance of previously
useful units. Urban sociologists must therefore seek compromises which
produce simplified but sociologically important analyses of urban communities. Before we turn to an extended discussion of basic ecological patterns,
let us briefly review the types of ecological units that have received most use.

1. natural areas

One of the earliest concepts of urban ecology is the natural area, an
unplanned segment of urban development marked by definable physical
features (topography, and boundaries supplied by hills, rivers, railroad
tracks, streets and highways) and a high degree of cultural uniformity
among the resident or functioning population.[8] Because of these features, the
natural area usually has a pointedly descriptive name, which does not cor-

---

8 Robert E. Park, *Human Communities* (New York, The Free Press of Glencoe,
1952), Chaps. I, II, XIV; Paul K. Hatt, "The Concept of Natural Area," *American
Sociological Review*, 11 (August, 1946), pp. 423–428; Harvey W. Zorbaugh, *The Gold
Coast and the Slum* (Chicago, University of Chicago Press, 1929).

respond to administrative designations (i.e., 2nd ward, 10th Assembly district, etc.). Some natural areas possess distinctive connotations, not only to the sociologist, but to the layman as well. Consider, for example, the Gold Coast, Skid Row, the Black Belt, Wall Street, the Bottoms, Little Sicily, Bohemia, and Downtown or the Loop. With some local modifications, these areas can be identified in many urban communities, which lends great weight to their usefulness. However, natural areas are rather large and sometimes difficult to delimit sharply. Furthermore, a considerable portion of the urban community fails to fit into any of the more clearly identifiable natural areas; the resultant islands provide a picture of urban discontinuity that perhaps over-estimates the genuine gaps in the urban fabric.

2. concentric zones

The division of the urban community into circular zones radiating from the central business district is a classic device first used extensively by Burgess and others at the University of Chicago. Basically, the zonal unit may be variable in width, but most often it has been arbitrarily (and conveniently) conceived in terms of one or two-mile bands. In general, zones have been used to detect gradients (patterns of increase or decrease) in such community phenomena as crime and delinquency, divorce, mental disorders, land values, etc.[9] It is assumed that urban development is relatively uniform in all directions from the center, though topographical features (rivers, lakes, hills) are recognized as distorting factors. On the whole, the zonal approach must be considered a useful orientation to ecological organization, rather than a source of functional ecological parts.

3. sectors

As a realistic supplement to, and modification of, zonal units, Homer Hoyt's analysis of radial sectors is of great value.[10] Using rental figures and surveys of housing quality, Hoyt found that urban growth could be substantially described as a series of residential fingers expanding in radial fashion around major transportation routes toward the outskirts of the city. Each sector tends to reflect segregation of population groupings according to income and social status and thus helps to account for some of the deviations from expected zonal patterns. In a sense, sectors correspond to elongated natural areas, with relatively homogeneous physical, cultural, and social characteris-

---

[9] The classic reference is Ernest W. Burgess, "The Growth of the City," in Robert E. Park *et al.*, eds., *The City* (Chicago, University of Chicago Press, 1925), pp. 47–62. A good discussion and bibliography may be found in Quinn, *op. cit.*, Chap. VI.

[10] Homer Hoyt, *The Structure and Growth of Residential Neighborhoods in American Cities* (Washington, Federal Housing Administration, 1939), pp. 74–78; Arthur M. Weimer and Homer Hoyt, *Principles of Urban Real Estate* (New York, Ronald Press, 1939), pp. 61–68.

tics in each type of sector. Since more than a third of the city's land area is devoted to residential usage, sector patterns furnish helpful clues to fundamental ecological organization.

4. nuclei

Zones and sectors perhaps simplify urban ecological patterns without sufficient regard for deviations and irregularity of urban development. Many cities seem to develop typical clusterings of population and activities that defy their easy inclusion in zones or sectors. These clusters, which have been called urban nuclei,[11] appear to arise in portions of the urban landscape that are peculiar to specific types of nuclei (as we shall see later). Some obvious examples are the central business district (and its specialized subareas), the wholesale district, distinctly high status and low status residential areas, dormitory suburbs, and heavy industrial concentrations. Urban nuclei likewise seem to be a form of natural area, though the influence of rational planning is often considerably stronger in the former.

5. census tracts

In the last thirty years, the emphasis on convenient ecological units has resulted in widespread use of census tracts. The popularity of this approach is indicated by the fact that 136 cities (of 50,000 population or over) in the United States had been officially divided into census tracts, while 37 urban regions (Standard Metropolitan Areas) had been completely tracted by early 1955.[12] The census tract is a relatively small, clearly defined area of the city (or its dependent area) which is designed to encompass a resident population that is demographically and culturally homogeneous and limited in size to a few thousand persons. Since tract boundaries remain officially fixed, various types of information (income, sex and age distributions, etc.) for any and all tracts can be studied for possible changes or trends over a period of years or decades.[13] However, several criticisms of tracts as ecological units have appeared, to which no adequate reply has yet been made. (a) Tracts tend to be too numerous—60 to 150 tracts seems to be the range for most cities—to aid in supplying a comprehensible picture of relevant conditions in the community. Consequently, census tracts are often supplemented by some grouping method (e.g., zones) to retrieve some recognizable pattern from a

[11] Chauncey D. Harris and Edward L. Ullman, "The Nature of Cities," in Hatt and Reiss, *op. cit.*, pp. 229–232. See also the analysis in James E. Vance, Jr., *Geography and Urban Evolution in the San Francisco Bay Area* (Berkeley, University of California Press, 1964), pp. 68–78.

[12] Calvin F. Schmid, "Research Techniques in Human Ecology," in Pauline V. Young, *Scientific Social Surveys and Research*, 3rd ed., (Englewood Cliffs, N.J., Prentice-Hall, 1956), p. 418.

[13] *Ibid.*, pp. 418–423.

puzzling mosaic of small units. (*b*) Census tracts tend to be arbitrary units, separately constructed without serious consideration of their relation to the larger entity. (c) Closely related, finally, is the recent discovery (long suspected, however) that individual census tracts contain measurable and perhaps significant internal variations in demographic and social characteristics.[14] It is not clear at this point that this variability can be interpreted as a recent development or a defect in the original tracting.

6. social areas

The most recent attempt to combine convenience and sociological distinctiveness in ecological units is called social area analysis. Based on the initial use of census tracts, this method classifies tracts according to three sets of significant characteristics—*social rank* (in terms of occupational distribution, formal education, and rent), *urbanization* (measures of fertility, housing types, and proportion of women in the labor force), and *segregation* (derived from figures on racial composition). In its first application to Los Angeles, the tracted area was divided into nine types of areas, representing different combinations of urbanization and social rank scores (see Fig. 4). Each of these nine areas was further distinguished into high and low areas

figure 4

Typology of Social Areas in Cities, by Social Rank and Degree of Urbanization

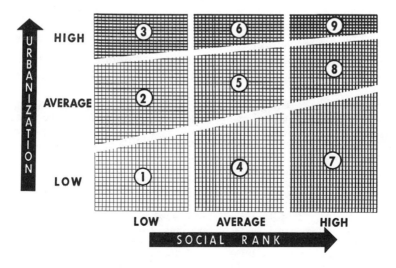

SOURCE: Shevky and Williams, *The Social Areas of Los Angeles*, p. 64.

[14] John H. Mabry, "Census Tract Variations in Urban Research," *American Sociological Review*, 23 (April, 1958), pp. 193–196.

of segregation, giving in all, eighteen types of units. In this way, a city map could graphically present clusters of census tracts having similar characteristics, as well as the spatial distribution of different types of social areas. Thus far, social area analysis has been mainly descriptive; we shall have to await its application to problems of explanation and understanding.[15]

Before we can decide which type of ecological unit (or units) is most helpful, one basic fact about urban ecology should be noted. Whether we explore urban space on foot, by auto, or from a low-flying plane, or carefully study zoning and land use maps, we are uniformly confronted with an overall *segregation of major activities and functions*. Most commonly, residential, commercial, industrial, and civic functions tend to be sharply separated from one another in a spatial division of labor that is possible only in increasingly extensive territories. The general pattern (or patterns) of this segregation, however, often defies simplified description. To obtain reasonable order from this complexity, therefore, we shall approach urban ecological organization as a product of relative emphases on two major social motivations: *status* and *rational-functional needs*.

status and ecological organization

The choice of distinct patterns of location and segregation according to definite criteria of status is well known. In general, status is most intimately connected with residential location and development,[16] though status considerations are not absent in location of specialty shops and professional establishments. Essentially, the status factor may be detected whenever any of the following can be demonstrated as motives for location: the quest for amenities—desirable scenery and an impressive view, the selection of an elevated or commanding site, an emphasis on space for the sake of space

[15] Eshref Shevky and Marilyn Williams, *The Social Areas of Los Angeles* (Berkeley, University of California Press, 1949); Eshref Shevky and Wendell Bell, *Social Area Analysis* (Stanford, Stanford University Press, 1955). See the critical evaluation of Amos Hawley and Otis D. Duncan, "Social Area Analysis: A Critical Appraisal," *Land Economics*, 33 (November, 1957), pp. 337–345. Several studies have applied the Shevky-Bell approach, with rather mixed results: Theodore R. Anderson and Janice A. Egeland, "Spatial Aspects of Social Area Analysis," *American Sociological Review*, 26 (June, 1961), pp. 392–398; Theodore R. Anderson and Lee L. Bean, "The Shevky-Bell Social Areas: Confirmation of Results and a Reinterpretation," *Social Forces*, 40 (December, 1961), pp. 119–124; J. Richard Udry, "Increasing Scale and Spatial Differentiation: New Tests of Two Theories from Shevky and Bell," *ibid.*, 42 (May, 1964), pp. 403–413.

[16] Harold A. Gibbard, "The Status Factor in Residential Succession," *American Journal of Sociology*, 46 (May, 1941), pp. 835–842; Peter Collison, "Occupation, Education, and Housing in an English City," *ibid.*, 65 (May, 1960), pp. 588–597; Otis D. Duncan and Beverly Duncan, "Residential Distribution and Occupational Stratification," *ibid.*, 60 (March, 1955), pp. 493–503; Arnold S. Feldman and Charles Tilly, "The Interaction of Social and Physical Space," *American Sociological Review*, 25 (December, 1960), pp. 877–884.

alone, or location at a comfortable distance from nuisance activities; a desire to locate or remain close to persons and groups of similar status; and a desire to locate in areas of established high reputation, regardless of accompanying inconveniences (e.g., commuting time).

Suburban developments and the recent growth of exurban areas, which we shall discuss in the next chapter, are obvious examples of the status factor in location. Likewise, the presence of a "Gold Coast" in many major American cities—despite their proximity to slum areas—is at least partly understandable when we consider that they often contain tall buildings with magnificent views of a lake, river, or impressive bridges—all of these being particularly attractive on clear evenings. We have, furthermore, the evidence of such otherwise disparate communities as Boston, Massachusetts and Bangalore, India, in each of which high status groups (and the newly rich) have chosen to remain in old, familiar residential areas rather than relocate in roomier suburbs.[17] Indeed, the status motive is so persistent that families may distinguish sharply between street designations in the same neighborhood. In Norfolk, Virginia, the named streets in the upper West Side have more attraction for status-conscious families than the numbered streets. Therefore, the latter often contain houses of lower market value, despite comparable accommodations.

functional needs and ecological organization

Urban activities, by their very nature, exhibit a characteristic emphasis on rational, economic motives. Location of specific activities and organizations is consequently guided by more or less practical attempts to link tangible objectives and available facilities. Indeed, the most obvious criterion of rational-functional location is expressed in the choice of sites that give access to personnel, materials, or services considered vital for the operation of a given group or organization. This is clearly indicated in such instances as: the location of industries in spacious, peripheral areas, close to railway spurs or trucking routes; the tendency for families to consider homes and apartments in terms of their proximity to schools, shopping facilities, and transportation lines; and the development of shopping centers at presumed points of greatest convenience to their respective clienteles. The rational factor is also prominent in the clustering of competitive firms (to keep an eye on competitors) and in the calculated settlement of dissimilar but complementary activities in adjacent locations (e.g., a variety of service establishments near college campuses, restaurants near the theater district).

[17] See Walter Firey, *Land Use in Central Boston* (Cambridge, Harvard University Press, 1947); Noel P. Gist, "The Ecology of Bangalore, India: An East-West Comparison," *Social Forces*, 35 (May, 1957), pp. 356–365.

the principle of median location

To the extent that urban groups and organizations pursue rational standards of functioning, given the opportunity to locate themselves without restrictions, the patterns of actual distribution tend to confirm Quinn's hypothesis of median location.[18] Simply stated, this generalization asserts that various kinds of urban activities assume patterns of location at points which minimize effort and cost in use of necessary services and/or furnishing services to clients, customers, or adherents. This, of course, assumes equal availability of these central locations and accurate knowledge of costs for alternative locations so that rational decisions can be made. Significantly, the hypothesis of median location provides a common foundation for the apparently divergent development of zones, sectors, and nuclei. All three rest to some degree on rational-functional motives, but each reflects different ecological consequences because each uniquely ignores or takes account of additional factors (e.g., the sector pattern stresses radial transportation routes and facilities).

Ecological patterns for concrete cities are consequently products of differential emphasis on status and rational-functional criteria of segregation. Since the actual combinations are quite numerous, we can only hope to identify here a few basic types of urban ecological structure.

1. the orthodox type

In general, the more recently established cities of the Western world —and particularly those in politically stable societies—tend to stress functional standards of ecological distribution. The orthodox type, which has been diligently studied by sociologists at the University of Chicago since the early twenties, consists of rough zonal divisions corresponding to successive time periods—the outer zones being more recently developed, as modified by geographic obstacles, the complementary growth of two or more residential sectors, and the concomitant rise of commercial and industrial nuclei. Status factors are by no means absent, but operate in intermittent patterns. For example, the early development of intermediate and outer zones stems from the migration of high status families to more spacious areas. This permits commercial expansion from the central business district and a consequent need for connective transportation facilities. Status factors in part intrude again in the growth of residential sectors and in suburban residential nuclei located in a peripheral zone. Within this basic pattern, deviations from the functional

[18] Quinn, *op. cit.*, pp. 86–94, 105–106, 279–289; William L. Garrison *et al.*, *Studies of Highway Development and Geographic Change* (Seattle, University of Washington Press, 1959).

figure 5
The Orthodox Ecological Structure of Cities

**1.Central business district 2. Low class residential
3.Middle class residential 4.Higher class residential
5. Manufacturing (light or heavy)**

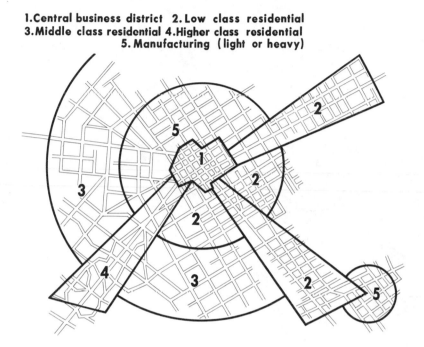

emphasis tend to be minor, since a competitive advantage normally lies with the financially superior rational-functional organizations (business corporations of various types). Only with the advent of community-wide planning is the orthodox pattern potentially subject to significant change.

2. the symbolic type

By comparison with the orthodox ecological pattern, the symbolic type appears to be without perceptible organization. Zones and sectors are especially difficult to identify. However, we might properly characterize the symbolic type as a continuation of early ecological patterns or a reflection of organized resistance to the liberation of rational, competitive motives in allocation of land. In place of zonal and sector developments, the symbolic type is compounded of a series of nuclei, which are maintained in roughly their traditional form by the stubborn immobility of high status families. Under these circumstances, residential nuclei (both high and low status types) are evaluated symbolically, in terms of past associations, not as areas to be manipulated for future development or exploitation. At this point, it is not

figure 6

The Symbolic Ecological Structure of Cities

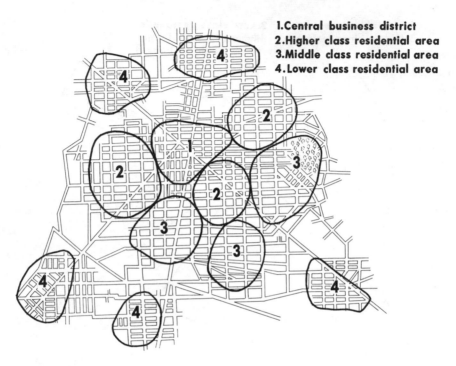

1.Central business district
2.Higher class residential area
3.Middle class residential area
4.Lower class residential area

necessary to distinguish the operation of private and public (governmental) organizations in applying symbolic evaluations to urban subareas.

Several features are distinctive of the symbolic type, as presented in rather simplified form in Figure 6. (a) There is a tendency for the core business district to be somewhat large and not well differentiated internally. Business establishments appear to be only vaguely separated according to type; and complementary (symbiotic) activities fail to achieve adjacent locations. In Bangalore, for example, banking facilities are highly dispersed, as are the finer hotels, which also are quite distant from the major shopping areas and the railway terminal. (b) High status families prefer to reside in a series of attractive nuclei close to the central business area. There is, consequently, no clear inner zone of transition in this type. (c) Middle and low status families tend to locate in scattered residential nuclei beyond high status areas. Low status areas are generally "outer slums," leftover areas that often possess otherwise desirable but undeveloped geographic features (hills, scenery).[19]

[19] Gist, *loc. cit.*; Leo Kuper, *Durban: A Study in Racial Ecology* (London, Jonathan Cape, 1958); G. Balandier, "Urbanism in West and Central Africa," in *Social*

New Orleans: an example of symbolic ecology [20]

While New Orleans deviates to a considerable extent from some of the previously listed features, it has been one of the best American instances of urban symbolic ecology. It is likewise particularly interesting as a unique blend of topographical and cultural factors in the development of a distinctive ecological structure. Situated between a bend in the Mississippi River and Lake Pontchartrain, New Orleans is marked by low-lying land that is separated by two major ridges. One ridge, running east and west, is about midway between river and lake; the other, running north and south, extends to the river near the French Quarter.

By 1900 or so, New Orleans had developed primarily as a gateway city. For over one hundred years, a succession of rather distinctive population groupings had been incorporated into the growing community by informal but highly patterned residential segregation (see Fig. 7). The earliest and most persistent residents, the Creoles (French) possessed—or claimed to possess—high status and an attachment to the convenient "French Quarter." Despite increasingly crowded conditions, many families remained in this district, though others moved steadily northward into the "new Creole" district. The American businessmen, who were considered culturally inferior by the Creoles, first settled in substantial numbers immediately west of the business district and then moved farther westward (but still at a convenient distance from the business district) to the so-called Garden District. Irish immigrants, imported to allay a labor shortage, gradually moved into the area vacated by business families, which came to be known as the Irish Channel. Meanwhile, other nationality groups—notably Germans—took up truck-farming and residence in the spacious, neglected area east of the Creole sector. New Orleans therefore developed a noticeable "T" pattern,

Implications of Industrialization and Urbanization in Africa South of the Sahara, International African Institute (Paris, UNESCO, 1956), pp. 496 ff.; Gideon Sjoberg, The Pre-Industrial City (New York, The Free Press, 1960), Chap. 4; T. G. McGee, The Southeast Asian City: A Social Geography of the Primate Cities of Southeast Asia (London, G. Bell, 1967), pp. 100, 128; Nathan Keyfitz, "The Ecology of Indonesian Cities," American Journal of Sociology, 66 (January, 1961), pp. 151–154; Xavier de Planhol, The World of Islam (Ithaca, Cornell University Press, 1959), pp. 348–354; Janet Abu-Lughod, "Tale of Two Cities: The Origins of Modern Cairo," Comparative Studies in Society and History, 7 (July, 1965), pp. 420–457; Emrys Jones, A Social Geography of Belfast (London, Oxford University Press, 1960), Part 2; Theodore Caplow et al., The Urban Ambience: A Study of San Juan, Puerto Rico (Totowa, N.J., Bedminster Press, 1964), pp. 17–33; H. Hywel Davies, Land Use in Central Cape Town: A Study in Urban Geography (Cape Town, Longmans, 1965).

[20] Harlan W. Gilmore, "The Old New Orleans and the New: A Case for Ecology," American Sociological Review, 9 (August, 1944), pp. 385–394; Earl F. Niehaus, The Irish in New Orleans 1800–1860 (Baton Rouge, Louisiana State University Press, 1965), pp. 27–28.

figure 7

The Symbolic Ecology of New Orleans (*ca.* 1940)

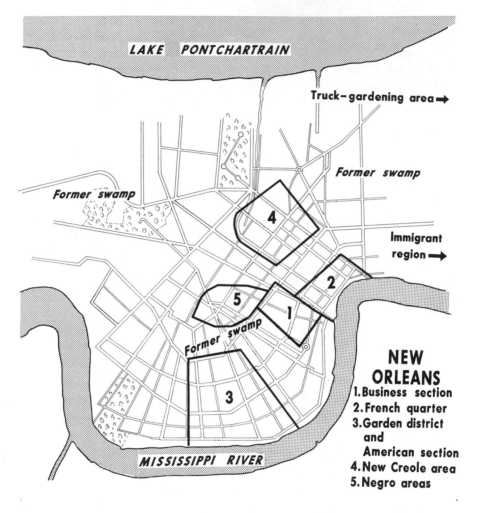

SOURCE: Adapted from Harlan W. Gilmore, "The Old New Orleans and the New," *American Sociological Review*, 9 (Aug., 1944).

which stemmed from the special sentiments and cultural conflicts of its component nationalities.

Urban ecology should therefore be approached as a relatively dynamic patterning of spatial allocation and coordination. At any point in time, the ecological structure of a given community represents a temporary equilibrium (or compromise) of rational and status factors, which constitutes a limiting framework for subsequent ecological developments. But, in varying degrees, urban areas of the world have tended to emphasize the rational factor, with unanticipated nonrational consequences. In the following chapter, and at various points in the remainder of this book, we shall try to analyze and explain ecological dynamics as a significant aspect of urban community organization. In particular, we shall be concerned with those factors that sustain given ecological patterns as well as those that help to account for substantial variations in structure.

selected references

ALIHAN, Milla A., *Social Ecology* (New York, Columbia University Press, 1938).

BARTHOLOMEW, Harland, *Land Use in American Cities*, 2nd ed. (Cambridge, Harvard University Press, 1955).

FIREY, Walter, *Land Use in Central Boston* (Cambridge, Harvard University Press, 1947).

FOGELSON, Robert M., *The Fragmented Metropolis: Los Angeles, 1850–1930* (Cambridge, Harvard University Press, 1967).

McKELVEY, Blake, *The Urbanization of America, 1860–1915* (New Brunswick, Rutgers University Press, 1963).

MAYER, Harold M., and KOHN, Clyde F., eds., *Readings in Urban Geography* (Chicago, University of Chicago Press, 1959).

PARK, Robert E., *Human Communities* (New York, The Free Press, 1952).

QUINN, James A., *Human Ecology* (Englewood Cliffs, N.J., Prentice-Hall, 1950).

RATCLIFF, Richard U., *Urban Land Economics* (New York, McGraw-Hill, 1949).

THEODORSON, George A., ed., *Studies in Human Ecology* (New York, Harper and Row, 1961).

6

the dynamics of urban ecological patterns

From the urban sociologist's standpoint, the nature of ecological facts is crucial to the understanding of significant changes in ecological organization. Following the distinctions suggested by MacIver, we may best describe ecological patterns as resultants of conjunctural social phenomena.[1] Essentially, conjunctural phenomena derive from a host of individual attitudes and activities of subtly interdependent persons and social groups. The overall consequences of these actions are largely unpremeditated but nevertheless important structures or patterns, which usually represent some division of rewards, facilities, opportunities, and responsibilities among the implicated persons and groups. In many instances, the development of a national economic system, patterns of social disorganization, and systems of social stratification seem to be primarily comprehensible in these terms.

Two aspects of conjunctural phenomena must be emphasized in analyzing ecological patterns. First, the location and movement of persons, groups, or activities always rests on more or less perceived social and cultural motivations. "Availability," "access," and "opportunity" have no meaning unless persons and groups recognize "availability," etc.—and proceed to act on that recognition. Second, individual and group decisions about settlement or relocation inevitably produce—simultaneously—restrictions on the decisions of other groups by occupying desired areas, and opportunities for occupancy in vacated areas. These are inevitable consequences because expansion of densely settled urban areas is limited by time-cost factors in transportation and provision of public utilities and services, and the buildings and facilities of vacated areas are relatively permanent investments. Under these circumstances, ecological patterns can best be understood as somewhat temporary resultants of facilitating and restrictive factors influencing the separate but interdependent actions of subgroups in the urban community.

---

[1] See the important discussion of distributive, collective, and conjunctural phenomena in the social sciences by Robert M. MacIver, "Social Causation and Change," in Georges Gurvitch and Wilbert E. Moore, eds., *Twentieth Century Sociology* (New York, Philosophical Library, 1945), pp. 121–125; and Robert M. MacIver, *Social Causation* (Boston, Ginn and Company, 1942).

Ecological changes, therefore, assume meaning only when considered as deviations from preexisting patterns or trends. But these deviations or changes must be examined from two aspects: (*a*) what accounts for alterations in facilitating and restrictive factors that make possible initial variations in a given ecological pattern; and (*b*) how do these initial variations affect the motivations and opportunities for decision of other groups in the evolving ecological structure?

ecological processes

The traditional approach to these general problems has been a descriptive account of the basic ecological processes.[2] These processes, however, are rarely investigated as processes in the strict sense of the term, i.e., as a succession of understandable changes through a given period of time. It is extremely difficult and costly to pursue a genuinely processual study. Consequently, urban ecologists normally assemble and analyze the products of ecological redistribution. The availability of comparable data, however, is generally limited to (*a*) population figures—with respect to size and distribution; and (*b*) urbanized types of activity, in the form of economic statistics, religious data, deviant behavior, etc.

Ecological change consists of several facets or problems, for which specific ecological processes provide some clarification and understanding. One aspect of change is the relative *size* of the urban community. A second type of ecological dynamics concerns changes in the *interrelations* among component areas in the community or region. Finally, and perhaps most fundamental, is the focus on changes in the *geographic position* of individuals, groups, and their material equipment (e.g., factories, stores, homes).

1. processes related to relative size

Aggregation refers to the increase in population units (and their property) within a defined area over a specific time period. This is reflected in changing density of population and is related to the process of *expansion*, which involves the growth of useable, populated areas beyond previously defined limits.

2. processes related to interrelation of subareas

Bridging processes of the previous type and the present category, *concentration* reflects the relatively higher rates of aggregation for specific subareas, as compared with other subareas in the community. Thus, in the early

2 James A. Quinn, *Human Ecology* (Englewood Cliffs, N.J., Prentice-Hall, 1950), Part III.

stages of urban development, inner areas were the focus of concentration processes. More recently, outer zones have been more clearly marked by processes of concentration.

Centralization, which is sometimes confused with concentration, is the process of accumulating important functions and services in one (or a limited number of) strategic subareas. The result is an increasing dependence on these highly specialized areas on the part of the remaining areal units in the community. An obvious example is the development of the central business district.

While both concentration and centralization emphasize positive processes of interrelations, *segregation* as an ecological process describes the conscious or unconscious development of separable and specialized areas in the community. In this process, particular population categories and types of activities assume identifiable concentration in specific areas. The segregation of racial and nationality groupings in given neighborhoods is merely a dramatic instance of a pervasive and inevitable process in urban communities. Segregation also occurs, for example, in the distinction between residential, industrial, and commercial areas, in the differentiation of low, medium and high status residential areas, and in the emergence of such specialized areas as "Skid Row," the red light district, and the civic center.

3. processes related to changes in relations between subareas

The last ecological processes to be mentioned here are normally dependent on prior processes of segregation, centralization, and concentration, which serve to establish a referential ecological structure. *Invasion* refers to a visible shift in population or function from one area to another (often adjacent areas) in a community. This encroachment is illustrated in the expansion of commercial activities into surrounding residential areas, and of course the emotion-charged movement of previously segregated racial and/or nationality groupings into informally forbidden areas. Invasion is followed by *succession* (and perhaps subsequent processes of invasion) when the invading function or population grouping becomes dominant, and concomitantly motivates the withdrawal of previously dominant groups or functions.[3]

Underlying all ecological processes is the crucial process of *migration*, which also provides an important link between demographic and ecological aspects of community organization. Migration simply refers to the physical

---

[3] Invasion and succession are well analyzed in the works of Robert E. Park and his disciples. See Robert E. Park, "Succession, An Ecological Concept," *American Sociological Review*, 1 (April, 1936), pp. 171–179; R. D. McKenzie, "Ecological Succession in the Puget Sound Region," *Publications of the American Sociological Society*, 23 (1929), pp. 60–80; Paul Cressey, "Population Succession in Chicago," *American Journal of Sociology*, 44 (July, 1938), pp. 59–69; Otis D. Duncan and Beverly Duncan, *The Negro Population of Chicago: A Study of Residential Succession* (Chicago, University of Chicago Press, 1957).

movement of individuals and groups from one location to another. The effects of such movements, however, rather than the movements themselves, are of particular interest to the urban sociologist. One such effect, often called the process of *ecological mobility*, involves the rate of redistribution of population and functions within a given area—or between areas. Mobility in this sense is not necessarily equivalent to *social mobility*, which refers to changes in social relationships—quite apart from changes in spatial position.

These ecological processes, as previously suggested, provide descriptions of changes in ecological patterns; they are important but preliminary devices for studying these changes. Essentially, an analytic approach to ecological dynamics must seek to explain both maintenance and change in ecological organization of urban communities. Ecological organization is a complex product of ecological processes, but these in turn are reflections of social, cultural, and psychological variables. Perhaps we can suggest the basic interconnection of these variables by approaching ecological dynamics as a reflection of community organization and of the social and cultural changes that challenge existing modes of organization. Since this broader set of processes is quite intricate, we shall try to select a few illustrative aspects of ecological dynamics in the urban community, with particular attention to the sociocultural context in which ecological changes occur.

changes in industrial location

The industrial function of cities during the nineteenth century was largely performed in or near central areas. Several reasons for this early pattern are clear. In that period, with limited transportation facilities, a central location provided maximum accessibility to labor supply, transport, and source of power. Before the expansion of housing and other land-competitive activities, the central area was not yet inflated in value, nor was considerable space required for most industrial operations. Then, too—and this must not be ignored—there was little or no attempt to challenge (let alone restrict) patterns of industrial location.

Since World War II, with varying degrees of clarity, the ecological niche of urban industries has been progressively shifted toward outer areas [4] —both in the relocation of existing plants and in the selection of sites for new plants. In general, light industries (involving limited equipment and a small labor force) have remained near the central business district, though a Detroit study indicates that some light industries seek the convenience of

---

[4] Evelyn M. Kitigawa and Donald J. Bogue, *Suburbanization of Manufacturing Activity Within Standard Metropolitan Areas* (Oxford, Ohio, Scripps Foundation for Research in Population Problems, 1955); Allen R. Pred, *The Spatial Dynamics of U.S. Urban-Industrial Growth, 1800–1914* (Cambridge, MIT Press, 1966).

one-story plants in suburban areas. Heavy industry, on the other hand, has rather consistently tended to find peripheral locations more desirable than those in inner zones. This is especially evident in the largest urban centers, and for those industries that produce durable goods (appliances, machinery, etc.). Some outstanding examples of this trend are the huge Fairless Plant of United States Steel in the Philadelphia area, and General Electric's appliance park near Louisville.[5]

This new pattern of location is a direct consequence of several changes in urban life and in the character of modern society. Most obviously, industrial location is motivated by rational-functional needs (more plant space, lower land values and tax rates, and less traffic congestion). But increasingly, industrial corporations are discovering that efficiency is also dependent on concern for their workers and the technical and professional staff. The suburban trek of residences for a widening range of status groupings is a highly important factor in problems of hiring competent personnel. Furthermore, an increasing demand for highly trained professional persons necessarily involves attention by the corporation to the normal residential and community aspirations of this segment of the labor force. Their desire for the amenities (space, modern homes, scenery, etc.) and for adequate and convenient schools, churches, and shopping areas is an increasingly powerful argument for peripheral location. We must not forget the impact of the city and regional planning movement, sponsored by a variety of public and private organizations, which has diligently encouraged the newer locational trends for industry.[6] Often, attractive tax benefits are offered by county, township, or state units with the hope of improving the economic base of predominantly residential areas.

changes in residential patterns

It is by now well known that changes in residential patterns have been in the form of zonal and sector developments, and also in outer, nucleated locations. Much of this trend reflects the *successive relocations* of urban residents, who try to match occupational and financial success with higher status residential location. But, as we have seen in Chapter 4, the character of *rural-urban migration* is related to residential patterns. Several important changes in migration trends are particularly relevant here.

1. Most obviously, the immigration restrictions of 1920 and 1924 (with minor modifications since 1950) have sharply reduced the stream of foreign-born, rural immigrants, who had traditionally settled in the zones of transi-

[5] *The New York Times*, March 15, 1953; Detroit Planning Commission study, cited by Noel P. Gist and L. A. Halbert, *Urban Society*, 4th ed. (New York, Thomas Y. Crowell, 1956), p. 110.

[6] See Part IV.

tion of American cities.[7] The lone, dramatic exception to this restrictive trend is the Puerto Rican influx of the past ten years. As a result, inner zones of cities are generally losing population—proportionately and often absolutely.

2. In the United States there is some evidence—for Chicago at least—that migrants to cities have tended to shift their initial location from the cheap rent, transitional zone to broader and more varied residential areas. During the period 1935–1940, migrants to Chicago were disproportionately concentrated in a long, narrow band along Lake Michigan. Significantly, foreign migrants were also attracted to this extensive migrant zone, a large part of which consisted of high rent areas. Various types of comparisons indicate that native migrants to Chicago in this period tended to locate in those portions of the migrant zone that were most similar to the social characteristics of the migrants. Thus, migrants from other cities (who were generally in service and middle-class occupational categories) settled in the high rent areas of the narrow band. Migrants from rural communities (mainly from the South) tended to locate in or near the zone of transition.[8]

While supporting data for other cities is lacking, this provisionally noted shift in migrants' location is understandable. In view of the changing character of American industry and the urban occupational structure (which is discussed more fully in Chapter 13), we can expect relatively more migrants with higher educational and occupational status, more persons migrating in family units, and more migrants with previous experience in other urban or suburban communities. Indeed, with the major exception of southern Negro migrants, the reservoir of distinctively rural migrants is rapidly diminishing, since the farm population continues to decrease as a result of past rural-urban migrations. From the standpoint of urban residential patterns, these demographic trends are accompanied by value systems and financial resources that impel migrants to seek locations that are both convenient and physically desirable.

minority residential patterns

Perhaps the most instructive aspect of changes in residential patterns is the dynamics of residential segregation of minority groups [9]—especially Negroes. But an overall picture of trends in residential segregation is not

---

[7] Donald J. Bogue, *The Population of the United States* (New York, The Free Press of Glencoe, 1959), Chap. VII.

[8] Ronald Freedman, *Recent Migration to Chicago* (Chicago, University of Chicago Press, 1949).

[9] For a summary of trends among Chinese in the U.S. see Rose Hum Lee, "The Decline of Chinatowns in the United States," *American Journal of Sociology*, 54 (March, 1949), pp. 422–432; and her *The Chinese in the United States of America* (New York, Oxford University Press, 1960).

yet available. One study of 23 cities, using census tracts as units of measurement, found a slight tendency toward decentralization (desegregation) of nonwhites from 1940 to 1950. By contrast, a study based on analysis of block statistics for 185 cities for the same period seems to demonstrate some increase in residential segregation of nonwhites.[10] In view of these inconsistent findings, it is probably too early to draw conclusions of a general nature. However, the processual aspect of residential segregation may be clarified by focusing briefly on a few representative instances.

1. Chicago

Several studies agree in demonstrating an increase in Negro segregation in Chicago during the 1940–1950 decade.[11] An overwhelming proportion of Chicago's Negro population is concentrated in the so-called Black Belt, which is a well-defined, deteriorated rectangle on the South Side. Unlike Philadelphia, which has a number of minor Negro areas, Chicago has retained and intensified racial segregation. But what explains this persistence of ecological pattern? Prejudice and discrimination are undoubtedly factors —but not adequate answers. Several conditions must be kept in mind. (1) The major Negro district was originally located in an area that was vacated by whites and relatively accessible to firms requiring unskilled labor, i.e., the Loop and the stockyards.[12] (2) As the Negro population expanded through migration following World War I, opportunities for residential movement were limited by Lake Michigan on the east and stockyards on the west. (3) Negro migration continued at high levels, since the depression and the mechanization of southern agriculture intensified the already precarious economic position of many Negroes. (4) Various attempts by Negro families to settle in white areas have been met by informal but effective rebuffs, or the use of violence. Ecological change in Negro residential patterns has, in short, been blocked by social and geographical obstacles.

2. New Orleans

A good example of a major shift in Negro residential patterns may be found in several southern cities. However, the process is especially clear in

---

[10] Richard W. Redick, "Population Growth and Distribution in Central Cities, 1940–1950," *American Sociological Review*, 21 (February, 1956), pp. 38–43; Donald O. Cowgill, "Trends in Residential Segregation of Nonwhites in American Cities, 1940–1950," *ibid.*, pp. 43–47.

[11] Redick, *loc. cit.*; Cowgill, *loc. cit.* A more detailed study may be found in Otis D. Duncan and Beverly Duncan, *The Negro Population of Chicago* (Chicago, University of Chicago Press, 1957). A contrasting trend in Washington is analyzed in George D. Nesbitt, "Dispersion of Nonwhite Residence in Washington, D.C.: Some of Its Implications," *Land Economics*, 32 (August, 1956), pp. 201–212.

[12] Homer Hoyt, *One Hundred Years of Land Values in Chicago* (Chicago, University of Chicago Press, 1933), pp. 97, 215–216, 315.

New Orleans (see the earlier discussion, pp. 91–92).[13] During the early part of the nineteenth century, each of the major residential areas had Negro slaves living on the premises, as well as a fringe of Negro residences. This general dispersion of Negroes was temporarily challenged by the settlement of Americans, who wished to live near their ethnic rivals, the Creoles, and apparently were not concerned about proximity to Negro areas. However, since the turn of the century, two community developments were followed by a significant change in Negro location. Drainage of former swamp areas north of the older residential districts greatly expanded the area available for residences. During the same period, the use of the electric street car facilitated transportation to various parts of the city. Consequently, Negroes increasingly moved from their former residential fringes to a voluntarily concentrated area north of the business district, from which they could conveniently reach their jobs.

3. Durban, South Africa

The residential distribution of nonwhites (Indians and native Africans) in Durban has for a long time been quite divergent from urban patterns in the United States.[14] In general, Durban's nonwhite population has been concentrated in several dispersed districts, with a considerable degree of residential intermingling in Durban's approximation to the familiar zone of transition. Table 33 summarizes patterns of segregation by distinctive sociographic zones, which are also approximately scaled in terms of desirability

table 33

Percentage of Ethnic Distribution of Population in Durban According to
Sociographic Zones, 1951

SOCIO-GRAPHIC ZONES	EUROPEANS	COLOREDS	INDIANS	AFRICANS	ALL NON-EUROPEANS
Alluvial flats	4.81	4.81	56.59	33.79	95.19
Peripheral	12.48	2.75	39.70	45.07	87.52
Inland transitional	23.18	7.76	57.66	12.00	76.82
Seaward transitional	65.91	7.18	17.22	9.69	34.09
Sea front	67.43	0.62	5.83	26.12	32.57
Central Berea Ridge	88.59	0.43	1.78	9.20	11.41
Total	*32.75*	*4.01*	*36.28*	*26.96*	*67.25*

SOURCE: Leo Kuper *et al., Durban: A Study in Racial Ecology,* p. 110.

[13] Harlan W. Gilmore, "The Old New Orleans and the New: A Case for Ecology," *American Sociological Review,* 9 (August, 1944), pp. 385–394.
[14] Leo Kuper, *Durban: A Study of Racial Ecology* (London, Jonathan Cape, 1958).

and status. Essentially, the nonwhite population is located in middle or outer zones—away from the refreshing ocean breezes and the major commercial district.

Since 1950 the City Council, representing the Europeans, has been developing plans for a more sharply segregated system of residential location. The underlying idea is to establish well-defined group areas (i.e., racially distinct areas), with the desirable inner areas reserved for Europeans, and a rough band of outer areas north and south of the central area for Africans and Indians. Such a program would require extensive resettlement of non-Europeans, but in addition many Europeans would face the annoyance of relocation. As a result, some resistance from Europeans—on grounds of expediency rather than humanitarianism—has caused review and modification of these plans. In view of the prevailing political climate in South Africa, some drastic resettlement along racial lines will undoubtedly be attempted. At present, the nonwhites seem to be more interested in expanding economic opportunities and health services than in stability or change in residential patterns per se.

changes in commercial location and function

Since 1945, the mammoth suburban or semisuburban shopping center has become a familiar accompaniment to the rapid growth of suburban residential areas. Until a few years ago, these new commercial nuclei primarily catered to the daily and weekly needs of their customers—drugs, groceries, laundry and dry cleaning, etc. Consequently, the significance of these centers was limited to competition with commercial clusters in older neighborhoods.[15] With the increasing location of department store branches in suburban centers, however, a genuine ecological revolution is at hand, a reversal of the multiform commercial dominance of the central business district.

The clearest and most advanced case of this revolution can be found in the New York City region. Macy's, Gimbel's, Lord and Taylor, and others have invested heavily in suburban branches in New York, New Jersey, and Connecticut. Lord and Taylor, a moderate-sized enterprise for many years, furnishes an interesting example of expansion. Founded in 1820 on Fifth Avenue, the first suburban branch was opened in Manhasset, Long Island in

[15] See Harold M. Mayer, "Patterns and Recent Trends of Chicago's Outlying Business Centers," *Journal of Land and Public Utility Economics*, 18 (February, 1942), pp. 4–16; Homer Hoyt, "Classification and Significant Characteristics of Shopping Centers," in Harold M. Mayer and Clyde F. Kohn, eds., *Readings in Urban Geography* (Chicago, University of Chicago Press, 1959), pp. 454–461; Mabel Walker, *Business Enterprise and the City* (Princeton, Tax Institute, Inc., 1959), pp. 108–144; J. Ross McKeever, *Shopping Centers Re-Studied: Part 2, Practical Experiences*, Urban Land Institute, Technical Bulletin No. 30, (Washington, D.C., 1957).

1941. A Westchester branch opened its doors in 1948, soon to be followed by others in West Hartford (1953), Bala-Cynwyd (1955), and Garden City (1956).

Federal Reserve figures for the New York region convincingly show that suburban department stores sales rose dramatically in the early fifties—as compared with a very modest rise for the downtown stores. Currently, it is not clear that these suburban increases have been achieved at the expense of the parent stores. It has been suggested that suburban branches have instead invaded the previous commercial monopoly of smaller, local competitors.[16] In any case, the convenience and variety now available to suburban families in peripheral centers (in 15–30 minutes' driving time) undoubtedly signifies a commercial decentralization that presents vexing problems for downtown merchants.

A dramatic aspect of this general trend—at least for New York City— is the closing of several large department stores in downtown areas.[17] Since 1952, eight such establishments have gone out of business in Manhattan and Brooklyn. The reasons are obvious to merchandisers. These stores failed to provide a modernized, attractive setting for a new generation of shoppers; the traditional, hard core of steady customers, who had received personal attention from favorite sales personnel, who once cared little for superficial physical improvements in the store, are virtually gone—because of death, removal to other cities, and even the competition of the more modern stores. The young, middle-class homemakers (the heaviest spenders in department stores) have moved to the suburbs and require extraordinary methods of enticement to shop downtown. Some stores, notably McCrory's, had emphasized a narrow range of merchandise—e.g., linens and materials by the yard—which is too restricted for the newer style of living. It is interesting to note that, with one exception, none of these stores had previously established suburban branches. Only one of the newly closed stores, Lewis and Conger (specializing in a stimulating variety of housewares), has as yet moved to a suburban location.

Somewhat less sensational but also symptomatic of ecological changes is the growing crisis of business offices in downtown districts. Since World War II, there has been a shortage of competent secretarial and clerical employees. A partial explanation lies in the recent development of new business offices in suburban areas. To this must be added the familiar fact that many potential typists and secretaries are suburban residents and refuse to bear the expense and inconvenience of commuting. Furthermore, a growing proportion of young women (suburban or urban) is college-trained, and therefore desires more creative positions than switchboard operator, typist,

16 Walker, op. cit., p. 110; The New York Times, February 5, 1956; George Sternlieb, The Future of the Downtown Department Store (Cambridge, MIT Press–Harvard University Press, 1962), pp. 116, 158.
17 The New York Times, February 17, 1957.

or stenographer. In desperation, several New York offices have migrated to the suburbs. But they have been confronted with a rebellion of their urban employees, who miss the opportunity of downtown shopping during the lunch hour.[18]

ecological dynamics: a summary

Significant changes in urban ecological patterns normally develop over a span of decades, since most of the unit decisions in this process are made without extensive knowledge and evaluation of other decisions. Despite the popular fiction of the calculating urbanite, considerable time often lapses before the opportunities for change are noted and acted upon. Ecological patterns are therefore of varying clarity to the urban sociologist, and at the same time apparently are rarely of conscious significance to most residents.

Nevertheless, we may conclude that the key to urban ecological dynamics is the social and cultural structure of given regions—at least after the initial location and settlement have been achieved. Essentially, as our previous discussion has illustrated, a major change in land use, population distribution, and the interrelations between subareas derives from changes in valuation or changes in the techniques of applying existing values. As examples of the first type, we may mention industry's recent concern for more space and for more desirable living conditions for its employees, the increasing emphasis on visible signs of status ascent, and a persistent change in taste in emulation of the traditional leisure class. On the other hand, changes in techniques of realizing values—particularly accessibility and convenience —can be seen in a variety of transportation improvements (automobile, bus, street car, modern highway system) and in the use of numerous electrical appliances (e.g., the recent "Dogomatic," which grills six frankfurters). Ultimately, then, ecological change depends on valuational change and the technical and financial ability to translate values into action. The latter condition, in turn, is related to specific institutional structures of the region and society—which will be discussed in Part III.

Altered valuations and technical resources may be considered facilitating factors in ecological change. Resistance to ecological change—whether conscious or unconscious—rests on adherence to traditional values that are immune to competition, or on outmoded facilities that defy change except through drastic methods. For example, Tokyo has a heavy industrial concentration in three inner areas, which are linked with outer residential areas by a comparatively small number of very narrow streets, which were haphazardly laid out to follow ancient goat paths. The resultant traffic congestion could be reduced by either relocating Tokyo's industrial establishments or

[18] *Ibid.*, February 24, 1952.

widening a limited number of key streets, and opening the Imperial Palace area to public transportation. But neither approach has yet been seriously considered. Financial problems are of course involved, though tradition seems to be the major obstacle.[19]

ecological change and planning

It seems likely that the era of uncoordinated operation of facilitating and restrictive factors in ecological change is coming to a close, though not without opposition. City and regional planning bodies, the focus of Part IV, constitute a new aspect of urban social organization. They seek—with varying success—to guide ecological changes with conscious concern for reducing undesirable by-products of change for the region as a whole. But the essential factors in ecological dynamics remain. Planning merely introduces the possibility of new combinations and more responsible attention to varied community and regional needs.

[19] *Ibid.*, April 26, 1959; Homer Hoyt, "The Structure and Growth of American Cities Contrasted with the Structure of European and Asiatic Cities," *Urban Land*, 18 (September, 1959), pp. 3–8.

selected references

BREESE, Gerald, *Urbanization in Newly Developed Countries* (Englewood Cliffs, N.J., Prentice-Hall, 1966).

GILCHRIST, David T., ed., *The Growth of the Seaport Cities, 1790–1825* (Charlottesville, University Press of Virginia, 1967).

HAWLEY, Amos H., *Human Ecology* (New York, Ronald Press, 1950), Part IV.

QUINN, James A., *Human Ecology* (Englewood Cliffs, N.J., Prentice-Hall, 1950), Part III.

THEODORSON, George A., ed., *Studies in Human Ecology* (New York, Harper and Row, 1961), Part II, Section C.

7

emergence and structure of the urban region: suburb, satellite, and fringe

The urban region, which is a continuously evolving entity, is slowly gaining serious recognition as the most important and strategic unit in modern society. However, the identification of urban regions requires some major alterations in our patterns of thought and our evaluation of public and private affairs. In general, the development of the urban region reflects a continuing tension between traditional political organization and boundary lines, on the one hand, and rapidly changing radii of personal and institutional relations in pursuing needs and providing services, on the other hand. The urbanite unconsciously faces this problem almost every day in referring to his area, and particularly so when talking to visitors or chance acquaintances. If he lives in a well-defined suburban area, the name of the locality certainly has meaning, but this is normally accompanied by the frequent reminders of metropolitan mass media that he is a resident of "Chicagoland," the Los Angeles area, Greater New York, etc. Indeed, as I sit here, several miles from the current municipal limits of Atlanta—in a densely populated, unincorporated suburban belt—I cannot help realizing that many necessary services are supplied for me and/or my neighbors by organizations located in downtown Atlanta: e.g., jobs, gas and electricity, the telephone, bus service, theatrical performances, concerts, varied restaurants, professional sports (baseball, football, basketball, soccer), radio, and television. Furthermore, such other services as are provided by our county (police, fire protection, schools, water) are largely financed by taxes derived from incomes earned in the central city.

Under these conditions, the name of the central city has constantly enlarged applications and reference points. Perhaps this phenomenon is most clearly illustrated by the London Region, which consists of the following zones,[1] all of which possess in their special fashion the "London" label:

[1] Albert Lepawsky, "The London Region: A Metropolitan Community in Crisis," *American Journal of Sociology,* 46 (May, 1941), pp. 826–834; J. B. Cullingworth,

figure 8

A Simplified Ecological Diagram of the Urban Region

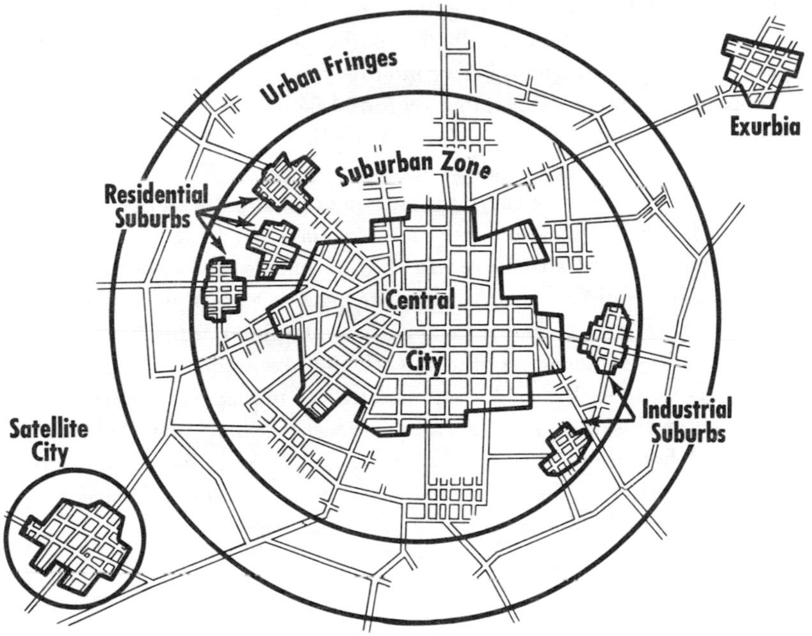

1. *The City of London* (central area): about one square mile.

2. *The Borough of London:* about 10 square miles.

3. *The Inner Ring* (the remainder of London County): about 107 square miles.

4. *The Suburban Ring* (also known as the conurban ring): about 605 square miles.

5. *The Outer Ring* (regional ring or Greenbelt): about 3,690 square miles.

6. *The London Region* (including the preceding areas, plus adjacent areas administered by the Greater London Council): about 4,412 square miles.

The London region and its functional planning zones exemplify the basic nature of urban regions: a cumulative but changing system of related

Housing Needs and Planning Policy (London, Routledge and Kegan Paul, 1960), Chap. 8; T. W. Freeman, *The Conurbations of Great Britain* (Manchester, Manchester University Press, 1959), Chap. 2; Peter Hall, *London 2000* (London, Faber and Faber, 1963), pp. 17–20; Donald L. Foley, *Controlling London's Growth* (Berkeley University of California Press, 1963), pp. 74–89.

urbanized areas, each of which receives different combinations of services from the central city, the counties, local units, and the regional governmental body (in this case, the Greater London Council). In the past, urban regions developed by exporting specific functions to peripheral areas (e.g., industry, special residential facilities, shopping). In this historic process, "encroachment" on existing towns and villages in the periphery was quite common,[2] thereby initiating or intensifying economic and other ties to the central city and other units of the developing region. Likewise, open spaces were converted to urban usages, though the availability of such space is now quite limited in the larger metropolitan regions.

In the processes of exporting and encroaching, a series of new (or newly significant) areas have become familiar supplements to the central city. Each part or specialized area in the urban region has acquired distinctive characteristics that seem to reflect its peculiar position and function in the region. As Figure 8 shows in a highly simplified form, these parts are typically arrayed in an intelligible though mainly unplanned manner, which in essence constitutes the ecological pattern of modern urban regions. The major tasks of this chapter, therefore, consist of analyzing the emergence, features, and functioning of suburbs, the urban fringe, the satellite city, and the exurban area, and then reviewing and assessing the evidence for their interdependent operation as regional entities.

the suburb

Though the suburb is an ancient phenomenon in human communities— for example, the suburbs of the Greek *polis* and the merchants' quarter of the late medieval town—it is only with the flowering of the modern metropolis (*ca.* 1870 in the United States; *ca.* 1800–1850 in Europe) that the suburb has increased in number and importance. The modern suburb is at the same time a creature of, and a reaction to, the complex development of the central city. Essentially, suburban growth has been made possible by successful expansion of a variety of commercial and industrial enterprises and the consequent creation of a rising middle class, improvements in communication and transportation, and the perceptive investments of real estate subdividers and builders, who have produced residential facilities and a tantalizing concept of gracious living, formerly limited to a favored minority.[3]

[2] R. D. McKenzie, *The Metropolitan Community* (New York, McGraw-Hill Book Company, 1933), pp. 70–76, 313.

[3] Chauncey Harris, "Suburbs," *American Journal of Sociology*, 49 (July, 1943), pp. 1–13; Leo F. Schnore, "The Growth of Metropolitan Suburbs," *American Sociological Review*, 22 (April, 1957), pp. 165–173; C. Wright Mills, *White Collar* (New York, Oxford University Press, 1950), pp. 251–258; H. Paul Douglas, *The Suburban Trend* (New York, Appleton-Century-Crofts, 1925); Carl Von Rhode, "The Suburban Mind," *Harper's Magazine*, 192 (April, 1946), pp. 289–299.

To these opportunities have been added the necessary motivations of urbanites: the desire for space, scenery, home ownership, proximity to social equals, and a communal identity distinct from the visible controls of the big city.[4] The ubiquitous result is suburbia, particularly in its residential form.

But how may we distinguish suburbs from other parts in the outer portions of modern urban regions? As a beginning, we may define suburbs as those urbanized nuclei located outside (but within accessible range) of central cities that are politically independent but economically and psychologically linked with services and facilities provided by the metropolis. By "urbanized nuclei" we mean those areas outside the central city that have relatively substantial population densities, a preponderance of nonrural occupations, and distinctly urban forms of recreation, family life, and education.[5] In addition, the economic and social structure of urbanized nuclei can be shown to reflect continuing bonds of dependence on the opportunities, selected services, and essential values of the central city. It should be pointed out that most of the territorial expansion of the central city since 1890 has been accomplished by political annexation of existing or potential suburban areas.

With this initial characterization as a guide, we may turn to a more detailed review of suburban features. However, there is a popular view of suburbia, which is a caricature of suburban areas, because it fails to take account of important types of suburban developments. The first distinction to be made is based on variation in suburban functions. There are predominantly *industrial suburbs, residential suburbs,* and *recreational* or *resort suburbs.*

However, residential (and quasi-residential) suburbs likewise differ among themselves in several important and interlocking respects:

1. *Origins*: developed from a previously isolated village or newly carved out of farm land or unused areas in the fringe; planned or improvised recently.

2. *Dominant strata*: semi-aristocratic families; successful professional and managerial groupings; clerical and skilled working-class families.

3. *Political structure*: incorporated or unincorporated and served by county governments.

4. *Availability of institutional facilities*: schools, shopping centers, variety of churches, recreational facilities, etc.

[4] This is the theme of Robert C. Wood, *Suburbia: Its People and Their Politics* (Boston, Houghton Mifflin, 1959).

[5] Otis D. Duncan and Albert J. Reiss, Jr., *Social Characteristics of Urban and Rural Communities* (New York, John Wiley and Sons, 1956), pp. 117–119; Nathan L. Whetten, "Suburbanization as a Field for Sociological Research," *Rural Sociology,* 16 (December, 1951), pp. 319–328; Robert C. Schmitt, "Suburbanization: Statistical Fallacy?" *Land Economics,* 32 (February, 1956), pp. 85–87.

5. *Dominant motives of migrants*: escape from city; social mobility; job opportunities.

6. *Current relation to central city*: *direct*, as reflected in commuting patterns to jobs, recreation, etc., in central city; *indirect* or tendency toward self-sufficiency following the initial attraction of developing within range of a central city.

Before we attempt to classify suburbs by means of these dimensions, it is quite evident that a reasonable perspective on suburban features in general is overdue. Since the early fifties popular and semi-professional sources have created intriguing but largely caricatured critiques of suburbia, usually based on arbitrarily selected cases and dubious impressionistic forms of observation. While a definitive, comparative review of suburban forms is not yet available, several general conclusions merit continued attention.

1. Historically, suburbs have been a major mechanism of urban growth through specialization. Suburban quarters usually contained specialized occupational groups (merchants, artisans, religious practitioners) who were initially necessary but socially unassimilable in the city structure.[6] It is interesting to note that before the 18th century, suburbanites were principally workers and marginal merchants;[7] only in the modern era in western nations have suburbs attained desirable status for secure and economically successful categories. In non-Western nations, however, suburbs remain as reservoirs of the marginal and impecunious, particularly those who have migrated from tribal or rural village communities.

2. It should be recalled that central cities themselves are resultants of long-term annexation of suburban settlements. Indeed, in some cities the modern core area was originally a suburb.[8] In earlier generations, extension of municipal boundaries was not fiercely contested; identity was then not as important as the advantages of suburban inclusion. Currently, in the Netherlands, suburbs are planned by city officials and are annexed before population growth and development attain problematic status.[9] Therefore, much of suburban history reveals collaboration in municipal growth, in establishing the modern contours of cities. Only when central cities and their services become firmly based and extensive (i.e., important facilities and

[6] W. G. Hoskins, *Local History in England* (London, Longmans, Green, 1959), pp. 82–89; H. J. Dyos, *Victorian Suburb* (Leicester, Leicester University Press, 1961), pp. 36–38; Pierre Francastel, ed., *Les Origines des villes polonaises* (Paris, Mouton, 1960), pp. 33–36.

[7] Edgard Kant, "Suburbanization, Urban Sprawl, and Commutation," in David Hannerberg *et al.*, eds., *Migration in Sweden: A Symposium* (Lund, C. W. K. Gleerup, 1957), p. 245.

[8] Francastel, *op. cit.*, pp. 36, 198; Sam B. Warner, Jr., *Streetcar Suburbs* (Cambridge, Harvard University Press, 1962), pp. 57–127.

[9] Joseph F. Mangiamele, "How Europeans Mold Their Cities," in Goodwin F. Berquist, Jr., ed., *The Wisconsin Academy Looks at Urbanism* (Milwaukee; Wisconsin Academy of Sciences, Arts and Letters, May, 1963), p. 49.

services are easily exportable) can suburban areas seek and maintain their apparent independence.

3. Contemporary suburban migrants are not unformed wanderers, empty vessels awaiting the distinctive contents of their new location. They are socialized representatives of family, occupational, religious, and status categories—though they may differ in some respects from their status peers in premigration communities. Suburbanites select suburbs for one or more of several definite personal and cultural reasons, and appear to evaluate suburban residence in terms of those reasons or motives. No study has yet documented a clear-cut "conversion effect" on suburban migrants (e.g., a change in values, birth patterns, political orientation). As Ktsanes and Reissman aptly and accurately phrase it, suburbia is "new houses for old values."[10]

4. But suburban areas exhibit significant changes in a very visible way: the diversification of family and status categories over time. Though the pattern is not equally clear in all types of suburbs in the U.S. and Western nations, the following seems to be a basic sequence in suburban development.

(a) First to locate in the area are "pioneer" residents from established middle or upper status categories, who can afford the relatively scarce housing facilities and the cost of commuting.[11] The major exceptions to this pattern have occurred since World War II and derive from two sources. One variation can be explained by suburban or fringe relocation of industry, such as in California, Sydney, Long Island.[12] Migrants, therefore, tend to be primarily skilled workers and their families. But a second variation derives from large scale planned suburban areas (public or private), which are designed specifically for lower class or modest middle class families. The Levittowns in Long Island, Pennsylvania, and New Jersey are notable examples, while English and Scotch housing estates illustrate the public form of this variation.[13]

---

[10] S. D. Clark, *The Suburban Society* (Toronto, University of Toronto Press, 1966), pp. 48–97; Herbert J. Gans, *The Levittowners* (New York, Pantheon Books, 1967), pp. 24, 224–239; Bennett M. Berger, *Working-Class Suburb* (Berkeley, University of California Press, 1960), Chap. 6; Robert C. Wood, *Suburbia: Its People and Their Politics* (Boston, Houghton Mifflin, 1959); Carl Werthman *et al., Planning and the Purchase Decision: Why People Buy in Planned Communities* (Berkeley, Center for Planning and Development Research, University of California, July, 1965, mimeo), pp. 12–14, 166–167; Thomas Ktsanes and Leonard Reissman, "Suburbia—New Homes for Old Values," *Social Problems*, 7 (Winter, 1959–1960), pp. 187–195.

[11] Warner, *op. cit.*

[12] Berger, *op. cit.*; T. Brennan, "Urban Communities," in A. F. Davies and S. Encel, eds., *Australian Society: A Sociological Introduction* (New York, Atherton Press, 1965), p. 299.

[13] William M. Dobriner, *Class in Suburbia* (Englewood Cliffs, N.J., Prentice-Hall, 1963), Chap. 4; Gans, *op. cit.*; E. I. Black and T. S. Simey, eds., *Neighbourhood and Community* (Liverpool, University Press of Liverpool, 1954), Part I (The Liverpool Estate), Part II (The Sheffield Estate); John Spencer, *Stress and Release in an Urban Estate* (London, Tavistock Publications, 1964); Ruth Durant, *Watling: A Survey of Social Life on a New Housing Estate* (London, P. S. King, 1939); Michael Young and

(b) As more homes are built and as public facilities are made available (roads, schools, shopping areas), younger families in lower middle and lower status categories constitute a contrapuntal migrant stream, if restrictive zoning is absent. Normally, the second stream locates at the edges of the older suburb, where land costs are lower or where enterprising subdividers provide housing developments at moderate cost and with palpably inaccurate though picturesque names.

(c) On the heels of this second suburban invasion come marginal families who are primarily small proprietors, unskilled workers, and semi-skilled clerical employees. These are marginal not only in terms of income but also in their expressed uncertainties about objectives and residence in the area. Obviously, this category directly refutes the alleged "middle-classness" of suburbs.[14] But, in a sense, middle class suburbanites unwittingly establish the bases for such a paradoxical migrant category. Of course, some of these marginal families simply are old residents of areas that have been infiltrated by movements summarized in (a) and (b).[15]

(d) In suburban areas or zones where commercial and/or industrial developments have *followed* the population trends just described, a second wave of professional, managerial, and technically proficient occupational categories tends to augment the pattern of diversification. At this point, the scarcity of suburban land arrests the prodigal subdivision of one-family homes on one- to four-acre lots. Instead, we find the increasing resort to high-rise apartments and most recently, a more economic use of land in town houses, whose high cost often represents a triumph of fashion over spaciousness.[16]

5. The formerly dominant concept of dormitory suburbs, once quite accurate, is much less applicable during the past 20 years in the U.S. and Western Europe. Only in the peripheral slums of Latin America and Africa is the traditional journey to work to the central city still pervasive. But this involves commuting by unskilled, marginal suburbanites, rather than the voluntary daily hegira of the natty middle class professional, executive, or white collar worker. In recent years, suburban job opportunities for managerial, professional, and skilled persons have greatly expanded, encouraging

---

Peter Willmott, *Family and Kinship in East London* (London, Routledge and Kegan Paul, 1957), pp. 97–135; Peter Willmott and Michael Young, *Family and Class in a London Suburb* (London, Routledge and Kegan Paul, 1960); Ronald Frankenberg, *Communities in Britain* (Baltimore, Penguin Books, 1966), Chaps. 7, 8.

[14] Alvin Boskoff, "Social and Cultural Patterns in a Suburban Area: Their Significance for Social Change in the South," *Journal of Social Issues*, 22 (January, 1966), pp. 85–94.

[15] Nelson N. Foote *et al.*, eds., *Housing Choices and Housing Constraints* (New York, McGraw-Hill, 1960), p. 164.

[16] Anshel Melamed, "High-Rent Apartments in the Suburbs," *Urban Land*, 20 (October, 1961), pp. 1–6.

urbanites to locate in convenient suburban areas and also motivating suburbanites to become long-term settlers in suburban zones [17] (unlike the stereotype of the restless suburbanite, who allegedly uses the suburb as a way-
station in his relentless ascent on the social ladder).

6. Most important, however, are the cultural and organizational consequences of the developed suburb. Contrary to the institutional aridity of
the dormitory suburb and its "suburban sadness," more suburbs are developing local sources of recreation, uplift, education, desired retail services,
banking, and voluntary or formal associations. In short, to an extent that is
not generally recognized, suburbs tend to become indistinguishable in operation (rather than location) from portions of the central city.[18]

7. Consequently, whatever distinctive features suburbs may possess initially (relative homogeneity, commuting patterns, spaciousness, low taxes),
these seem to be transitional. Functionally, suburbs begin as spatial additions to urban cores. Increasingly, they tend to become distant subcenters
of urban populations and activities. The only remaining distinction of any
meaning seems to be political independence through incorporation.

suburban types

Since suburbs are products of varied motives, pressures, and facilities,
and likewise exhibit historical development or change in population, it does
not seem satisfactory to use the prevailing distinction between residential
and industrial or employing suburbs.[19] Instead, we may begin with this distinction (direct vs. indirect relation to the central city) and further sub-
divide each in terms of two important dimensions: dominant motives or
goals of residents; and dominant social class patterning of an area. The
resulting 12 types are presented in Figure 9, primarily as a conceptual map
for organizing available data, but also as a base for future investigation of
suburban phenomena.

As yet only six of these suburban types can be identified empirically,
though other "cells" may be found to be appropriate to areas familiar to
other students of urbanism. With unavoidable oversimplification, let us try
to focus on the special features of each type.

[17] Lowdon Wingo, Jr., ed., *Cities and Space* (Baltimore, Johns Hopkins Press, 1963),
p. 90; Sidney Goldstein and Kurt B. Mayer, *Residential Mobility, Migration, and Commuting in Rhode Island* (Providence, Rhode Island Development Council, September,
1963), p. 18; Brennan, *op. cit.*, p. 299.

[18] Clark, *op. cit.*, pp. 12–14; Gans, *op. cit.*, pp. 288, 409.

[19] Leo F. Schnore, "Satellites and Suburbs," *Social Forces*, 36 (December, 1957),
pp. 121–129. Cf. Charles S. Liebman, "Functional Differentiation and Political Characteristics of Suburbs," *American Journal of Sociology*, 66 (March, 1961), pp. 485–490.

figure 9

A Suggested Classification of Suburbs

DOMINANT CLASS STRUCTURE	DIRECT RELATION TO CITY		INDIRECT RELATION TO CITY	
	Escape Motives	*Positive Motives*	*Escape Motives*	*Positive Motives*
Upper	1 Traditional suburb	4	7	10
Middle and mixed	2 Identity conscious suburb	5 Stable suburb (Levittown)	8	11 Stable suburb (DeKalb County, Ga.)
Lower	3	6 Housing estate Suburban slum	9	12 Industrial suburb

1. traditional upper-class suburb

This type, so ably dissected by Cleveland Amory,[20] is numerically small and increasingly untypical of recent trends in suburban development. Essentially, this type is marked by a preponderance of long established, high-status families, comparatively little turnover in population, location near towns or villages that have extensive, independent histories, and an understandable concentration in the Northeast (e.g., near Boston, New York City, and Philadelphia).

2. the identity-conscious suburb

This is a highly obtrusive and controversial type of suburb—and a continuing object of fictional and journalistic diagnosis. Most of these suburbs were carved out of fringe areas following World War II, while some were developed as recently as a decade ago. The major feature or tone seems to be one of recently acquired or desired upward mobility, which is connected with a pervasive distaste for the central city in its spatial, political, and demographic aspects. Most families in this suburban type are commuters who appear to identify their personal independence with the political isolation of their community. In general, residents are in professional and

[20] Cleveland Amory, *The Proper Bostonians* (New York, E. P. Dutton, 1947).

managerial occupations and tend to be in the late 30s and 40s age categories. The residential character of the area and the maintenance of relative status homogeneity are prime considerations.[21]

3. the mass-produced suburb

This is perhaps the most representative and numerous of contemporary suburban forms. Its residents are predominantly interested in good, reasonably priced housing, which is unobtainable in their respective central cities. Indeed, they retain some attachment to the city beyond the necessity of commuting to offices and shops in the city. For many, this dual allegiance involves some strain, as reflected in considerable interest in local social participation (civic organizations, etc.) and in campaigns for obtaining local urban facilities from limited tax funds or voluntary contributions.[22] The typical resident (usually in the salaried professions, lesser administrative posts, or in moderately successful businesses) plans to settle in the suburb, rather than to seek higher status by frequent moves. However, the major problem—and challenge—seems to be the newness of such developments, with a resultant inadequacy in varied cultural facilities. Good examples may be found in Levittown, New Jersey, and several British housing estates near London, Liverpool, and Sheffield.

4. the suburban slum

The foremost illustration of this type is the Latin American favela or barriada and the bidonville of African urban concentrations. Such areas are marked by makeshift, unimaginably crowded housing for impoverished Negro or Indian migrants from rural areas. These suburbanites, unable to afford urban apartments, live with or near relatives or acquaintances from home communities and participate in informal networks of aid and recreation with neighbors and kinsmen. Work opportunities tend to be largely in unskilled jobs in the city, with the journey to work a noisy and uncomfortable experience by ancient bus or train.[23] Clearly, the expected amenities of suburban living are simply not available. More important, these suburbs seem to show neither improvement nor development, only continued cramming of more migrants.

[21] Good examples of this type are discussed in John R. Seeley et al., *Crestwood Heights* (New York, Basic Books, 1956); Alvin H. Scaff, "The Effect of Commuting on Participation in Community Organizations," *American Sociological Review*, 17 (April, 1952), pp. 215–220; William H. Whyte, Jr., "The Transients," *Fortune* (May-August, 1953); William H. Whyte, Jr., *The Organization Man* (New York, Simon and Schuster, 1956), Part 7.

[22] See references in note 13.

[23] Philip M. Hauser, ed., *Urbanization in Latin America* (New York, Columbia University Press, 1961), Chaps. 6, 8, 9.

5. the stable variegated suburb

Apparently this type of suburb has developed without much notice, probably during the last ten years. It seems to have derived either from the identity-conscious or mass-produced type because of one or more local attractions (e.g., considerable space for expansion, quality of local education, scenic features, or presence of a high status facility such as a university, prestige hospital, etc.). Whatever the specific reasons, the original settlers discourage the rapid addition of new subdivisions from nearby vacant lots and farms. The more recent migrants represent a wide span of professional and white collar occupations and have previous experience in suburban or city living.

Perhaps the crucial element in this suburban type is the increasing location of appropriate jobs within the suburb or in adjacent suburban areas. While daily commuting to the city persists, an appreciable proportion of suburbanites come to reside near their jobs. Consequently, a reciprocal interest in the character of the suburb tends to develop in suburban employers and suburban residents. Both emphasize the necessity of local facilities (schools, shopping, civic organizations, the arts) as a means of encouraging continued residence and community stability. But with increasing facilities, the more attractive this suburb becomes for different social categories, from both city and fringe areas. Thus, the basis for a considerable population mix (largely excluding nonwhites) is firmly established.

Since few detailed studies of this suburban type are available, it may be helpful to summarize a relevant case in the Atlanta metropolitan region.[24] In DeKalb County, which lies on the eastern border of Atlanta and its county, a suburban crescent (largely unincorporated) has developed in the western portion during the last 20 years. The average family income for the county is among the top 20 counties in the nation. But in the suburban area under consideration, occupational and income differences are considerable. However, careful interviews with a sample of 101 families revealed several family types or life-styles.

Essentially, information was gathered on occupation, place of work, shopping habits, patterns of voluntary association membership and participation, reasons for moving to the areas, aspirations for family members, and patterns of friendship. Assuming that basic values and allocation of effort are reflected in marital patterns of organization membership over time, we classified families into the following types:

Consistent involvement: both mates belonged to associations before and after the suburban move.

Interchangeable responsibility: either mate (husband or wife) had con-

[24] Boskoff, *op. cit.*, pp. 85–100.

tinuous membership, while the other had discontinuous (past but not present, or present but not past) associations.

Attempted mobility: one mate, or both, had acquired voluntary affiliations after the suburban move.

Social Resignation: one mate or both had previous but no present affiliations.

Conflict: relatively few instances in which one mate had continuous affiliations, while the other maintained consistent isolation from voluntary groups.

Significantly, these family types were not well correlated with occupational categories. More important, each type seemed to possess a relatively distinctive complex of behavioral and attitudinal patterns. Very briefly,

1. *Consistent involvement* families, more than others in the sample, tend to work in the suburban zone rather than in downtown Atlanta. Indeed they have largely moved into the area to be near their place of work. In general, these families emphasize their health and the future of their children rather than status. Furthermore, they tend to have more friends, who are rather dispersed geographically. There is a strong tendency to participate in varied activities with different friends. The consistent involvement type seems reasonably content and able to maintain balanced involvements. (The interchangeable responsibility type is very similar in these respects.)

2. *Attempted mobility.* This category fits the stereotype of suburbanite in many respects. It contains the largest proportion in our sample who are status conscious—as reflected in reasons for moving to the suburb (and specific areas in the suburban zone) and in high status aspirations for the family. A high proportion of the husbands commute to jobs in downtown Atlanta. While these families maintain about the same number of active friendships as other suburban types, the proportion of multipurpose friendships (i.e., varied activities with the same person) is somewhat less, perhaps indicating less intense involvement. Furthermore, in comparison with other types, attempted mobility families tend to have friends away from their immediate neighborhood, even when length of residence is taken into account. The overall style seems to be future-oriented, instrumental, and cosmopolitan.

3. *Resignation* families were too few in number for any definitive conclusions. However, they seem to have no focal reason for moving to the suburbs, nor are their aspirations very articulate. We may suspect that their occupational status (primarily in clerical and lower managerial jobs) is perceived as immutable and that the suburb is a refuge from the complexities and pressures of urban competition.

4. *The conflict type.* This is a particularly intriguing set of families, which is not normally associated with suburbia. In this sample, the husbands were predominantly small proprietors, whose places of business were often in the suburban zone. Yet comparatively few respondents were specially con-

cerned about living near (or convenient to) their work. Comparatively more attention was instead given to availability of various services and adequate housing (more space, reasonable financing). There is considerable evidence of personal and family uncertainty; responses to questions on aspirations contained very high proportions (33–64 percent) of "don't know." Of those with definite answers, it is difficult to identify consistent ideas about the future. Wives desired more status for themselves and for their families, but not for their husbands. The major concern about their children was that they be good citizens and have stable personalities, rather than that they achieve success. But very significant is a highly circumscribed friendship pattern. Conflict families have fewer friends than the other types, more of whom (two-thirds) are in the immediate neighborhood. Indeed, this small circle of friends is involved in a wide range of activities, which is perhaps part of the general insulation of the conflict type from the suburb and the urban region.

As suburban areas become more populated, existing suburbs may be expected to develop toward the stable variegated type. Unfortunately, specific suburbs have not been studied over long periods of time, so that we might identify processes of suburban change. Yet we may hypothesize that economic and industrial relocation into suburban areas will be followed by increasing diversification of status levels and family types within the same suburban area or zone. In that case, suburbs tend to re-create the structure of the central city and can no longer be viewed as ecologically or functionally distinct.

6. the industrial suburb

It is quite apparent that the industrial or employing suburb has been relatively ignored in recent years as an object of urban studies, in favor of the residential or dormitory type. Perhaps two features of the industrial suburb, however, can be considered well established. (a) Understandably, the occupational and social class distributions of industrial suburbs are weighted toward the skilled and semiskilled categories, and likewise toward lower and lower middle status groups. (b) In recent years, the relative population growth of industrial suburbs has been significantly smaller than that of residential suburbs. This is true for all sections of the nation, for all sizes of central city and suburb, and for all distances from the central city. Perhaps these comparative trends reflect an approximation to saturation in growth of industrial suburbs, particularly of the larger and older suburbs. The rate of growth is lowest, for example, in the Northeast and highest in the newer industrial suburbs of the West and South.[25] Suburban growth in general

[25] Leo F. Schnore, "The Growth of Metropolitan Suburbs," *op. cit.*, pp. 29–34. A recent study of an industrial suburb in California is Bennett M. Berger, *Working-Class Suburb* (Berkeley, University of California Press, 1960); Robert E. Dickinson, *The West European City* (London, Routledge and Kegan Paul, 1951), pp. 85, 229–231.

seems to depend on expansion of residential areas, rather than on employment opportunities in industrial suburbs.

the roles of suburban forms

The social and cultural differentiation in suburban areas should curb the over-confident comparisons and distinctions between city and suburban entities. Indeed, such comparisons—based on census data—are really between central cities and rings (i.e., noncity portions of given Standard Metropolitan Areas), so that suburbs are unfortunately lumped with fringe areas and villages. However, if we make use of available data with some caution, the following overall differences between city and ring can be identified (though it may be presumed that these are decreasingly valid patterns).

1. Population increase is decidedly greater in ring areas as a consequence both of migration from central city and migration from fringe and small town areas (outside the SMA) to the suburbs. In 1950, ring areas accounted for over 21 percent of metropolitan population, while the most recent estimate is almost 30 percent. Central cities have generally had net population losses, or very slight increases. Even greater population losses have been masked by annexation of suburban fringe areas since 1950.[26]

2. Sex ratios are somewhat higher in ring areas, particularly in comparison with commercial central cities. This is related to the characteristics below.

3. Marriage rates tend to be higher in ring areas, probably as a consequence of selective migration of family units to such areas.

4. Age distribution is somewhat more skewed toward younger age categories in ring areas.

5. Income and occupational distributions show larger concentrations in higher or more prestigeful categories in ring areas.

6. Educational levels in ring areas for those 25 years and over are higher than in cities. Nonwhites in ring areas, however, have in the past had lower educational levels than these city counterparts, perhaps indicating selective migration of skilled and semi-skilled nonwhites to industrial suburbs.

In view of suburban variety and the diminishing differences between central city and suburb, what can we conclude about the contributions of suburbs to modern urban regions? Perhaps the basic consideration is a distinction between early and developed phases of urbanization and the related notion of differential significance of suburbs according to phase of urbanization.

[26] Duncan and Reiss, *op. cit.*, pp. 119–123; Leo F. Schnore, "Municipal Annexations and the Growth of Metropolitan Suburbs, 1950–60," *American Journal of Sociology*, 67 (January, 1967), pp. 406–417.

In earlier urban waves, and in the first phases of urban development during the past 150 years, suburbs seem to have operated as specialized outposts of the city, as potential or actual substitutes for activities or facilities the city could not conveniently provide. For example, industrial suburbs enabled the core to serve its commercial and administrative-governmental needs without the encroachment of factories. Likewise, early suburban forms enabled higher status categories to experiment with the fruits of their achievement in ways that were impossible in the built-up portions of the city. One consequence, of course, was the heightening of status distinctions, and also the implicit provision of tangible goals or vehicles of urban achievement and social mobility. However, the epiphenomenal or auxiliary character of these suburbs largely prevented serious concern for a local range of urban services and facilities. They could not function as communities in the full sense of the term, which perhaps accounts for the long-standing criticism of suburbia.

More recently, the previously analyzed suburbs have been supplemented by developed suburban forms, which seem to function in a different manner. It is quite likely that the stable, variegated suburb provides an alternative and more satisfactory setting for family living and child rearing in terms of more space, more and newer facilities, better public education, and more flexibility. It is by no means utopia, but it may represent a resurgence of satisfying family life for many acquainted with the urban frustrations of the Great Depression. Perhaps the suburban birth rate and the emphasis on activities for children and youths reflect a collective appreciation of the "new suburbia."

In addition, the variegated suburbs permit or encourage the broadening of middle social categories in the urban region by providing space for various segments of middle life-styles, and allowing for direct and indirect communication and participation among these categories. Perhaps this explains the immense popularity of suburban PTAs and similar groups, in which are mixed such emphases as concern for children, participation in family units, identification with the local area, and civic rather than class or status responsibility. Furthermore, though there are some signs of change, the central city has been generally perceived as uncongenial to middle class ideals. Consequently, migration from central cities (or from suburb to suburb) can be interpreted, not as antiurban, but as a search for a substitute for the city. Such a quest can only be satisfied in the variegated suburb and thus we would predict the largest suburban population increase in Western nations in this type of suburb.

Finally, to the extent that these functions are successfully performed, the developed suburbs may be interpreted as the prime socializer of the professional, managerial, and technical personnel required for the continued and expanding operation of metropolitan entities. As cities progressively increase their demand for tertiary occupational categories, the dependence of cities on such suburbs will likewise grow, simply because cities have not been consciously or consistently designed for retaining ambitious and capable families.

Taken as a whole, suburban variety reflects the typical urban opportunity for experimentation, specialization, flexibility, and change. Urban regions develop largely through the mechanisms of suburbanization, often without control or understanding of these processes. The immediate effects of suburbanization on the central city are either added costs for provision of services, or reduced revenues (which instead flow to county or other non-municipal units). However, urban economists are not agreed on the actual long-term financial burden which suburban growth imposes on city governments.[27] In any case, urban and suburban populations are both directly and indirectly dependent on one another. Suburban growth eases population pressure on the central city, thereby providing opportunities for alert cities to replace slum areas and substandard housing, as well as to plan for the future availability of desired services and facilities. Suburbs, on the other hand, are the beneficiaries of preexisting urban concentrations of capital, skills, and expensive facilities.

If earlier suburbs, with their specialized facilities, formalized their interdependence through annexation by the metropolis, the more balanced suburbs of the current era face the same issue: does spatial separation justify autonomy or does the continued attractiveness of suburbia depend on joint financing and planning of regional networks of facilities and resources?

the urban fringe

It is to be expected that the nature of the urban region becomes increasingly difficult to identify and analyze as one moves from the city proper to the region's periphery. At the present time, the urban fringe (and closely related labels for this type of area) is therefore understandably vague, or so variably defined that its characteristics do not form a coherent whole. But there is enough valid information to conclude that the fringe is not chaotic, but a meaningful entity in the urban regional complex.

If we recall the imputed nature of the urban region as a system in continuous operation, involving the basic processes of growth, differentiation, and coordination, then the fringe can be initially approached as that part of the region most immediately relevant to regional expansion and therefore least subject to the process of regional coordination. From a purely geographic

[27] Amos H. Hawley, "Metropolitan Population and Municipal Government Expenditures in Central Cities," *Journal of Social Issues*, 7 (1951), pp. 101–108; Ruth L. Mace, *Municipal Cost-Revenue Research in the United States* (Chapel Hill, Institute of Government, University of North Carolina, 1961); Harvey E. Brazer, *City Expenditures in the United States* (New York, National Bureau of Economic Research, 1959), Occasional Paper #66, p. 58.

standpoint, most of the fringe area thus defined is peripheral. But, as many urban land inventories have shown, there are fringe areas or islands in the suburban zone, and even within the city limits.[28]

Since suburban areas develop from previously fringe territories, it is clearly necessary to distinguish these two regional parts from one another. The fringe possesses several identifying features.

1. Its general location is beyond the suburban zone or cluster, but normally near main highways or watercourses.

2. The land use pattern of the fringe is a crescive, uncoordinated accumulation of residential, commercial, manufacturing, and special service (private hospitals, cemeteries, etc.) types, with considerable amounts of vacant land.

3. The residential facilities of the fringe tend toward lower levels of attractiveness and physical repair (e.g., tourist cabins, trailer homes).

4. The employed population tends to be drawn from lower status categories than are found in the residential suburb.

5. Since the fringe as an urban appendage is relatively new, or in early stages of development, it normally lacks both urban services (e.g., pressurized gas for cooking and heating, adequate water systems, paved streets, etc.) and local social organization, such as its own government, school system, police and fire protection, and churches. Firey and Wehrwein have therefore called the fringe "an institutional desert." [29]

6. The outer rim of the fringe, also called the extended fringe, is adjacent to, or intermixed with, more or less active agricultural areas.

7. Because of the encroachment of more settled suburban areas, the fringe is in constant change with respect to boundary lines. In general, however, fringe areas and fringe population are declining.

the role of the fringe

The importance of the fringe is considerable, though comparatively little definitive data are available. Essentially, the urban fringe has been a major source of urban expansion, from which have eventually emerged the residential and industrial suburbs. In addition, the fringe provides an interesting but still unexplored locus of social and cultural contacts between urban and rural families, since population movements to the fringe involve families from

---

[28] See Richard B. Andrews, "Elements in the Urban Fringe Pattern," *Journal of Land and Public Utility Economics*, 18 (May, 1942), pp. 169–183; George S. Wehrwein, "The Rural-Urban Fringe," *Urban Geography*, 18 (July, 1942), pp. 217–228; Walter Firey, "Ecological Considerations in Planning for Urban Fringes," *American Sociological Review*, 11 (August, 1946), pp. 411–421.

[29] Wehrwein, *op. cit.*, p. 223; Walter Firey, *Social Aspects of Land Use Planning in the Country-City Fringe* (East Lansing, Michigan State College Agricultural Experiment Station, June, 1946).

farms and villages, as well as from the central city.[30] On the other hand, the absence of effective social controls (either from the city, county, or local area) tends to make the fringe attractive to irresponsible land developers, criminals, gamblers, and nuisance activities (roadhouses, dumping areas)—all of which may interfere with the orderly expansion of the urban region and with the search for adequate residential accommodations.

satellite cities

At the outer edge of the fringe, but often in a segment of the fringe of the largest cities, are located one or more satellite communities whose status and functional importance to the urban region are somewhat unique. Known variously as independent cities (i.e., not within census-defined regions), employing satellites, hinterland cities, and subdominant communities, the satellite city is in some respects a miniature version of the central city.[31] However, the satellite should be distinguished both from the central city and the industrial suburb (with which it has sometimes been confused). For simplicity, it may be helpful to classify satellite cities into two categories—large: 100,000 population or over; and small: 10,000 to 100,000 population, thus enabling us to note gross variations in characteristics related to size whenever the data permit.

In general, satellite cities appear to have their origin prior to and therefore independent of the rise of central cities. Many satellites once had pretensions to urban grandeur, but newer and more favorably situated cities (both geographically and politically) have come to overshadow their older, less fortunate competitors. Thus, the satellite, as the name implies, operates in a functionally restricted manner in the regional complex. This is substantially true for both size categories.

Unlike most suburbs but in line with central cities, satellite cities are politically independent, formally organized communities. They generally supply their residents with the normal range of community services—often with distinct quality in the larger satellites—but are rarely able to afford such urban accomplishments as art museums, symphony orchestras, etc.

The relative location of smaller satellite cities is normally beyond the fringe and frequently at points roughly intermediate to contiguous urban regions. Consequently, the satellite tends to have an exposed or marginal location, in contrast to the relatively shorter distance between the suburb and central city. In some instances (i.e., the larger satellites), the satellite is

[30] Myles W. Rodehaver, "Fringe Settlement as a Two-Dimensional Movement," *Rural Sociology*, 12 (March, 1947), pp. 49–57.

[31] Donald J. Bogue, *Population Growth in Standard Metropolitan Areas 1900–1950* (Washington, Housing and Home Finance Agency, December, 1953), pp. 40–45.

almost adjacent to its central city—across a river or bay (e.g., Council Bluffs, Iowa and Omaha, Nebraska; Jersey City and New York City; Camden, N.J. and Philadelphia).

By comparison with either residential or industrial suburbs, the satellite tends to have a larger average population size. This results from the greater life span of the satellite, but more significantly from the greater range of activities and services.

The satellite city, unlike the residential but somewhat similar to the industrial suburb and the central city, is a predominantly employing area of the urban region, as measured by the proportion of residents who work in the community as against those who commute to the central city for employment. Recent studies indicate that satellites specialize both in manufacturing and various types of retail trade, with a preponderance of manufacturing in northern and midwestern satellites, and diversified retail trade in the south. As Schnore points out, satellites provide few employment opportunities in transportation, resort and recreational functions, or wholesale activities.[32] Consequently, while the satellite resembles the central city as a source of jobs, it functions as a supplement, rather than a competitor, to the metropolitan center.

There is some evidence that satellite communities possess distinctive population characteristics, which seem to be intermediate to those of the central city and suburban areas. On the basis of incomplete data, the satellites seem to lie between the city and suburb on such features as percent of non-whites, sex ratio, proportion of married males, and proportion of younger persons. Other studies point to the comparatively lower status levels of satellite populations, as measured by median rentals and property values.[33]

In general, satellite communities show an average population increase considerably below that of suburbs, though comparable to or higher than that of central cities. The relative stability of satellites probably indicates a continuing specialization in a few economic functions, with a consequent de-emphasis on residential expansion (which is currently the greatest source of population increase).

The role of the satellite city in urban regions has been well described as "subdominant." [34] It is important as a specialized though unofficial agent of the central city which aids in furnishing services and organization to the distant subareas of the region. This function is neither planned nor voluntary,

[32] Schnore, "Satellites and Suburbs," loc cit.; Grace M. Kneedler, "Functional Types of Cities," in Paul K. Hatt and Albert J. Reiss, Jr., eds., Reader in Urban Sociology (New York, The Free Press of Glencoe, 1951), pp. 49–53; Clarence F. Ridley et al., eds., The Municipal Year Book 1953 (Chicago, International City Managers Association, 1953), pp. 54–56.

[33] Duncan and Reiss, op. cit., pp. 171–175; Schnore, "Satellites and Suburbs," loc. cit.

[34] Donald J. Bogue, The Structure of the Metropolitan Community (Ann Arbor, Mich., Horace H. Rackham School of Graduate Studies, University of Michigan, 1949), pp. 18–20, 61–62.

but it is probably the major basis for survival of satellite communities. The unintended result is a strengthening of the invisible bonds which maintain a regional identity. Not only does the satellite flourish under this division of labor, but the central city is thereby relieved of some of its staggering responsibilities in providing facilities for urbanites beyond municipal limits. It should be recalled that a substantial proportion of the population in the urban fringe (as defined by the Census Bureau)—20 percent—resides in incorporated areas each having 2,500 population or over.[35] These areas are often what we have referred to as satellite communities.

exurbia

The farthest thrust of the urban region is both relatively recent and somewhat rare.[36] Only the very largest cities—New York City, Chicago, and Los Angeles—seem to develop one or more exurban outposts, which are located well beyond the fringe in what were originally rural or village communities. The exurban area may or may not be geographically continuous with the more familiar segments of the urban region. But it is nevertheless closely linked with the central city.

Exurbia is generically similar to suburbia, although the exurbanite often refuses to consider himself in the same universe with the suburbanite. Both types represent a basic ambivalence toward the big city; both wish to escape —but not too far (either physically or psychologically) from the cultural magnetism of the metropolis. Exurbia and suburbia differ, however, in their opportunities to express this ambivalence and in the means used to implement it.

The exurbanite, by virtue of his occupation, has superior opportunities for escape. He (or she) is typically in the creative branches of the vast urban communications industry—advertising, commercial art, radio, television, films, magazines, and playwriting. From an ecological standpoint, given the desire to escape, these occupations are significant in that they do not require daily attendance at a downtown office or studio. In addition, they yield comparatively large salaries—$20,000 and up, with an average probably around $50,000. Consequently, the exurbanite can easily arrange to live at a considerable distance from the central city, unlike the typical suburbanite.

If exurbia is therefore both residence and workshop, how are specific locations selected? Escape involves physical distance, of course, but also physical contrast with the city and some link with previous marks of successful escape. These conditions are satisfied by rural and semirural areas where

[35] Bogue, *Population Growth in Standard Metropolitan Areas*, p. 43.
[36] The following discussion is primarily based on A. C. Spectorsky, *The Exurbanites* (Philadelphia, J. B. Lippincott, 1955).

artists and writers of the recent past lived and worked—e.g., Bucks County, Pennsylvania and Fairfield County, Connecticut.[37] Exurbia is therefore a specialized, modernized, financially successful version of the artists' colony, located 40–50 miles from the commercial center with which it maintains a sustained symbiotic relationship.

It is difficult to appraise the role of exurbia in the urban region. However, some relevant inferences can be made from the fragmentary information now available. Exurbanites, far out of proportion to their numbers, control (or at least significantly channel) the tastes and underlying ideals of urbanites in general. This is inherent in their occupational role, though many exurbanites would rather be "artistic" than merely expert tools of persuasion and amusement. In addition, as a special status group (based on their "glamorous" occupations, high incomes, and semibohemian living), exurbanites are among the pacesetters of urban fashion. The foreign car as a status item (rather than a more economical form of transportation), for example, was first adopted by exurbanites. Finally, exurban populations seem to be unwitting agents of a restrictive urban regionalism, while trying to retain the low density and high social status of "snob zoning" (such as requiring a minimum of four acres and $30,000 homes).[38]

the urban region as a functional entity

Throughout the preceding analyses of specialized parts in the urban region, it was difficult to ignore linkages between parts, and also the interrelations between specific parts and the central city. Indeed, the development and special character of each type of regional part could only be understood as a cumulative set of adjustments to some aspect (or aspects) of the central city. However, urban sociologists regard the central city as the dominant unit, not only with respect to influence on any one type of subdominant community, but as the subtle integrator of interrelations in the entire regional complex. In other words, the urban region is approached as a functional unity based on a territorial-social division of labor more or less influenced by the operation of the central city; and on recognizable patterns of coordination among the parts, which are directly or indirectly imposed by ongoing processes (social, cultural, and ecological) within the central city. Since this coordination and regional organization are highly complex, at present we can only try to indicate their essential character through research evidence that is illustrative and inferential, rather than conclusive.

---

[37] Boston seems to have acquired an exurban area in Hillsborough and Rockingham Counties of New Hampshire. See *The New York Times*, February 5, 1961.
[38] *The New York Times*, November 11 and December 16, 1956.

dominant ecological patterns

'   With some variations by region and size of central city, the basic dominance of the metropolis is most clearly evident in the familiar constellation of specialized zones or rings around the central city (see Fig. 8). This remarkably consistent pattern of differentiation is usually interpreted as a consequence of attempts (conscious or unintended) to accommodate to the centralized economic and political influence of the metropolis.

It has been suggested, furthermore, that specialized zones closest to the central city should therefore show greater internal specialization (i.e., sharper differences between community units) than that of more distant zones. This is based on the theory that the power of an organizing center decreases with distance, and that its power over dependent units is reflected in varying degrees of specialization (which is viewed as an adjustive mechanism) within such units. Recently, some evidence has been presented which supports this theory for a sample of 24 SMAs.[39] Suburban communities closest to the central city were found to exhibit greater variations among themselves than were discovered in outer suburban areas in such relevant factors as occupational distribution (particularly in percent of professionals and operatives), average monthly rental and physical condition of dwellings, concentration of non-whites, and voting behavior. Perhaps theses differences can be explained as a consequence of the urban emphasis on status distinctions, which presumably diminishes as urbanization decreases.

patterns of population distribution

Theoretically, metropolitan dominance should be indirectly expressed in the overall pattern of population density and distribution in the urban region. More specifically, the various areal parts of the region should exhibit predictably different population features as a consequence of their respective relations with the central city. For example, we would expect the urban fringe to have a lower density of population than the residential and industrial suburbs and a greater prevalence of urban population features in areas most accessible to the central city.

In general, these expectations have been fairly well substantiated by Bogue in studies of 67 of the largest urban regions of the U.S.[40] Not only does population density tend to decrease with distance from the metropolis, but the larger the metropolis (and therefore the greater the presumed influence)

[39] Leslie Kish, "Differentiation in Metropolitan Areas," *American Sociological Review*, 19 (August, 1954), pp. 388–398.

[40] Bogue, *The Structure of the Metropolitan Community*, pp. 31–54.

the greater the relative density. As expected, Bogue also demonstrates a relative concentration of persons with urban features in areas closest to central cities. A special analysis of sectors radiating from the metropolis to the regional periphery further shows that population density is considerably higher in sectors containing highways to other major cities and in those marked by the presence of satellite cities than in sectors which had neither feature. Central cities, therefore, seem to operate as latent regulators of regional population patterns, a situation that perhaps facilitates the economic dominance of the metropolis.

economic dominance

A growing fund of investigations concerned with metropolitan dominance emphasizes the direct and indirect economic dependence of the so-called hinterland on the central city. The pioneer formulations of this approach were made by Gras, McKenzie, and several urban geographers, but it is only recently that economic control has been verified by Bogue and others.[41] In the decade 1940–1950, central cities tended to provide disproportionately higher amounts of wholesale, retail, and diversified services (e.g., repairs, warehousing facilities) than other components of the urban region. Bogue found that population groupings within a 35-mile radius of the metropolis were specially dependent on the latter for retail commodities and diversified services, while dependence on wholesale services was even more marked for a 65-mile radius from the city. Beyond a 65-mile radius, in sectors containing either intermetropolitan highways or satellite cities, this dependence of the hinterland gradually declined. As summarized by McKenzie and Bogue, these economic patterns indicate that satellite cities, suburbs, and the fringe specialize in activities which do not directly compete with the superior resources of the metropolis.

Metropolitan dominance is not maintained without cost to the city population, however. Based on information for 76 cities of 100,000 population or over in 1940, it was discovered that per capita cost of city governmental services increases somewhat with increases in the proportion of regional population residing in the hinterland.[42] It would be interesting to know whether or not this situation persists, as well as the comparative changes in

---

[41] N. S. B. Gras, *An Introduction to Economic History* (New York, Harper and Brothers, 1922), Chaps. V, VI; McKenzie, *op. cit.*, pp. 70–84, 313; Eugene Van Cleef, *Trade Centers and Trade Routes* (New York, Appleton-Century-Crofts, 1937) ; Harold M. Mayer and Clyde F. Kohn, eds., *Readings in Urban Geography* (Chicago, University of Chicago Press, 1959), Sections 7, 10; Bogue, *The Structure of the Metropolitan Community*, pp. 38–40, 54–60; Melvin E. DeFleur and John Crosby, "Analyzing Metropolitan Dominance," *Social Forces*, 35 (October, 1956), pp. 68–75.

[42] Hawley, *loc. cit.*

governmental costs for central cities and for hinterland communities since 1940.

miscellaneous facets of metropolitan dominance

Several indirect measures of metropolitan influence should also be noted. The effective range of significant contact with the central city has been fairly well established by studies of relative frequency of telephone calls to or from the city, origin and destination surveys of automobiles and other traffic surveys, and analysis of daily and Sunday newspaper circulation.[43]

Let us briefly examine newspaper circulation. Following the pattern of earlier studies by Park and McKenzie, recent research indicates that a declining rate of readership of metropolitan newspapers accompanies increasing distance from the central city.[44] By itself, newspaper circulation does not provide clear-cut limits to the urban region; but circulation rates seem to be closely related to degrees of dominance in retail trade. Since advertising policy (e.g., the space given to local merchants and regional branches of metropolitan firms) affects circulation patterns, this relationship is understandable. But it remains to be established that either advertising policy or special features in metropolitan dailies (syndicated columns, fuller news coverage, etc.) are more attractive to hinterland residents. Another consideration is the rapid rise of local community and neighborhood papers,[45] which corresponds to the recent development of peripheral population movements and new outlying business centers. It is too early to estimate the degree of competition these local papers offer, but it may be symptomatic that in North Hollywood, California, about 65 percent of the readers of the *Valley Times* (circulation of 50,000) read no Los Angeles paper at all.[46]

[43] James A. Quinn, *Human Ecology* (Englewood Cliffs, N.J., Prentice-Hall, 1950), Chap. VIII.

[44] Robert E. Park, "Urbanization and Newspaper Circulation," *American Journal of Sociology*, 35 (July, 1929) pp. 60–79; McKenzie, *op. cit.*, Chap. VIII; Noel P. Gist and L. A. Halbert, *Urban Society*, 4th ed. (New York, Thomas Y. Crowell, 1956), pp. 223–224.

[45] Morris Janowitz, *The Community Press in an Urban Setting* (New York, The Free Press of Glencoe, 1951).

[46] *Newsweek*, April 1, 1957.

selected references

BOGUE, Donald J. *The Structure of the Metropolitan Community* (Ann Arbor, Horace Rackham Graduate School, University of Michigan, 1949).

DICKINSON, Robert E., *City Region and Regionalism* (London, Kegan Paul, Trench and Trubner, 1947).

DOBRINER, William, ed., *The Suburban Community* (New York, G. P. Putnam's Sons, 1958).

DUNCAN, Otis D. *et al.*, *Metropolis and Region* (Baltimore, Johns Hopkins University Press, 1960).

GEDDES, Patrick. *Cities in Evolution*, new and enlarged ed. (New York, Oxford University Press, 1950).

HALL, Peter, *The World Cities* (New York, McGraw-Hill, 1966).

HOOVER, Edgar H. and VERNON, Raymond, *Anatomy of a Metropolis* (Cambridge, Harvard University Press, 1959).

McKENZIE, R. D., *The Metropolitan Community* (New York, McGraw-Hill, 1933).

MURPHY, Raymond E., *The American City: An Urban Geography* (New York, McGraw-Hill, 1966).

WURSTER, Catherine B., *Housing and the Future of Cities in the San Francisco Bay Area* (Berkeley, Institute of Governmental Studies, University of California, 1963).

8

the urban regional system: a theoretical approach to urban specialization and imperfect coordination

To many people from all sorts of occupations and ways of life, the modern urban community seems like a disordered giant, a fascinating but cancerous growth. They are understandably bewildered by its size, by its impetus, its multifaceted interests and forms, and by the numerous problems that daily accompany its functioning. From the viewpoint of the sociologist, however, the primary fact about the urban community is that it is a complex human phenomenon, a human invention in process. Consequently, it must possess some underlying patterns or regularities, however unintended, which require considerable probing in order to fashion a realistic picture of uniquely urban order. We may call this set of patterns an evolving system, a persistently imperfect unity, or perhaps a changing sociocultural equilibrium. All refer to the same theme: subtle, dynamic order.

Many sociologists, social philosophers, and other students of urban life have searched for adequate ways of expressing the basic structure of urban systems. As a result, the annals of urban sociology contain a number of provocative but often competing theories of urban organization. We can only attempt to outline a sample of this diversity, in the hope that this will provide useful clues to a modern conception of urban regions as systems of fact and of analysis.

cultural and institutional approaches

Several theories seem to place great emphasis on the major institutions as coordinators of urban systems, particularly in earlier urban waves. Max Weber gave special prominence to *military organization* and its political and economic consequences in classical cities. In the medieval and early modern cities of Europe, however, he noted a decisive shift to the economic focus of commerce and the dominant influence of merchant associations.[1] A similar view has been meticulously detailed by the great Belgian historian, Henri Pirenne.[2] In a most convincing fashion, Fustel de Coulanges interpreted the history of the ancient city as a process fundamentally marked by changes in urban *religion*. The development of cities was first accompanied by community religions, in place of family and tribal deities. With the rise of class conflicts and internal urban revolutions, religion itself receded as an instrument of order. Henceforth, secular government became dominant, guided by varying conceptions of the "public interest." [3]

Still another institutional theory has been available in the works of Oswald Spengler, the poet-philosopher of a troubled urbanism. To Spengler, the city is a late phase in the cyclical workings of world history—the high point of complexity before the inevitable decline to simpler communities based on blood and tradition. The city, in Spengler's view, is organized around the twin structures of a money economy and an expansive science, which together breed democracy and, eventually, disorganization.[4]

Perhaps the most radical and challenging conception of the city, one that sharply diverges from that of Spengler, is the notion of urbanism as a creator of *concentrated institutional functioning*, as a "mobilization, mixture, and magnification" of previous institutions toward a new, "purposive social complexity." In short, according to Mumford, the essence of the city lies in continuous devising of social arrangements for human interaction and spiritual communion. Thus, in a modern translation of the ideas of Fustel de Coulanges and Durkheim, Mumford interprets the city as an expansive religion transcending the realms of economy, kinship, and politics.[5]

functional approaches

Unlike institutional explanations of urban structure, the functional approach emphasizes the city as a continual arena of division of labor and

[1] Max Weber, *General Economic History* (New York, The Free Press of Glencoe, 1950), pp. 316–324, 333–354.

[2] Henri Pirenne, *Medieval Cities* (Princeton, Princeton University Press, 1925), Chap. IV.

[3] Fustel de Coulanges, *The Ancient City*, 10th ed. (Boston, Lee and Shepard, 1900), pp. 167–170, 423–429.

[4] Oswald Spengler, *The Decline of the West* (New York, Alfred A. Knopf, 1937), 2 vols. Cf. the discussion in Georg Simmel, *Philosophie des Geldes* (Leipzig, Duncker und Humblot, 1900) and his "The Metropolis and Mental Life," in *The Sociology of Georg Simmel*, Kurt H. Wolff, ed. (New York, The Free Press of Glencoe, 1950), pp. 409–424.

[5] Lewis Mumford, *The Culture of Cities* (New York, Harcourt, Brace and World, 1938), p. 6; and his *The City in History* (New York, Harcourt, Brace and World, 1961), pp. 9–10, 31, 35, 95.

specialization on the one hand, and imperfect coordination and degree of interdependence on the other. Robert Park regarded the city as primarily reflecting competition for space and the consequent development of numerous specialized social types (such as the hobo, the rooming-house resident, the delinquent, and the saleslady). These types inevitably establish symbiotic relations with one another, i.e., they come to have indirect dependence on one another in an impersonal, unplanned manner. But Park recognized that these relations were insufficient; therefore, he placed great emphasis on *mass communications* (the newspaper in particular) as a source of superimposed integration.[6]

Students of Park worked out a somewhat modified and yet more detailed functional theory of urban structure. McKenzie, and more recently Bogue,[7] have envisaged the urban region as a *network of economic dominance and subdominance*; each urban area, zone, or sector is shown to be bound by one or more economic ties to the central city or the central business district. Even the distribution of population in urban regions demonstrates the effects of economic specialization and interdependence. Thus, in effect, McKenzie and Bogue have interpreted the urban system as an evolving unity whose functioning is mediated by the economic institution through manufacturing, wholesale, and retail activities.

urbanism as mass society

One of the most persistent theories of urban structure focuses on the presumably inevitable texture of urban living from the standpoint of individual participation. According to Wirth's classic formulation of this approach,[8] the development of urban centers proceeds through increasing size, density, and functional specialization. These processes in turn encourage social and geographic mobility, impersonality, anonymity, and fragmented concerns. Furthermore, urbanites become disengaged from compelling, intimate social affiliations (family, neighborhood), thus acquiring first, a standardization or unanticipated commonness by default, and then receiving the crucial reinforcement of mass communications media. To Wirth, mass communication is both effect and cause in urbanism. It becomes a practical necessity because of the sheer number and diversity of people involved in economic, civic, educational, recreational and other matters. But mass media serve to level urbanites by subtly requiring them to adjust their ideas, prejudices, per-

[6] Robert E. Park, *Society* (New York, The Free Press of Glencoe, 1955), Part II.

[7] R. D. McKenzie, *The Metropolitan Community* (New York, McGraw-Hill, 1933); Don J. Bogue, *The Structure of the Metropolitan Community* (Ann Arbor, Mich., Rackham School of Graduate Studies, University of Michigan, 1949).

[8] Louis Wirth, "Urbanism as a Way of Life," *American Journal of Sociology*, 44 (July, 1938), pp. 3–24.

ceptions, and abilities to the average that seems to insure successful communication.

Wirth seems to have envisaged an urban pattern in which, paradoxically, the management of specialization and heterogeneity produces a large, passive, and homogeneous mass. Under these circumstances, urban areas can only operate by a central power elite which maintains control of all or most of local communication channels. On occasion, small subcategories of urbanites may organize temporary and rather specialized interest groups but these normally compete with one another and therefore fail to satisfy the urbanites' quest for integrity (whole men) and achievement. Consequently, behavior tends to be erratic and apparently irrational, erupting into public attention in the social problems that are presumed to accompany the iniquitous cities—crime, corruption, suicide, marital difficulties, and mental disorders.

By implication, therefore, "urbanism as a way of life" is a schizophrenic syndrome of over-organization (centralized control of communication) and under-organization (inadequate or unsatisfying social affiliation). Further developments of urban regions would appear to be virtually impossible since (a) those in control must be both willing and able to produce and implement significant innovations in technical and coordinative problem areas, a rarely experienced phenomenon and (b) sources of either innovation or support from the urban mass would be weak or erratic. Yet, as we shall see in succeeding chapters (particularly Chapters 9 and 10), these predictions of 30 years ago simply do not jibe with the accumulating data of urban regions.

urbanism as the expression of the middle class

This theory, though quite ancient, has never been explicitly formulated and therefore cannot be accurately attributed to a specific theorist. However, from clues provided by such disparate sources as Aristotle, Sombart, Pirenne, Marx, and Holcombe,[9] the outlines of a middle class theory of urbanism may be briefly sketched. Perhaps the basic notion is the crucial role of commercial, entrepreneurial, and professional categories in developing urban centers from military, religious, or local trading nuclei to dynamic, expansive multi-functional entities. The practical prominence of these categories (which we may call for convenience middle classes or white collar strata) was recognized as early as Aristotle, who argued that middle classes were the major source of social order in the city-states of his knowledge.

Fifty years ago, Sombart asserted a three-way relation among cities,

[9] Aristotle, *Politics* (New York, Random House, 1943), pp. 191–195, 219–221; Werner Sombart, *Luxury and Capitalism* (Ann Arbor, University of Michigan Press, 1967; orig. ed., 1913); Henri Pirenne, *Medieval Cities* (Princeton, Princeton University Press, 1925), Chap. 6; Arthur N. Holcombe, *The Middle Classes in American Politics* (Cambridge, Harvard University Press, 1940).

middle classes, and capitalism.[10] Briefly, he concluded that the bourgeoisie blossomed in late medieval towns by encouraging luxury items, waste, credit, and indebtedness. The town became the permanent location of resourceful but previously peripatetic producers or traders. Indeed, according to Sombart, capitalistic forms were invented to regularize and sustain middle class (bourgeoisie) exploitation of urban resources and populations. Thus, towns and cities became vehicles for the economic and political interests of middle classes.

In the same vein but with different intentions, students of suburbanization have also tended to view urbanism and its development as essentially middle class phenomena.[11] Thus, it can be recalled that (in Western urban areas, at least) middle class groupings—or those which acquired middle class characteristics—generally initiated suburban settlements, while much of the continuing movement from inner zones of the city has until recently also derived from well-to-do professionals and businessmen. In addition, the needs and tastes of suburban areas (despite a considerable infusion of varied status levels) have significantly restructured the public and private problems of urban regions. More specifically, the dispersion of middle class styles of life has led to increased attention to housing and locational problems, highway and expressway construction, multi-nucleated retail patterns, the changing character and location of urban religious organizations, and increased concern for education, recreational areas, and the arts.[12] Carried to its extreme, this general viewpoint might equate the future of urbanism with the success of the middle class ("what's good for the middle class is good for the city"). But a subtle form of this orientation is also represented in programs or campaigns to develop lower status urbanites into a cultural middle class (advertising, Poverty Programs, etc.).

the verdict is disorganization

Some students and critics of modern urbanism, on the other hand, are unable to detect a basic urban order. They point to the loss of its clear-cut institutional and ecological structure, which was dominant a century or more ago, and they also assert that the city is decaying internally, as evidenced by the urbanite's increasing withdrawal to the suburbs and beyond. Furthermore, Martindale suggests that, unlike past periods of urban glory, the modern city is no longer largely autonomous, or dominant over a region of dependent communities in its hinterland. Instead, he notes a trend toward national (and

[10] Sombart, *op. cit.*, pp. 117–118, 168–170.
[11] William M. Dobriner, *Class in Suburbia* (Englewood Cliffs, N.J., Prentice-Hall, 1963), Chaps. 1, 2.
[12] Raymond Vernon, *The Myth and Reality of Our Urban Problems* (Cambridge, MIT Press, 1962).

state) intervention in urban affairs and problems. Somewhat glumly, Martindale offers the prediction: "The age of the city seems to be at an end." [13]

urbanism, transition, and organic solidarity

There is some truth in all these explanations and interpretations. But most of these theories contain an implicit picture of some past urban order, or of some desired order. The basic fact about modern urbanism is its transitional nature, its irregular movement toward a newer, more complex structure.[14] In this process, institutions change at varying paces, and inconsistencies crop up with noticeable frequency. Yet, as T. H. Marshall has wisely observed, "human society can make a square meal out of a stew of paradox without getting indigestion—at least for quite a long time." [15] Perhaps we can attempt an interpretation of the "urban stew" by considering in more detail the basic configuration of urban social processes and some variations in urban structuring as "semi-finished" materials for the refinements of theory. Hopefully, we may begin to develop a theoretical framework for explaining the phenomenon of workable but imperfect functional entities called urban regions.[16]

urban processes

processes of growth and specialization

Urbanism as process is perhaps best characterized as development through specialization. However, specialization may be expressed in several forms in complex human systems.

1. *Specialization of function.* This universal process—which is particularly visible in formal organizations and urban systems—involves the assignment of a definable task (old or new) to single or limited numbers of persons, positions, or subgroups. Normally, specialization arises and is extended as a consequence of the pursuit of some standard of efficiency, convenience, or

[13] Don Martindale, "Preface," in Max Weber, *The City*, trans. by Don Martindale and Gertrud Neuwirth (New York, The Free Press of Glencoe, 1958), p. 62.

[14] Howard W. Odum, *Understanding Society* (New York, Macmillan, 1947), Chaps. XII, XX, XXIX; Alvin Boskoff, "Social Indecision: A Dysfunctional Focus of Transitional Society," *Social Forces*, 37 (May, 1959), pp. 305–311.

[15] T. H. Marshall, *Citizenship and Social Class* (Cambridge, at the University Press, 1950), p. 84.

[16] Cf. Warner Bloomberg, Jr., "Community Organization," in Howard S. Becker, ed., *Social Problems: A Modern Approach* (New York, Wiley, 1966), pp. 366–372, 406–415.

rationality. Certainly, when numerous objectives and/or multiple skills are thought to be desirable, specialization or division of labor is a practical necessity.

At least three kinds of skills seem to crystallize in processes of specialization. Most obvious perhaps are *technical skills* involving learned and directly applicable behavior with respect to tools, machines, and aspects of the physical environment. Urban skills of this variety include computer programming, auto repairs, typing, stenotyping, golfing, elevator operating, etc. Obviously, technical skills proliferate with advances in science and related technological innovations. A second type of skill is *social-organizational*, the distinguishing mark of which is ability to influence, direct, or manipulate persons (directly or indirectly) in structured settings. Some examples are: political skills (recruiting subordinates and staff members, delegating responsibility, etc.); entrepreneurial skills (obtaining financial support from patrons, clients, philanthropic organizations; obtaining and using competent advice on organizational problems); educational skills (influencing definable audiences to accept and use specified attitudes and skills in participating in some organized activity such as the arts, an occupation, political structures, etc.). Finally, we may identify *ideational* skills—those by which values, perspectives, feelings, and concepts are created, revised, or manipulated so as to produce potentially satisfying guides to behavior. Artists, composers, dramatists, editorial writers, scientists (as distinct from technicians), philosophers, theologians, some educators (how many and which ones are favorite controversial issues), and varied kinds of demagogues (faith healers, street-corner orators, and advertising copywriters) illustrate the range of specialties in this skill category.

2. *Relocation and areal expansion.* Historically, specialization in the urban community has often entailed spatial segregation as well, with many new specialties planted or exported to outlying areas. Merchant quarters, artisan sections, religious nuclei (called *suburbia* in the medieval records), high status residential areas, in some instances enclaves of racial or nationality groupings, and in recent years, industrial parks—all have added in their own way to a historically limited urban mosaic.[17] The reasons for these specialized expansions seem to have been either security, economic considerations (convenience, cost), desire for privacy and seclusion, or simply the lack of space in older sectors. But the significant point is the heretofore continual recourse to areal expansion given the availability of peripheral land. Apparently, without the spur of the booster psychology ("the bigger the better"), urbanism has meant concatenated accretions.

3. *Articulation and autonomy of subareas.* As both functional and spatial specialization proceed, the opportunity for localization of interest, authority, and even sources of support likewise tends to expand. This is

[17] Pierre Francastel, ed., *Les Origines des villes polonaises* (Paris, Mouton, 1960), pp. 33–36, 185–198.

particularly true for metropolitan regions of the West, where the more diffuse government structures permit certain types of local decision making. From the standpoint of the urban regions, however, the mundane facts of subareal autonomy (e.g., county or small municipality education systems, suburban zoning, peripheral recreation facilities, the practice of defensive incorporation) challenge the subtle interdependencies that are presumed to characterize (and justify) the metropolitan form. Autonomy in apparently limited and undramatic matters is practical only when a fundamental consensus on goals for the overall entity (the metropolitan area) exists. Most studies indicate that such consensus is either embryonic or anemic.[18]

4. *Negative Specialization: The Intensification of Social Problems.* The prevalence of social problems in urban areas is certainly widely recognized, publicized, and bewailed. But perhaps it is not typically viewed as a "normal" or expectable set of specializations in the urbanized milieu. It may be useful to approach social problems—from the perspective of the urban sociologist—as reflecting attempts to cope with the peculiar opportunities and limitations of urbanism. Some problem behavior involves considerable technical and organizational skill (e.g., robbery, fraud, embezzlement, effective use of narcotics). Other forms of deviant behavior seem to involve little or no technical or organizational skill, but rather skill in developing immunity from detection (e.g., mental disorders, alcoholism, promiscuity, homosexuality) or unconscious etherial skill in destroying others' self-confidence (as in marital difficulties, minority group relations).

There is some controversy over the urban region's role in the development of problem behavior. Some students contend that the size and anonymity of cities tend to attract disturbed or inadequate persons from other areas (the import hypothesis). Others, however, assert that the complexity, uncertainty, and strains of urban living ultimately create deviants from otherwise normal human materials (the production-line hypothesis).[19] In any case, there is some evidence of the specialized location of certain problem types in certain zones (e.g., drug addicts, prostitutes).

But whatever the causes of deviant behavior types, the primary significance of such behavior, apart from the moral aspects, is the effective removal

[18] Scott Greer, *Metropolitics* (New York, Wiley, 1963), Chaps. 1, 2; John C. Bollens, ed., *Exploring the Metropolitan Community* (Berkeley, University of California Press, 1961); Wallace Sayre and Herbert Kaufman, *Governing New York City* (New York, Russell Sage Foundation, 1960); James Q. Wilson and Edward C. Banfield, "Voting Behavior on Municipal Public Expenditures: A Study in Rationality and Self-Interest," in Julius Margolis, ed., *The Public Economy of Urban Communities* (Baltimore, Johns Hopkins Press, 1965), pp. 74–92.

[19] Marshall B. Clinard, *The Sociology of Deviant Behavior* (New York, Holt, Rinehart and Winston, rev. ed., 1963), Chap. 3; Robert E. L. Faris and H. Warren Dunham, *Mental Disorders in Urban Areas* (Chicago, University of Chicago Press, 1939); Mildred B. Cantor, ed., *Mobility and Mental Health* (Springfield, Illinois, Charles C. Thomas, 1965).

of implicated persons and social categories from participating in or contributing to the operation of positively valued specialties and the intricate timing that makes urban variety so attractive. In short, these forms of specialization tend to impede the normal course of urban development by blunting the effectiveness of more desired specialties. If one values continued urban development, then social problems and deviant behavior merit criticism, treatment, or action. But if it is argued that urban development has at some point overstepped the bounds of feasibility and must therefore be contained or curbed, one may conceivably treat deviant behavior (as in Malthus) as a latent beneficent phenomenon. However, others may question the price to the deviants in misery, contempt, and abuse, for their alleged "contribution." Certainly, if desired, there are more direct and less humanly costly methods of achieving urban control. Indeed, as we shall see in some detail in the last part, urban planning has been conceived as a functional alternative to the paradoxical disabilities of urban social problems in modern times.

Rationalization. Based on increasing knowledge, rationalization as a typical urban phenomenon involves attempts to calculate needs and to adjust behavior in line with anticipated responses of other actors. Tradition and "sacred" practices or premises tend to be ignored or dismissed in the quest for more efficient means. For example, rationalization is expressed in location of expressways through previously stable residential areas, in marketing analysis of consumer tastes, in relocation of churches as their congregations move to outlying areas, in providing public transit routes, in maintaining evening and Sunday shopping hours for those with daytime occupational or family responsibilities, and in "united appeal" campaigns for a multitude of private social welfare agencies.

Generalization. The process of generalization involves two aspects that are often inseparable from the operation of complex social structures. First, there is conceptualization of a significant technique, objective, or situation. This involves the ability and willingness to abstract or select certain features from experience in line with some sort of focused interest. Certainly, specialized roles demand particular kinds of conceptualizing. But second, generalization entails the practice of applying a given abstraction to wider and wider ranges of phenomena, under the assumption that the concept is workable with these additional data or experiences. In the urban regions, generalization is illustrated in various types of law, in advertising techniques for different products, and in merit or civil service systems. Parenthetically, generalization may be extended beyond the bounds of efficiency or desirability, in which case we often identify the result as bureaucracy or stultifying uniformity.

Innovation. Urbanism and innovation are virtually inseparable, as almost any historical period can bear witness. To a large degree, the opportunity and the support for innovating are heightened by complex division of labor and the normal resultant of indirect, impersonal control of behavior. The process of innovation, in sociological terms, contributes new or revised means, objectives, or criteria for evaluating means or goals, and thus constitutes a potential or actual change in the interactions of urban participants. We should distinguish between positively valued innovations (if somewhat controversial) —such as expressway systems, television, community colleges—and negative or undesirable innovations—such as check-kiting schemes and other frauds, tax evasion skills, and the experimentation with drugs for hallucinatory purposes. Finally, it is necessary to note that innovations tend to have multiple effects on the operation of urban regions (e.g., technical efficiency, conflict of interest, status uncertainty, enhanced power or dependence). Innovating, therefore, presents a distinctly radical challenge to the subtle interdependencies which characterize urbanism.

Mobility and Motility. Relative freedom of personal decision-making and of perception and aspiration have always been attractions of urban centers. From the standpoint of individuals and social categories, these processes have meant (*a*) opportunity to change geographic location (motility) for whatever personal complex of reasons seemed important and (*b*) the opportunity of taking advantage of predictable or unpredictable changes in access to valued experiences (mobility). Motility is directly related to spatial expansion of urban areas and variations in the implementation of relevant space. Mobility, on the other hand, is more directly dependent on some preexisting specialization of skills and rewards, plus the effects of processes of innovation, which serve to expand the range of urban specialties and to alter the scale of status differences. However, mobility and motility are not merely variables for a given urban population; we find differentials in these processes for given social categories—in direction, speed, distance, and in impact on behavior. In short, mobility and motility contribute to variety, potential change, and also to transitional processes of apparent confusion, uncertainty, and misunderstanding.

Obviously, all of the preceding processes are generative, expansive, even explosive in nature; they stretch the notions of system and organization to the edge of practicality and endurance. Indeed, they seem destined to produce an unbearable density of stimuli, a satiation of alternatives, or a rash of adjacent anarchies. But, despite dire predictions and endless references to Sodom and Gomorrah, urban areas persist and, in many parts of the world, are encompassing a rapidly enlarging segment of national political entities. Therefore, we may well ask: what accounts for the skeletal patterning of urban structure? How are the intricate interdependencies, the numerous indirect effects of urban processes, encouraged and yet constrained? In short, how does apparently incessant variation sustain rather than destroy the operation of distinctive urban systems? [20]

[20] Cf. Richard L. Meier, *A Communications Theory of Urban Growth* (Cambridge, MIT Press–Harvard University Press, 1962), pp. 84–142, 171–177.

urban coordination mechanisms

Many values and perhaps most instances of social organization (networks of regular influence on behavior of a definable set of persons) tend to lag behind current experience, particularly in social systems which implicitly or explicitly encourage variation and innovation. In simple systems, this discrepancy can be ignored because the practical difficulties are minor and often unnoticed. But in complex systems such as urban regions, social organization in practice normally involves several processes of coordination which implicitly (*a*) impose limits on otherwise autonomous urban processes and (*b*) reduce in some degree the gap between practical difficulty and available solution in organization.

We may profitably distinguish between processes of coordination that (*a*) prevent interference between potentially or actually interdependent parts and (*b*) positively create and/or sustain connections between these parts. While these kinds of coordination may be found in preurban and nonurban communities, the urban versions of these processes are usually marked by greater visibility and frequency in application.

1. coordination by noninterference

(*a*) *Timing*. The multiplicity of specialized activities for large numbers of persons in a relatively limited area demands a concern for timing and promptness in carrying out time obligations that nonurbanites cannot really comprehend. The clock is certainly important, but more vital are the decisions by which allocations of time are made. Perhaps the key decision is determination of the workday for the gainfully employed—9–5, 8–4, or other combinations. This preempting of time shifts other valued activities to other time periods; recreation, visiting, education, and family religious participation are largely confined to evenings and weekends. The lack of a formal mechanism for adjusting nonwork time to work times should not be viewed as a sign of accident or randomness. Clearly, the perceived needs of commerce, industry, and certain professions (given the state and costs of their respective technologies) are reflected in the setting of work times by administrators and bosses. On the other hand, twice a day with unwavering fidelity, the timing mechanism threatens to break down—the traffic jam (erroneously called "rush hour").

(*b*) *Spacing*. While timing operates by ordering activities in the same space or location, spacing distributes simultaneous activities (and persons) in different areas. Spatial allocation represents both specialization and coordination as well, because the regularities in spatial segregation allow competing activities to develop and to make their special contribution to other, later urban processes. The phenomena of spacing are partly fortuitous (that is, due either to historically irreversible locations or geographic barriers), but increasingly, processes of spacing depend upon formal decisions of officials (zoning, use permits) and the informal but highly effective decisions of land developers and landlords. In addition, of course, the patterning of spatial allocation is made possible in many instances by previous or accompanying decisions about the availability of transportation and communication lines.

2. coordination by connectives

(a) *Relating.* Processes of relating necessarily involve both strategic locations and an assigned or assumed responsibility to adjust the operation of some activity or organization to one or more other patterns in the urban region. For example, decisions on the location of shopping centers near residential nuclei and major arteries obviously establish some coordination among these three activities. Similarly, coordination is achieved by routing public transit facilities and by providing networks of public utilities (electricity, gas, telephone, water). Somewhat less obviously, the relating process is an important aspect of the mass media, particularly in the edited and interpreted availability of varied information and experiences that are not otherwise accessible to urban residents. Of course, governmental agencies perform a number of relating functions by law, such as resolving conflicts in the courts, converting revenues into a set of public services, and exchanging services with autonomous sub-units in the urban region. With such overwhelming evidence of relating processes, however, the patterning of connections presents a serious problem. Much of the criticism of urban functioning stems from the dominance of numerous limited kinds of relating, rather than of an overall, coherent framework of coordinating. But this latter form is closely akin to the following process.

(b) *Anticipation.* In a closed and slowly developed system, relating is a normally adequate form of coordination. On the other hand, complex, open systems such as urban regions require the additional use of anticipatory coordination. Essentially, this is planning, i.e., the ordering of decisions about coordinative processes in terms of a meaningful time-sequence. More specifically, anticipation is reflected in budgeting, the preparation of comprehensive city plans, surveys of potential need in community services, and the operation of "united appeal" campaigns for a group of private social service agencies.

The complex interaction of specialization and coordination processes in effect links the contributions of four major dimensions to the subtle patterning of urban regions. These dimensions are: the *demographic* (population resources in terms of number, location, composition); the *spatial* (culturally defined delineation of units of land); the *technological* (methods of using land and persons for specific goals); and the *social organizational* (the needs, resources, effectiveness of variably potent groups and associations, as reflected in their ability to affect the choices of others). We may well call this complex set of linkages "urban interdependencies" or, following Durkheim's classic conception, "organic solidarity." [21]

As several sociologists have observed, interdependence or integration (*a*) is a matter of degree and (*b*) comprises at least three important dimensions. One dimension concerns the facilitative or complementary affect of one activity or social process on the operation of other processes within the same system. This may be called the *functional aspect* of interdependence. If we focus, however, on the conscious attempts to create or regularize the practical interconnections of activities, this dimension may be distinguished as the *political aspect*. Thirdly, to the extent that specialized participants perceive, positively evaluate, and identify with the network of interrelated activities, we may refer to the *consensual* or *symbolic dimension* of interdependence.[22]

Though Durkheim did not intend to analyze and explain urbanism, his writings can be interpreted as providing a general theory of organic solidarity, for which urban regions may be considered special cases or forms. Perhaps the key underlying supposition in Durkheim's analysis is the probability that functional interdependence "produces" both political and consensual interdependence as well. For Durkheim, specialization normally develops within a preexisting system, with rules, rights, and duties as emergents that guide subsequent functioning and interrelationship of roles.[23]

Let us instead view Durkheim's position as one empirical possibility; Durkheim himself recognized "abnormal" or imperfect forms of organic solidarity. In Figure 10 (upper portion), three combinations of the dimensions of interdependence are posited. We may assume that these form a rough scale of interdependence, with the highest degree in Type I. In the lower portion, the lack of significant functional interdependence disqualifies all three possibilities for the urban designation, though each possesses some interest of its own.

Focusing on the three urban types, we may theorize that Type 3 interdependence is a consequence of the dominance of resources in the processes of specialization described above. To the extent that coordinating processes are in evidence, however, these are predominantly of the noninterference type (timing, spacing). Historical accounts—primarily in Western Europe and North America—suggest the hypothesis that Type 3 arises in periods

[21] Emile Durkheim, *The Division of Labor in Society* (New York, The Free Press, 1947), pp. 131–132, 147–154, 181–190.

[22] Werner S. Landecker, "Types of Integration and Their Measurement," *American Journal of Sociology*, 56 (January, 1951), pp. 332–340.

[23] Durkheim, *op. cit.*, pp. 302, 365, 406.

figure 10

Types of Integration

		Functional	Political	Consensual	
Planned region	I	X	X	X	
Contemporary cities	II	X	X		Urban types
Traditional ecological model	III	X			
Backward rural community	IV		X	X	
Rule by terror	V		X		Nonurban types
Utopian colony	VI			X	

of private (officially nonlegitimated) decisions and normally when competing private interests and organizations abound—or when competing public organizations inhibit the formation of effective overall coordinative mechanisms.

Type 2 interdependence is the prototype of the "community power structure" described by Hunter and others (see Chapter 12 below). In this type, urban centers function with a clearcut, persistent decision-making clique of private persons who identify themselves with the public realm (i.e., responsive to but not responsible for matters directly affecting a range of activities and social categories). The coordination thus achieved is, from the standpoint of many specialized segments, imposed, arbitrary, and legitimated by default rather than by referential values.

Type 1 interdependence, which approximates Durkheim's ideal, is also the ultimate goal of the literary efforts of urban planners such as Lewis Mumford. It is somewhat controversial, since some would claim that this is a self-contradictory type, in the sense that political and consensual integration or interdependence probably leads to declining functional interdependence and to desiccation of the processes of specialization. Whatever the merits of these arguments, this level of organic solidarity has never been achieved in larger, highly complex urban centers. However, it may be hypothesized that successful functional interdependence, however temporary, tends to produce psychological dependence on this patterning. Consequently, beneficiaries of functional interdependence press for or accept organized attempts to insure continued operation of indirect but effective functional complementation. This, it seems, serves to explain the swelling acceptance of more centralized public decision making—on practical rather than ideological grounds. The sticky theoretical question now appears: what are the processes by which Type 2 is converted into an approximation of Type 1?

It is reasonably clear that the social sciences are as yet unable to provide a satisfactory answer—perhaps because the end product is inherently elusive. On the other hand, we can recognize that urban regions increasingly exhibit conflicting nuclei of coordination which in effect arrest urban interdependence at the Type 2 level. Essentially, then, the problem of urban interdependence levels is related to the mechanisms of resolving intraregional conflicts, which is the phenomenon of social power. But as several analysts have shown, power can be expressed in several forms.[24] Since the urban area has been developed around technical and scientific accomplishments, a fruitful way of conceptualizing and classifying power phenomena might well consider strategies based on (a) beliefs about cause and effect relations and (b) preferences about outcomes of decisions.

In Figure 11, four types of operational power or decision making are identified, following an important clue of Thompson. While this typology has not yet been applied to urban coordination, it may be tentatively

figure 11

Types of Power Structures

BELIEFS ABOUT CAUSE AND EFFECT	PREFERENCES ABOUT OUTCOME	
	Certainty	*Uncertainty*
Certain	Computational strategy (expert)	Compromise strategy (politician)
Uncertain	Judgmental strategy (consultant)	Inspirational strategy (charismatic leader)

[24] James D. Thompson, *Organizations in Action* (New York, McGraw-Hill, 1967), pp. 134–140; Talcott Parsons, "On the Concept of Political Power," *Proceedings of the American Philosophical Society*, Vol. 107 (1963), pp. 237–261; Richard A. Schermerhorn, *Society and Power* (New York, Random House, 1961), Chap. 2.

suggested that the most frequent historical sequence is inspirational strategy→judgmental strategy→compromise strategy, with the next "new" phase (if and when it occurs) marked by computational strategy.

Essentially, inspirational and judgmental forms of decision making in urban contexts are only capable of temporary effectiveness, since the former is highly personal and unpredictable, while the latter is technically deficient. The compromise strategy, however, possesses comparatively more longevity— possibly because this type of decision making is flexible about specific objectives and yet employs techniques of persuasion and management that can be shown to work. Political skill (i.e., consistent use of the compromise strategy) in urban regions is thus the closest approximation to coordination we have heretofore known, regardless of ideological distaste for its inherent limitations. But when functional interdependence becomes endangered—for example, by riots, strikes, lethal air or water, or any other impediment to the coordination mechanisms previously discussed—the compromise strategy likewise becomes impractical. It is for many a moot question whether or not this situation has indeed arrived for urban areas of the U.S. and Great Britain. To the extent that (*a*) a genuine city manager system is instituted, (*b*) a comprehensive metropolitan administrative framework is seriously discussed, and (*c*) urban planning (as a rational allocation of resources to anticipated sets of needs over meaningful spatial units) is judged to be desirable and operational—then we may discern the early and problematic stirrings of the computational strategy of coordination.

From these kinds of considerations, it seems reasonable to conclude (for the present) that urban areas and regions develop complicated forms of organization; that processes of specialization are accompanied (or closely followed) by minimally workable coordinative devices; that the major forms of coordination thus far identified are subsequently unequal to the unregulated successes of specialization; and that imperfect coordination represents not a major defect in urbanism, but perhaps the cost of persisting urbanism and of the quest for change.

deviations from organic solidarity

Despite these important processes, the organic solidarity of urban regions is far from stable; the incessant and sometimes sudden introduction of cultural and social changes appears to offer a constant threat to complex, precarious order. Urban regions therefore exhibit obvious and widespread gaps or lags in their structure, more than occasional malfunctioning of such critical subsystems as families, public agencies, and distributional mechanisms, and consequently, a continuing repertory of well-known social problems (see Part IV).

To understand the deficiencies in urban order, we must keep in mind that modern urban regions are rather novel inventions in the history of the human community and transitional systems that face the task of mediating between two forms of community—in Matthew Arnold's somewhat gloomy words, "one dead, the other powerless to be born." Indeed, the transitional nature of urban regions can be grasped by recalling the tenacity of feudal, semifeudal, or theocratic types of community throughout the world. In Western Europe and North America, though feudalism had been in precipitous decline since the seventeenth century, it was not before the first third of the nineteenth century that all of the social and political restraints of a feudal past were removed. In Central and Eastern Europe, on the other hand, the old regime was even more persistent; German, Austrian, Hungarian, and Polish cities did not join the ranks of modern urban regions until the twentieth century, primarily after World War I. As for Russian cities, a Czarist feudalism has been superseded by Soviet controls, which apparently amounts to putting "old wine in new bottles." Turning to the vast continents of Asia and Africa, to Central and South America, and to the new Pacific nation of islands—Indonesia—we can see that the tentacles of their respective feudalisms are still in process of being loosened, if not removed.

If modern urbanism can be interpreted in part as liberation from an older order, toward what new system is it evolving? The bare fact that in general we do not know is the essential dilemma of transition. Of course, if urbanism were returning to some previous type of system—as largely occurred during the Dark Ages—some definite predictions about the future might be reasonably made. But, clearly, the nature of modern urban regions gives little evidence of regression in an objective sense (evaluations of tastes, morality, etc. present great problems in interpreting facts, of course), unless one assumes the extinction of urban regions by nuclear warfare. Instead, modern urbanism is marked by a set of characteristics that cannot be distinguished in previous waves of urbanism and that therefore is difficult to evaluate as to its consequences. These features include the high prestige and considerable autonomy of economic motives and economically oriented organizations; a widespread receptivity to change (both quantitative and qualitative) as a necessary and desirable aspect of experience; the tendency toward urban expansionism in its hinterland by peaceful, indirect means; and a somewhat flexible stratification system, with uniquely vague but attractive opportunities for social mobility.

In this context, the transitional nature of modern urban regions lies in the practical difficulty of assimilating and coordinating these trends in an evolving order without noticeable strain and dissatisfaction. This problem is expressed most basically in the circuitous development of an intermediate morality for urbanites, a practical morality distinct from the reassuring rigidities of tradition (e.g., knowing one's place, the code of the gentleman), and yet pointing toward a new and more complex communal morality whose outlines are still far from clear. As we have already noted at various places, the transitional morality of modern urbanism is marked by great aspiration (for productivity, progress, and possession) and the peculiar ethics of ambiguity and compromise. It is a morality that, in practice, implicitly assigns responsibility to individual judgment. The organization man is an apparent exception; yet he represents merely the substitution of an autonomous corporate focus for an emphasis on individual choice.[25] Furthermore, this intermediate and experimental morality cannot, by virtue of its special origins, possess the comprehensive range and reassuring certainty of traditional moralities. There is, we must admit, an unavoidable dash of anomie in urbanism, an absence of distinct norms and standards of evaluation as guides to repeated behavior in such areas as personal honesty, responsibility for aged relations, advertising, public service vs. private interests, and sexual relations.[26]

The transitional morality of urbanism, which contains both latitude for individualism and a presumably open invitation to anomie, is evident in most aspects of urban life. However, its relative strength cannot be easily determined. As we learn more about the interrelation of facts (rather than opinions) in modern urbanism, we may have to conclude that transitional morality is a haunting, perhaps annoying, second melody, not the dominant theme, in the complex, polyphonic score of urban regionalization. Yet two forms of expression of transitional morality deserve some attention at this point as implicit and unintended obstacles to organic solidarity. First, there is the continuing growth of powerful, often nonaccountable private organizations bent on achieving their own ends, under the plausible assumption that activities not proscribed by law are therefore clearly admissible and perhaps even praiseworthy. Such groups as labor unions, real estate developers, contractors, industrial corporations, political parties, transportation companies, among others, have at times equated their individual fortunes with the welfare of the urban region as a whole. Unravelling the merits of such claims would exhaust the wisdom of many Solomons. But more important, while these groups press their respective legitimate interests, there is an inevitable competition that strains a precarious urban consensus and sustains the transitional morality discussed above.

The second example of transitional morality is more subtle, but no less significant: it concerns the familiar phenomenon of uncontrolled population movements within and between urban regions. Of course, the right to change one's residence is long cherished by urbanites. Freedom to move is basic to the growth of urban regions, and to the typical urban quest for more de-

25 William H. Whyte, *The Organization Man* (Garden City, N.Y., Doubleday and Company, 1956), Parts II, III, V.
26 Edwin H. Sutherland, *White Collar Crime* (New York, Dryden Press, 1949); Marshall B. Clinard, *The Black Market* (New York, Holt, Rinehart and Winston, 1952). For a general discussion of "transitional morality," see Alvin Boskoff, "Postponement of Social Decision in Transitional Society," *Social Forces*, 31 (March, 1953), pp. 232–234.

sirable styles of living. Yet individual (and family) decisions to move are motivated by probable advantages to the individual or family, without much reference to the moves of other residents or to the eventual consequences of such moves for the neighborhood and the region as a whole.[27] To suggest alternative grounds for moving or not moving would certainly invite indignation and anger. However, the rather high mobility of urbanites, which is often preceded by little advance notice (though the desire may have a long history), has extensive effects on such major services as public education, welfare, police and fire protection, as well as on vital sources of taxation. Budgets, programs, personnel, and buildings are normally geared to the recent past and to a future of one to ten years. In short, the availability and quantity of urban community services depend heavily on estimates of needs that are based on recent trends, projections of these trends, and considerable guessing. A great number of individual moves, collectively considered, can therefore confound responsible computation of needs and services. For example, the largest single public expenditure in urban regions is for education. As a result of these population movements, most cities contain some schools that have become too big for their student bodies, while other schools in suburban areas are already fated for obsolescence and overcrowding before the foundations are laid. This situation, repeated in most public aspects of urban organization, stems from urban freedoms that latently challenge organic solidarity and occasionally create local crises (e.g., the Puerto Rican invasion of New York City, and traffic snarls in most major cities).

It appears that urban regions are transitional in another important respect that may help us understand continuing problems of urban order. In general, the major Western cities have developed an increasing independence from ecclesiastical and feudal controls, principally from the thirteenth or fourteenth centuries till the late nineteenth and early twentieth centuries. To the middle classes and the legally emancipated artisans and laborers, the autonomy of the city was the ultimate objective. But political and economic forces that were nurtured by the newly autonomous cities gradually created dominions and empires that have begun to impinge on the relative independence of urban regions. A prime interloper in most European cities has been the national state, which has inevitably interfered in the operations of major urban centers (particularly national capitals)—sometimes with needed financial aid, sometimes by political determination of urban legal or economic policy. An excellent example of the latter may be found in the case of London, whose government during the eighteenth and nineteenth centuries was not allowed to acquire adequate responsibility because of a hostile Parliament.[28] On a somewhat reduced scale, Washington, D.C., suffers from

[27] Motives for moving are discussed in Peter Rossi, *Why Families Move* (New York, The Free Press of Glencoe, 1955); Richard Dewey, "Peripheral Expansion in Milwaukee County," *American Journal of Sociology*, 53 (May, 1948), pp. 118–125.

[28] William A. Robson, *The Government and Misgovernment of London* (London, Allen and Unwin, 1939).

frustrated aspirations that can be traced to the refusal of Congress to yield its rule over the nation's capital.

selected references

Bogue, Donald J., *The Structure of the Metropolitan Community* (Ann Arbor, Mich., Horace Rackham School of Graduate Studies, University of Michigan, 1949).

McKenzie, R. D., *The Metropolitan Community* (New York, McGraw-Hill, 1933).

Mumford, Lewis, *The Culture of Cities* (New York, Harcourt, Brace, and World, 1938), Introduction, and Chap. V.

iii

social organization and cultural foci of the urban region

9

primary groups

As we have seen in Part II, the urban region exhibits a rather complex underlying structure, which we call its ecological organization. But ecological organization is not an independent or autonomous aspect of the urban regional system; we have already mentioned several typical instances in which specific group interests and general value systems clearly affect, and even alter, ecological organization (see pp. 86–92). Indeed, one of the themes of this book is the continual interplay between the basic ecological structure of the urban region and its distinctive social and cultural patterns.

As a backdrop to the discussion of urban social organization, let us briefly review the general nature of urban regions. First, the urban region encompasses a large, densely populated, irregularly shaped area. Partly as a consequence of its extent and population size, but very closely tied to its variety of services, is the development of highly specialized and increasingly segregated patterns of population location and activities. This division of regional labor—into subareas of the city and also in the form of specialized communities—often gives an impression of isolation, parochialism, and a defensive impersonality. A third feature is the impressive dominance of the central city over the region and, at the same time, a restless resistance to such dominance in the form of peripheral settlement and the frequent reluctance to support annexation. Finally, the basic organization of the urban region reflects a strong emphasis on rationality and efficiency, and a resultant pressure for expansion and change. The overall picture, then, is one that highlights a desired complexity, greater levels of performance, conscious or semiconscious forms of competition or emulation, and a strain toward coordination.

The present chapter and succeeding chapters in Part III will examine major segments of modern social and cultural organization in the urban region in terms of a few recurrent questions. How has the basic character of urban regions influenced the structure and operation of preexisting types of social organization, especially those found in the rural community? What new types of social groups and cultural forms have been developed in the urban region? Can these new forms be better understood as adjustments to the special character of the urban region? And finally, what are the consequences of these sociocultural innovations for urban ecological organization and the life-style of the urbanite?

The primary group is an extremely essential form of social organization in any community. It is normally marked by relatively few members, personal relationships, the concern for a variety of its members' needs and interests, informal and often unstated controls over individual behavior, an emphasis on personal qualities rather than performance, and the provision of emotional security.[1] Obviously, these features are in essential contradiction to the underlying patterns of the urban region. Consequently, we would expect rather substantial changes in urban primary groups. Yet we might also anticipate that the great psychological and social importance of the primary group would tend to limit or retard dramatic changes. Since the focal primary group relationships are in the family, the clique, the gang, and the various forms of association related to the practice of youth culture, each of these will be analyzed for distinctive clues to the understanding of primary groups in urban regions.

family relations in urban regions

After a generation of analyzing and discussing modern urban families, there is little doubt in most people's minds that the urban family has changed considerably since World War I, and that it greatly deviates from the traditional rural family.[2] While this general impression is substantially correct, several warning signals should be raised to avoid the dangers of oversimplification.

First, we should recognize that much of our knowledge about urban families concerns relatively superficial aspects (e.g., purchasing patterns) and family interaction in crisis situations (wartime separation, unemployment).[3] Second, a good deal of information is gathered from children and

---

[1] See Charles H. Cooley, *Social Organization* (New York, Charles Scribner's Sons, 1909) ; William F. Whyte, *Street Corner Society* (Chicago, University of Chicago Press, 1943) ; George C. Homans, *The Human Group* (New York, Harcourt, Brace and World, 1951).

[2] Well-known texts that discuss these changes include: Ernest W. Burgess and Harvey Locke, *The Family*, 2nd ed., (New York, American Book Company, 1960) ; Clifford Kirkpatrick, *The Family: As Process and Institution* (New York, Ronald Press, 1955) ; Joseph K. Folsom, *The Family and Democratic Society*, 3rd printing (New York, John Wiley and Sons, 1945).

[3] Mirra Komarovsky, *The Unemployed Man and his Family* (New York, Dryden Press, 1940) ; Robert C. Angell, *The Family Encounters the Depression* (New York, Charles Scribner's Sons, 1936) ; Ruth S. Cavan and Katherine H. Rank, *The Family and the Depression* (Chicago, University of Chicago Press, 1938) ; Reuben Hill, *Families Under Stress* (New York, Harper and Brothers, 1949) ; Samuel A. Stouffer and

students, rather than the parents themselves. Third, it is very difficult to generalize about the urban family—since there are some important variations in family life related to social class level and location in the urban region.[4] Fourth, family life in the urban milieu is influenced by fashion and fad; consequently, there are cycles of change which sometimes appear to represent little change, if the intermediate phases are ignored. Finally, it is important to distinguish among the identifiable changes in family life those which are significant for understanding urban social organization from those which are merely incidental (e.g., the television furor of the past ten or twelve years).

Urban families have in general developed three fundamental patterns that are by now obvious and crucial to any serious analysis of family relations. First, virtually all urban occupations are pursued away from the home and family members. This separation of work and domestic relations, which is contrary to the typical rural pattern, is both physical and cultural. In effect, it isolates the breadwinner from his family; specifically, it hampers meaningful communication between these two worlds of experience. The father-husband who lacks sympathy with minor household crises and the numerous details of child-rearing is not a brute, but a partial outsider. This is often matched by the family's ignorance of the skills and frustrations connected with the husband's job or career. A further consequence of this separation, however, is that the time patterns of the job (and the necessary journey to work)[5] inevitably influence the scheduling and coordination of home activities. It may not be too extreme to suggest that one of the most important material inventions for urban families is the multi-bathroom home or apartment.

A second general pattern in urban families is their voluntary abdication of responsibility for many functions formerly identified with the home. Religion, formalized education, recreation, design and manufacture of clothing, baking (and sometimes cooking) are largely provided by specialized organizations beyond the influence of the individual family. As many students of family life have indicated,[6] this stripping of disposable functions allows

---

Paul Lazarsfeld, *Research Memorandum on the Family in the Depression*, Social Science Research Council, Bulletin 29 (New York, 1937).

[4] See Ruth S. Cavan, *The American Family* (New York, Thomas Y. Crowell, 1953), Part II; *American Journal of Sociology*, 53 (May, 1948), entire issue.

[5] Kate Liepmann, *The Journey to Work* (New York, Oxford University Press, 1944); George P. Stevens, Jr., "Sample Study of Residential Distribution of Industrial Workers in an Urban Community," *Land Economics*, 28 (August, 1952), pp. 278–283; Louis K. Loewenstein, *The Location of Residences and Work Places in Urban Areas* (New York, Scarecrow Press, 1965), pp. 112, 190, 232; John B. Lansing *et al.*, *Residential Location and Urban Mobility* (Ann Arbor, Survey Research Center, June, 1964).

[6] Cavan, *op. cit.*, Chap. IV; Burgess and Locke, *op. cit.*, Chaps. I, II; William F. Ogburn and Meyer F. Nimkoff, *Technology and the Changing Family* (Boston, Houghton Mifflin, 1955); John Sirjamaki, *The American Family in the Twentieth Century* (Cambridge, Mass., Harvard University Press, 1953).

for (but does not insure) greater stress on child care and affectional relationships in the home.

Third, the urban family tends to be streamlined in size and in range of routine family relationships. In contrast to the traditional rural family, with its normal complement of three (or more) generations and numerous close relatives—resembling the clans or gens of the anthropologist—urban families have become essentially independent conjugal units, made up of husband, wife, and offspring. This conjugal or nuclear form of family is relatively isolated from other relatives; with some exceptions, it is the principal unit of child care, of consumption, and of social status in the urban region.

In general, these features are most evident in middle income and status families. Both lower and upper status families have tended to retain traditional family organization and values, though several changes in the lower status levels will be noted later. Inherent in the urban regional complex, however, is the central importance of middle class groupings—their aspirations, values, and problems—despite the fact that they account for little more than a third of the urban population. Consequently, we shall largely restrict our analysis of urban family adjustments to this category. In addition, we shall give special attention to middle status families living in the outer ring (suburbs and fringe) of the region, since these families are becoming increasingly representative of life in the urban region.

roles of the wife-mother

One of the most widely noted changes in the urban middle class family is the growing variety (and often contradiction) of social roles assumed by the wife-mother.[7] She is typically adding to her responsibilities, either voluntarily or under pressure from social peers and superiors, the following roles.

1. *The Glamor Girl Role*, in which she must keep in step with fashion in clothes and cosmetics, and when on public display give the impression of eternal, vivacious, assured youthful attractiveness. Much of the advertising industry seems to be dedicated to reminding her—incessantly—of her responsibilities in maintaining a gracious appearance, not to her family but to social equals.

2. *The Civic Role*, in which she has the obligation to devote part of her spare time to one or more worthy causes in the community—religion, education, welfare, fine arts, political activity, etc.

3. *The Copilot or Companion Role.* This involves a persistent and intelligent interest in the husband's quest for occupational advancement. Essentially, the wife is expected to provide informal, understanding attention to his

---

[7] See Talcott Parsons, *Essays in Sociological Theory Pure and Applied* (New York, The Free Press of Glencoe, 1949), Chap. XI.

occupational problems. Ideally, she should appreciate the special demands which the job makes on her husband and be willing to endure minor or major sacrifices in scheduling her time, entertaining, and sharing her husband with his business or professional associates. It is well known that several large corporations are as interested in the wife's readiness to assume this role as in the husband's own qualifications for executive responsibility.

4. *The Career Role.* With the social and cultural emancipation of the female has come the opportunity to follow a career in business or one of the professions, even after the wedding ceremony, and often after the birth of one or more children. Recent reports from the Census Bureau indicate that working wives in career roles are mainly concentrated in middle class families.[8] This probably reflects greater educational opportunities and achievement, higher motivation for self-expression, and greater facility in reassigning household duties.

5. *The Economic Supplement Role.* The working wife in her career role works for challenging experiences and to display or sharpen personal skills —not for income. On the other hand, many wives have taken jobs, either full-time or part-time, to supplement the husband's salary. This role seems to be found in families where the husband is unemployed; and it is somewhat more prevalent in cases of low family income.[9]

It is not yet possible to evaluate the impact of this variety in role demands on the urban wife. Many laymen believe, however, that the rather vague definition of the "good wife" in the urban region inevitably produces family irritations and instability. Indeed, one study of divorced couples in Chillicothe, Ohio, suggests that the major underlying condition of marital difficulties is continuing disagreement about proper roles of both wife and husband.[10] Yet in an investigation of working wives and family relations in Michigan, the expected role conflicts did not materialize. It was discovered instead that the wife's job tended to develop more equalitarian attitudes toward authority in the home, among wives and husbands. Furthermore, a significant adjustment to the wife's employment role was the fact that husbands in these families assumed greater responsibility for housework.[11] The key to the Michigan findings is perhaps the type of family studied. About 90 percent were on the middle class level. More than 50 percent had completed a year or more of college. Finally, 96 percent of the working wives

[8] Bureau of the Census, Current Population Reports, *Family Characteristics of Working Wives: March 1957* (Washington, D.C., U.S. Government Printing Office, March, 1958), pp. 2–3.

[9] *Ibid.*, p. 1. See also F. Ivan Nye and Lois Hoffman, eds., *The Employed Mother in America* (Chicago, Rand McNally, 1963).

[10] Alvin H. Jacobson, "Conflict of Attitudes Toward the Roles of the Husband and Wife in Marriage," *American Sociological Review,* 17 (April, 1952), pp. 146–150.

[11] Robert O. Blood, Jr., and Robert L. Hamblin, "The Effects of the Wife's Employment on the Family Power Structure," *Social Forces,* 36 (May, 1958), pp. 347–352.

were employed as teachers or in white collar jobs, indicating that the career role was at least partially involved in this sample. The tentative conclusion can be drawn that middle class families have tended to accommodate themselves to the urban milieu with some success.

This conclusion is partially corroborated by recent statistics on divorce in urban regions. Contrary to popular notions, divorce rates are substantially higher among lower class families. The lowest rates are found among professionals, proprietors, and white collar workers.[12] If we also consider the rather high desertion rates among lower class families, the impression of relatively successful adjustment among urban middle class families is even further strengthened.

By contrast, wives in lower status families retain the simpler repertory of roles of traditional rural housewives. According to Rainwater's studies in Chicago, Louisville, Tacoma, and Trenton, the typical demands on wives center on the children, care of the home, and responsibility for financial management. In sharp contradiction to the themes of advertising, then, family routine is dull and uninspiring. There is, furthermore, a sense of isolation from the roles and interest of the husband, a situation which is increasingly unacceptable to middle class wives. Perhaps this perceived vacuity and role limitation accounts for a strong emphasis on religion—in beliefs rather than church-going—which indicates the psychic rather than the social function of religion for many wives in this category.[13]

urban parent-child relationships

Because of our widespread sensitivity to the family as an emotional milieu for the child, and also as a consequence of the comparatively small size of urban families, much attention has been given to parent-child relationships and child-rearing practices in the urban region. However, a considerable folklore, perhaps once true, has been woven about this essential and somewhat intangible aspect of urban family life. We often hear about child neglect in the lower class, maternal overprotection in the middle class, neurotic tendencies in middle class children, etc.[14] But what does a review of the available evidence suggest?

Studies in Detroit, Chicago, New Haven, San Francisco, and Washington during the past 15 years fail to provide a sharply etched picture of

[12] William J. Goode, "Economic Factors and Marital Stability," *American Sociological Review*, 16 (December, 1951), pp. 802–812; J. A. Livingston, "Divorce Totals Upset Notion That Workers Live on Love," *Norfolk Virginian-Pilot*, February 19, 1956.

[13] See Lee Rainwater *et al.*, *Workingman's Wife* (New York, Macfadden Books, 1962); Mirra Komarovsky, *Blue Collar Marriage* (New York, Random House, 1964).

[14] David Levy, *Maternal Overprotection* (New York, Columbia University Press, 1943); Arnold W. Green, "The Middle Class Male Child and Neurosis," *American Sociological Review*, 11 (February, 1946), pp. 31–41.

parent-child relationships. Havighurst's study of southside Chicago families in the early forties seemed to point to substantial differences between lower and middle class rearing of children. The major conclusion was that middle class parents were more demanding, more restrictive with their children, while lower class parents were more permissive.[15] Recently, a careful analysis of family practices in two New England suburbs also uncovered significant differences between lower and middle class parents, but a perplexing finding was that the lower class mothers were more demanding than middle class mothers.[16] Perhaps a decade or more had produced new motivations among urban families. On the other hand, perhaps relative location in the urban region (central city vs. suburb) accounts for differential child-rearing practices within the same class level. Still a third possible explanation of these incompatible findings is the unwitting neglect of social and attitudinal differences among families on the same status level in the same urban setting.

A tentative path through the wilderness has been laid out by an ingenious set of interviews with mothers in the urban region of Detroit.[17] Although middle and lower class families remain the focus, the social orientation of the family also receives special attention in analyzing child-rearing practices. Thus, on each class level an entrepreneurial type is contrasted with a bureaucratic orientation toward social experience. In the former, parents engage in risk-taking, small economic ventures (e.g., small proprietors), or recently come from farm areas where a similar economic ideology prevails. The bureaucratic type, on the other hand, places relatively more emphasis on adjustment to large, complex organizations, on security, group morale, and "togetherness."

What is the effect of social orientation on child-rearing? Within the middle class families, entrepreneurial mothers are somewhat more demanding with youngsters than are bureaucratic mothers; they put greater emphasis on feeding babies on a regular schedule; they begin toilet training earlier (normally before eleven months); they use symbolic punishment (stressing self-control, guilt, and shame) more than direct, material rewards or punishments. However, there is little difference in weaning practices. Among lower class mothers in this sample, such differences are much less marked between bureaucratic and entrepreneurial types, although once more the bureaucratic type seems more permissive. In a comparison of bureaucratic middle class and bureaucratic lower class families, similarities in child-training greatly outweigh

[15] Robert J. Havighurst and Allison Davis, "A Comparison of the Chicago and Harvard Studies of Social Class Differences in Child Rearing," *American Sociological Review*, 20 (August, 1955), pp. 438–442.

[16] Robert R. Sears, Eleanor E. Maccoby, and Harry Leven, *Patterns of Child Rearing* (Evanston, Ill., Row, Peterson and Company, 1957), pp. 426–446; Melvin L. Kohn, "Social Class and Parent-Child Relationships: An Interpretation," *American Journal of Sociology*, 68 (January, 1963), pp. 471–480.

[17] Daniel R. Miller and Guy E. Swanson, *The Changing American Parent* (New York, John Wiley and Sons, 1958), pp. 97–153.

differences. The net result is a surprisingly marked convergence in parent-child relations among bureaucratic middles, and bureaucratic and entre-preneurial lowers—all of which have apparently geared their child-training to the modern tone of the urban region. In contrast, the entrepreneurial middle type clings to an earlier urban ideal of inner direction, personal responsibility, and initiative.

As Martha Wolfenstein has shown in her illuminating review of suc-cessive editions of "Infant Care," there have been definite changes in the recommended styles of child care.[18] We do not have much information on the practical application of these recommendations—particularly of reactions to revised recommendations—though the widespread sale of this bulletin in its editions of 1914 through 1951 probably indicates considerable attention to its views. It seems likely that urban families have experimented with various techniques and that there is now a trend toward the bureaucratic orientation. While this represents a shift from the traditional rural family and its relatively entrepreneurial emphasis, the middle class urban family has also reverted (or perhaps retained) several rural features which support the growing impression of a new, composite type of family organization in the urban region.

Contrary to prevailing urban folklore, there is some evidence that "neigh-boring" and informal visiting are quite common among urbanites. Studies in Detroit and Los Angeles, for example, report very substantial degrees of home visiting on all status levels with friends, relatives, neighbors, and co-workers. In general, the amount of visiting with neighbors, etc., tends to be greater in higher status families, but these differences are not very sharp.[19]

familism

In middle class families—and especially in suburban and fringe areas—an urban variety of familism is being discovered piecemeal by urban so-ciologists. A New Haven study casts some doubt on the isolation of the nu-clear family. Among white, Protestant middle class, and probably semibureau-cratic families, strong affectional and economic ties were found between middle-aged parents and their married children. The former provided mod-erate economic assistance to the latter in the form of gifts, loans, and baby-sitting. In addition, as a moral and financial obligation, 120 of 195 married couples exchanged nursing care with their parents—mainly during illness and

[18] Martha Wolfenstein, "Fun Morality: An Analysis of Recent American Child-Training Literature," in Margaret Mead and Martha Wolfenstein, eds., *Childhood in Contemporary Cultures* (Chicago, University of Chicago Press, 1955), Chap. X.
[19] Scott Greer, "Urbanism Reconsidered: A Comparative Study of Local Areas in a Metropolis," *American Sociological Review*, 21 (February, 1956), pp. 19–25; Morris Axelrod, "Urban Structure and Social Participation," *ibid.*, pp. 13–18.

childbirth. On the other hand, sons were given opportunities in family businesses in only 18 of 90 cases.[20]

As mentioned above, several studies point to the prevalence of visiting patterns among urban families. In particular, extensive visiting with relatives —at least once a week—was found in all social class levels, with the most frequent family contacts reported in middle status urban families. Indeed, on almost all status levels, visits to relatives substantially exceeded visits to friends or neighbors.[21] This in itself is fairly good evidence of the resurgence (or merely continuation) of urban familism.

Since World War II, birth patterns in urban regions seem to suggest a revival of familism. For example, the overall increase in birth rates for urban regions is less significant for present purposes than the increase in third and fourth births among middle class groups from 1942 to date. Since contraception is widely practiced, these added births probably reflect a desire for larger families, a crucial element in familism.[22]

Closely connected to the preceding feature is the increasing emphasis on the home and family-related activities. The former is illustrated by rising rates of home ownership in central cities and suburban zones and in increasing sales of household furnishings. As for family-related activities, it is uncertain whether urban families show greater participation as a unit in home-centered occasions—meals, entertainment, etc. But among middle class families, there is widespread involvement of parents in activities related to the status and welfare of their children. Some common instances are: membership in Parent-Teacher Associations; baby-sitting pools, cooperative nurseries; private music lessons; Boy Scout and Girl Scout organizations; and Sunday Schools.

An interesting issue concerning the relation between urbanism and family structure has generated thoughtful discussion and some unexpected data. Briefly, it had been postulated that the social and psychological pressures of urban living tend to encourage conjugal or nuclear families, rather than the complex family networks of rural and small town communities (the extended family type).[23] Goode has assembled a considerable amount of information from developing (urbanizing) nations, such as China, India, the Near East, Western and Southern Africa, which suggests either a lack of expected reorganization of family forms in response to industrialization and urbaniza-

[20] Marvin B. Sussman, "The Help Pattern in the Middle Class Family," *American Sociological Review*, 18 (February, 1953), pp. 22–28.
[21] Axelrod, *loc. cit.*; Greer, *loc. cit.*
[22] Ronald Freedman, P. J. Whelpton, and Arthur A. Campbell, *Family Planning, Sterility, and Population Growth* (New York, McGraw-Hill, 1959), Chaps. IX–XI.
[23] Talcott Parsons, *Essays in Sociological Theory* (New York, The Free Press, rev. ed., 1954), Chap. 9; Ethel Shanas and Gordon F. Streib, eds., *Social Structure and the Family: Generational Relations* (Englewood Cliffs, N.J., Prentice-Hall, 1965), Chaps. 4, 5, 13; Jesse R. Pitts, "The Structural-Functional Approach," in Harold T. Christensen, ed., *Handbook of Marriage and the Family* (Chicago, Rand McNally, 1964), pp. 88–94, 101–108.

tion, or changes toward conjugal forms which cannot be connected with such processes. Similarly, Litwak argues with some empirical support that upward mobility—one of the expected accompaniments of urbanization—is often achieved by traditional (extended) family types.[24] At this point, however, the analysis of urban family forms is only at the threshold of sophistication. We must await the difficult task of disentangling the effects of ethnic background, length of urban experience, social status, stage in the family cycle, etc. on the development or modification of both (1) workable, effective families and (2) problem or maladjusted families in urban regions.

friendship and clique groups

Apart from rather superficial information on frequency of visits, surprisingly little is known about the patterns of friendship in modern urban regions. However, the stereotype of the cold, unfriendly, and socially isolated urban resident is increasingly remarkable for its persistence, despite its disregard of many personal observations to the contrary. Perhaps also the stereotype survives because urban sociology has not extensively examined the nature of urban friendship. Yet a few available studies enable us to suggest that friendship and clique formations constitute an important source of primary group relations in the urban region.

Turning first to friendship groups, it is becoming apparent that the urban region, as compared to rural and small town areas, provides a wider range of friendship-producing situations. Unlike the traditional ruralite, the urbanite is not bound by the proximity factor in choosing friends. In general, the greater mobility of the urbanite permits any or all of four major sources of close friendship or more than casual acquaintance.

1. In childhood and young manhood, school and college are frequent "gardens of friendship," even though some educational systems are called educational wastelands. Compulsory public education, or an equivalent form of private education, is a process of almost inevitable social mixing and common experiences. Friendships thus formed seem to be based on similarities in social class, ethnic background, and religion [25]—not on accessibility of residence or personality type. School chums are often memorable for one reason or another, but it is not known what proportion of these friendships

[24] William J. Goode, *World Revolution and Family Patterns* (New York, Macmillan, 1963); Eugene Litwak, "Occupational Mobility and Extended Family Cohesion," *American Sociological Review,* 25 (February, 1960), pp. 9–21; Eugene Litwak, "Extended Kin Relations in an Industrial Democratic Society," in Shanas and Streib, *op. cit.,* pp. 290–323.

[25] George A. Lundberg and Lenore Dickson, "Selective Association Among Ethnic Groups in a High School Population," *American Sociological Review,* 17 (February, 1952), pp. 23–35.

survive graduation. It may be reasonably suspected that the mobility of urbanites severely restricts the number of one's friends who first became congenial in a school setting.

2. Church affiliation, particularly among middle status urbanites and in the suburban ring, is a consistent factor in stimulating close personal ties for young people, and to some extent for adults. Indeed, most congregations encourage their young members to participate in a variety of social events —Sunday School, discussion groups, dances, bazaars, parties, musical activities, etc.

3. For the urban adult, office, shop, and factory are not only economic locations, but also excellent opportunities for informal contacts with fellow workers. Considerable research in industrial plants demonstrates an almost inevitable formation of workers' cliques, the members of which come from the same crew, department or section. In offices and commercial establishments, coffee breaks, lunch hours, and normal work routines provide numerous opportunities for personal chatter and closer acquaintanceship.[26] According to the Detroit study mentioned above, visiting with co-workers (off the job) is a substantial part of the informal associations of urbanites. In fact, about one-third of the Detroit sample spent part of its leisure time with fellow workers at least once a month.[27] It would be useful to know if informal contacts with co-workers are greatly affected by proximity of residence, to which we shall now turn.

4. Several recent studies—mainly in the newer areas of the urban region and among medium status families—strongly suggest that urban friendships with close neighbors and with families within a limited radius of blocks are more numerous than had been expected.[28] This is clearly shown in postwar housing projects and in newer suburban areas, where intimacy of contact seems to be related to proximity of residence, the availability and choice of playmates among children, and similarity in socioeconomic status. Whyte's widely discussed picture of friendship patterns in Park Forest, a suburb of Chicago, offers a sympathetic and yet objective account of the web of friendship among junior executives' families, which can be understood in terms of such accidental causes as juxtaposition of apartment units, location of play areas, and placement of driveways and lawns.[29] In a study of Lansing, Michigan, friends appeared to be chosen almost equally between neighbors

[26] F. J. Roethlisberger and W. J. Dickson, *Management and the Worker* (Cambridge, Mass., Harvard University Press, 1939); Delbert Miller and William H. Form, *Industrial Sociology* (New York, Harper and Brothers, 1951); William F. Whyte, *Human Relations in the Restaurant Industry* (New York, McGraw-Hill, 1948).

[27] Axelrod, *op. cit.*, p. 16.

[28] William H. Whyte, Jr., "The Transients," in Llewellyn Miller, ed., *Prize Articles, 1954* (New York, Ballantine Books, 1954), pp. 39–112. This appeared in four installments in *Fortune* (1953). See also William H. Whyte, Jr., *The Organization Man* (Garden City, N.Y., Doubleday and Company, 1956), Part VII; Sylvia F. Fava, "Suburbanism as a Way of Life," *American Sociological Review*, 21 (February, 1956), pp. 34–37.

[29] Whyte, "The Transients," pp. 81–95.

and nonneighbors. But it was found that close neighborhood friendships were more prevalent in higher socioeconomic groupings and areas.[30] The apparent explanation is that the greater average length of residence in an area for middle and upper status families permits more intimate friendships than those for the relatively more mobile lower status families.

cliques as quasi-primary groups

It is sometimes difficult in specific instances to distinguish between informally organized friendship groups or circles and the somewhat more specialized, quasi-primary groups known as cliques. Both types of group possess little formal organization; both types are normally composed of persons from the same status level; both types, finally, emphasize personal relations among members.

On the other hand, the clique is unique in several respects by comparison with other primary groups. Unlike the family or friendship group, the clique relationship is limited to a fairly specific set of activities; there are cliques in professional circles, in commercial and industrial organizations, in amusement and recreation, in politics and public administration, in private community services, and in the specialized realm of status per se. A second distinctive trait of the clique is its tendency toward exclusiveness, often perhaps a rekindled consciousness of its distinctiveness to assure desirable social segregation from outsiders. Consequently, cliques possess rather sharp though informal criteria of recruitment. Generally, entrance into cliques depends more on an individual's status than on personal qualities or achievements. Thirdly, the clique normally forms as an unanticipated component of a larger, more formal organization. Indeed, it may be suggested that modern cliques operate either to circumvent or promote the efficiency of complex social organizations (e.g., factories, universities, government agencies) or abstract collectivities (social classes, communities).

The adult clique is a venerable form of social organization, which is found both in rural and urban communities. In rural areas and small cities, cliques tend to supplement and even strengthen the existing social order. This conservative function of cliques rests on the fact that many are formed among upper status persons, who regard the clique as an effective and desirable form of social control. This is the case, for example, in such otherwise varied communities as Middletown, Yankee City, Plainville, Elmtown, and Old City (southern town).[31]

---

[30] Joel Smith, William H. Form, and Gregory P. Stone, "Local Intimacy in a Middle-Sized City," *American Journal of Sociology*, 60 (November, 1954), pp. 276–284.

[31] Robert S. Lynd and Helen M. Lynd, *Middletown in Transition* (New York, Harcourt, Brace, and World, 1939); W. Lloyd Warner and Paul S. Lunt, *The Social Life of a Modern Community* (New Haven, Yale University Press, 1941); James West, *Plainville, U.S.A.* (New York, Columbia University Press, 1945); Allison Davis, Bur-

But what is the nature of cliques in larger urban settings? From the limited number of available investigations, it is possible to identify some urban cliques as essentially rural survivals, as far as their function is concerned. Baltzell's study of the Philadelphia elite, Amory's delightful scrutiny of the "Proper Bostonians," and Hunter's demarcation of Atlanta's informal leadership are surprisingly similar in demonstrating the basic conservatism of the most visible cliques.[32] They are rural survivals in their respective attachments to earlier, "sacred" periods of community organization, but also in their common attempt to bypass or nullify such modern urban features as mass media and mass tastes, complex and impersonal bureaucracies (particularly in government), and the free play of romantic love.

In the last few years, a relatively unique form of clique or quasi-clique has developed among young adults in the central city. This is the "swingle set" of single, employed, college educated, recent migrants (male and female) to New Orleans, Atlanta, Birmingham, Charlotte, Memphis, Jacksonville, etc., who participate in a personal, mass culture of partying, dating, swimming, and all the sex the market will bear.[33] Two ingredients are indispensable: (1) a convenient apartment complex, designed for singles (but unofficial though temporary additions are quite common), with spacious swimming pools and indulgent neighbors, and (2) one or more "in" restaurants in the vicinity, which encourage singles to use the facilities (food, drink, and dance floor) as a focal meeting-place. It has been asserted, with some accuracy, that these otherwise favored migrants are isolated from the family life and the suburban residences of their co-workers and office mates. Consequently, the swingles form their own subculture, which, it has been suggested, is not unlike the pace and flavor of fraternity and sorority life in college.

While many urban cliques are found among adults and on upper status levels, the clique type of organization is also a favorite device among adolescents in the middle and lower status categories. However, these cliques seem to have an entirely different significance for their members. In general, they function not as supplements to existing social order, but as contrived reactions to deficiencies in social order, as radical innovations in the interstices of the evolving urban sociocultural complex. For this reason, we shall call such cliques "counter-cliques," the major forms of which are represented by urban gangs.

The gang is unfortunately a much misunderstood phenomenon in modern society and one which has been studied more often by journalists than by

---

leigh B. Gardner, and Mary Gardner, *Deep South* (Chicago, University of Chicago Press, 1941).

[32] E. Digby Baltzell, *Philadelphia Gentlemen* (New York, The Free Press of Glencoe, 1958); Cleveland Amory, *The Proper Bostonians* (New York, E. P. Dutton, 1947); Floyd Hunter, *Community Power Structure* (Chapel Hill, University of North Carolina Press, 1953).

[33] Atlanta *Journal-Constitution*, June 30, 1968; Sandra Grimes, "The Supersingles," *Atlanta* (May, 1968), pp. 47–50.

social scientists.[34] Since there are at least two types of gangs—a fact that is often overlooked—a preliminary definition of gangs in general is certainly desirable at this point. The gang is a form of clique organization which emphasizes fairly regular social contacts among its members, attracts members who are remarkably similar on such items as sex, age, social class level, and often, nationality, and perhaps most significantly, functions as a potential or actual competitor to the prevailing social order of adults. There is considerable variation among gangs in degree of organization, yet most urban gangs reflect in their individual operation an overarching set of organizing values, which has been accurately called youth culture.

Gangs and youth culture are predominantly urban, though rural areas have had both gangs and the partial intrusion of youth culture in recent years. Youth culture consists of a series of innovations in values and activities which enable adolescents to achieve status and a measure of independence from the adult world of responsibility, impersonal organization, and deferred gratification. In the process of creating and sustaining the technical specialization that marks urban organization, the adolescent has been a forgotten man, a marginal person, no longer a child, but not yet an adult. The urban family has been largely unable to provide adequate links to future experience; it is itself typically isolated. The same limitation of specialization is evident in the school, the church, and in economic groups.

The paradox of urban youth culture is that it is simultaneously impersonal and generalized, and the basis for the proliferation of specific quasi-primary organizations among adolescents (counter-cliques). Essentially, youth culture reflects the transitional, problematical status of urban adolescents. Its major values are the intrinsic importance of fun, amusement, recreation; withdrawal from "responsible" activities and concerns, as defined by adults; an emphasis on physical skills, such as complex dancing steps, sports, driving and dismantling automobiles; a love of constant minor novelties in dress, jargon, amusements; the acceptance of conformity to peer group standards; and the emphasis on gregariousness, on direct personal interaction with one's peers, accompanied by an apparent fear of isolation or extended privacy.[35]

Youth culture, which is largely the property of youth groups that resemble the previous definition of cliques, is practiced by two general types of gang. The first and less obvious type may be called—more for simplicity

[34] The journalists are well represented by Dale Kramer and Madeline Karr, *Teen Age Gangs* (New York, Holt, Rinehart, and Winston, 1953); Harrison E. Salisbury, *The Shook-Up Generation* (New York, Harper and Brothers, 1959); and Herbert Asbury, *The Gangs of New York* (New York, Alfred A. Knopf, 1928).

[35] Talcott Parsons, *Essays in Sociological Theory*, pp. 101–102, 189–190, 342–345; James S. Coleman, *Adolescent Society* (New York, The Free Press, 1961); David Gottlieb and Charles Ramsey, *The American Adolescent* (Homewood, Dorsey Press, 1964), Chap. 2; F. Musgrove, *Youth and the Social Order* (Bloomington, Indiana University Press, 1965), Chap. 3.

than accuracy—the normal or approved gang.[36] While many would hesitate to call these groups "gangs," it is becoming increasingly clear that many noncriminal organizations of adolescents share with their unapproved contemporaries in many values of the youth culture, basic social organization features—e.g., leadership, and meeting similar social and psychological needs of their members. The normal gang is found among lower and middle class adolescents, and appears to be an essential part of the adolescent's transition to adult status.

Among middle class urban youngsters, the normal gang sometimes arises within specific neighborhoods (in the form of athletic groups), but more often the high school or college provides the opportunities for social contacts that culminate in this type of gang. Such groups are commonly referred to as crowds, circles, cliques, or the bunch. From the admittedly scanty information available, the middle class normal gang appears to have a loose but recognizable organization as a clique or counter-clique, with three kinds of focal activities.

One type may be called the sports gang, since it involves habitual association of like-minded boys either for playing one or more sports (but not necessarily as an organized team) or for attending sports events as a nucleus of spectators. The sports gang probably has a relatively brief history and a minimum of clique-like features.

A second type of middle class normal gang operates at the borders of social approval. Its focus is semiuninhibited diversion, adolescent hilarity, and boisterousness as ends in themselves. Boys in these gangs meet in public establishments (such as drive-ins, ice cream parlors, drug stores—often near school grounds) to the mixed amusement and annoyance of other customers. Occasionally, these gangs erupt into minor roughhouse behavior, with some damage to crockery, windows, and clothing, but this is unplanned and regretted by most members.

Finally, and perhaps most significantly among middle class normal gangs, there is the dating gang, an urban innovation which has enormous implications for family organization, the amusement industry, and advertising. Dating, as distinct from courtship, is a characteristic expression of youth culture. But it is erroneous to consider dating as the mere pairing of youngsters for fun and amusement. Typically, dating occurs within circumscribed reservoirs of desirable males and females; dates are exchanged, succeeded, and resumed largely in well-defined crowds whose members more or less accept common standards of exclusion and inclusion. These standards are explicit and easily verbalized. Most dating gangs—and in particular those developed on college campuses and in high schools—reflect common concern for status (social level of parents, academic and social status on campus), up-to-date dancing skills, as well as consensus on proper attire and physical

[36] One of the few recent studies of this type is Herbert Bloch and Arthur Niederhoffer, *The Gang* (New York, Philosophical Library, 1958).

attractiveness. In such circumstances, clique members view the date both in terms of personal enjoyment and in comparison with the dating experiences of other members. The latter concern is the source of Willard Waller's graphic designation, "the rating and dating complex," for such groups and activities.[37] Parenthetically, dating gangs have generally looked with disfavor at the current epidemic of "going steady," perhaps because these personal monopolies signify independence from, and therefore a challenge to, the adolescent clique.

Gangs among middle class youngsters are generally mild counter-cliques, functioning as acceptable and temporary protests against the restraints of family and formal education. These gangs are conventional, expedient, and dispensable to their members, who soon exchange their brief period of rebellion for higher degrees in conformity. But lower class adolescents likewise develop many approved gangs, usually the sports and seminuisance type, though these rarely receive the publicity reserved for delinquent associations.

The classic sociological account of approved gangs is that of the Corner Boys in a lower class neighborhood of Somerville, near Boston.[38] The Corner Boys are especially interesting to those who want a balanced picture of the urban gang. For one thing, the Corner Boys are essentially a normal, law-abiding form of primary association in an immigrant area that lacked legitimate social organization beyond the family and the settlement house. In a sense, then, the gangs served to counterbalance neighborhood inadequacies. Indeed, the gangs were so necessary to their members that they spent most of their time in gang hangouts and—significantly—remained as members well beyond adolescence. Finally, unlike delinquent groups, the Corner Boys were largely concerned with sports activities and approved forms of entertainment (one exception: betting on numbers).

The second type of urban gang, the delinquent or criminal gang, seems to be a lower class urban phenomenon. In general, as Thrasher demonstrated in his classic study of about 1300 Chicago gangs in the twenties, these gangs arise in zones of transition, in areas of mixed racial and nationality groupings. The distinguishing features of these gangs are extreme sensitivity to status frustration and a consequent repudiation of middle class values. In practice, then, the gang as a primary group is geared for and thrives on conflict with the symbols and vehicles of respectability, and also with rival, similarly irritable gangs. As Cohen, and more recently, Cloward and Ohlin have suggested, delinquent gangs are both creators and creatures of delinquent subcultures, whose major themes are violence, malice, impulse, and "face." But even delinquent gangs exhibit specialization in objectives and

[37] Willard Waller, "The Rating and Dating Complex," *American Sociological Review*, 2 (October, 1937), pp. 727–737; E. W. Burgess and Paul Wallin, *Engagement and Marriage* (Philadelphia, J. B. Lippincott, 1953), Chap. III.

[38] William F. Whyte, *Street Corner Society* (Chicago, University of Chicago Press, 1943), especially pp. 115–118.

techniques. The *criminal gang* seeks economic success through organized theft. By contrast, the *conflict gang* is more idealistic; it wages organized warfare with other gangs for morale and honor. Finally, the *retreatist variety* seeks the substitute satisfaction of narcotics, as a desperate alternative to failure in both normal and delinquent pursuits.[39]

the aged and their emerging subculture

Because of greater longevity and the isolation (voluntary or involuntary) of aged parents, private and public decisions are increasingly tending toward physical and social segregation of elderly urbanites in (*a*) homes for the aged, (*b*) subcommunities or retirement communities, and (*c*) special apartment complexes. In general, congregation of the elderly is most pronounced among those who possess reasonably adequate resources and enjoy good health. Unfortunately, it is difficult to determine what proportion of retired persons currently participates in these age-graded housing units.[40]

The available research on social adjustment of the urban aged is somewhat mixed in character and in findings, but it is becoming clear that social interaction is largely limited to those of similar age, in the various forms of congregate housing mentioned above. According to Rosow,[41] this is particularly marked for lower class persons in Cleveland, though studies in other communities do not provide strictly comparable data on this point.

Clearly, as Rosow and others have recognized, the substratum of retirement and old age is loss of previously central social roles and status (worker, active parent). Consequently, the aged subculture (or subcultures) is practically geared to provisional substitutes in social interaction. One such pattern is alienation and isolation, both from the larger community and from age-mates. But another pattern is recreational; it involves regular (but not necessarily frequent) social visiting and participation in games, perform-

[39] Frederic Thrasher, *The Gang* (Chicago, University of Chicago Press, 1927); Albert K. Cohen, *Delinquent Boys* (New York, The Free Press, 1955); Richard Cloward and Lloyd Ohlin, *Delinquency and Opportunity* (New York, The Free Press, 1960), pp. 20–27; Lewis Yablonsky, *The Violent Gang* (New York, Macmillan, 1962); Gilbert Geis, *Juvenile Gangs* (Washington, D.C., President's Committee on Juvenile Delinquency and Youth Crime, June, 1965); Malcolm W. Klein and Barbara G. Myerhoff, eds., *Juvenile Gangs in Context* (Englewood Cliffs, N.J., Prentice-Hall, 1967), Part 1; James F. Short, Jr., and Fred L. Strodtbeck, *Group Process and Gang Delinquency* (Chicago, University of Chicago Press, 1965).

[40] Glenn H. Beyer, *Housing and Society* (New York, Macmillan, 1965), Chap. 13; Irving Rosow, *Social Integration of the Aged* (New York, The Free Press, 1967), Chap. 1; Rosabelle P. Walkley *et al.*, *Retirement Housing in California* (Berkeley, Diablo Press, 1966); Ernest W. Burgess, ed., *Retirement Villages* (Ann Arbor, Division of Gerontology, 1961).

[41] Rosow, *op. cit.*, Chap. 7.

ances, and hobbies. According to Rose, this focus is allied to emphasis on health and on awareness of a unique position in society.[42]

From studies in California and Florida urban areas, it appears that the aged or retirees participate in this emerging subculture if they are among the "younger" category (60s and early 70s), in good health, financially comfortable, and in subcommunities located in the urban fringe.[43] We might expect similar primary-like groupings among residents of the newer, carefully designed homes in central cities, rather than among those who are dispersed throughout a given urban area. Gerontologists are currently studying the associational patternings of the elderly, who are growing both in absolute and relative numbers, and we must await their findings for a much needed comparison with the social adjustments of the aging in other urban regions of the world.

summary and interpretation

Perhaps two generalizations may be drawn from the preceding discussions of urban primary groups. First, it is quite evident that primary group relationships are difficult to sustain as isolated segments of experience; complex organizations and impersonal social processes inevitably intrude on preexisting primary forms, such as the family and the traditional neighborhood. Consequently, urban primary groups have been faced with the need for re-formation, for adjustment to the special circumstances of urban regional life. Changes in family structures, and the personal and social problems that accompany these changes, are dramatic illustrations of such adjustment. In addition, relatively new kinds of primary groups—adult and adolescent cliques, and counter-cliques—may also be interpreted as organizational adjustments to gaps or deficiencies in the complex but loose structure of the urban region.

Second, although the problem aspect of urban primary groups was not specially emphasized (this will be discussed in Chapter 16), it is becoming clear that urbanites implicitly recognize that primary groups are unequal to the task of satisfying numerous, specialized needs. The underlying quest for more conscious, more formal organization of urban activities therefore con-

---

[42] Arnold M. Rose and Warren A. Peterson, eds., *Older People and Their Social World* (Philadelphia, F. A. Davis, 1965), Chaps. 1, 2; Ruth Bennett and Lucille Nahemow, "Institutional Totality and Criteria of Social Adjustment in Residences for the Aged," *Journal of Social Issues*, 21 (October, 1965), pp. 44–78.

[43] Two studies of an Atlanta subcommunity for the aged are: David G. Asquith, *Factors Associated with Social Interaction in a Private Home for the Aged* (M. A. Thesis, Department of Sociology, Emory University, 1967); Alvin P. Short, *Some Friendship Attraction Patterns in a Retirement Community* (M. A. Thesis, Department of Sociology, Emory University, 1968). See also P. From Hansen, ed., *Age with a Future* (Copenhagen, Munksgaard, 1964), section on social science and welfare.

stitutes one of the dominant themes in the urban order. In succeeding chapters, we shall examine several important variations of this theme, beginning with the so-called voluntary associations.

selected references

BOTT, Elizabeth, *Family and Social Network* (London, Tavistock Publications, 1957).

CLOWARD, Richard and OHLIN, Lloyd E., *Delinquency and Opportunity* (New York, The Free Press of Glencoe, 1960).

COHEN, Albert K., *Delinquent Boys* (New York, The Free Press of Glencoe, 1955).

FARBER, Bernard, ed., *Kinship and Family Organization* (New York, Wiley, 1966).

FESTINGER, Leon *et al.*, *Social Pressures in Informal Groups* (New York, Harper and Brothers, 1950).

GANS, Herbert J., *The Urban Villagers* (New York, The Free Press, 1962).

MILLER, Daniel R. and SWANSON, Guy E., *The Changing American Parent* (New York, John Wiley and Sons, 1958).

RIESMAN, David, *The Lonely Crowd* (Garden City, N.Y., Doubleday and Company, 1953).

SEARS, Robert R. *et al.*, *Patterns of Child-Rearing* (Evanston, Row, Peterson and Company, 1957).

THRASHER, Frederic, *The Gang* (Chicago, University of Chicago Press, 1927).

WHYTE, William F., *Street Corner Society* (Chicago, University of Chicago Press, 1943).

WHYTE, William H., Jr., *The Organization Man* (Garden City, N.Y., Doubleday and Company, 1956).

10

voluntary groups and formal associations

For many persons, the calendar and the date book have become indispensable items in the routine of urbanized living. This is not a result of faulty memory or a compulsive desire for order, but merely a consequence of the increasing load of organizational activities to which the urbanite is committed. In the urban region, these activities are largely separate from the direct pursuit of one's occupation, and therefore are channeled through specially created groups called voluntary groups or formal associations. The urban milieu is liberally sprinkled with such groups; indeed, they seem to be proliferating at such a rate and constitute such a firm, semiobligatory part of urban living, that some students occasionally question the designation "voluntary." Whatever the proper label, these associations are increasingly significant components of urban organization.

In its essential form, the formal association is a highly specialized, explicitly organized group composed of persons with a common interest (though not necessarily common degrees of interest) that cannot be satisfactorily pursued individually, or by preexisting forms of social interaction. For example, John Smith may have some interest in reading and gaining appreciation of the classics or "Great Books." Yet he may feel unable to spare the necessary time; he may even doubt his ability to accomplish much on an independent basis. At the same time, he may also be reluctant to enroll in one or more courses at a local college. If the interest persists despite these obstacles, he is a likely prospect for a Great Books Reading Group, a very popular variety of voluntary association in urban regions. The variety of voluntary or formal associations is so great that several central features must be given special attention.

characteristics of voluntary and formal associations

It may be useful to approach voluntary organizations as an intermediate type of social organization, somewhere between primary groups on the one hand and firmly established, highly bureaucratized groups on the other. Unlike primary groups, voluntary associations tend to function with limited sets of definite objectives or interests, and exhibit rather visible attempts at formalized organization. However, as in the case of most primary groups, membership is normally voluntary; entrance and withdrawal are dependent on personal decisions of high interest or of frustrating disaffection with the specific aims or methods of a given organization. Yet if voluntary associations resemble highly formalized and well-established groups in such respects as specialization, formal structure, and general impersonality, two important distinctions nevertheless recur. Understandably, the highly institutionalized groups are often older, more conservative, and perhaps defensive, more fully legitimated, and therefore exercise a more encompassing control over one's experience. As a result, these groups tend to inhibit deviant opinions and values among members, either by providing no regularly approved channels for creativity or disagreement, or by specifically penalizing unapproved variations (e.g., dismissal for insubordination on the job, excommunication for heretical beliefs, fines and imprisonment for disobeying current but unpalatable laws). Voluntary associations, by contrast, emphasize (or try to) some degree of freedom for change, deviation, creativeness, or merely variation from routine responsibilities.

This intermediate position of voluntary associations (or as Voltaire called them, private associations) is probably a consequence of the fact that they arise and function to supplement—not supplant—both existent primary groups and highly institutionalized groups. While the latter forms of social organization are certainly indispensable—their absence would be unthinkable and impractical to the highest degree—they have apparently been judged inadequate by themselves to provide the range and quality of organization deemed necessary for coping with the desired complexities of urban living. Therefore, voluntary associations fill a gap in urban organization, by experimental blends of primary group and institutionalized group traits.

Voluntary associations may be simply classified into two major types, according to dominant objectives or functions perceived by their members.[1] One important type, called expressive associations by Rose, provides regular opportunities for self-expression, creativity, and perhaps innocent deviation. In this type, the members merely desire to exchange ideas and experiences in some limited field of interest. Garden clubs, literary societies, hobby groups, fraternal lodges, many veterans' organizations, and book clubs are fundamentally constructed in terms of this general set of goals.

Many expressive associations seem, upon close examination by outsiders, to pursue their stated interests in a somewhat haphazard way. This leads to the suspicion that these associations are more important as facili-

[1] Arnold Rose, *Theory and Method in the Social Sciences* (Minneapolis, University of Minnesota Press, 1953), pp. 55–66. See also his *Sociology* (New York, Alfred A. Knopf, 1956), Chap. X.

tators of social interaction, of expression, and even of sociability than for the content of expression and interaction. Where this suspicion is well founded, it probably indicates that expressive associations are essentially supplements to one's stock of primary group experiences—perhaps even substitutes for inadequate or frustrating primary group relations.

A second type of voluntary association—possibly the more dominant variety—is organized to initiate or encourage desired changes in local, national, or international institutional organization. Instead of providing a forum for mutual expression of opinions, ideas, and information, this type attempts to influence persons and organizations beyond the particular association to accept and implement proposed changes. Obviously, politics is marked by innumerable social action or influence associations (taxpayers' groups, independent voters' leagues, and various lobbying groups). But these are also found in education, religion, intergroup relations, welfare, medicine, industry, agriculture, and even the issue of possible calendar reform. If expressive associations supplement primary groups, social action associations try to repair or improve the major institutional arrangements. However, social action associations inevitably develop counter-associations, when threats to established patterns become increasingly difficult to ignore. As social action associations achieve some success and momentum, they become the foci of social movements [2] and thus constitute one of the most important levers of social and cultural change in modern society.

As both Robin Williams and Arnold Rose have perceptively remarked, voluntary associations in the urban region arise and persist in a social environment of diffuse power.[3] However, it is doubtful that this "permissive power situation" is inherent in urban regions in general. In France, for example, Rose found considerably less diversity of, and participation in, such organizations than in American cities. The apparent explanation is that the cultural dominance of the Catholic Church—and perhaps the vastly greater authority of the national government in French cities—either makes these organizations unnecessary, or implicitly discourages the emergence of competing groups and loyalties.[4] On the other hand, in American cities, the government has not tended to be greatly concerned with private affairs (despite the general enlargement of government functions); and many of the established religious organizations have not been able to match the pervasive influence of the Catholic Church over its adherents. The result is vast opportunities for new, specialized organizations.

[2] Ralph Turner and Lewis Killian, eds., *Collective Behavior* (Englewood Cliffs, N.J., Prentice-Hall, 1957), Part IV; Rudolph Heberle, *Social Movements* (New York, Appleton-Century-Crofts, 1952); Kurt Lang and Gladys E. Lang, *Collective Dynamics* (New York, Thomas Y. Crowell, 1961), Chaps. XVI, XVII.

[3] Robin M. Williams, Jr., *American Society*, 2nd ed. (New York, Alfred A. Knopf, 1960), pp. 497–500; Rose, *Theory and Method in the Social Sciences*, pp. 58–61.

[4] Rose, *Theory and Method in the Social Sciences*, Chap. IV.

Under these facilitating conditions, voluntary associations have developed and attracted members for a variety of reasons. Indeed, an important characteristic of such organizations is the fact that both collectively and individually, they may satisfy a diversity of motives.[5] Some urbanites join voluntary associations because of a consuming interest in literature, lower taxes, or improved public education. Others are attracted to these groups because they bolster or enhance personal status. Still others feel a personal obligation, a sense of social responsibility or service toward civic groups and action organizations. We must recognize that some persons desire additional opportunities for social contacts—often of a quasi-personal character —and perhaps as antidotes to unsatisfactory primary group relations. Thus, as in other forms of social organization, voluntary associations serve both rational and nonrational purposes. Despite these variations in organizational aims and individual motives for membership, the urban voluntary association has developed a characteristic structure that dovetails with the general features of urban living.

1. In many cases, the voluntary association exhibits a semibureaucratic form—official positions, definite responsibilities, records, minutes, and often parliamentary procedures at formal meetings. Yet this surface formality of structure is often accompanied by personal interaction among members (in the organizational framework as well as in other social contexts) through use of first names, exchange of family information, pooling of transportation to meetings, and in consideration of members' other responsibilities in allocating duties in the association. Thus, the voluntary association implicitly permits the pursuit of a specific interest without the annoyance of unrelenting pressure to subordinate personality and personal problems to organizational demands.

2. The scheduling of regular meetings—once a week or once a month —is perhaps a small detail, but an important one. In the vague competition of activities and responsibilities that marks urban living, specification of definite meeting times well in advance performs at least two functions for members. First, it supplies or strengthens a feeling of continuity despite the time-consuming attention to routine responsibilities (the job, household chores, etc.). Primary groups (e.g., friendships) generally operate more haphazardly, since their underlying assumption is that members should interact spontaneously, rather than by design. Perhaps, in the urban setting, many friendships expire or drift away for lack of minimum design, rather than through conflicts or divergent interests. It appears that voluntary associations avoid some of the limitations of primary groups by recognizing that interest must be supplemented somewhat by an appropriate routine.

A second function of regularly scheduled meetings is the opportunity

5 Williams, op. cit., pp. 499–501; Ronald Freedman et al., Principles of Sociology, rev. ed. (New York, Holt, Rinehart and Winston, 1956), pp. 450–452.

to plan for participation in other activities and the discharge of other obligations. Few things are more productive of annoyance to the urbanite than unexpected, hastily called meetings, whatever the justification. The necessary rearrangements may involve a chain reaction of irritation among family members, plus several strategic telephone calls. Indeed, relatively infrequent meetings (once a month, or less often) have the latent consequence of allowing many persons active affiliation with several associations concurrently, thus permitting a small core of interlocking memberships in a given community.[6]

3. It is a current truism that a few persons do most of the work in most organizations. This is often true in bureaucratic groups. But perhaps the relatively clear-cut division of responsibility and authority in such groups accounts for differences in genuine participation. On the other hand, voluntary associations also tend to have a core of active participants ("live wires") and a large proportion of peripheral, semiapathetic members. An adequate explanation of this feature is not yet available. However, it seems probable that the voluntary nature of the association implicitly tolerates great variations in participation. Though information is lacking, experience suggests that lower levels of participation are often found among new members and that greater turnover in membership tends to inhibit active participation. A final consideration: since personal motives for joining vary a good deal, we might reasonably expect corresponding differences in involvement in associational functions. The pressure to conform is more likely to reveal itself in superficial matters for most members—paying dues and attending meetings. Perhaps the lack of genuine emphasis on intensive participation is unconsciously attractive to many urbanites, whose primary identification is with the family or the job.

4. To fulfill its basic function, either as a forum for various creations of its members or as a pressure group working for some cause, the voluntary association normally requires two closely related patterns—committees and programs. The formation of committees, their deliberations, and reports are symbols of the need for efficiency and the eager recourse to internal specialization. These committees have received their share of ridicule from cartoonists, whimsical social scientists, and intellectuals in general.[7] But these critics have principally evaluated committees from the standpoint of tangible results (in which case the consequences are often trivial), not from the standpoint of latent contributions.

In view of the necessary infrequency of regular meetings, the voluntary association achieves much of its continuity and part of its ability to

---

[6] W. Lloyd Warner and Paul S. Lunt, *The Social Life of a Modern Community* (New Haven, Yale University Press, 1941), Chap. XVI.

[7] One of the best critiques is C. Northcote Parkinson, *Parkinson's Law* (Boston, Houghton Mifflin, 1957).

compete with other social obligations of its members through a succession of committees. Membership on committees gives urbanites an opportunity for limited responsibility without the necessity of crucial achievement. To many persons, this is a pleasant contrast to the routine, imposed responsibilities of home and office. Not to be ignored is the fact that participation in committees also furnishes opportunities for more personal relations with members of the larger organization, for converting mere similarities of interest into subtle patterns of acquaintance and friendship. Of course, involvement in committee work does not reach an overwhelming proportion of the membership; the distinction between the dedicated and the apathetic "hanger on" in voluntary associations as a whole applies with particular force at this point as well. Nevertheless, the trend in all but the most hidebound or personally dominated associations is toward encouraging wider participation through committee assignments, and through performance in one or more programs.

Since meetings of many associations are typically infrequent but yet regularly spaced, each formal meeting assumes great importance for the vitality of the association. Purely routine meetings—concerning business matters, election of officers, etc.—tend to clash with the ultimate aims of the organization and with one or more personal motives for joining. Consequently, a key feature is the avowed necessity for several programs during the organizations's yearly round. A program is essentially a dramatic deviation from routine, an opportunity for display and temporarily heightened activity. The pattern is simple and often effective. An outside dignitary is invited to give a provocative talk. Sometimes one or more members are plucked from the fringes of participation to discuss a crucial issue, to recount their achievements, or to display some skill. This is followed by open discussion, appreciation and criticism, and often by refreshments. When properly planned and executed, the program stimulates or maintains interest, provides sanctioned freedom for self-expression, and lends a personal flavor to the formalized aspects of organization.

5. A great many voluntary associations are affiliated with their counterparts in other communities in regional, national, or international federations. Whether a local association boasts an independent origin or was founded by the efforts of some parent organization is for present purposes a minor issue, a matter of historical detail. More important, it seems, is the sense of linkage with a wider world of experience and the occasional feeling of vicarious power that is a tonic to further participation.

Voluntary associations in urban regions are to a large extent attuned to the special traits of urban social organization. But how do they collectively operate in urbanized society? Direct information on this problem is, unfortunately, meager. However, we can profit from such indirect evidence as

table 34

Differential Membership in Formal Organizations, by Residential Category and Population Type, 1953

PERCENT OF FAMILIES WHOSE MEMBERS BELONG To:	METROP. COUNTIES (WITH CITY OF 500,000 OR MORE)			OTHER URBANIZED COUNTIES (WITH CITY OF 10–50,000)			PRIMARILY RURAL COUNTIES (NO TOWN OF 10,000)		
	Urban	Rural nonfarm	Rural farm	Urban	Rural nonfarm	Rural farm	Urban	Rural nonfarm	Rural farm
No organization	42	40	67	46	46	53	54	52	70
One organization	33	37	21	36	34	28	27	24	21
Two or more organizations	25	23	12	18	20	19	19	24	9
Total	100	100	100	100	100	100	100	100	100

SOURCE: Charles R. Wright and Herbert H. Hyman, "Voluntary Association Memberships of American Adults: Evidence From National Sample Surveys," *American Sociological Review*, Vol. 23 (June, 1958), p. 290.

the extent of participation in voluntary associations and the concentration of membership in specific social categories of the urban region.

Several recent investigations indicate that relatively small proportions of urban males belong to no voluntary associations at all. In the Detroit area, 37 percent were nonmembers, while in the San Francisco region, only 23 percent were in that category.[8] An often cited study by Komarovsky in New York City during the depths of the depression, on the other hand, found that between 50 percent and 60 percent of the males (and between 63 percent and 88 percent of the females) questioned had no formal group affiliation apart from church membership. Similarly, a national sample survey of the National Opinion Research Center (in 1953) provided the incidental finding that 64 percent of the respondents belonged to no voluntary association, excluding unions.[9]

These striking differences can be largely discounted, if a few basic points are considered. The Komarovsky study was mainly confined to the central city and was carried out in a depression period, when motivation for voluntary association was understandably low. In addition, though this study was one of the first of its kind, it did not attempt to draw a representative

[8] Morris Axelrod, "Urban Structure and Social Participation," *American Sociological Review*, 21 (February, 1956), p. 15; Wendell Bell and Maryanne T. Force, "Urban Neighborhood Types and Participation in Formal Association," *ibid.*, pp. 27–28.

[9] Mirra Komarovsky, "The Voluntary Associations of Urban Dwellers," *American Sociological Review*, 11 (December, 1946), pp. 686–698; Charles R. Wright and Herbert H. Hyman, "Voluntary Association Memberships of American Adults: Evidence from National Sample Surveys," *ibid.*, 23 (June, 1958), p. 287.

sample of adults—as Wright and Hyman have remarked. As for the NORC study, we do not know with any assurance that the sample adequately represents urban regions in the United States. Indeed, a special tabulation of respondents from metropolitan counties and rural counties furnishes results that diverge significantly from the overall findings. As the accompanying table shows, associational membership is considerably less marked in the rural farm segments of metropolitan counties. Consequently, it seems likely that—in the contemporary urban region—participation in at least one voluntary group is widely distributed, perhaps accounting for 60 to 70 percent of adult males.

Despite this rather broad involvement in urban voluntary groups, the various social categories of the urban region do not seem to be equally represented. With virtually no exceptions, studies on this point indicate that status level (measured in several ways) is highly correlated with participation. In particular, the middle and upper status groupings have a significantly greater involvement in the range of available associations than lower status categories. This pattern has been identified in such widely dispersed areas as New York City, Detroit, Spokane, Los Angeles, San Francisco, Columbus (Ohio), Evanston, Denver, and Columbia (South Carolina).[10]

As Table 35 shows, these differences in participation persist regardless of the specific measure of status levels—family income, occupation, formal education, and type of neighborhood. Obviously, too, these measures do not reveal equally sharp distinctions in participation (compare lines 3 and 4). Income seems to be one of the more useful indicators of differential participation, in addition to occupation. This casual conclusion is corroborated by a careful analysis for Spokane. In addition to demonstrating that class level is correlated with membership, Freeman and his associates found that salary was more intimately related to membership than such status measures as the Index of Status Characteristics, rent, or subjective identification.[11]

Many studies of the membership of voluntary groups also find that people in middle and upper status categories tend to belong to a greater

[10] Komarovsky, loc. cit.; Morris Axelrod, "Urban Structure and Social Participation," American Sociological Review, 21 (February, 1956), pp. 13–18; Scott Greer, "Urbanism Reconsidered: A Comparative Study of Local Areas in a Metropolis," ibid., pp. 19–25; Wendell Bell and Maryanne T. Force, "Urban Neighborhood Types and Participation in Formal Associations," ibid., pp. 25–35; Alfred C. Clarke, "The Use of Leisure and its Relation to Levels of Occupational Prestige," Ibid., 21 (June, 1956), pp. 301–307; Howard E. Freeman, Edwin Novak, and Leo G. Reeder, "Correlates of Membership in Voluntary Associations," ibid., 22 (October, 1957), pp. 528–533; Leonard Reissman, "Class, Leisure, and Social Participation," ibid., 19 (February, 1954), pp. 76–84; James H. Williams, "Close Friendship Relations of Housewives Residing in an Urban Community," Social Forces, 36 (May, 1958), pp. 358–362.

[11] Freeman et al., op. cit., p. 531; Robert Hagedorn and Sanford Labovitz, "An Analysis of Community and Professional Participation Among Occupations," Social Forces, 45 (June, 1967), pp. 483–491; Nicholas Babchuk and C. Wayne Gordon, The Voluntary Association in the Slum (Lincoln, University of Nebraska Studies, #27, October, 1962).

table 35

Differences of Formal Group Participation for Selected Status Characteristics in the Detroit Area

Status Factor	Percent Who Are Members	Percent Who Are Very Active
Family income		
Under $3,000	42	8
$3,000–$3,999	66	9
$4,000–4,999	67	14
$5,000–5,999	62	12
$6,000–6,999	65	12
$7,000 and over	81	21
Education		
0–6 years	52	2
7–8 years	60	9
9–12 years	63	14
Some college	78	19
Occupation of family head		
Service worker or laborer	50	19
Operative	40	9
Craftsmen, foremen, etc.	40	11
Clerical, sales, etc.	62	21
Professional, managers, and proprietors	61	11

SOURCE: Morris Axelrod, "Urban Structure and Social Participation," *American Sociological Review*, Vol. 21 (February, 1956), p. 15.

number of such associations than do lower status persons. It is not yet clear that sheer number of memberships is a significant fact. Therefore, important clues may well be sought in the types of associations selected by persons in each status level, on the assumption that identifiable and meaningful differences exist between status levels. In Komarovsky's investigation, carried out in 1934–1935, several such differences were sufficiently clear to permit the following "class profiles" of membership to be identified: [12]

Economic (occupational) Level	*Associational Pattern*
1. Unskilled	Only 32 percent belong to any group; social and athletic club; fraternal lodges.

[12] Komarovsky, *loc. cit.*

2. Skilled	44 percent belong to one or more groups; labor unions and fraternal lodges.
3. White collar	47 percent belong to one or more groups; lodges, social clubs, religious groups; secondarily, Masons, fraternities, military groups, unions.
4. Business	67 percent belong to one or more groups; fraternal groups, Masons, economic groups, civic and cultural associations.
5. Professional	68–98 percent (depending on salary) belong to one or more groups; professional groups, cultural and civic types, Greek letter societies.

More recently, Bell and Force have searched for possible relations between broad types of organization (according to focus of interest) and status level of members.[13] Voluntary organizations were classified into three types: (a) general interest—devoted to the public good rather than a particular segment of the community (e.g., Rotary, Kiwanis); (b) special stratum interest—devoted to particular status groups, such as veterans groups, labor unions, the Parent-Teacher Associations, business groups; (c) special, individualized interest—involving either a nonstatus interest of members (such as hobby groups) or aiding a specific grouping not represented within the membership (e.g., charitable organizations for underprivileged boys, for the crippled, the aged, etc.).

Several suggestive patterns were found in comparing four neighborhoods in San Francisco. General interest and specially individualized interest associations were not greatly represented in either high or low status areas. However, general interest associations were somewhat more popular with high status males, while special stratum interest associations were more often found among low status males. In general, then, high status persons seem to show a greater diversity of associational interests, as well as greater inclination to participate in community-conscious groups. It is interesting to note also that apartment dwellers in high status areas have the highest proportionate participation in charitable groups. Whether these patterns reflect conscious motives (either of an altruistic or selfish nature) or imitation of one's peers has not been investigated.

family association types

As we have already noted in Chapter 7 (pp. 116–118), membership in voluntary organizations may also be classified in terms of continuity of

[13] Wendell Bell and Maryanne T. Force, "Social Structure and Participation in Different Types of Formal Associations," *Social Forces*, 34 (May, 1956), pp. 345–350.

mates' affiliations. Indeed, in a suburban sample,[14] we found that neither number nor types of affiliations yielded significant distinctions. However, the following patterns could be readily identified:

1. Both mates had past and current affiliations (consistent involvement).

2. One mate had both past and current affiliations, while the other had either past or current affiliations (interchangeable responsibility).

3. One or both mates had current but no past affiliation (attempted mobility).

4. One or both mates had previous but no present affiliations (resignation).

5. One mate had both past and current affiliations, while the other had neither (conflict).

The relation between associational type and status was suggestive, when broad occupational categories were used as a means of indicating differential paths of recruitment. Professionals were most typically in the attempted mobility category, while managerial families tended toward the consistent patterns (i.e., consistent involvement or interchangeable responsibility types). Though the number of cases was small, proprietors seemed to be roughly split between conflicting and relatively continuous patterns of affiliation. Clerical and skilled persons, finally, seemed to function with the least patterning of voluntary affiliations.

Because this was a suburban sample, of relatively small size, it is difficult to interpret these results. We would obviously need comparable data for various parts of the central city. But it seems evident that, if voluntary memberships have meaning for urbanites, the study of voluntary associations must give greater consideration to changes, continuities, and contradictions in participation, and to the factors that help to account for these differences (e.g., stage of the family cycle, the nature of geographic mobility, occupational experiences, and marital role definitions).

voluntary associations in the new nations

In general, the current situation among urban lower status categories in the United States appears to discourage much participation in voluntary groups. But some instructive exceptions should be noted. (1) Lower class Negroes have relatively high rates of participation, particularly in political action groups. In addition, their devotion to local religious groups may be interpreted as a functional equivalent to participation in civic and cultural

[14] A summary of some aspects of this study is contained in Alvin Boskoff, "Social and Cultural Patterns in a Suburban Area: Their Significance for Urban Change in the South," *Journal of Social Issues*, 22 (January, 1966), pp. 86–90.

groups. (2) In previous generations, immigrant nationality groups (Irish, Italian, Polish, etc.) developed a prodigious network of ethnic voluntary associations during their years of early struggle up the urban status ladder. (3) As Babchuk and Gordon have shown for Rochester, N.Y., lower class persons can be attracted to organizations for adults, children, and senior citizens, if the initiative for formation comes from reputable and sincerely interested community agencies.[15]

From these clues, it may be possible to infer that voluntary associations constitute an effective and desired means for lower class adjustment to cities during the first generation of urban residence. As they find it possible (and congenial) to cast off previous cultural traits (rurality, traditional religion, foreign language), urban migrants enter a period of transition in which organizational energies are focused on occupation and fraternal activities. Adolescents, on the other hand, confront this process of transition without the structural opportunities of their elders. Consequently, gangs and peer groups serve as "voluntary association-surrogates" for lower status urban youth.[16] For those youth who adequately traverse the crucial channels of formal education and occupational advancement, voluntary associations later become comfortable accoutrements of achievement, rather than means of adjustment.

If this general orientation is tenable, we would expect an extensive network of voluntary associations in the booming cities of the newly developed or underdeveloped nations in Africa, Asia, and Latin America. The evidence for this prediction is already unmistakable. Little and Banton have documented the rise and development of voluntary associations in West African cities (mutual aid associations, drum clubs, and church-affiliated groups), while Mayer, Southall, M. Wilson, and others clearly describe the same processes in South African cities. Similar studies are available for Lima, Bangkok, Tripoli, and several Indonesian cities.[17]

---

[15] Nicholas Babchuk and Ralph V. Thompson, "The Voluntary Associations of Negroes," *American Sociological Review*, 27 (October, 1962), pp. 647–655; Murray Hausknecht, *The Joiners* (New York, Bedminster Press, 1962), p. 85; Robert E. Park and Herbert A. Miller, *Old World Traits Transplanted* (New York, Harper, 1921).

[16] Cf. Bartolomeo J. Palisi, "Ethnic Generation and Social Participation," *Sociological Inquiry*, 35 (Spring, 1965), p. 222.

[17] Kenneth Little, *West African Urbanization* (Cambridge, at the University Press, 1965); Michael Banton, *West African City* (London, Oxford University Press, 1957); Philip Mayer, *Townsmen or Tribesmen* (Cape Town, Oxford University Press, 1961); Aidan Southall, ed., *Social Change in Modern Africa* (London, Oxford University Press, 1961), esp. pp. 28–29; George H. Kimble, *Tropical Africa* (New York, Twentieth Century Fund, 1960), 2 vols., Chap. 18; Hilda Kuper, ed., *Urbanization and Migration in West Africa* (Berkeley, University of California Press, 1965), pp. 102–103; Richard J. Coughlin, *Double Identity* (Hong Kong, Hong Kong University Press, 1960), pp. 60–65; William P. Mangin, "The Role of Regional Associations in the Adaptation of Rural Migrants to Cities in Peru," in Dwight B. Heath and Richard N. Adams, ed., *Contemporary Cultures and Societies of Latin America* (New York, Random House,

Voluntary associations seem to serve as intermediaries between migrants from tribal areas and the complexity and impersonality of urban institutions. Consequently, these relatively recent groups recruit migrants from the same or similar tribes and give great emphasis to personal support. On this base, voluntary associations provide information about urban conditions (jobs, proper dress, punctuality, the handling of money, etc.) and give a protected form of varied social interaction with other migrants. On the other hand, the role of such organizations should not be exaggerated. For example, Schwab found them somewhat ineffectual in Nigeria. Likewise, Germani reports rather weak involvement in such groups by recent migrants to Buenos Aires. In other Latin American cities (e.g., Lima, São Paulo), the urbanizing function of formal groups is limited by the physical and health problems associated with living in suburban slums.[18]

intra-regional variations in membership

Since the urban region is composed of several interrelated areas, as discussed in Chapter 7, we might reasonably expect participation in voluntary groups to vary among central city, suburb, and fringe areas. Only two studies provide information on this matter, however. Zimmer and Hawley discovered that residents of Flint, Michigan's fringe area had fewer associational memberships than the residents of Flint.[19] Very probably, Flint's population size and economic structure are not representative of American urban areas. It is also likely that its fringe and suburban populations do not correspond to the general features of comparable areas throughout the nation. As a result, it is unwise at this point to draw any conclusions about intraregional patterns of membership.

On the other hand, in the previously cited study by Wright and Hyman, special tabulations of associational membership by size of county and type of residence within counties contain very suggestive and possibly meaningful patterns of difference. In general, smaller urban centers have higher proportions of families without associational membership, as compared with cities of 50,000 or more population. Conversely, larger cities have higher proportions of families with two or more memberships. Furthermore, within two of the three size categories of county sampled, the sharpest difference

---

1965), pp. 311–323; Monica Wilson and Archie Mafeji, *Langa* (Cape Town, Oxford University Press, 1963).

   [18] Banton, *op. cit.*, Chaps. 9, 10; Kuper, *loc. cit.*; Gino Germani, "Inquiry into the Social Effects of Urbanization in a Working-Class Sector of Greater Buenos Aires," in Philip M. Hauser, ed., *Urbanization in Latin America* (New York, Columbia University Press, 1961), pp. 225–226.

   [19] Basil Zimmer and Amos H. Hawley, "The Significance of Membership in Associations," *American Journal of Sociology*, 65 (September, 1959), pp. 196–201.

is between farm residents, and urban and rural-nonfarm (suburban) areas. Perhaps the most significant finding—one that contradicts our plausible hypothesis—is that patterns of associational membership are quite similar in urban and rural-nonfarm areas, particularly so in the metropolitan counties studied.[20]

migration and membership

Some attention has been given to the possible impact of mobility on associational membership, since migration and commuting are widespread processes in the urban region. Survey data for Denver, analyzed by Wright and Hyman, show comparatively small differences between migrants and long-term residents. Furthermore, roughly similar degrees of participation were found in the various commuting zones. The largest difference was between a nearby zone (less than 25 minutes travel time) and a 35–44 minute zone, with the latter showing the higher participation rate. Yet Scaff's study of Claremont, a suburb of Los Angeles, indicates that length of residence is closely related to associational membership. Relative newcomers to the community (an average of 7.6 years residence) participate less in various organizations than the more established residents (average residence of 13 years). A specially interesting fact is that newcomers to the area are very likely to be commuters to other cities and suburbs of the Los Angeles region, thus combining two important facets of urban mobility. Consequently, the commuter category is on the average less involved in voluntary groups than noncommuters. And in contrast to the Denver study, among commuter families, rate of participation in organizations declines sharply as commuting distance increases.[21]

It may very well be that these studies fail to take account of important subgroups in the migrant or commuting category. Freedman's analysis of migrants to Chicago in 1935–1940, for example, demonstrated that important differences in migrants could be related to regional variations and type of community background.[22] This approach has been applied to an analysis of associational memberships in a Midwestern community of about 20,000 population. In general, it was found that membership increases with length of residence, and that younger migrants (those under 40) attain higher rates somewhat more rapidly than older migrants. But participation is also dependent on the types of migrants involved. Migrants from farm areas had

[20] Wright and Hyman, *op. cit.*, p. 292.
[21] Alvin H. Scaff, "The Effect of Commuting on Participation in Community Organizations," *American Sociological Review*, 17 (April, 1952), pp. 215–220.
[22] Ronald Freedman, *Recent Migration to Chicago* (Chicago, University of Chicago Press, 1949), Chaps. IV, V.

decisively lower rates of participation during the first two years of residence, as compared with those from urban and rural-nonfarm areas. Furthermore, migrants from the latter areas tended to increase participation more rapidly than did rural migrants. Even after twenty years' residence, rural migrants still showed less participation than the urban category. These differences in participation probably are closely related to educational and occupational differences among migrants, and possibly to the difference in availability of voluntary associations for each migrant category.[23]

social attitudes and social participation

While all the preceding differences in participation seem plausible and coherent with respect to one another, there is a continuing lack of information on the attitudinal and motivational factors that may make these patterns more meaningful. A few clues are available that deserve further investigation. In a sample of Protestants from Columbus, Ohio, Dynes discovered that membership in voluntary groups was significantly related to basic religious attitudes. Persons with sectarian attitudes (characterized by relatively complete integration of religion and social life, and illustrated by emotionalism, evangelism, and other-worldliness) belonged to fewer nonchurch organizations than those with church-institutional attitudes toward religion (i.e., separation of religion from other major facets of social life). Dynes suggests that the sectarian feels comparatively little need for formal organizational membership, since he is more likely than the nonsectarian to establish friendships within his religious group, and also participates in more organizations within his religious group. In fact, Dynes found that sectarians derived considerably greater satisfaction from their religious affiliation than did the nonsectarian.[24] Unfortunately, this study did not attempt to relate participation and religious attitudes to status differences.

Another motivational clue may be found in the previously cited study of Spokane by Freeman and associates. While social class differences were most closely related to patterns of participation in voluntary groups—as expected, attitudes toward the community also seemed to be moderately significant in distinguishing gross differences in participation. In particular, those who indicated general satisfaction with the size and operation of the community, as well as optimistic attitudes about the community's future, were somewhat more likely to belong to two or more voluntary associations. It is likely that these attitudes have some basis in the class position of the

[23] Basil Zimmer, "Participation of Migrants in Urban Structures," *American Sociological Review*, 20 (April, 1955), pp. 218–224.

[24] Russell R. Dynes, "The Consequences of Sectarianism for Social Participation," *Social Forces*, 35 (May, 1957), pp. 331–334.

persons studied, as Freeman suggests, but at this point a clear picture of the basic factors in community attitudes is not available.[25]

the place of voluntary groups in urban regions

The rise and multiplication of voluntary associations provide fairly good illustrations of latent consequences in human behavior—those largely unplanned, unpremeditated patterns of values, activities, and organizations that nevertheless satisfy one or more important needs of individuals and of their social organizations. If any single voluntary association seems to reflect conscious planning, awareness of purpose, and recruitment of membership, these facts should not obscure the underlying similarities, the implicit common features, that have been analyzed in this chapter. Let us briefly review these features.

1. A fundamental feature of most voluntary groups is their generally effective *compromise* between formal and personal relationships. Since the dominant tendency of urbanization has been a separation of primary and secondary relationships, of private and public spheres, the voluntary association may be interpreted as an organizational invention that aids in the continual transitional process of urbanization by *combining complementary social experiences.*

2. As previous discussion has suggested, though voluntary associations are well distributed throughout the urban region, there is increasing evidence that voluntary associations have not been equally attractive to various subgroupings (class, religious, residence status, etc.). If the voluntary group is fundamentally a means of adjusting to the special nature of the urban region, it surely follows that membership will be most meaningful and desirable to those who are most motivated by uniquely urban goals. Mere residence in the urban region does not insure urban culture.[26] Essentially, voluntary groups are supported by middle class persons who share a *basic social stability* (reflected in respectable or responsible occupations, moderately long residence in the community, and in general, optimism about community prospects), plus an accompanying emphasis on *personal and community progress* (reflected in concern for education and upward mobility, a secularized religion that does not resist the necessity for change, and a somewhat greater involvement in broader, service organizations).

By contrast, other social categories—recent migrants (especially from

[25] Freeman *et al., loc. cit.;* Reissman, *op. cit.,* pp. 81–83. See also Dorothy L. Meier and Wendell Bell, "Anomia and Differential Access to the Achievement of Life Goals," *American Sociological Review,* 24 (April, 1959), pp. 189–201.

[26] Adolph S. Tomars, "Rural Survivals in American Life," *Rural Sociology,* 8 (December, 1943), pp. 378–386.

rural areas), lower status persons, adherents of sectarian religious forms—seem to have a more limited identification with urban values, and therefore —on the average—less need for and appreciation of voluntary associations as a normal part of their experience. Perhaps the essential difference between associational members and nonmembers lies in understandable variations in frustration, pessimism, and uncertainty in achieving success—what has been called anomia. Meier and Bell, for example, found several striking differences in participation patterns related to anomia. Taking males of low socioeconomic status, they discovered higher proportions of anomia among those who identified themselves as "lower or working class" rather than "middle class." Anomia tended to be higher among older males, regardless of class identification, but more important to our discussion is the finding that anomia was somewhat more pronounced among lower status persons who did not belong to voluntary groups. For persons in middle and high status categories, the difference in anomia was even sharper between participants and nonparticipants.[27]

3. In short, voluntary associations as a whole appear to serve a generalized function of more enduring value than the explicit purposes of any single association. Paradoxically, they provide a continuing source of *morale* for the supposedly heartless, impersonal, and fragmented urban region. To be more exact, voluntary associations bolster the social and psychological stability of an otherwise precarious urban middle class. This is accomplished, without plan, in two ways. Positively, the associational contacts of middle class families inspire and sustain a sense of responsibility and purpose, of movement and progress, which are so closely related to the middle class ethos. But voluntary associations have an important negative function as well, as Robin Williams has noted. There is a very popular variety of expressive association (e.g., the fraternal order or service organization) that is particularly congenial to middle class persons because they provide a refreshing contrast to the competitive routine of the dominant business and professional pursuits in the middle classes.[28] Thus, to the extent that the urban region relies on its middle classes for leadership and stability, the voluntary association is an unheralded but indispensable component of urban social organization.

[27] Meier and Bell, *op. cit.*, p. 195.
[28] Williams, *op. cit.*, p. 499. See also Benjamin B. Ringer, *The Edge of Friendliness* (New York, Basic Books, 1967), Chap. 11.

selected references

BANTON, Michael, *West African City: A Study of Tribal Life in Freetown* (London, Oxford University Press, 1957).

LANG, Kirk and LANG, Gladys E., *Collective Dynamics* (New York, Thomas Y. Crowell, 1961), Chaps. XVI, XVII.

ROSE, Arnold, *Theory and Method in the Social Sciences* (Minneapolis, University of Minnesota Press, 1953), Chaps. III, IV.

STACEY, Margaret, *Tradition and Change: A Study of Banbury* (Oxford, Oxford University Press, 1960), Chap. V.

11

social class divisions in urban regions

At many points in previous chapters we have noted the importance of status and status differences in the operation of the urban region. Perhaps without using the proper technical terms, many of us have also impressionistically encountered differences in status as we walk or drive from one neighborhood to another, observe obvious differences in housing quality, scan the covers and inside pages of prominently displayed magazines, examine the variety of work space and facilities for employees in a large office or bank, or simply compare the clothing of people on major urban thoroughfares. In this chapter, the realm of status and social class as a focal component of urban social organization receives special attention.

"Status" and "class" are relative terms; they refer first to different degrees of importance or value assigned to specific persons and categories of persons in a community or society. Thus, we may rightly speak of parental status as distinct from child status, managerial status and employee status, faculty status and student status, married status and single status. In practice, status differences mean differences in opportunities (material and social), in motivations, and in responsibilities and rewards. Consequently, there is, secondly, a tendency for persons of similar status to recognize their similarities, more or less consciously, and to be aware of their cultural and social separation from persons on other status levels.

In simpler types of communities, types of status distinction are relatively few in number—age, sex, skill, physical prowess, and family are the most frequent. More important, in such communities, specific distinctions do not normally coincide with one another. Thus, a person who is noted for physical prowess may come from a family of low repute. Social classes arise and become visible when people are evaluated, and judge themselves, in terms of a commonly used complex of status distinctions, which is applied to persons regardless of their sex or age. When these distinctions are formalized in law and sanctioned by a dominant religion, one's social position is permanently fixed in a social caste system, or an approximation to a caste system. However, throughout the past three centuries and in widening portions of the world, caste systems have been diluted and eventually replaced by more flexible types of social positions—social classes.[1] In the modern urban community, social classes constitute the key to its characteristic maze of status distinctions.

If class and caste are more adequately conceived in comparison with single status distinctions, urban classes are perhaps more meaningful in contrast to rural and small town classes. In Plainville, a village-centered community in Missouri, the residents recognized a basic division into two classes that were separated by differences in family background, wealth, morality, and, most visibly, by manners. More recently, a study of Gosforth, an English village, also found a basic division into two social classes. However, the upper and lower classes were further separated by a buffer category of persons of indeterminate position (called intermediate by the researcher). Furthermore, each major class seemed to possess subdivisions or secondary distinctions, which suggest that rural residents in recent years do not fit the stereoype of bucolic equalitarianism.[2] The same general picture emerges from the frequently cited study of Prairie Town, which found a fairly distinct set of three class strata.[3] Essentially, people in Prairie Town evaluated one another in terms of stability of residence in the community, permanence of occupation, and economic independence. Thus, the highest social stratum consisted of large landholders and successful businessmen. A middle category contained small shopkeepers, retired farmers, independent craftsmen, and a few professional persons. At the bottom rank, consequently, were unskilled workers, ex-farmers, and former farm hands.

How, then, may we characterize in general terms a typical rural or small town class structure? Despite the obvious variations just noted, several features seem specially distinctive.

First, the limited size of the community gives residents rather intimate knowledge of the rest of the population. Consequently, judgments of relative status tend to be sharp and inclusive of all residents.

Second, most rural studies have discovered only two or three broad strata, with little or no development of finer distinctions within a major social division. This relative simplicity is partly explained by the size of the community, but more probably by the high degree of cultural and occupational homogeneity of the population.

[1] Useful discussions of status and class systems may be found in Bernard Barber, *Social Stratification* (New York, Harcourt, Brace, and World, 1957), Chaps. I–IV; Joseph A. Kahl, *The American Class Structure* (New York, Holt, Rinehart, and Winston, 1957), Chaps. I, II; E. T. Hiller, *Social Relations and Structures* (New York, Harper and Brothers, 1947), Part VI; Gunnar Landtman, *The Origin of the Inequality of Social Classes* (Chicago, University of Chicago Press, 1938).

[2] James West, *Plainville, U.S.A.* (New York, Columbia University Press, 1954); W. W. Williams, *Gosforth: The Sociology of an English Village* (New York, The Free Press of Glencoe, 1956), Chap. V.

[3] John Useem, Pierre Tangent, and Ruth Useem, "Stratification in a Prairie Town," *American Sociological Review*, 7 (June, 1942), pp. 331–342.

A third feature is especially noteworthy: in genuinely rural communities, status lines are drawn with an implied finality and permanence. To the ruralite, initial position is not viewed as subject to much change by effort, striving, or imitation. Indeed, except for outmigration, the opportunity for changing social position is obviously limited.

Fourth, because of its small size, relative homogeneity and stability, there seems to be a higher degree of consensus about the standards of differential evaluation and social position.

Finally, rural and small town standards of evaluation tend to emphasize the more personal and subjective aspects—family background, length of residence, morality—in short, items that are difficult to measure but are nevertheless easily available to the judgment of most community participants.

Urban class systems cannot be expected to possess the relative simplicity or consensus of their rural counterparts. Basically, the heterogeneity and dynamic nature of the urban region have not produced a clear-cut system of social strata, but rather a series of shifting fragments that recurrently appear to represent a hierarchical complex of responsibilities, rewards, opportunities, and power. Most of our earlier investigations of urban social strata have failed to consider these issues because they were made in comparatively small, slowly changing urban areas. Yankee City (Massachusetts) and Elmtown-Jonesville (Illinois), which are frequently cited as illustrations of urban class systems, each had a population of 10,000 (or less) when studied.[4] Only Middletown (Muncie, Indiana) approaches a more typical phase of urban development. When the Lynds restudied Middletown in 1935–1936, it had grown to almost 50,000 population. But more important, Middletown was a relatively new city in the midst of vast economic and social changes derived from the general industrialization following World War I and the crisis of the Great Depression.[5]

the distinctiveness of urban stratification

What, then, are the distinctive traits of urban stratification, which we can consider as meaningful reflections of the modern urban region?

Probably the most important is the increasing trend toward spatial segregation between families of different statuses. As we have already seen in Chapter 5, the urban region is becoming a mosaic of class-linked areas and neighborhoods, the suburb perhaps being the purest form of recent segregation by class level. Consequently, apart from fleeting contacts in offices and

---

[4] W. Lloyd Warner and Paul S. Lunt, *The Social Life of a Modern Community* (New Haven, Yale University Press, 1941); A. B. Hollingshead, *Elmtown's Youth* (New York, John Wiley and Sons, 1949); W. Lloyd Warner, ed., *Democracy in Jonesville* (New York, Harper and Brothers, 1949).

[5] Robert S. Lynd and Helen M. Lynd, *Middletown* (New York, Harcourt, Brace, 1929); and *Middletown in Transition* (New York, Harcourt, Brace, 1937).

plants, in retail outlets and in provision of services to the home, urbanites are increasingly insulated from direct and sustained knowledge of persons on other social levels.[6] A generation ago, it was considered proper among comfortably situated families to ask "how the other half lives." More recently, personal knowledge of other class levels has become not so much a matter of distaste or impropriety as one of disinterest. The overall result is that urbanites tend to be more conscious of their own position and opportunities (or frustrations) than of a system of graded positions. This is a form of class consciousness that Marx and his followers simply could not comprehend.

Closely related to this spatial segregation of status categories is a general inability to evaluate the position or status of more than a small fraction of residents in the urban region. Not only does segregation restrict interaction between status levels; it also tends to blur otherwise meaningful connections between the community or region as a unit and the activities of numerous specific persons and families. To the urbanite, beyond a limited circle of neighbors, relatives, friends, and associates, other urbanites are paradoxically familiar strangers who are accepted as "givens" in the urban context. Just as the urbanite is notoriously (and understandably) poor in giving street directions, so is he basically uncertain about the social standing of anyone who cannot be easily identified with either extreme of the social scale.

Nevertheless, urban custom and experience demand that evaluation of status be made for all who enter a field of potential interaction, no matter how tenuous or impersonal. Therefore, the urbanite necessarily acquires standards of evaluation that are simple, quick, "objective," and easily applicable to large numbers of persons. In short, urban status criteria are characteristically material, rather than behavioral or motivational, since the latter are only feasible in situations of prolonged contact and intimacy. As Simmel and others have shown, the simplest, most objective measure in the urban community is money (whether inherited, earned, or borrowed).[7] Yet income or wealth is not directly visible. Consequently, a number of indirect but normally visible (external) standards have become part of the urbanite's evaluation apparatus: occupation, material possessions, residential area and type of housing, formal education, travel, and membership in formal associations.[8]

This urban emphasis on a variety of status criteria inevitably yields

[6] A good discussion of the excluding nature of class divisions is Carl E. Ortmeyer, "Social Interaction and Social Stratification," *Rural Sociology*, 17 (September, 1952), pp. 253–260.

[7] Georg Simmel, "The Metropolis and Mental Life," in Kurt H. Wolff, ed., *The Sociology of Georg Simmel* (New York, The Free Press of Glencoe, 1950), pp. 409–424; Talcott Parsons, *Essays in Sociological Theory Pure and Applied* (New York, The Free Press of Glencoe, 1949), pp. 178–180.

[8] Barber, *op. cit.*, Chap. VIII; Kahl, *op. cit.*, Chaps. III, IV.

some discrepancies between one's ratings on the above mentioned standards. It is becoming increasingly difficult to discover close connections, for specific persons, between such criteria as income, formal education, type of housing, and material possessions. Unfortunately, we do not know the extent of this inconsistency of statuses (what Lenski calls low status crystallization). Yet several studies have shown that evidence of inconsistency exists on all traditional class levels.[9] The significance of this aspect of urban stratification should not be misconstrued, though it is specially tempting to do so. The facts of status inconsistency do not allow us to dismiss social classes as outmoded or purely imaginary conceptions. There is, for example, considerable evidence of status consistency (which will be discussed below). Perhaps two useful cautions can be derived from this brief discussion. First and foremost is the recognition that urban stratification systems tend to be more complex, more fluid than those found in older, more tradition-bound communities. Secondly, the use of judges or raters of family status in specific urban areas is inevitably of limited value unless some means of compensating for status inconsistencies is devised—in which case the raters are unnecessary.

Quite characteristic of urban open class systems is the rather general finding that urbanites on all status levels tend to share similar valuations about the nature and personnel of the highest and lowest status positions, but disagree on the criteria of distinction for a broad, intermediate range of statuses.[10] This vagueness about a fluid middle status range results from the varied criteria of status, limited social experience with other strata, and a more or less constant cultural emphasis on the desirability of movement, progress, and opportunity for those assumed to be at middle status levels. Urbanites are somewhat disturbed and gratified by this fluidity of definition. In fluidity there is hope of social ascent. Perhaps the increasing residential segregation by status reflects in part a search for status consistency in reaction to vagueness and fluidity. A few studies indicate that people tend to overestimate the size of the status level with which they identify.[11] This, too, may represent a desire to extend the boundaries of familiar status into the no man's land of the muddled middle.

In view of all the preceding features, a rather unique aspect of urban

[9] Gerhard Lenski, "Status Crystallization: A Non-Vertical Dimension of Social Status," *American Sociological Review*, 19 (August, 1954), pp. 405–413; Gerhard Lenski, "Social Participation and Social Status," *ibid.*, 21 (August, 1956), pp. 458–464. See the earlier discussion of this problem by Emile Benoit-Smullyan, "Status Types and Status Interrelations," *ibid.*, 9 (April, 1944), pp. 151–161.

[10] Gregory P. Stone and William H. Form, "Instabilities in Status: The Problem of Hierarchy in the Community Study of Status Arrangements," *American Sociological Review*, 18 (April, 1953), pp. 149–162; O. A. Oeser and S. B. Hammond, eds., *Social Structure and Personality in a City* (New York, Macmillan, 1954), Chap. XXII; Allison Davis, Burleigh B. Gardner, and Mary Gardner, *Deep South* (Chicago, University of Chicago Press, 1941).

[11] Oeser and Hammond, *op. cit.*, p. 281.

stratification should be quite understandable. With some oversimplification, it appears that the urban open class structure stimulates (or permits) upward social mobility, but principally by providing opportunities for imitating higher status levels, rather than techniques for achieving validated entrance into higher strata. This is at first glance a surprising conclusion, perhaps because we are still accustomed to thinking of classes in the European or the American small town setting. Yet the nature of the modern urban region —its complexity and heterogeneity, extensiveness, stress on segregation of activities and groups, and the importance of mass media of communication —tends to remove the process of social mobility from a personal to an impersonal plane. With the decreasing opportunity for contacts between clearcut social levels, with the development of superficial, tangible criteria of status, with the incessant promptings of merchandisers and advertisers—status movement (the "status game") inevitably becomes depersonalized, a competition for symbols of position rather than the positions themselves.[12]

Indeed, the imitative, impersonal nature of urban social mobility has become so marked in American urban regions that personal competition for higher status is largely muted. "Keeping up with the Joneses" is a wearisome game of matching possessions within a circle of neighbors; it is of no status value to its participants beyond that circle. One of the striking findings in recent years is the discovery of a "keeping *down* to the Joneses" attitude,[13] a fear among neighboring families of similar social status of creating local jealousies by converting outwardly invisible status increments into visible form too quickly.

It is, of course, a moot question whether or not mobility by imitation is mobility at all. If it appears dubious to an observer, urbanites place great faith in its potential, as evidenced in their persistent resort to two channels of status imitation (which may be considered by-products of distinctively urbanized forms of stratification). There is the obvious and ubiquitous process of *imitation by status objects*. This simply involves acquisition of those objects, appliances, and gadgets that are most closely identified with higher status positions (expensive cars—until recently, foreign cars—large homes, clothing, etc.). During the early years of commercial television, it was not uncommon to find, in cities of the northeastern United States, rows of roofs adorned with television aerials, unaccompanied by television receivers in the apartments below. Advertising and installment buying assume special significance as technical foundations for this form of status imitation.

But an impressively growing form—and perhaps ultimately the more

[12] This is brought out in several ways by C. Wright Mills, *White Collar* (New York, Oxford University Press, 1951), especially Chap. XI: Vance Packard, *The Status Seekers* (New York, David McKay, 1959); Lucy Kavaler, *The Private World of High Society* (New York, David McKay, 1960); Pierre Bleton, *Les Hommes des temps qui viennent: essai sur les classes moyennes* (Paris, Editions Ouvrières, 1956).

[13] William H. Whyte, Jr., *The Organization Man* (Garden City, N. Y., Doubleday and Company, 1956), Chap. XXIV.

successful form—has been *imitation by formal education.* From the urban-ite's standpoint, an inherent limitation of imitation by status objects is that it is both an endless process and difficult to convert into opportunities for higher status contacts. Formal education, on the other hand, can provide both entrance into higher occupational level and opportunities for vocational and social contacts with higher status persons. As far as mobility is concerned, urban education therefore consists of two essential acquisitions: vocational or technical skills; and the broader, cultural skills appropriate to each major occupational level. Many people cynically declare the second more important than the first for mobility. This has not yet been investigated, however. Yet the cultural skills (which are part of style of life, to be discussed later) are more difficult to acquire in the typical educational setting—or almost any-where beyond the family. Hence the importance of the college and university. On the other hand, formal education as a means of imitation is dependent on an expanding economy. In Calcutta, thousands of university students are dis-covering that limited job opportunities are rapidly making a mockery of the status value of formal education.[14] The same situation in the Germany of the twenties was a source of great social instability.

For our purposes, a final aspect of urban classes concerns the dominant type of relations between persons on different class levels. As analyzed by Ortmeyer, these interrelations may take some combination of three forms: (*a*) The "circumscribing or excluding" type emphasizes social distance, segre-gation of classes. (*b*) The "manipulating" type is marked by exploitation of one class by another. (*c*) In the "nurturing" form, currently found in several South American communities, one class feels obligated to provide protection and aid to members of a subordinate class.[15] While all three kinds of relation-ships can be found in modern urban regions, in the more complex regions of Western Europe and North America the opportunity (and perhaps the moti-vation) for pursuing the manipulatory and nurturing types is being gradually but surely reduced. Political ethics, education, the growth of private organiza-tion, and the institutionalization of welfare activities largely explain this trend.[16] Much of the evolving urban class system—which is a system by courtesy—as reflected in behavior and verbalized aspirations, seems to be focusing around the issue of impersonal but informal exclusion. Those on higher levels wish to promote or protect minimal social distance, for various reasons. We find this in typical forms of segregation—racial, residential, educational, and in formal associations. On the other hand, in view of the fluid aspects of urban stratification, those on comparatively lower status levels seek to contract social distance by using genuine channels of mobility (such

---

14 *The New York Times,* December 27, 1959.
15 Ortmeyer, *loc. cit.*; Melvin M. Tumin, *Caste in a Peasant Society* (Princeton, N.J., Princeton University Press, 1952), pp. 127–129.
16 See a fictional treatment in Edwin O'Connor, *The Last Hurrah* (Boston, Little, Brown, 1956).

as education). Those who cannot do so successfully become resigned to, or oblivious of, social distance, and instead content themselves with imitation by status objects.

urban social strata and styles of life

The nature of urban stratification, as summarized in the last few pages, does not permit the identification of a well-ordered hierarchy of social classes in the urban region—such as may be found in smaller cities and in European and many non-Western cities. The main tendency is instead toward the demarcation of four roughly defined status spheres, in each of which subspheres have appeared with fluid boundaries. It is often difficult to determine the relation between subspheres; in some instances, they are more coordinate than hierarchical. In any case, these status spheres and subspheres (or social classes) rarely exhibit the organization or class consciousness that are found in more static stratification systems. Urban classes, to the extent that they can be reliably identified, are primarily expressed through a series of distinctive life-styles, which are rather difficult to copy and therefore constitute a fairly useful means of conceptualizing class differences.

Style of life may be conceived as a more or less implicit expression of shared status features, which, it will be recalled, entail definable opportunities, learned perceptions and usages of such opportunities, and some range of expected rewards. If a class or stratum is identified by one or more related opportunity variables (education, income), then a related style of life may be identified by the special manner in which opportunities are used, evaluated, and rewarded by a relevant reference group. Thus, we might suggest that objective status characteristics are necessary conditions, while style of life features constitute sufficient conditions, in the production of class phenomena in urban regions.

From various studies of stratum-linked behavior and attitudes, we may interpret a style of life as a product of experience in trying to provide adequate means of adjusting to available facilities, resources, limitations and frustrations. Each developed life-style possesses (1) its own dominant values or goals, (2) a distinctive orientation to the prevailing power situation, and toward authority, (3) a characteristic viewpoint on social mobility, and (4) some judgment about the kinds of persons deemed appropriate for acquiring detailed and intimate knowledge of its network of norms and practices. Since a given style of life is a meaningful composite, it cannot be imitated piecemeal without some embarrassment to the imitator and scorn from those being imitated. In general, a distinctive style of life takes years to develop—and years to unlearn—and therefore is an important source of stability in the flux of urban stratification. Indeed, it is quite likely that traditional class labels (lower class, upper crust, bourgeoisie, etc.) and self-identification with a given stratum are less useful than analysis of life-styles themselves in capturing the fundamentals of urban stratification systems.

But what are the most useful ways of reliably distinguishing styles of life in urban regions? Impressionistic analyses of life-style have emphasized such matters as consumption patterns, formal education, travel, leisure and recreational pursuits. Mass production, mass marketing, and extensive availability of formal education in recent years, however, may encourage the conclusion—perhaps a very superficial one—that most urbanites share a common life-style and that class differences represent a semantic hangover from an irrelevant past.[17] While the above-mentioned clues to differences in style of life should not be ignored, there are at least three other indicators which deserve more exploration in the urban regional setting.

1. *Training.* As distinct from formal education, in the sense of number of years' schooling completed, training refers to the actual level and type of acquired skills that can be attributed to some category of persons. Two varieties can be briefly noted: (a) those skills that concern ability to perceive opportunities—verbal facility, practical logic, etc.—and (b) those that emphasize use of opportunities—job or technical skills, knowledge of community resources, decision making, manipulation of persons. Life-styles differ in the relative emphasis on these kinds of skills and on the kinds and levels of responsibility which such emphasis entails.

2. *Patterns of associational affiliation.* It may be assumed that basic perception of social opportunities is translated into more or less conscious decisions about participation in voluntary or formal associations (see Chapter 10). Each style of life may be conceived as a collective guide to preferred forms of (a) pursuing opportunities, (b) compensating for limitations, and (c) receiving confirmation or reinforcement from status peers. Therefore, we would expect specific patterns of participation to provide indirect but useful clues to styles of life. However, the number of formal affiliations and types of organizations seem helpful primarily in discriminating extremes in life-styles. But one study in a suburban area (see Chapter 7) found time patterns of participation by conjugal units a particularly helpful and reliable means of studying life-styles.

3. *Dominant role conception.* Style of life, as defined above, may also be interpreted as a selective ranking of available legitimate (and in some instances, nonlegitimated) roles. Each life-style signifies to the typical adherent (male or female) some range of role choices and a distinctive hierarchy of such roles. For example, Table 36 shows the way a national sample of housewives was classified, according to their responses to 26 items relating to

[17] Robert A. Nisbet, "The Decline and Fall of Social Class," *Pacific Sociological Review*, 2 (Spring, 1959), pp. 11–17. See the opposing viewpoint in Rudolph Heberle, "Recovery of Class Theory," *ibid.*, pp. 18–24.

table 36

Life-Styles in a National Sample of Housewives, 1960

TYPES OF ROLE FOCI

LIFE STYLE PATTERN	Sociability	Home and Family	Self-Develop-ment	Political Interest	Career	N
A. Cosmopolitan	+	+	+	+	+	121
B. Responsible activist	+	+	+	+	−	149
C. Satisfied exploiter	+	+	+	−	−	180
D. Familistic	+	+	−	−	−	154
E. Surface adjustment	+	−	−	−	−	238
F. Resignation-insulation	−	−	−	−	−	137
Total						979

SOURCE: Data were supplied by The Psychological Corporation. Their assistance and interest are gratefully acknowledged.

activities they considered as personally important in some degree.[18] While the items probably did not exhaust all relevant role possibilities, it seems reasonably clear that housewives differ in their interpretation of their roles, responsibilities, and opportunities. Perhaps more important, these differences in role conceptions are not markedly related to differences in income, husband's occupation, or formal education.

In recent years, sociologists have come to question the prevailing characterization of classes or strata in terms of one objective dimension (e.g., occupation), or a composite of such dimensions (income, education, and occupation). For one thing, the explanatory values of these indicators is generally low. In addition, the exclusive use of such variables assumes that persons within the same range of income or occupation share the same perceptions, values, and goals—a notion that is opposed by stubborn fact in most studies of class-linked behavior (voting, leisure, fertility). Consequently, attempts have been made to salvage "occupation" by grouping similar skills into "situses," [19] which makes the assumption that broad occupational types more closely approximate genuine status differences (as defined previously). Also, occupations have been simply and arbitrarily divided into manual and nonmanual types, a device which unwittingly converts occupation into a training difference (see above) and thus produces a style of life difference. Recently, Duncan has shown that the manual-nonmanual distinction is

[18] Don A. Davis, Jr., *"Style of Life" vs. Objective Status Variables in Relation to Expenditure Patterns and Financial Decision-Making* (M. A. Thesis, Department of Sociology, Emory University, 1967), pp. 20, 27.

[19] Paul K. Hatt, "Occupation and Social Stratification," *American Journal of Sociology*, 55 (May, 1950), pp. 533–543; Raymond J. Murphy and Richard T. Morris, "Occupational Situs, Subjective Class Identification, and Political Affiliation," *American Sociological Review*, 26 (June, 1961), pp. 383–391.

largely accounted for by educational differences. And in an international comparison of manual-nonmanual differences, Marsh found that a common major factor was a distinction in leadership and symbolic skills.[20]

In developed urban regions, and in newly urbanized regions, basic status divisions are increasingly reflected in the subtleties of life-styles. Admittedly, there is no master classification of life-styles. But we may study life-styles with some justification as relatively unique kinds of collective management of, or adjustment to, perceived differences in opportunities and limitations. In short, according to this orientation, a style of life is simultaneously (but not necessarily consciously) a mechanism for participating in and responding to the prevailing power patterns in given communities and regions. For convenience, urban status and style of life categories may be summarized approximately as follows;

1. *The consummatory style.* The underlying goal is full utilization of correctly perceived high levels of opportunity, with an accompanying satisfaction with such opportunities. The exercise of power by adherents tends to be confident, responsible, and self-limited.

2. *The striving style.* The dominant note is expanding (a) the utilization of existing opportunities or (b) the range of available opportunities. Consequently, many activities tend to be extrinsically valued; behavior seems directly practical, with an absence of subtle symbolism. Power, therefore, is eagerly sought and threats to power are rather directly countered. Such a life-style is in many respects a civilian form of military strategy.

3. *The resistant-rebellious style.* Essentially, this is a negative life-style, one designed to derogate or discredit either the consummatory or striving styles. It is marked by deliberate attempts to constrict otherwise available opportunities, or to employ them in unconventionl ways. Discipline and denial seem to be implicit master values, while the phenomena of power are disdained as unworthy or superfluous.

4. *The derivative-vicarious style.* This life-style seems to be based on the confluence of relatively ambitious aspirations and comparatively low perception of opportunities. The result is a compromise, in which a favored but unattainable life-style is imitated symbolically, or in which adherents of the desired life-style are consistently followed from afar by empathetic identification with *their* opportunities and achievements. Experience tends to be mediated by the referent life-style, which serves as a filter that protects against striving or resignation.

5. *The resignation-alienation style.* Correctly or incorrectly, this style of life is based on the perceptions of limitations outweighing opportunities.

[20] Otis Dudley Duncan, "Methodological Issues in the Analysis of Social Mobility," in Neil J. Smelser and Seymour M. Lipset, eds., *Social Structure and Mobility in Economic Development* (Chicago, Aldine, 1966), pp. 87–89; Robert M. Marsh, *Comparative Sociology* (New York, Harcourt, Brace and World, 1967), p. 176. See also Mary W. Herman, "Class Concepts, Aspirations and Vertical Mobility," in Gladys L. Palmer *et al.*, *The Reluctant Job Changer* (Philadelphia, University of Pennsylvania Press, 1962), p. 124.

figure 13

Major Urban Life-Styles and Related Strata

Consummatory style	The Social Elite
Striving style	Nouveaux riches Exurbanites Organization men
Derivative-vicarious style	Old middle class New middle class Stable poor (copers)
Resistant-rebellious style	Bohemian Fugitives
Resignation-alienation style	Unstable poor Social outcasts Indolent-apathetic

The resultant value cluster negates the need for risk, achievement, or variety. It nurtures isolation, fatalism, distrust of outside help, and also frequent ventures in violence and undisciplined affect. When practical decisions (public or private) are necessary, futility and powerlessness are dominant feelings that are expressed in indecision, inaction, or erratic hostility.

These life-styles may be considered a very rough hierarchy of reference points, but since modern urban stratification is typically fluid in the intermediate layers or strata, it is unwise to search for strict, crystallized hierarchies. Instead, we may tentatively locate currently identified strata, or fragments of strata, in the set of life-styles, with the understanding that (a) the base for such allocations are still not fully developed and (b) old and somewhat stereotyped status labels (the poor, the middle class) will at first glance be unconventionally and inscrutably placed in such a scheme (see Fig. 13).

consummatory

the social elite; traditional upper class [21]

This stratum is perhaps least representative, both numerically and culturally, of the modern urban region. The way of life of the social elite is in

[21] Warner and Lunt, *op. cit.*, pp. 422–430; Baltzell, *op. cit.*, Chaps. X, XII, XIII; Kahl, *op. cit.*, pp. 187–193; Stephen Birmingham, *"Our Crowd": The Great Jewish*

many respects reminiscent of an earlier urbanism, partly medieval and partly the rarefied urbanism of royal capitals. Perhaps this special cultural ancestry helps to explain both the immense social distance from other contemporary urban strata and the social and cultural attachment to social elites in more static societies (e.g., England, France, pre-Nazi Germany, nonfascist Italy).

Style of life is ultimately dependent on the happy accident of inherited wealth, and on the assurance and unimpeachable position normally guaranteed by this form of wealth. Striving and social climbing, therefore, are not only conveniently relegated to the past, but any evidence of current social striving is viewed as improper and in poor taste. Inherited wealth, with some exceptions, leads to the underlying viewpoint that stability is preferable to potentially disruptive innovations; conservatism, not reactionary ideals, is visible in a variety of fields—including politics.

Conservatism to the social elite means a deep respect for the past, but in particular that portion of the past that is most significant to the elite. Almost all evidence points to the family line and family tradition as the primary focus; it is the acknowledged source of support, position, facilities, and continuity. The family name is perhaps the major object of worship, though the elite is prominent in the more public forms of religion. Emphasis on family background normally restricts choice of mates to families of equivalent status, though a dearth of proper candidates may be remedied by permitting marriages with members of the next highest stratum. Stratum endogamy among the so-called Proper Bostonians is clearly revealed by the "royal family" spate of intermarriages among the Cabots, Amorys, Saltonstalls, and Lodges. And a careful analysis of society marriages would indicate a similar process of marital segregation.

Members of the urban elite should not be confused with the leisure class as acidly described by Veblen more than sixty years ago. Upper-upper class persons tend to follow a modern version of the Protestant Ethic, which demands industriousness and serious attention to some sphere of business enterprise. The playboy is an exception, a deviant case, in contemporary elite circles. With all the assured financial resources of inheritance and devotion to enterprise, the elite—particularly the elder members—refuse to engage in conspicuous consumption and material display. They tend to be parsimonious in routine family expenditures, though few probably equal the attitude of the Proper Bostonian who seriously complained about the price of batteries for his hearing-aid.[22] This parsimonious attitude also extends to the question of publicity, for the members of the elite generally maintain pride in privacy and do not seek frequent inclusion in society columns of metropolitan newspapers. However, their names invariably appear in the Social Register (or its

---

Families of New York (New York, Harper and Row, 1967); Stephen Birmingham, *The Right People: A Portrait of the Social Establishment in America* (Boston, Little, Brown, 1968); Nathaniel Burt, *The Perennial Philadelphians* (Boston, Little, Brown, 1963).
[22] Amory, *op. cit.*, p. 206.

figure 12
A Schematic Version of the Structure of Urban Life-Styles

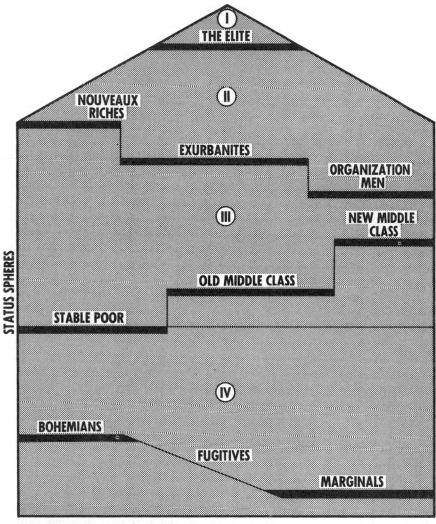

I Consummatory Sphere
II Striving Sphere
III Derivative-Vicarious Sphere
IV Resignation-Alienation and Resistant-Rebellious Sphere

local equivalent) and often in *Who's Who*. This is considered a proper and expected form of publicity.

Another aspect of the elite style of life concerns a special sense of social responsibility, *noblesse oblige*, toward the community and region, and often the nation. This is expressed in several ways: as consistent patrons of the expensive arts (museums, symphony orchestras, opera, etc.) ; as major contributors to various welfare activities; and as members of long-established formal organizations. This responsibility is rarely reflected in the pursuit of political office unless there is a family tradition of this sort, as in the case of the Lodges or Saltonstalls of Boston.

Finally, there is a predominant yet simple focus on gracious living, not as a sought after antidote to the routine of career and upward mobility (as in the middle strata), but as the basis and justification of success. Comfort, assurance, continuity, balance in interests as ends in themselves, rather than as means of display or rivalry—these are the components of gracious living that are not only desired, but are readily available. Travel, for example, means a renewal of contact with acquaintances, places, and objects. It is a normal, necessary part of the elite round of life, an experience worthy in itself—not a symbol of success or a useful conversation piece.

striving

nouveaux riches; the lower-upper life-style [23]

This stratum is one of the most representative of urban stratification processes and one which probably has had the greatest changes in membership during the last 20 years. The quality of dynamism is perhaps the basic theme in a wearing style of life that eventually produces opportunities to enter the elite, or psychological casualties for those who cannot do so.

Lower-upper persons acquire a distinctive life-style when success in a business or professional career reaches (or gives promise of reaching) well beyond the average expectation of income, responsibility, and power. The desire to convert worldly success into acceptance by the elite becomes the fundamental ideal, though they are often mistakenly and superficially criticized as materialistic. The ideal is pursued by various routes and with a special cluster of guiding attitudes. Most prominent is the emphasis on a definite career, with intense striving and competitiveness as indispensable personal traits. Formal education is principally viewed as preparation for a

[23] Few studies of this stratum are available. See Warner and Lunt, *op. cit.*, pp. 430–434; Kavaler, *op. cit.*; Aline Saarinen, *The Proud Possessors* (New York, Random House, 1958) ; S. N. Behrman, *Duveen* (New York, Random House, 1952).

career and upward social mobility, not as a link with the experience of past generations or as a means of developing a rounded personality.

This life-style is hopefully viewed as transitional or preparatory, a kind of implicit social probation. Consequently, the lower-upper category strives to give evidence of current achievement. One avenue is active participation in voluntary associations, principally those in the public eye. Another is the necessity of being among the first to follow new fashions in clothes, housing, appliances and gadgets, and leisure. For whatever is achieved or purchased, adequate publicity and display are particularly important. Thus, at the height of this life-style, considerable emphasis is given to collecting (and advertising) valuable and notable art objects—often acquired through the services of a knowledgeable agent who is necessarily given carte blanche. (Several of the leading art galleries and private museums had their origins in this process.)

The recently rich and successful do not yet assume the elite's devotion to lineage and family name. Instead, as an accompaniment of striving, they foster a belief in individual talent and initiative, and the value of optimism. Increasingly since World War II, the individualistic emphasis has been modified by the recognition of large organizational contexts (corporations, political parties, institutes and foundations), but this is a strategic move that does not blunt the acuteness of striving.

Perhaps the growing corps of rising junior executives, so well depicted by William Whyte, provides a social reservoir from which new adherents to the lower-upper ideal will be recruited. It is interesting to note that this category is in many instances still too young, too undecided about open striving and conspicuous consumption, too limited in income and achievement, to adopt more than fragments of another style of life. But the organization man does place considerable emphasis on career and an uncomfortable degree of striving, which is reflected in his willingness to move or to be transferred (upward, of course) and even in his moderately numerous shifts to other organizations. In view of the distinctive nature of modern urban economic systems, it is reasonable to expect that a sizeable portion of lower-uppers will necessarily come from the ranks of properly motivated organization men.

the exurban life-style

A relatively new stratum and style of life has appeared at the edge of the urban region, almost as an exile from the status whirl of the city and suburb.[24] Because it is so new, it is difficult to locate on the urban scale of status. Yet the exurbanite seems to be just within the upper status sphere, distinct from and yet not completely unrelated to the recently rich.

The exurban style of life is based on a compound of artistic aspirations

[24] A. C. Spectorsky, *The Exurbanites* (Philadelphia, J. B. Lippincott, 1955).

and employment in the vast and expanding communications industries of modern urban regions. Since these elements are ultimately incompatible, an immediate compromise is necessary—the exurban life-style. Closely dependent on city affairs, the exurbanite settles in semirural retreats and pursues a superficially bucolic way of life by owning split-rail fences, quaint lanterns, hitchingposts near the driveway, and coffee tables made from cobbler's benches.

Exurbanites are also "recently rich." Their income ranges from $20,000 to over $100,000, with a median income probably above $50,000. This wealth is principally used for display among other exurbanites—in the rural articles previously mentioned, in week-end parties with substantial liquor bills, and foreign cars. But exurbanites think of themselves as frustrated artists and writers; they want to compose great works, rather than saleable ones. Their exurban residence presumably provides the conditions for creativity (time, space, quiet, and very infrequent commuting to the job), yet the wish is often unequal to these conditions (or to creative abilities). As a result, exurbanites are also strivers, but mainly for esthetic ideals, not social reputation, power, or entrance into the elite.

the organizational men

The life-style of the rising junior executive and salaried professional, on the other hand, seems to stress the somewhat contradictory goals of security and mobility. Their income level is peculiarly marginal: it provides enough for current security, but frequently offers only limited possibilities of status increase (through possessions, memberships, etc.). The striving for upward mobility, however, is partly satisfied by the knowledge that in many cases mobility in the corporation or bureaucracy is moderately well assured. Perhaps these twin goals explain a deepening involvement—almost a fanatical dependence on—continuous installment buying and a dethronement of the traditional virtues of thrift and savings. With the recent creation of revolving credit by department stores and the giant mail order houses, mortgaging of the future has become even easier.[25] In fact, revolving credit is available to a fairly wide category of families, which may thereby imitate important aspects of this life-style.

derivative-vicarious

the new middle class

Generally denied more than token opportunities for increased social responsibility, the new middle class stresses respectability and morality, as

---

25 William H. Whyte, "Budgetism: Opiate of the Middle Class," loc. cit.

well as security.[26] Several items point to this central set of themes. There is a serious adherence to organized religion and participation in church-related activities, particularly in fringe areas of the larger metropolitan regions. Formal education—increasingly college—is highly valued, not only for related occupational opportunities, but as a mark of culture. In the same way, home ownership assumes intrinsic value, despite the financial sacrifices that often accompany purchase of a house. Perhaps, the addiction to membership in various voluntary groups, book clubs, and the like can be interpreted as another aspect of the quest for respectability.

Mills has discovered among some white collar workers a special ideology of security through regular contacts with higher status persons—the "reflected glory" theme. For example, sales personnel in medium-sized cities appeared to borrow (however tenuously) the prestige of their patrons, and also derived a feeling of momentary power in influencing their patrons' selection of articles.[27]

the old middle class

The so-called old middle class category of small, independent proprietors and independent professionals seems to be gradually losing its identity in the American middle status sphere, probably as a result of the centralization and bureaucratization of business and industry. However, the few available studies of this stratum in recent years indicate that its distinctive life-style is focused on mobility and respectability. While the income level is often comparatively high (on a par with upper ranges of white collar and lower ranges of the *nouveaux riches*), thus providing economic security, the social origins of many small proprietors seem to be in the lower strata. Proprietorship signifies a rise in independence and income, but not necessarily in life-style. Consequently, this stratum tends to develop two related themes. There is, first, the rejection of lower status memories through converting income into higher status possessions (home, auto, appliances) and by intermarriage with girls from more substantial middle class families. Second, there is a tendency to view economic trends and community issues from the standpoint of the elite and the *nouveaux riches*.[28] This identification with the higher status businessman and entrepreneur may be interpreted as an unconscious quest for vicarious respectability, by emulating their opinions, even if the heights of influence and acceptability remain unattainable.

[26] Kahl, *op. cit.*, pp. 202–205; Mills, *op. cit.*, Chaps. X–XII.
[27] C. Wright Mills, "Middle Classes in Middle-Sized Cities," *American Sociological Review*, 11(October, 1946), pp. 520–529.
[28] Mills, "Middle Classes in Middle-Sized Cities," *loc. cit.*

the stable or respectable poor

Realistically, the dominant situation of the unskilled, the poorly educated, and the marginal wage worker is the comparatively low probability of upward mobility. But it is the reaction to this situation that is crucial in distinguishing a general working class style of life, and variations in the basic style. The solid or stable working class family clearly recognizes its position, but either accepts it philosophically or makes limited gestures toward preparing for a son's occupational ascent.[29]

Adjustment to immobility normally entails a meaningful cluster of values, activities, and avoidances. A frequent source of comfort—perhaps of harmless fantasy—is a vaguely defined possibility of owning a small business, "working for myself." This tends to lose psychological value with increasing age, but even such a modest hope has important consequences. Inclinations toward thrift, for example, though difficult to implement, may be traced to the hope of some independence. Likewise, this level of aspiration generally prevents the development of more ambitious but unrealistic strivings (great wealth, extensive power, or social acceptance by the elite). Thus, this lifestyle reflects realism, undramatic dignity, and an unconscious quest for respectability.

A major facet of this style of life is reluctance to participate in community affairs, politics, and in more than one or two voluntary associations. Instead, there is considerable emphasis on maintaining the nuclear family and on retaining close family ties. Since 1940, at least in the United States, home ownership has come to be both an aspiration and a reality. Several studies have also shown a marked inclination toward hobbies involving either the home or friends.[30]

Recently, considerable attention has been given to distinguishing the various accommodations made by lower-income families to their economic and social limitations.[31] The "stable poor," the "respectable poor," the "copers,"

---

[29] Kahl, *op. cit.*, pp. 205–210, 287–288; James S. Coleman, "The Adolescent Subculture and Academic Achievement," *American Journal of Sociology*, 65 (January, 1960), pp. 337–347.

[30] See Chapter 10 for references on voluntary associations. For evidence of an emphasis on hobbies and home ownership see John M. Mogey, *Family and Neighbourhood* (New York, Oxford University Press, 1956); Michael Young and Peter Willmott, *Family and Kinship in East London* (London, Routledge and Kegan Paul, 1957); T. Cauter and J. S. Downham, *The Communication of Ideas* (London, Chatto and Windus, 1954); Bennett M. Berger, *Working-Class Suburb* (Berkeley, University of California Press, 1960); Glenn H. Beyer, *Housing: A Factual Analysis* (New York, Macmillan, 1958), pp. 151–168.

[31] S. M. Miller, "The American Lower Classes: A Typological Approach," in Frank Riessman *et al.*, eds., *Mental Health of the Poor* (New York, The Free Press, 1964), pp. 139–154; Marshall B. Clinard, *Slums and Community Development* (New York, The

etc. represent labels for social categories that should not be confused with low-income families enmeshed in life-styles to be discussed shortly.

the resistant-rebellious type

the fugitives and unfindables

Some slum areas provide a haven for social drop-outs, who either fail to assume the available discipline of striving or react to a real or imagined bar to greater opportunities. In the first case, we have those who choose poverty (and its urban locale) as an appropriate camouflage for deviant roles, thereby absolving themselves from "responsibility," "morality," and "dependability." Seeley calls this life-style fugitives and unfindables, though the line of criminality or illegality may often be difficult to discern. A classic case, probably genuine, is the "hero" of *Subways Are for Sleeping,* who maintained an ingenious race with middle class respectability by constant movement and intermittent unskilled work.

the bohemian and its variations

Unlike the fugitive life-style, the Bohemian represents an open and sometimes an articulate avowal of a "deviant" value system—either in the realm of aesthetics, sociopolitical ideology, or social arrangements (communal economics or variably institutionalized sexual liaisons). Limited income and Spartan material accommodations come to attain symbolic value, as identifying marks of independence. The Greenwich Village–Latin Quarter life-style is a rather old form of Bohemianism. But, despite some differences in the selection process, the hippy movement of recent years likewise falls in this category —as well as the "beats."

resignation-alienation type

the marginals

In urban regions, the lowest status (by every index or standard known to social scientists) is held by those who are unwilling or unable to adjust to

Free Press, 1966), p. 45; Lola M. Irelan, ed., *Low-Income Life Styles* (Washington, D.C., Division of Research, Welfare Administration, 1966), Publication #14; John R. Seeley, "The Slum: Its Nature, Use, and Users," *Journal of the American Institute of Planners,* 25 (February, 1959), pp. 7–14.

relative social immobility. Families—and often unattached persons—in this situation are plagued by intermittent employment. They view a job as an eternal evil, an interlude of no intrinsic value, as the price of getting a little money. Typically, there is no longing for a cherished past, no hope for a brighter future; only the immediate present has meaning. Such a life-style derides respectability and deferred gratification. In the informal world of stratification, this lowest status is equivalent to no status. Only the formal network of courts, police, and social agencies recognize the marginal life-style by assigning its practitioners the negative statuses of criminal, hopeless alcoholic, hardened delinquent, and hard-core families.

Apparently, the marginal style occurs most often among those migrants to urban regions who lack proper cultural preparation for urban living and its system of regularized employment. Probably, a disproportionate number come from the ranks of rural Negroes, Puerto Rican migrants, or Mexican-Americans. However, many persons in these migrant streams manage to overcome marginality and become indistinguishable from older participants in other urban life-styles.

Unlike the previous life-styles, the marginal category is largely negative and barely structured.[32] It seems to encompass such overlapping subtypes as the following.

1. *Indolence-apathy*. Seeley calls this the adjusted poor because they seem to accept without bitterness or regret the barely habitable quarters and their low or irregular hourly wages.

2. *Social outcasts*. These are the practitioners of illegal or shady professions, who try to insulate themselves from the normal community by locating in the depths of urban slums (e.g., winos, hustlers, pimps, prostitutes, drug addicts). The common life-style is geared to the basic conditions of secrecy, irregular income, and the evaluation of all motives in harsh, monetary terms.

status phases and social mobility

Urban styles of life, as already suggested, form a subtle hierarchy of desirability and social opportunity, particularly in the more developed and dynamic metropolitan centers of Western nations. But a more or less explicit feature of urbanism (and modern metropolitan functioning) is the legitimate encouragement of individual and segmental improvement in life-style. Essentially, then, urban living simultaneously promotes location in a given stratum or life-style and variably potent attraction to more expansive life-styles—that is, upward social mobility. One consequence of this duality is some variability of behavior among members of a class or style of life, which tends to belie the prevalent notion that status is essentially rigid.

[32] Seeley, *op. cit.*

In recent years, stratification in urban areas has been approached more consciously as a continuous process of allocation and adaptation to available opportunities. It therefore has become necessary to link stratification and mobility by means of a series of status phases or types of perception and use of social opportunities. From scattered clues in the traditional literature of stratification, and from several exploratory studies, the following phases may be identified.[33]

1. Learning and adherence to a referential life-style—through socialization by parents, neighbors, and selected educational channels.

2. Extended or significant exposure to an alternative (and "higher") style of life—through mass media or contacts with dramatic representatives of that life-style.

3. Development of definite mobility aspirations.

4. Identification and use of one or more channels of mobility.

5. Status inconsistency as a consequence of substantial success in these channels of mobility.

6. Reduction in social affiliation with persons who practice the referential life-style.

7. Aspiration for acceptance by adherents of the desired life-style.

8. Learning the complexities of the desired life-style.

9. Validated acceptance by the responsible practitioners of the desired life-style.

Obviously, it is extremely difficult to follow a substantial number of urbanites through most or all of the status phases mentioned above. Consequently, most of the available research in urban mobility deals either with movement through two or three adjacent phases, or social mobility (expressed in occupational terms) from Phase 9 of fathers to Phase 1 of sons. Studies on three continents indicate that considerable occupational mobility is typical of urban centers and that the overall degree of such mobility has not been lessening. However, it is reasonably clear that the greatest focus of mobility is in the amorphous middle occupational status sphere.[34] This dominant pattern of mobility very probably reflects an underlying process of controlled mobility, which operates by three interrelated means.

1. Mobility aspirations, achievement motives, and deferred gratification patterns tend to be less stressed in lower status and occupational categories, as

[33] Alvin Boskoff, "Status Phases, Social Mobility, and Differential Behavior," paper given at the meetings of the American Sociological Association, September, 1965.

[34] Seymour M. Lipset and Reinhard Bendix, *Social Mobility in Industrial Society* (Berkeley, University of California Press, 1960), Chaps. II, IV; Natalie Rogoff, *Recent Trends in Occupational Mobility* (New York, The Free Press of Glencoe, 1953); D. V. Glass, ed., *Social Mobility in Britain* (London, Routledge and Kegan Paul, 1954). For an exceptional case see A. B. Hollingshead, "Trends in Social Stratification: A Case Study," *American Sociological Review*, 17 (December, 1952), pp. 686–697.

reported by several sociologists.[35] This tendency is visible in student achievement in primary and secondary schools, and in verbalized plans for further education and future jobs. In most cases, family status and values, rather than abilities or perceived opportunities, are the bases for the individual's decision "to strive or not to strive."

2. The formal educational system tends to be specifically geared to students with aspirations for mobility, or those from families that can afford the expense of a continued education. For example, appropriate academic counseling and vocational advice are more often given to students from middle status families than from lower status families. The resultant drop-out rate is, therefore, consistently higher for the latter category.[36] Likewise, college entrance and graduation largely remain the prerogative of middle and upper status categories.

3. A final limitation on opportunities for mobility is the extent of inter-marriage between urban status levels. Studies of residential propinquity and marital choice among middle status persons indicate that approximately half of these marriages involve persons from the same or very similar status levels (in terms of religion, family reputation, and occupation).[37] But what is the preponderant type of intermarriage in the remainder of urban marriages? Though the evidence is not always free of contradictions, studies in the United States and Great Britain seem to show that urban males tend to marry more often below their status level than above. In Great Britain, this pattern is particularly marked among middle and upper status males.

In recent years, considerable interest has been given to the effects of social mobility (usually measured by occupational change within or between generations) on the behavior of urbanites. Though it is often difficult to establish the time order of mobility and the behavior under study, some tentative generalizations may prove to be quite adequate.

Downward mobility—or its functional equivalent, blocked status ascent—is reflected in the following.[38]

[35] Bernard C. Rosen, "The Achievement Syndrome: A Psychocultural Dimension of Stratification," *American Sociological Review*, 21 (April, 1956), pp. 203–211; Russell R. Dynes *et al.*, "Levels of Occupational Aspiration: Some Aspects of Family Experience as a Variable," *ibid.*, pp. 212–214; William H. Sewell *et al.*, "Social Status and Educational and Occupational Aspiration," *ibid.*, 22 (February, 1957), pp. 67–73; Jackson Toby, "Orientation to Education as a Factor in the School Maladjustment of Lower-Class Children," *Social Forces*, 35 (March, 1957), pp. 259–266; Frank Bonilla, "The Urban Worker," in John J. Johnson, ed., *Continuity and Change in Latin America* (Stanford, Stanford University Press, 1964), p. 189.

[36] Lipset and Bendix, *op. cit.*, pp. 92–101, 194–197.

[37] Glass, *op. cit.*, pp. 326–328; A. B. Hollingshead, "Cultural Factors in the Selection of Marriage Mates," *American Sociological Review*, 15 (October, 1950), pp. 619–627; Richard Centers, "Occupational Endogamy in Mate Selection," *American Journal of Sociology*, 54 (May, 1949), pp. 530–535.

[38] Harold L. Wilensky and Hugh Edwards, "The Skidder: Ideological Adjustments of Downward Mobile Workers," *American Sociological Review*, 24 (April, 1959), pp. 215–231; Bruno Bettelheim and Morris Janowitz, *The Dynamics of Prejudice* (New York, Harper and Row, 1950); Fred B. Silberstein and Melvin Seeman, "Social Mobility

1. Conservative ideology about the class system.

2. Comparatively less interest in job conditions.

3. Greater emphasis on leisure as a status-compensating device or immersion in mass media and mass culture.

4. Somewhat higher levels of prejudice against minorities, if downward mobility occurs among those who value upward mobility as an end in itself.

5. Suicide—though the available evidence does not allow us to conclude that downward mobility is a major factor in male suicides.

6. Schizophrenia.

Upward mobility, on the other hand, seems to have the following consequences or accompaniments for urban categories.[39]

1. More liberal economic-political views than those in one's new status level. European data tend to support this pattern, it has been suggested, because the upwardly mobile tend to retain close contacts with their earlier status peers. Lipset, however, finds upward mobility from middle class occupations in the United States to be associated with greater conservatism (i.e., a shift from Democratic to Republican preferences).

2. With respect to fertility, the "common sense" hypothesis that mobility leads to reduced births seems unwarranted. In a study of eight large metropolitan areas in the United States, Westoff and his associates found no relation between desire for a small family and either achieved mobility or mobility aspirations. Parenthetically, they discovered religion to be more significant than class or mobility in explaining fertility differentials. Likewise, Tien did not locate a consistent pattern of reduced fertility among a sample of Australian academics who had achieved varying degrees of occupational success.[40]

3. Social participation patterns show quite varied and puzzling relations to mobility. Curtis found no relation for a Detroit sample between occupa-

and Prejudice," *American Journal of Sociology*, 65 (November, 1959), pp. 258–264; R. Jay Turner and Morton O. Wagenfeld, "Occupational Mobility and Schizophrenia: An Assessment of the Social Causation and Social Selection Hypotheses," *American Sociological Review*, 32 (February, 1967), pp. 104–113; Warren Breed, "Occupational Mobility and Suicide Among White Males," *ibid.*, 28 (April, 1963), pp. 179–188; Harold L. Wilensky, "Work, Careers, and Social Integration," in S. N. Eisenstadt, ed., *Comparative Social Problems* (New York, The Free Press, 1964), pp. 306–319.

39 Edward O. Laumann, *Prestige and Association in an Urban Community* (Indianapolis, Bobbs-Merrill, 1966), p. 144; Seymour M. Lipset and Reinhard Bendix, *Social Mobility in Industrial Society* (Berkeley, University of California Press, 1959), p. 66; Henry Valen and Daniel Katz, *Political Parties in Norway: A Community Study* (Oslo, Universitetsforlaget, 1964), p. 177.

40 Charles F. Westoff *et al.*, *Family Growth in Metropolitan America* (Princeton, Princeton University Press, 1961), p. 260; H. Y. Tien, *Social Mobility and Controlled Fertility* (New Haven, College and University Press, 1965).

tional mobility and religious observances. On the other hand, mobile persons tend to reduce their informal visiting until the age of 50, but older mobiles either fail to curtail acquaintanceships or come to resume former levels of sociability. In a more recent Atlanta study,[41] upward mobility seemed to be accompanied by less visiting with relatives (controlling for geographic location), though the differences were not statistically significant if mobility was measured against father's occupation. But intragenerational mobility (current occupation compared with occupation at marriage) did yield evidence of a significant reduction of visiting among upwardly mobile males.

1. effects of phase location as an indicator of mobility

A major problem in studying the effects of mobility is the assumption that either occupational change for a cohort of males or occupational differences between successive generations is adequate evidence of social mobility. Certainly, this is a difficult assumption to test; perhaps we must regard it as a temporary, pragmatic device. However, if we assume that the meaning of occupational affiliation varies by one's location in the status phase sequence described earlier, then we can compare (a) the behavior of the same persons in different status phases or (b) persons of the same occupational category who can be reliably classified in different status phases. The latter strategy was used in an exploratory study of suburban families in the Atlanta metropolitan region, with results that seem worthy of further specification and refinement.[42]

As might be expected, the suburban sample was largely composed of professional, managerial, and white collar occupational categories. Adequate numbers for analysis were found in only two status phases, Phase 6 (reduction in former social affiliations) and Phase 9 (validated acceptance into a desired life-style). Consequently, we compared (a) occupational categories in the same status phase and (b) status phases within the same occupational category, in terms of attitudes toward a set of proposed changes. These were the major findings.

(a) Overall, difference in status phase was substantial for white collar workers (averaging 14 percent), moderate for managerial persons (averaging 9 percent), and quite small for professionals (averaging 3 percent).

(b) For seven issues, differences between status phases were significant in three, while occupational differences were significant in only one issue.

(c) In general, status phase differences were significant on issues dealing with local community affairs, while occupational differences were more marked on larger political issues.

(d) Greater acceptance of change was found in Status Phase 9 among

---

[41] Unpublished paper.

[42] Linda L. Wilock, *Status Phase Location and Differential Attitudes and Behavior* (M.A. Thesis, Department of Sociology, Emory University, 1967).

professionals and white collar respondents. Conversely, managers were more open to change in Phase 6. By implication, then, mobility seemed to produce greater conservatism among managers, greater liberalism among white collar workers, and to a smaller extent, among professionals.

2. decline of class conflicts

Though there are obvious differences in life-style and interests between urban status categories, it is very significant (but not so obvious) that class conflicts are becoming less frequent and less bitter than in previous urban waves, or even as recently as 40 years ago in England, 25 years ago in the United States.[43] An apparent exception is labor-management difficulties in the form of strikes, lockouts, etc. Yet industrial disputes are more often settled by bargaining than by violence or serious threats of violence.[44] Even the hostile statements of labor and industrial leaders seem to be more for newspapers than for one another.

On the whole, however, urban stratification in operation (not in theory) has simultaneously raised invisible status boundaries and yet muted conflicts by a prevalent ideology of mobility. In general, urbanites accept the mixture of fluidity and rigidity in the status realm; they seem to reserve their hostility for individuals at any status level who practice snobbery (i.e., who over-emphasize distinctions in a personal manner) or who strive for ascent with "indecent" speed and with inadequate cultural preparation ("he thinks money can buy anything"). Urbanites have come to concern themselves more with security and comfort than with power differences and historical issues of exploitation. Perhaps this shift in attention reflects an era of prosperity and inflation, and greater ease in status imitation.

3. poverty, race, and protest

On the other hand, it is impossible to ignore the concentrated phenomena of organized and semi-organized protest and violence in urban areas since about 1964.[45] Clearly, these represent frustration with formally available but practically unattainable opportunities for upward mobility in the visible chan-

---

[43] For an interesting theory of the mutual opposition of class conflicts and racial conflicts, see Theodore W. Sprague, "The Rivalry of Intolerances in Race Relations," *Social Forces*, 28 (October, 1949), pp. 68–76.

[44] Arthur Kornhauser *et al.*, eds., *Industrial Conflict* (New York, McGraw-Hill, 1954); William F. Whyte, *Pattern for Industrial Peace* (New York, Harper and Row, 1951); Neil H. Chamberlain, *Social Responsibility and Strikes* (New York, Harper and Row, 1953); Joseph Shister and William Hamovitch, *Conflict and Stability in Labor Relations* (Buffalo, Department of Industrial Relations, University of Buffalo, 1952).

[45] See Arnold M. Rose, ed., "The Negro Protest," *Annals of the American Academy of Political and Social Science* (January, 1965); Raymond J. Murphy and Howard Elinson, eds., *Problems and Prospects of the Negro Movement* (Belmont, Calif., Wadsworth, 1966), Part 3.

nels of housing, education, and occupation. Likewise, these activities may be regarded as a new form of conflict between the resigned-alienated and the consummatory and striving urban life-styles. But the conflict is not wholly one of life-styles. Clearly, white members of the resigned-alienated category are not conspicuously involved in such protests. Negroes have recently developed a racial ideology of mobility that appeals to selected portions of urban Negroes—in particular, to those who have not clearly adopted any of the low status life-styles described in preceding pages.

At this point in our knowledge, urban Negro protests seem to be fragmented into at least four components. First and oldest is the legalistic approach of the NAACP and the Urban League, which represent consummatory, striving, and derivative-vicarious segments. A second form is the Black Muslim movement, whose ideology of violence and Negro revolution is largely verbal and whose appeal is difficult to trace. However, recent migrants from rural areas seem to be a major source of adherents. Third, there is the symbolic, nonviolent protest of the Southern Christian Leadership Conference (SCLC), formed and led by Martin Luther King, Jr., who was assassinated in Memphis on April 4, 1968. Despite its growth and success, we are unable to specify with any accuracy its major sources of support. Finally, we can identify semi-organized and unorganized expressions of "black power," expressed either in threats or calls for violence, or in actual, variably developed incidents of destruction, looting, and killing (e.g., Watts, Newark, Milwaukee).

From the comparatively slight evidence now available,[46] the more consistent protests among Negroes in cities stem from striving (and at least partly successful striving), moderately well-educated and employed Negroes. On the other hand, among those who are unemployed or earn very meager wages, and among those whose jobs and educational levels are consistent with one another, a resignation-alienation life-style seems to prevail. Generally, the latter category of urban Negroes either eschews militance or is involved in isolated, fitful incidents of unpremeditated violence or disturbance. In short, life-style differences among urban Negroes may well be closely related to the form and intensity of racial status conflicts in contemporary urban areas.

4. the role of spatial segregation

As we have previously noted, urban stratification is increasingly accompanied by residential segregation of status spheres. Contacts between status levels seem to be largely temporary, impersonal, and indirect. It is quite likely that this degree of social insulation helps to diminish status conflicts by minimizing personal frictions and frustrations. But such an arrangement is rapidly erasing a sense of community, which is at best difficult to sustain in

[46] Gary T. Marx, *Protest and Prejudice* (New York, Harper and Row, 1967), pp. 59–61, 118.

such a large, complex entity as the urban region.[47] The insularity and provincialism of many urbanites is by now well known; knowledge of other communities is distorted by ignorance, prejudice, and the attractive inaccuracies of films and other mass media. Even more striking to the social scientist and public administrator, however, is the urbanite's immersion in purely local neighborhood affairs and their relation to a specific style of life (e.g., suburban middle class segments). Los Angeles was once facetiously defined by J. B. Priestley as "six suburbs in search of a city." The modern urban region, especially in the United States, might well be defined—though not so humorously—as "a fumbling metropolis deserted by dozens of 'independent' localities hopefully searching for private Utopias." Consequently, a latent result of urban stratification is an added intensification of problems of coordinating developments and devising workable planning programs for urban regions.

[47] Good discussions and evidence for this phenomenon can be found in: C. Wright Mills, *The Sociological Imagination* (New York, Oxford University Press, 1959), pp. 172–173; Morton Grodzins, *The Metropolitan Area as a Racial Problem* (Pittsburgh, University of Pittsburgh Press, 1958); Morton Grodzins, "The New Shame of the Cities," *Confluence*, 7 (1958), pp. 29–46; John M. Foskett, "The Influence of Social Participation on Community Programs and Activities," in Marvin B. Sussman, ed., *Community Structure and Analysis* (New York, Thomas Y. Crowell, 1959), pp. 311–330.

selected references

BARBER, Bernard, *Social Stratification* (New York, Harcourt, Brace and World, 1957).

BAZELON, David T., *Power in America: The Politics of the New Class* (New York, New American Library, 1967).

FERMAN, Louis *et al.*, eds., *Poverty in America* (Ann Arbor, University of Michigan Press, 1965).

GLASS, D. V., ed., *Social Mobility in Britain* (London, Routledge and Kegan Paul, 1954).

HOLLINGSHEAD, A. B. and REDLICH, Fritz, *Social Class and Mental Illness* (New York, John Wiley and Sons, 1958).

KAHL, Joseph A., *The American Class Structure* (New York, Holt, Rinehart and Winston, 1957).

KAHL, Joseph A., ed., *Comparative Perspectives on Stratification: Mexico, Great Britain, Japan* (Boston, Little, Brown, 1968).

LIPSET, Seymour M. and BENDIX, Reinhard, *Social Mobility in Industrial Society* (Berkeley, University of California Press, 1959).

LYND, Robert S. and LYND, Helen M., *Middletown in Transition* (New York, Harcourt, Brace and World, 1939).

McKINLEY, Donald G., *Social Class and Family Life* (New York, The Free Press, 1964).

PORTER, John, *The Vertical Mosaic: An Analysis of Social Class and Power in Canada* (Toronto, University of Toronto Press, 1965).

REISS, Albert J., *Occupations and Social Status* (New York, The Free Press, 1961).

SHOSTAK, Arthur B. and GOMBERG, William, eds., *Blue-Collar World: Studies of the American Worker* (Englewood Cliffs, N.J., Prentice-Hall, 1964).

WARNER, W. Lloyd and LUNT, Paul S., *The Social Life of a Modern Community* (New Haven, Yale University Press, 1941).

WARNER, W. Lloyd *et al.*, *Social Class in America* (New York, Harper Torchbooks, 1960).

12

urban power structure: decision making on public issues

In the last chapter, social stratification was primarily viewed in an analytical way, that is, in terms of its differentiated parts or segments. Consequently, our focus tended to be on the more private aspects of urban stratification. However, to the extent that we can reliably identify a system of stratification, we would expect to find (1) some patterns of coordination among social strata and (2) reflection of this coordination in public or community concerns. Indeed the relation between the public and private aspects or expression of stratification has generated a good deal of useful controversy among social scientists, under the vivid label of "community power structure."

As an introduction to this very live issue, several rather obvious but important points merit some attention. First, urban areas, or communities that are becoming urbanized, necessarily face many varied practical problems, which relate to the entire population or a significant portion of that population. Second, normal processes of community change and development (economic, political, etc.) contribute additional problems or intensification of existing ones. Third, and likewise normal, urban areas encourage a high degree of specialization and heterogeneity among their residents. Consequently, we can expect highly variable concern for identifiable urban problems and, when widespread interest in a specific problem develops, some sharp differences about the definition and resolution of that problem.

Urban areas, therefore, are notable as arenas for experimental attempts to develop adequate forms of responsible and responsive leadership on community issues. But these forms seem to be wrought out of experience with three major kinds of dimensions.[1]

[1] See Karl W. Deutsch and Hermann Weilenman, "The Swiss City Canton: A Political Invention," *Comparative Studies in Society and History*, 7 (July, 1965), pp. 393–408.

1. *Types of issues or problems,* particularly with respect to their urgency, technical feasibility, moral or evaluational significance, costs.

2. *Dominant characteristics of decision makers,* such as official or unofficial status, social class background, length of residence in the area.

3. *Patterns of support for decision makers,* the groups or categories which are formally or tacitly allied with decision makers on some range of interests.

Since we have already distinguished three major historical types of urban complexity (the three urban waves discussed on pp. 15–25), it may be helpful to review the ways in which earlier urban areas devised leadership structures from these three dimensions. Thanks to the diligent and creative work of such historians as Pirenne, Petit-Dutaillis, Lestocquoy, Glotz, Thrupp, Pernoud, Bridenbaugh, and Bloch, we may characterize the classical and medieval forerunners of contemporary urban decision making with some confidence.

ancient or classical power structures [2]

During the first urban wave, towns and cities were principalities rather than municipalities. Their location and structure stressed defense from aggressors and marauders. Military prowess, coupled with religious virtuosity, identified leading families as worthy of office and decisive prestige. These patricians dominated the councils, proclaimed the laws, and determined participation in community affairs and ceremonials. With the growth of highly profitable trade, formerly weak or unclassed persons often achieved new prestige, and wherever permitted, election to public office. These new men were variably successful in acquiring power. In Greece and Rome, they gradually displaced or infiltrated the segregated ranks of the patrician families. On numerous occasions in Greek cities the heated contests between aristocrats and *nouveaux riches* ended in the exile of leading patricians and the imposition of a tyranny. The tyrants usually took an antiaristocratic viewpoint; they tended to favor lower strata, the encouragement of commerce, and the arts, as well as relations with other urban areas.

In general, a limited number of issues or problems were prominent in urban centers of the first wave. Adequate defense and the advisability of war with other cities constitute one recurring theme. A second urban issue of importance was continuity and change in community religious observances, particularly in Greek and Roman cities. Third, such economic problems as

[2] Fustel de Coulanges, *The Ancient City* (Garden City, Doubleday; orig. ed., 1864) ; Max Weber, *The City,* tr. by Don Martindale and Gertrud Neuwirth (New York, The Free Press, 1958) ; Max Weber, *General Economic History* (New York, The Free Press, 1950), pp. 320–321; A. Andrewes, *The Greek Tyrants* (London, Hutchinson's University Library, 1956).

taxation and the handling of debtor categories were particularly sore matters for political resolution. Finally, and perhaps an issue that modern urbanites find incomprehensible, ancient cities often wrestled with the desirability and specific application of official ostracism or exile for alleged enemies of the community. Greece was especially involved in this kind of problem, though a few medieval cities (Florence and Ypres in the 14th century) seem to have revived a similar device for alternately settling and generating urban difficulties.

In retrospect, classical cities produced few types of coalitions in community decision making. Portions of the landed aristocracy engaged in trade and collaborated with the new rich (merchants) in support of the tyrant against the old aristocracy. The latter often left their cities to foment interurban wars, thereby hoping to remove the tyrant. On the other hand, Greek tyrants intermarried with one another, thus creating strong external supports for specific ruling cliques. However, the tyrant (who was usually a renegade aristocrat) was ultimately succeeded in Greece by the demagogue, who was (or directly represented) an artisan or a minor merchant determined to diminish the political role of the wealthy landed class. Thus the demagogue sponsored numerous (and probably unnecessary) wars for the benefit of traders, sailors, and craftsmen.

medieval urban power structures

The medieval town was largely a European phenomenon of the period 900–1700 A.D., though some of its characteristics developed in Far Eastern cities as late as 1500 to 1900. Essentially, medieval towns represented the fruits of regional and international commerce, with the consequent addition of new and highly organized social categories to the urban polity. The major theme, however, was the decided shift from landed nobility and ecclesiastical influence to a constantly challenged dominance of wealthy, aggressive merchant families.

In the early phases of medieval town development (*ca.* 900–1200), merchants acquired power by organizing themselves as pressure groups, interceding in the selection of officials wherever possible and influencing public policies by the solidity of their accomplishments and by collective protests against arbitrary actions or ordinances. Venice is one of the earliest instances of a ruling merchant family (11th century), which was succeeded by five centuries of a caste-like mercantile aristocracy. But the period 1300–1500 was one of complex and somewhat confusing struggles for urban power.[3]

[3] Henri Pirenne, *Les Villes et les institutions urbaines* (Paris, Alcan, 1939), Vol. 1, pp. 55–58, and *Early Democracies in the Low Countries* (New York, Harper Torchbooks,

In Italian towns and cities, the older, established merchant families opposed the *nouveaux riches* and likewise one another. Florence, for example, was a 14th-century battleground between patricians and *nuovo gente* (the newly rich); the former supporting the Pope, while the latter constructed temporary alliances with artisans and small merchants, and supported the Ghibelline cause. Meanwhile, in Britain and France, wealthy merchants were supported by the Crown or by powerful dukes. The bourgeoisie, which had been sorely limited by legal experts representing the State, gradually and with the aid of bloodshed, developed a captive salaried officialdom (the "nobility of the robe"), which was generally well disposed to the rich merchants on such matters as taxation and freedom from government interference or control.[4] In the Low Countries, merchants established rather tight controls over land use and public works projects.

By the early 14th century, particularly in Italian and Belgian towns, workers and artisans had migrated in great numbers, thereby adding both new urban problems and a new element to the structure of urban power. In Venice, the workers were unorganized and politically apathetic; but in Florence, they were involved in continued rebellions (master-minded by dissident merchant families) against an entrenched merchant oligarchy.[5] However, in England, Belgium, and Germany, the development of the guild form, for merchants, producers, and craftsmen, tended to dispel the potential strength of dependent, semiskilled workers, while multiplying the opportunities for internal divisions and alliances within the entrepreneurial ranks.

The guilds were specialized power centers which were designed to protect the economic interests of each craft or type of merchandise. Community decisions, therefore, were made by the elected or appointed officials. But each guild legislated its own rules as to training, prices, labor supply, and welfare services to its members. On the other hand, specialization did not produce equality; guilds were involved in jealous competitions for prestige and influence, based on their relative size, age, and wealth.[6]

Ultimately, the industrial and commercial success of the towns became

1963; orig. ed., 1915); J. Lestocquoy, *Les Villes de Flandre et d'Italie* (Paris, PUF, 1952); Charles Petit-Dutaillis, *Les Communes françaises* (Paris, Albin Michel, 1947).

[4] James Cushman Davis, *The Decline of the Venetian Nobility as a Ruling Class* (Baltimore, Johns Hopkins Press, 1962); Gene A. Brucker, *Florentine Politics and Society 1343–1378* (Princeton, Princeton University Press, 1962); Nicolai Rubinstein, *The Government of Florence Under the Medici 1434 to 1494* (Oxford, at the Clarendon Press, 1966); Marc Bloch, *La France sous les derniers Capétiens 1223–1328* (Paris Armand Colin, 1958); Régine Pernoud, *Les Villes merchandes aux XIV et XV siècles* (Paris, Editions de la Table Ronde, 1948); David Herlihy, *Pisa in the Early Renaissance* (New Haven, Yale University Press, 1958).

[5] Lestocquoy, *op. cit.*, pp. 133–134; Régine Pernoud, *Les Origines de la bourgeoisie* (Paris, PUF, 1947), pp. 26–48; Gwyn A. Williams, *Medieval London* (London, Athlone Press, 1963), pp. 264–307.

[6] Williams, *op. cit.*, Chap. 6; Stella Kramer, *The English Craft Guilds* (New York, Columbia University Press, 1927); Pirenne, *Early Democracies*, pp. 176–177; Gerald Strauss, *Nuremberg in the Sixteenth Century* (New York, Wiley, 1966), pp. 97, 107, 123.

the key to the dissolution of the guilds and the end of urban autonomy. In France, England, and Belgium, the towns entered into a symbiotic relationship with the monarchy, exchanging financial support for the continued prestige and power of wealthy merchants and financiers. The 16th–18th centuries, therefore, were marked by internal dissension that was not well channeled, as well as by instances of royal interference in town affairs.[7] Perhaps the focus of urban problems was the restive, relatively young bourgeoisie, who in France writhed under the imposed bureaucracy of the king and the acquiescence of the local establishment. By translating their difficulties into the more general problem of liberty and wider opportunities, the urban bourgeoisie obtained support from artisans and laborers in public protests, local rebellions, and organized revolution. With the rise and maturation of industrialism and modern capitalism, the revival of internal urban issues was assured, since earlier leadership and alliance patterns were found to be unequal to the demands of rapidly expanding cities.

This admittedly oversimplified review of the vicissitudes of urban power structures should lead us to expect both complexity and change in patterns of decision making for cities that exemplify the third wave of urban development. Clearly, then, urban power structures can be profitably analyzed and interpreted only by taking account of: (1) the relative independence of larger social systems (state, province, national government); (2) the kinds of changes—internal or external—to which the urban area must adjust; and (3) the demographic and social composition of a city or urban region (for clues about potential leaders and coalitions).

But we must make explicit the phenomena to which the term community power structure applies. As currently used, community power structure refers to a presumed network of persons who can be identified as locating, resolving, and controlling the implementation of solutions to issues that affect a significant portion of an identifiable community or region. This conceptualization assumes that the three major aspects of power are principally determined by elites, influentials, and dominants, and that their actions either overcome any substantial resistance or acquire minimal levels of support from relevant categories in the community.

patternings of contemporary urban power

In the U.S., decision making in urban areas has been largely studied from the standpoint of the relative influence of elected and appointed officials and unofficial economic leaders. One commentator has concluded that studies by political scientists tend to emphasize official power, while investigations by

[7] Petit-Dutaillis, *op. cit.*, p. 341.

sociologists seem to focus on the effectiveness of economic elites.[8] The evidence, however, is far from unambiguous. Yet some tentative patterns may be identified.

1. In general, urban areas reflect experiments in devising workable combinations or compensatory dominance patterns for given time periods. An implicit theme in most studies of urban power is the relative competence and willingness of key individuals and groups to raise and/or direct the resolution of public issues. We may then distinguish four components of community leadership (see Fig. 14).

figure 14

Types of Power Structure

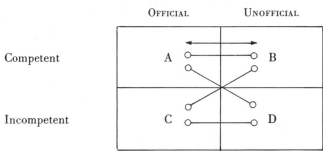

Descriptively, several combinations of these components may be noted.

(a) BC (the community power structure) represents legally or personally weak officialdom, whose role in decision making is performed by one or more knowledgeable and/or economically significant categories.

(b) AD (official power structure), the reverse of BC, is found where the mayor or city manager or city councilmen (or some combination) are skilled practitioners of legal responsibilities and the derived powers of official status. In addition, potential sources of alternative power (e.g., economic dominants) are either uninterested in many public issues or are internally divided so that effective, coordinated influence cannot be generated or sustained.

(c) AB is somewhat rare, if not practically improbable, in joining the talents and interests of career officials and strategically placed local elites.

(d) A↔B represents a struggle for power between official and unofficial leaders who differ on either identification of important issues or on

8 John Walton, "Substance and Artifact: The Current Status of Research on Community Power Structure," *American Journal of Sociology*, 71 (January, 1966), pp. 430–438; John Walton, "Discipline, Method, and Community Power: A Note on the Sociology of Knowledge," *American Sociological Review*, 31 (October, 1966), pp. 684–689.

means of providing appropriate solutions. Experience would seem to indicate that this type cannot long endure in most urban areas.

(e) Likewise rare or temporary is CD, which reflects a stagnant community in which neither officials nor private influentials are able to address themselves to a set of current issues.

2. With few exceptions, BC tends to appear either in smaller cities, industrially specialized cities, or in large cities that are relatively recent entrants into the category of complex, modern urban facilities and services. In these cities, apparently, the recruitment process does not typically attract or hold experienced and forceful officials. Consequently, the power vacuum is filled by elites who combine expertise with an acquired responsibility for urban progress.

3. However, one of the persistent findings in urban areas characterized by BC power structure is a tendency toward specialization in the influence of unofficial elites. As illustrated in studies in Syracuse, New Haven, Wichita, and Lansing, different types of issues stimulate high levels of interest in different occupational categories or geographic segments. In addition, specialized knowledge or experience on particular issues tends to induce a crucial advantage in decision making for each category of "experts." Thus, educational questions are often determined by school administrations, or PTAs, while physicians dominate in health issues, and downtown business groups are most effective on matters of transportation, parking, and taxation.

4. Few studies provide a sufficient historical breadth to determine the persistence or alteration of urban power patterns.[9] However, data from New Haven, the New York Metropolitan area, several Florida towns, and El Paso indicate that three factors affect the operation of preexisting power structures. Most obviously, changes in urban ethnic composition as a consequence of in-migration may result in intergroup competition and declining effectiveness of unofficial elites. In addition, recruitment to the unofficial elite tends to give more prominence to representatives of migrant categories (cf. Boston, New Haven). Second, significant change in urban government structure, particularly in methods of electing officials, can erode preexisting patterns of power. For example, election on a ward basis seems to interfere with the persistence of an effective official elite, except as a delaying or obstructive mechanism in public decision making. At the same time, a shift to or from ward elections alters the opportunities of economic dominants and/or specialized interest groups for claiming or acquiring widespread popular support. Finally, as Wood suggests,[10] increasing complexity in urbanization is accompanied by a greater number of perceived needs and an appreciable rise in public expenditures. These in turn multiply the number of issues and magnify competition in decision making among interested and capable private groups. In effect, then, urban expansion stimulates greater specialization of interest

[9] Robert A. Dahl, *Who Governs?* (New Haven, Yale University Press, 1961), Book I.
[10] Robert C. Wood, *1400 Governments* (Garden City, Doubleday, 1964), p. 48.

in community and regional isues and also strengthens the power position of officials, whose access to public funds (increasingly from federal agencies) enhances their ability to raise and resolve issues.

5. If we define an issue as a situation in which a decision is delayed by disagreement or controversy, then it is clear that relatively few matters for decision arouse either widespread interest or focused dissent. In smaller cities, few problems are controversial for any large segment of the population. Under these circumstances, power (whether by officials or unofficial elites) operates by default rather than by persuasion or imposition. Indeed, as several studies have shown, migration of middle and upper class persons to suburbs and fringe areas of urban regions tends to reduce the number and importance of core city issues. During the past decade, perhaps the most visible issues have been urban renewal, public housing for Negroes, annexation, and the suggestion of some form of semi-metropolitan consolidation of services, and most recently, rapid transit systems.[11] We may tentatively conclude that these issues favor official rather than unofficial elites, primarily because the evolving character of urban official roles tends to cause selection of persons (or advisors) who are competent to deal with complex data, massive sums, and the intricacies of local and federal bureaucratic channels.

6. Decision making in modern urban regions is neither random, chaotic, nor simply structured in power pyramids. It is instead a shifting resultant of achievements and resistances in five key processes.

(a) *Acquisition of power potential.* The opportunity to exercise power hinges on access to strategic positions, either through election to public office or through transferable prestige derived from achievements in some valued activity (industry, commerce, the high status professions, community service, or dedicated party work). Normally, selection of candidates for office reflects the preexisting patterning of power, but we must also recognize the continual possibility of political upsets or realignments, as these develop from party struggles and the changing social and ethnic composition of electorates. Achievements tend to point persons toward power when success occurs in activities that presumably involve numerous decisions affecting many persons (i.e., business).

(b) *Evaluation of power potential.* As some ethnographic data demonstrate,[12] opportunity for power does not necessarily produce desire to exploit power. In the case of urban economic elites (based on key organizational

---

[11] Henry J. Schmandt et al., *Metropolitan Reform in St. Louis: A Case Study* (New York, Holt, Rinehart and Winston, 1961); Harold Kaplan, *Urban Renewal Politics* (New York, Columbia University Press, 1963); Gladys M. Kammerer et al., *The Urban Political Community* (Boston, Houghton Mifflin, 1963); Oliver P. Williams et al., *Suburban Differences and Metropolitan Policies* (Philadelphia, University of Pennsylvania Press, 1965); Frank Smallwood, *Greater London: The Politics of Metropolitan Reform* (Indianapolis, Bobbs-Merrill, 1965).

[12] Cf. Margaret Mead, *Sex and Temperament in Three Primitive Societies* (New York, Mentor Books, 1950), Part I.

position, profits, etc.), a focus on power may compete with either continued social mobility (acceptance and participation among high status persons) or further economic achievement, or both. There is some evidence that locally raised economic elites (as compared with temporary or outsider categories of business leaders) are more likely to subordinate marginal additions to economic and social success to the satisfaction (whether selfish or benevolent) of determining community policies.[13] But legitimate mobility for officials lies only in seeking greater effectiveness in controlling policy. Obviously, too, reelection, reappointment, or the achievement of civil service tenure serves to reinforce and embellish decision-making capabilities.

(c) *Contacts and control of other dominants.* In the normal situation of diffusive power, a particularly significant mechanism of power is the ability to influence either the selection or the behavior of collateral power holders (either in official positions or private elites). Thus, Williams and Adrian noted that the economic elite maintained its influence in a middle-sized city by controlling the nomination of city councilmen. In Milwaukee, civic notables persuaded the governor to appoint a prestigious committee to investigate metropolitan water problems, thereby shifting the locus of decisions from local officialdom. However, this committee ultimately failed because it had no direct link with or influence over the center of official power, despite considerable support from commercial and industrial leaders. As reported by Kweder in his study of North Carolina cities, though city councilmen receive virtually no pressure from organized interest groups, councilmen admit that they are attentive to the known attitudes of influential citizens.[14]

(d) *Selection of issues.* In general, the responsibility for selecting urban issues more often rests with official leaders—particularly in larger cities and in cities where party competition and heterogeneity of population are found.[15] Though the evidence is far from clear on this point, most issues (i.e., questions concerning either routine decisions or future action) seem to be initially defined by an interest group that obtains the support of some unofficial leader. Usually, the unofficial elite informally sounds out strategic officials before exposing the issue to public scrutiny and possible attack. Failure to secure initial clearance indicates either prevailing subservience of public

[13] Dahl, *op. cit.*; M. Kent Jennings, *Community Influentials* (New York, The Free Press, 1964).

[14] Henry J. Schmandt, *The Milwaukee Metropolitan Study Commission* (Bloomington, Indiana University Press, 1965), p. 244; Oliver P. Williams and Charles R. Adrian, *Four Cities: A Study in Comparative Policy Making* (Philadelphia, University Press, 1963); B. James Kweder, *The Roles of the Manager, Mayor, and Councilmen in Policy Making* (Chapel Hill, Institute of Government, University of North Carolina, 1965), pp. 56–87.

[15] Edward C. Banfield, *Political Influence* (New York, The Free Press, 1961); Peter H. Rossi, "Power and Community Structure," in Edward C. Banfield, ed., *Urban Government* (New York, The Free Press, 1961), pp. 413–422. Cf. the findings in Carol E. Thometz, *The Decision-Makers: The Power Structure of Dallas* (Dallas, Southern Methodist University Press, 1963); Jack Langguth, "Group of Businessmen Rules Dallas Without a Mandate from the Voters," *The New York Times*, January 19, 1964.

leaders, or audacity on the part of an essentially peripheral or marginal leader. For example, the president of the private bus system in a southern metropolis recently submitted a plan for temporary rapid transit, using specially designed bus routes. But he had neglected to discuss the possible merits of his solution with relevant public officials or with key members of the unofficial elite in the Rapid Transit Committee. Consequently, the issue of rapid transit by bus was quickly defined as impractical and prohibitively expensive—a very complex technical judgment after two weeks of deliberation.

As Banfield and others have indicated, the profusion of problems, dissatisfactions, segmental needs, etc. overloads the decision-making potentialities of the urban region; the multiplicity of perceived difficulties and unsolicited solutions in effect mutes the significance of many of these competitive calls for action. This situation allows canny officials to ignore many issues, to control the appearance of those issues that cannot be ignored, and then to manage the rhythm by which a given issue develops.

(e) *Prosecution of issues.* Once an issue has been permitted the dignity of open discussion and reporting, specific mechanisms of power and influence tend to follow. In urban areas where economic dominants are key decision makers (such as Dallas), initial solutions usually come from lower echelons of business and professional leaders, whose major role is to transmit ideas to one or a few strategic members of a more or less informal private or nonelected elite. Then a study committee, appointed by a single top influential, analyzes the issue and the desirability of the suggested solution. When a definite recommendation is achieved, it is widely and deftly publicized in the mass media, thereby providing for preliminary sanctification and the illusion of popular support. Thereafter, the sponsoring top influential places his "favorite" project before his power peers for complementary support and for mobilizing relevant financial and technical means.[16] Because the private elite is an informal cluster of peers with differing interests, the sponsoring influential is assured moral and financial backing in return for subsequent support of other policies by other members of the elite. With this effective elimination of practical obstacles, the implementation of a policy decision proceeds by communicating the policy and its operational forms (specific programs, sources of financing, cooperation of specific strategic groups) to appropriate officials (mayor, city council). In the face of deliberate and responsible study, assured financing, and favorable publicity, officials may extend the period of debate, but usually offer their legal blessing to the new program.

Clearly, the pattern just described is an exceptional one. In large cities and in the organizational stage at which major sources of financing are in state and federal agencies, the balance of power and the techniques of decision making are somewhat more complex. The most important considera-

16 Thometz, *op. cit.*, pp. 60–69.

tion here is the fact that official leaders generally abhor the necessity of positive decision making, simply because such decisions threaten their exalted position by stimulating conflict and resistance. Consequently, official leaders confront issues by: first, procrastination and postponement, as long as possible; and second, by selecting prestigious individuals (from business, professional and civic groups) to serve as proponents and buffers against potential or actual opposition. Skill in decision making lies in determining which issues cannot be safely ignored and in recruiting appropriate civic influentials to either represent official viewpoints or to counter insistent demands for positive action. Power, then, involves manipulation of conflicting sources of power and influence.[17]

However, on issues for which official leaders seek to make definite policy commitments, several techniques may be identified. First, and increasingly important, is developing expertise in applying for extralocal sources of massive public funds (state and federal). Since such funds are legally expended only by public bodies or officials, an unassailable form of monopoly works to the advantage of officials. Second, the prevalent lack of coordination among economic elites, because of differing interests or differing levels of commitment to the community or region, allows capable officials to initiate lines of action (publicity, coalitions with other officials) without effective interference from specific businessmen, labor leaders, bankers, prominent old-line families, or vocal professionals. Third, public officials can utilize the data-gathering and scholarly interpretive services of private research organizations to bolster their policy conclusions on almost any issue.[18] In some cases, a similar role is played by such public research and advisory organizations as metropolitan planning commissions. And it has been suggested that, over periods of time, public officials may become quite dependent on the research organization, so much so that research administrators can inadvertently or consciously affect official decisions on given issues.

It is important to recognize that decision making requires few direct indications of support from the urban electorate. The referendum and the special bond issue are dramatic confrontations between power structures and citizens, but these are notable for their infrequency and the fact that officials largely determine when popular response to decisions can be made.

However, we have a limited number of studies that suggest explanations of both successful and unsuccessful attempts to obtain popular legitimation of official decisions. These studies suggest that only a limited range of issues is presented to the voter of metropolitan regions: school bonds (and bond issues for physical facilities); annexation; basic organizational change (such as metropolitan government); and such emotional issues as fluoridation and

---

[17] Banfield, *Political Influence*, p. 276; Wallace Sayre and Herbert Kaufman, *Governing New York City* (New York, Russell Sage Foundation, 1960).

[18] Edward F. Cooke, "Research: An Instrument of Political Power," *Political Science Quarterly*, 76 (March, 1961), pp. 69–87.

fair or open housing ordinances. Two or three general conclusions may be tentatively drawn about the implementation of power structure.

1. The greater the difference in status (occupational types and education, age, ethnic background) between elites and voters, the greater the probability of rejection of referenda or bond issues. For example, school bonds tend to be voted down in blue collar and rural-oriented constituencies.[19] In a recent study of a multipurpose bond issue in a suburban county near Atlanta, the highest levels of voter support came from those with higher incomes, those residing in urban and suburban portions as against those in fringe and rural areas, and those with higher perceived status.[20]

2. Voter turnout is an intriguing but not always predictable aspect of local power structuring. In general, the type of issue tends to attract voters from relevant portions of the community and disinterest other segments. It is quite clear that many referenda and bond issues are of primary interest to middle and moderately educated persons, while low income persons tend to avoid the polls unless there is a highly emotional and controversial matter at hand.[21] In the latter case, a higher than expected turnout may mean increased participation from lower status categories, with the consequence that the middle class viewpoint will be defeated (or narrowly avoid defeat).

3. By their ability to select issues for presentation to the voters, official and/or unofficial leaders affect the character of voter response. In other words, given a middle class issue (e.g., school bond issues for expanded facilities) and a substantial middle class electorate, a positive vote is assured without the need of complex processes of persuasion from decision makers. But if inordinate lethargy among middle class residents develops or any incident converts the issue from a routine to a sensational level, then the outcome may be uncertain.

Various descriptive clues in the literature indicate that the power of decision makers often hinges on the supportive efforts of specialized voluntary groups, whose major function is to activate the preexistent interests of middle status categories. Perhaps this explains the contemporary difficulty of effective decision making by official leaders. For, in general, official leaders possess little control over these intermediary voluntary associations (e.g., PTAs, Chambers of Commerce, Negro political associations, "good government" leagues). Unofficial leaders, on the other hand, usually maintain close contact with local businesses, professionals, or interest groups; indeed, they often sharpen their ability to handle issues by considerable periods of past and pres-

[19] Gary King et al., Conflict Over Schools (E. Lansing, Institute for Community Development and Services, Michigan State University, 1963); Richard F. Carter and William G. Savard, Influence of Voter Turnout on School Board and Tax Elections (Washington, D.C., Office of Education, Cooperative Research Monograph #5, 1961).

[20] Alvin Boskoff and Harmon Zeigler, Voting Patterns in a Local Election (Philadelphia, Lippincott, 1964), Chap. 3.

[21] Williams and Adrian, op. cit., p. 224; George Taylor, "Bond Issues Pass in the Big Cities," The Atlanta Constitution, November 9, 1967.

ent membership in such groups. Therefore, the structural basis of unofficial leadership must be seriously noted, if positive decision making is to be explained in the urban setting.

To what extent are these features of urban power systems unique to the U.S.? Urban areas are clearly affected by the larger political and economic setting in which they grow and confront the problems of development. Specifically, we would expect international differences in power structures as an accompaniment of variations in federal or state control, recency of national independence, rate of economic growth, and composition and rate of urbanward migration streams. There is a growing fund of comparative studies, often not directly addressed to this problem, which suggest the following kinds of variation from American experience.

1. In most European, Latin American, African and Asian cities, official leaders are in firm control of the decision-making processes described in the preceding pages. To a large extent, this form of dominance derives from centralized national governments and the development of federally selected local bureaucracies.[22] The familiar phenomena of influential businessmen and related professionals are relatively absent, either because these social categories have not yet emerged in sufficient strength (as in the case of under-developed nations) or because previously dominant elites (the gentry, certain merchant families, etc.) have been unequal to the administrative demands of modern urban systems. For example, in the Liverpool-Manchester area, local leadership has visibly shifted from old prestigious categories (the gentry) to persons trained in practical politics and the administrative professions.[23]

2. Though there is much evidence of specialized voluntary associations in urban areas throughout the world, a careful analysis of these groups indicates that they are predominantly ethnic or expressive in orientation. Newer African cities, for example, are marked by voluntary association of a tribal character or by athletic and recreational pursuits.[24] Thus few private organizations have political impact on their respective communities. Where potentially influential groups do exist (e.g., labor unions, professional societies, trade associations), the impact of a dominant national political party and the expertise of urban administrators tend to limit the role of interest groups to protests of decisions rather than participation in the formulation of decisions.

The exceptions to this generalization are instructive; they occur mainly in highly developed nations (Canada, Great Britain), where technical and

---

22 See for example: A. Banani, *The Modernization of Iran, 1921–1941* (Stanford, Stanford University Press, 1961); Leonard Binder, ed., *Politics in Lebanon* (New York, Wiley, 1966); K. H. Silvert, *The Conflict Society* (New York, American Universities Field Staff, 1966).

23 J. M. Lee, *Social Leaders and Public Persons* (Oxford, at the Clarendon Press, 1963).

24 See Chapter 10.

economic advances have not been determined by formal political systems. In English cities, for example, decision making seems to be a fluid process of debate and supplementation among city officials, businessmen, and labor leaders.[25] Miller's study of "English City" (population about 500,000, in the western part of England) also concludes that policy making is specialized; that is, each type of issue (education, taxation, welfare) is marked by a distinctive set of influentials whose interests and efforts tend to concentrate on a small range of community problems.

A highly interesting case study, which demonstrates the power of nongovernmental elites, concerns a recent attempt to achieve a major administrative reorganization for metropolitan London. As analyzed by Smallwood,[26] the initial proposal was drawn up by a Royal Commission for appropriate legislation by Parliament. However, in the interval between the submission of the report and final deliberations by Parliament, local elites of various kinds proceeded to criticize and suggest alternative versions of the reform. Ultimately, substantial changes were introduced which had the effect of weakening the original recommendations. But more important, in terms of our perspective at this point, is Smallwood's discovery that several "unofficial" groups were instrumental in revising the earlier, formal decision on metropolitan organization. Specifically, teachers' groups, local medical committees, architects, study groups from the London School of Economics and the University of London, and a newly formed prestigious pressure group (the Committee for London Government, led by prominent economists, actors, literary lights, architects, and journalists) were particularly effective in opposing the official position on a crucial metropolitan issue.

3. Closely related to the previous generalizations is the widespread dominance of nonbusiness (or nonindustrial) categories within the unofficial segment of non-Western urban power structures. In general, this pattern is more likely in nations of the Near East, India, Africa, and Latin America, where stratification systems retain strong elements of a religious base, a kinship-tribal base, or a semiautonomous military tradition. Under these kinds of circumstances, commercial and manufacturing interests have not yet attained the influence their counterparts have achieved in more highly urbanized nations of Europe and North America. Instead, social sources of power in urban areas tend to be located in (a) leaders of dominant religious groups, as in Iran and Lebanon, (b) prominent supporters of the prevailing

[25] Delbert C. Miller, "Decision-Making Cliques in Community Power Structures: A Comparative Study of an American and an English City," *American Journal of Sociology*, 64 (November, 1958), pp. 299–310; Irving A. Fowler, *Local Industrial Structures, Economic Power, and Community Welfare* (Totowa, N.J., Bedminster Press, 1964); Roscoe C. Martin *et al.*, *Decisions in Syracuse* (Bloomington, Indiana University Press, 1961); Donald O. Cowgill, "Power as Process in an Urban Community," in Richard L. Stanton, ed., *Approaches to the Study of Urbanization* (Lawrence, Kans., University of Kansas Publications, Government Research Center, 1964), pp. 168–175; Charles Press, *Main Street Politics* (E. Lansing, Michigan State University, 1962).

[26] Smallwood, *op. cit.*, Chaps. 5, 6, 8, 12.

political party, as in India, Tanganyika, Mexico, Israel, and Indonesia, or (c) a miscellaneous smattering of intellectuals drawn from segments of the military establishment, the leading universities, or the neighboring gentry.[27]

conclusion

The decision-making or power structures of urban regions are relatively new foci of concern for sociologists and other social scientists. Consequently, comparative studies of the past decade or so seem to indicate a diversity that disturbs the quest for therapeutic simplicity of a Hunter or a Mills.[28] Yet it may be suggested that a few provisional generalizations appear promising.

In general, however, and as a prelude to such generalizations, urban power structures tend to be more clearcut and visible in smaller urban regions, in more isolated urban regions, and in those that are relatively immune from processes of political, technological, and economic changes.

In addition, urban power structures are more stable in urban areas marked by simple polarization of populations, rather than by complex and subtly shifting specializations of skills and statuses.

Finally, and in line with the previous point, urban power structures become more visible to observers when (a) greater opportunities for decision making develop (i.e., more issues) and (b) the differentiated interests and skills of an urban population express themselves in some measure of active participation (agreement or resistance) in definable matters of public concern.

some provisional generalizations

Urban power structures can be distinguished into two parts: [29] (a) a nuclear core group of officially responsible leaders and (b) a set of potentially influential elites, whose concerns are largely specialized in terms of their occupational or "professional" experience.

1. In newly developed cities, where "satellite" elites are not consciously organized, public officials normally dominate processes of community decision making. Furthermore, since there is a marked tendency for newly developed

[27] Lucian W. Pye, *Politics, Personality and Nation Building* (New Haven, Yale University Press, 1962); Leonard Binder, ed., *Politics in Lebanon* (New York, Wiley, 1966); Karl von Vorys, ed., "New Nations: The Problem of Political Development," *Annals of the American Academy of Political and Social Sciences*, Vol. 358 (March, 1965).

[28] Floyd Hunter, *Community Power Structure* (Chapel Hill, University of North Carolina Press, 1953; Garden City, Doubleday, 1963); C. Wright Mills, *The Power Elite* (New York, Oxford University Press, 1956).

[29] Sayre and Kaufman, *op. cit.*, p. 710 ff.

cities to be located in centralized or one-party states, the dominance of urban officials reflects the system of control in the national capital.

2. In modern western cities, likewise, public officials tend to predominate in policy formation as a consequence of the lack of interest in many issues on the part of potentially influential elites (businessmen, professionals). This lack of interest may be attributed to immersion in business pursuits, to migration and identification with suburban areas, or to the absence of pressure for community participation from national corporations.

3. Again, in modern complex cities (particularly the largest metropolitan regions in the U.S.), a great variety of issues and relevant satellite groups in effect serves to limit the influence of such groups. Over time, these groups tend to cancel out their respective strengths, thereby according decisive power to public officials as brokers of power (cf. Banfield's analysis of Chicago; Sayre and Kaufman's study of New York). The "power of the purse" and the development of public bureaucracies in key agencies (education, health, transportation) also narrow the functioning of civic and economic elites.

4. Economic elites seem to attain decisive power in urban areas primarily in transitional phases of urban development. In general, economic elites predominate in smaller, slowly developing cities, in early stages of significant economic growth of larger cities (e.g., Dallas), and in cities where the governmental structure institutionalizes the diffusion of authority (as in weak mayor systems, the commission form); and in cities where coalitions of electoral blocs are necessary to provide adequate support for major officeholders. However, when these kinds of conditions change (normally, as a consequence of economic and demographic growth), the locus of power shifts from satellite groups to a nuclear grouping of officials.

5. The boss system (or the traditional machine system) is an excellent instance of the transitory nature of power in nonofficial elites. Essentially, urban bosses have been of two types. One sort, exemplified by Mayors Hague and Curley, solidified their power from the vantage point of strategic public office. Their strength lay in continual reelection and the related ability to buy votes. In a sense, this kind of boss was a private person in an official position; his primary responsibility was to a party or political association (Tammany Hall). A second type of boss operated from an unofficial but strategic position in the power network of the community. Essentially, this boss was content to control the nomination and election of major officeholders, thereby assuring policy decisions favorable to the financial and political interests of the boss and his cohorts.

Apparently, the city machine depends upon three permissive conditions. Most obvious is a great diversity of ethnic groups (religious, nationality, and racial), which, in their first generation of urban residence, possess little interest in public issues and little political experience. Second, the machine thrives on the absence of civil service or merit systems for public officials and employees—in short the absence of a secure, relatively independent bureaucracy. Third, unorganized, uninterested or ineffective business and professional participation provides little challenge to experienced bosses. However, developments in these three areas normally squeeze the lifeline of city machines. In addition, national sources of support for local welfare and service programs inevitably topple bosses from their crucial location as electoral entrepreneurs who solicit votes in return for promised favors to collaborators.

6. Paradoxically, the more developed and complex the urban region, the more likely its decision-making apparatus will become a series of exercises in collective interference or mutual checks on effective power. In short, the dominant tendency seems to be (a) the emergence of specialized elites capable of publicizing certain issues and projecting narrowly supported solutions and (b) the strategic development of cautious officials dedicated to the comforts of tenure rather than the demands of articulated and interdependent public programs.[30] The cumbersome process of piloting decisions through the heavily mined waters of competitive, narrowly concerned responsibilties has often cooled the fires of ardent reform, humanitarian vision, and even the righteous solutions of various urban interest groups. Therefore, we may expect either (a) drastic adaptation of urban power structures to the demands of inter-connected urban problems—perhaps in the direction of the planning orientations (see Chapter 17) or (b) violent eruptions from urban segments which refuse to accept inaction or ineffective action as the dominant theme in urban organization.

[30] *Ibid.*, p. 716; Wood, *op. cit.*, Chap. 3. See also Fred I. Greenstein, "The Changing Pattern of Urban Party Politics," *Annals of the American Academy of Political and Social Science*, 353 (May, 1964), pp. 1–13 (the entire issue, given over to "City Bosses and Political Machines," is relevant to our discussion).

selected references

BANFIELD, Edward C., *Political Influence* (New York, The Free Press, 1961).

CLARK, Terry N., ed., *Community Structure and Decision-Making: Comparative Analyses* (San Francisco, Chandler Publishing Co., 1968).

DAHL, Robert A., *Who Governs?* (New Haven, Yale University Press, 1961).

HUNTER, Floyd, *Community Power Structure* (Chapel Hill, University of North Carolina Press, 1953).

PRESS, Charles, *Main Street Politics* (E. Lansing, Michigan State University Press, 1962).

13

major urban institutions:
the political economy

The most public and therefore the most discussed aspects of urban social organization are the major urban institutions. In the evolving urban environment, these institutions are notable in several respects: (*a*) they are acquiring a greatly extended radius of influence and control—in terms both of area and population; (*b*) they have developed highly formalized and bureaucratic structures; (c) they are increasingly interdependent, despite the trend toward specialization; (*d*) they tend to be the practical foci of stability and change in urban regions, and therefore the basic nuclei of regional problems; and (*e*) they appear on the whole to represent groping adjustments to the complexities of dynamic urban regions.

In a sense, urban institutions may be viewed as organized attempts to create essentially rational patterns of land use, services, and their coordination within the limits of societal values—such as democracy, efficiency, equity, etc. However, since urban regions are simultaneously units of national societies in a shrinking world, cultural and social differences among the latter inevitably affect the rational role of evolving urban institutions. A recent United Nations survey indicates, for example, that rapid growth of cities is proceeding without the benefit of fundamental industrial and commercial growth, especially in Asia, Africa, and Latin America.[1] This trend suggests that urbanization in its earlier stages in the modern world must for a time operate without the aid of responsible urban institutions. Therefore, any analysis of urban institutions should take into account the stage of urbanization and the sociocultural differences between societies (e.g., stratification systems, level of technology, form of government, etc.).

Partly through choice, partly as a result of space limitations, we shall emphasize the urban institutions of Western nations and give prominence to the more developed urban regions. Since the full range of institutions cannot

[1] Harland Bartholomew, *Land Uses in American Cities,* 2nd ed. (Cambridge, Mass., Harvard University Press, 1955), p. 119; Julia J. Henderson, "Urbanization and the World Community," in Martin Meyerson, ed., "Metropolis in Ferment," *Annals of the American Academy of Political and Social Science,* 314 (November, 1957), p. 149.

receive adequate space in a work of this kind, it seems advisable to concentrate on the most distinctive and significant institutional spheres. These institutions, which the anthropologist Herskovits calls cultural foci, are significant in two respects: (*a*) they comprise the areas of greatest interest, variation, and development; (*b*) they are crucial in the continuing process of interpreting and assessing the desirability and application of new forms and ideas to the urban region.[2]

In the urban setting, the major institutions can be grouped into two categories: (*a*) the basic, sustaining institutions—economic, political, and familial, and (*b*) the supporting or supplementary institutions—e.g., religious, educational, social welfare. This chapter will consider the first category; the second category is the theme of the following chapter. Since the familial institution has already been discussed in Chapter 9—the family is unusually significant because of its primary group and institutional character —it will be omitted from the discussion to follow.

Though we have briefly analyzed institutions in Chapter 10 (pp. 172–173), it may be helpful at this point to define the concept more clearly. This is particularly necessary because "institution" is used in a variety of ways by laymen and social scientists. In the most general sense, institutions refer to organized and widely accepted solutions to the needs of individuals and groups in a community or society. Each institution possesses a set of characteristics or parts, which give it distinction as a human creation.

1. A specialized function or need, such as provision of physical security, maintenance of order, transmission of accumulated experience.

2. A more or less explicit set of guiding values (mores), which translate "needs" into recognizable objectives (e.g., equality, efficiency, the importance of love, emphasis on youth).

3. A special cluster of social roles and skills, which translate ultimate goals into specific duties and responsibilities for individuals.

4. The development of informal and formal coordination of social roles through formation of groups (primary groups, voluntary associations, and larger bureaucratic organizations).

5. Participation (direct or indirect) of an entire population (community, region, or national society) in this network of values, roles, and groups.

6. A more or less emotional commitment to, or internalization of, institutional values and responsibilities by a substantial portion of a population.

Our discussion will emphasize features 3 and 4 (and to some extent number 2), not only because the bulk of our knowledge of urban institutions refers to these aspects, but also since we can thereby most clearly trace important trends in the operation of institutions in urban regions.

[2] Melville J. Herskovits, *Man and His Works* (New York, Alfred A. Knopf, 1948), Chap. XXXII.

political economy

Throughout the past two centuries in Western urban areas, political and economic roles and goals have developed with some independence of (and even conflict with) one another.[3] In an important sense, economic principles have in practice emphasized production of goods and services for the profit of individual producers and suppliers. Political principles, on the other hand, have usually asserted the necessity of public (collective) allocation of services (and some goods), not for private profit or enjoyment, but for the welfare of the community or region. Neither the ideological merits of these contending principles nor the efficiency of their application is at issue here. Rather, it is important to recognize that emerging urban governments and economies have been practically compelled to adjust to one another, to mute the conceptually sharp distinctions in their goals, and, without much plan or design, to engage in a continual intersection of skills, roles, values, and organizations. We can now truly speak of a *political economy*[4] (or an economic polity) in urban regions, though we may still focus for convenience on political and economic institutional sectors.

What accounts for this pragmatic re-fusion of highly specialized interests and groups in developed urban areas? Very simply, though the process was probably not guided by a clear rationale, representatives of both spheres came to recognize that cities operate routinely on three undeniable bases.

1. the *employment* base—a set of paid skills and positions which produce the goods and services that constitute the raison d'être of urban areas.

2. the *sales* base—the internal market for a significant portion of these goods and services.

3. the *taxation* base—the capacity of urban residents and firms to support necessary public services by regular, legitimate contributions to authoritative agencies.

In practice, urban areas depend on successful maintenance or expansion of each of these sectors; but, equally important, the interrelation of all three may well be considered a crucial indicator of urban development and change. For most cities, vitality and attractiveness depend on the availability of varied experiences and opportunities, which means an appropriate employment base. But urban variety also requires public financing of auxiliary services (water, health, education, etc.) either from a local taxation base or

[3] Lorenz von Stein, *The History of the Social Movement in France, 1789–1850*, tr. by Kaethe Mengelberg (Totowa, N.J., Bedminster Press, 1964; orig. ed., 1850), pp. 55–70; Franz Oppenheimer, *The State* (Indianapolis, Bobbs-Merrill, 1914).

[4] Marshall E. Dimock, *The New American Political Economy* (New York, Harper and Row, 1962). Dimock's discussion is on the national level, but is directly relevant.

from an extraurban source (e.g., the national government, whose revenues likewise derive largely from urban populations). However, it is increasingly clear that (a) the greater the employment base, the greater the sales base, and (b) the greater the sales base, the greater the possibility of flexibility in expanding the local taxation base. Consequently, urban areas tend to operate with multiple feedbacks among initially separable economic and governmental processes, with the emerging necessity of regularizing, predicting and controlling the feedback processes [5] (cf. the concept of urban planning, as discussed in Chapter 17).

the economic aspect of urban political economy

the employment base

The normal precondition of viable and expanding urbanization—given the preexisting social and economic developments of the first two urban waves (see pages 15–23)—is technical proficiency in (a) converting natural resources into desirable form, (b) organizing the possible interconnections between technical skills, and (c) recruiting persons for appropriate positions in the urban mosaic of material and social skills. In the fledgling urbanization of the newly developed nations, as Breese has suggested,[6] technical proficiency is as yet too low to accomplish more than bare survival (subsistence urbanization) in urban-like agglomerations. But well-known scientific and technological advances in Western nations have added to or derived from urban perceptions of needs by creating new products, new techniques of production and distribution, thus stimulating experimentation with appropriate organizational forms (see pages 245–249 below).

Trends in urban occupational distributions show rather clearly the impact of increased technical efficiency on the jobs and career lines of metropolitan residents. If we further divide technical efficiency into (a) material (substantive) and (b) administrative or organizational forms, we can see the substantial increases in both types in Table 37. On an industry basis, public administration and the professions represent the largest gains, symbolic of advances in (and need for) organizational skills. However, in the case of material efficiency, job increases are most notable in the construction field, where newly created desires are not visibly matched by improved technical efficiency in the residential aspect, while business and industrial construction (the lion's

[5] Werner Z. Hirsch, "Urban Government Services and Their Financing," in Werner Z. Hirsch, ed., *Urban Life and Form* (New York, Holt, Rinehart and Winston, 1963), pp. 129–166.

[6] Gerald Breese, *Urbanization in Newly Developed Countries* (Englewood Cliffs, N.J., Prentice-Hall, 1966), p. 5.

table 37

Occupational Distribution of Employed Civilian Workers in the U.S., 1940–1960
(Selected Categories) and Projections to 1975

(IN PERCENT)

	1960	1950	1940	Increase 1940–50	Increase 1950–60
White collar	43.3	37.4	32.9	41.9	27.7
Professional, technical	11.8	8.8	8.0	37.5	47.0
Managers and proprietors	8.8	9.0	8.1	38.6	7.4
Clerical and kindred	15.1	12.5	9.8	58.7	33.8
Sales workers	7.5	7.0	6.9	26.8	18.7
Manual workers	38.6	40.3	36.7	36.9	5.8
Craftsmen	14.2	14.0	11.6	51.2	11.8
Service workers	11.7	10.2	11.9	7.9	25.6
Agricultural workers	6.4	12.1	18.5	−18.8	−41.3

(IN MILLIONS)

	1960	1970	1975
Wholesale and retail	11.4	14.0	15.6
Government employees	8.5	11.5	12.8
Service and miscellaneous	7.4	10.2	11.9
Transportation and public utilities	4.0	4.4	4.5
Manufacturing	16.8	19.2	20.3
Construction	2.9	4.0	4.4

SOURCES: *Monthly Labor Review* (November, 1962), pp. 1203–1213; Emma. S. Woytinsky, *Profile of the U.S. Economy* (New York, Praeger, 1967), pp. 128–129.

share of overall construction) does represent considerable use of new technologies (in the use of steel, preformed slabs, etc.).

By type of skill, too, the effects of technological change may be noted. The largest proportionate increase in urban areas has been in professional and highly specialized technical skills, closely followed by jobs involving machine and related skills. Managerial or administrative skills likewise assume an increasingly important share of the urban employment base.

Perhaps these general tendencies can be better evaluated by considering variations in occupational distributions, both in the United States and in selected nations. Clearly, urban areas differ in their concern for a certain type of technical efficiency. Commercial cities, for example, tend to develop employment increases primarily in clerical and sales positions. Industrial cities on the other hand, encourage craft and mechanical skills. Understandably, a governmental center such as Washington, D.C., tends to concentrate its employment in professional and clerical categories.

Employment characteristics, of course, depend on stage of urban career, as well as on current focus of economic specialization. (The two, however, are somewhat interrelated). As several economists have suggested on the basis of past economic patternings,[7] cities tend to mature economically by changing proportionate emphasis on goods and services for residents (and visitors) as compared with those for consumers and customers in other communities and nations. This is often called the *basic-nonbasic* dimension of urban economy. Though its utility has recently been questioned by some economists, it continues to sensitize us to the practical problems and achievements that accompany a relative emphasis on either exported or locally consumed products and facilities. Thompson [8] suggests in a tentative way four typical stages in urban growth (confining his discussion to industrial and/or commercial cities).

1. *Export specialization (basic)*. Primary economic products and a significant share of the labor force are organized around a limited set of commodities for other communities (examples: automobiles, wool, steel).

2. *Export complex.* The most significant share of urban income (wages and profits) derives from a diversified set of commodities and services for other communities (examples: insurance, magazines, precision machine products, airplanes, auto assemblies, processed food products). The crucial consequences of an export complex are expansion of the labor force (and therefore population expansion by migration) and a growing diversity in the backgrounds, tastes, and needs of the resident population.

3. *Economic maturation stage (nonbasic)*. With the preceding development as a base, the urban economy becomes increasingly concerned with its large home market and its effective demand not only for housekeeping goods and services (food, clothing, etc.), but also for the varied and infinitely expandable range of products originally designed for export. At this stage, urban areas attain a kind of economic and cultural balance, one which in effect hedges against fluctuations in external markets and also provides a stronger identification between residents and a functionally defined urban region.

4. *The regional metropolis.* A more complex urban economy may develop from the economic and demographic strengths of the preceding stage. Indeed, the assured successes that stem from dual markets (home and export)

---

[7] Benjamin Chinitz, ed., *City and Suburb: The Economics of Metropolitan Growth* (Englewood Cliffs, N.J., Prentice-Hall, 1964); Wilbur R. Thompson, *A Preface to Urban Economics* (Baltimore, Johns Hopkins Press, 1965); Mark Perlman, ed., *Human Resources in the Urban Economy* (Washington, Resources for the Future, 1963); John C. Bollens and Henry J. Schmandt, *The Metropolis* (New York, Harper and Row, 1965), pp. 116–117.

[8] Thompson, *op. cit.*, pp. 15–16.

stimulate the development of subtle and yet expansive services—principally in the realm of mass communications (newspaper, radio, and television) and financing (banking, credit, investment in enterprises in outlying areas, branch offices and outlets). Ultimately, some economic enterprises that were originally within the central city are transferred to peripheral locations, even to smaller cities within a manageable time-cost area. The result is, from an economic standpoint, a regional network in which economic operations (and related occupational skills) are conditioned by their contribution to the major goods and services of the central city. For example, small cities as much as 50–70 miles from a central city tend to persist by specializing in producing processed foods, drugs, educated youth, furniture, etc., which either flow into the nonbasic sector or utilize the strategic transportation, communication, and financial facilities of the city for export to far-flung regions.[9]

The major problem of urban areas, from this standpoint, can be identified simply as "to grow or not to grow" (in size and complexity). Essentially, the crucial decision is whether or not to move from export complex to economic maturation. If a positive decision is made, then the employment base must be enlarged—new firms or enterprises, new skills, and often new residents. It is important to recognize that these are largely political matters involving community-relevant decisions and questions of coordination by public bodies.

the sales base

It is perhaps old-fashioned to point to the obvious. However, it seems rather clear that the urban economic structure is designed to facilitate distribution to the growing market of urban consumers. In the Western world and to an increasing extent in the more traditional or underdeveloped countries, science and technology have conquered problems of production. Therefore, cities and urban regions for many centuries have been stimulants to innovation in economic organization, with considerable and growing attention to distribution. Indeed, modern capitalism itself is largely the creation of urban groups in Western Europe, based on such specifically urban features as mobile labor, rationalized technology, capital accumulation, "rational" legal systems, individual and group property rights, and instruments for commercial transactions (checks and drafts, bills of lading, stocks and bonds).[10] During the past 80 years, however, urban regions have become marked by an unique battery of economic organizations, which represent an un-

[9] Don J. Bogue, *The Structure of the Metropolitan Community* (Ann Arbor, University of Michigan, 1949); James L. Green, *Metropolitan Economic Republics* (Athens, University of Georgia Press, 1965).

[10] Max Weber, *General Economic History* (New York, The Free Press of Glencoe, 1950), pp. 276–313.

planned, experimental adjustment to metropolitan development. These organizations are the corporate form in industry and commerce; centralized and varied channels of distribution—the department store, the chain store, the mail order house; the advertising agency; various consumer credit facilities; and organized interest groups, such as the specialized trade association, chambers of commerce, and national labor unions.

Such an array of organizational forms, diverse as they may seem, can be profitably analyzed in terms of common problems and objectives in the urban milieu. For example, the basic pursuit of profit tends to require efficiency, optimum size of organization, and specialization in the context of a large, relatively accessible market. The variety of wants among urbanites and their comparative ability to spend present and foreseeable income has undoubtedly stimulated specialization as well. Not only variety, but a constant increase in variety of needs and desires, is significant for urban economic organization. The creation of new needs on any scale, however, is dependent on the expansion of leisure, which is perhaps most typical of urbanized lifestyles for large segments of the population.

Urban economic institutions cannot be fully understood only as reflections of profit motives, standards of efficiency, and the rational pursuit of progress. Perhaps two other values play supplementary roles in urban economics. As suggested by Galbraith, modern business enterprise (which includes all of the economic forms listed above) is not primarily attuned to the rigors of competition in the classical sense, but instead exhibits a "comprehensive effort to reduce risk." [11] To the producer and distributor in the urban market, risk lies in miscalculating consumer demand, promoting of obsolete products, overdependence on the success of limited types of products, and uncontrolled price variations.

Consequently, Galbraith argues, advertising is a necessary technique for controlling consumer tastes and preferences. In a highly efficient economy, productivity tends to outstrip consumer demand; advertising therefore becomes a conscious application of the formula "invention is the mother of necessity." Similarly, large organizations make possible a diversification of products, which may provide protection against instabilities in specific sales patterns. Research and development in industrial enterprises, while ostensibly aimed at greater efficiency and progress, is, in Galbraith's view, also dedicated to the corporate quest for minimizing market uncertainties, by insuring up-to-date (not necessarily better or cheaper or more efficient) products and methods of production. This process is partly a consequence of competition with similar firms, but also involves "self competition," i.e., to avoid loss of some desired proportion of sales and repute in the urban market. Finally, though it is difficult to document in many instances, reduction of risk is apparent in attempts to control or "administer" prices—whether informally

[11] J. K. Galbraith, *The Affluent Society* (Boston, Houghton Mifflin, 1958), pp. 101–102.

(as in the steel industry) or formally (as in utilities and transportation).[12]

A second value—somewhat related to risk reduction—is the emphasis on power or nonlegal controls over segments of the urban economy. In a negative sense, power in the economic sphere consists of attempts to determine economic decisions (wage and price levels, availability of technical ideas) apart from the classical "free play of the market." Theoretically, market decisions are made through the independent evaluations of individual units (buyers and sellers). Practically, urban economic power is expressed in a positive way by two widely used methods. The more public approach is through combination, collaboration, or merger of similar or related economic organizations. This is evident in the composite corporation (United States Steel, General Motors, General Foods), the national labor union and federated national unions, the trade association, and the chamber of commerce. "Power through combination" depends on comparatively greater financial resources, superior sources of market information, the increased ability to compete for favorable facilities, and the intangible effects of sheer size (since size and quantity are widely respected, sometimes feared, but rarely challenged effectively by individuals or smaller organizations). In the United States and Great Britain, this form of power is morally (and often legally) barred from extension to violence or open intimidation. This should be compared to the situation in the period 1870 to 1936, when such limits were not widely observed.[13]

Therefore, a second avenue of power has become important beyond measure, as an indispensable supplement to combination: informal influence of administrative and legislative bodies in the political sphere. Lobbying in the broad sense of representing a specific economic interest before an official or public authority is a major activity, particularly in the United States and Great Britain. Almost every economic interest in urban regions—real estate, industrial corporations, labor unions, retailers, wholesalers, professionals (physicians, teachers, lawyers)—maintains substantial budgets and staffs for acquainting legislators and officials with their respective needs and viewpoints. While lobbying was once regarded as a nefarious activity, in the United States it has become an accepted (if not respected) institutionalized linkage between the economic and political spheres. Federal and some state laws require formal registration of lobbying organizations and itemized accounting of their expenditures. However, in practice, these laws serve to recognize rather than control the activities of lobbyists.[14]

The full story of the role of economic pressure groups would fill several

12 Walton H. Hamilton, *The Pattern of Competition* (New York, Columbia University Press, 1940).

13 Robert A. Brady, *Business as a System of Power* (New York, Columbia University Press, 1943); Henry W. Ehrmann, *Organized Business in France* (Princeton, Princeton University Press, 1957).

14 Donald C. Blaisdell, *American Democracy Under Pressure* (New York, Ronald Press, 1957), Chap. VI.

libraries, but much of it is scattered in unread scholarly monographs, records of congressional hearings, and dusty newspaper files. But it is not necessary to digest this mass of essentially repetitive detail to recognize that economic influence groups are meaningful and pervasive responses to major economic and political trends in modern urban regions and their national societies. In general, the specialization and technological efficiency of urban economies create relatively new problems of surplus production. Since markets are increasingly complex, economic risks are too high to be left to chance or natural resolution. Consequently, some economic interests inevitably seek protection by favorable legislation and administration. Because of the interdependence of urban economies, however, lobbying creates real or imagined threats to other economic interests, and thus an apparently endless cycle of competitive influence ("politics") is characteristic of urban regions. In the United States, for example, where such a process is at its height, influence groups have successfully affected wages, prices, awarding of exclusive economic rights and government contracts, proper channels of distribution, and competition with other nations.[15]

the corporate form

Small proprietors and partnerships persist as the most numerous form of economic organization in urban regions, but the corporation is doubly significant as contributing a major (and still increasing) share of productivity and dollar value, and as the symbol of urban economic organization. Perhaps, then, the extent of corporate organization is a key index to the overall level of urbanism in a society. Generally, newly urbanized societies (India, Africa, the Near East) depend on familial, dynastic, or individualized economic units, while such nations as Great Britain, the United States, Germany, and Canada have had considerable experience in extending private corporate enterprise into virtually every aspect of the urban economy.

To the urban sociologist, the corporation is an excellent example of organizational adaptation to the urban region, as well as an unwitting stimulant to other social changes that have come to be closely associated with urban patterns. There is little question that the corporate form initially reflects attempts to maximize efficiency in financing and directing a variety of economic enterprises. This is accomplished by pooling and coordinating resources, facilities, and skills through the agency of a legally fictitious "person" that is miraculously separate from the identities of any and all individuals associated with it.

However, in practice, the corporation tends to confuse efficiency with impersonality to the point that impersonality comes to mean independence

[15] *Ibid.*, Chaps. VII, VIII, XIII–XV; Karl Schriftgiesser, *The Lobbyists* (Boston, Little, Brown and Company, 1951); Henry W. Ehrmann, ed., *Interest Groups on Four Continents* (Pittsburgh, University of Pittsburgh Press, 1958); Stuart Chase, *Democracy Under Pressure* (New York, The Twentieth Century Fund, 1945).

of the local urban region. This is of course recognized by corporate leaders, who try to superimpose personal, noneconomic features on corporate functioning. Most "institutional advertising," [16] the recent practice of streamlining financial statements, the facilitation of stockholders' meetings, and the lending of corporation executives for local civic duties seem to be designed to restore a quasi-personal flavor to the abstractions of prices, wages, profits, and production figures. But the fact remains that corporations inherently are impersonal and expansive, that in binding together a diversity of supplies, personnel, and areas they have become extraurban or interurban, absentee owners in a literal sense. One consequence of this impersonality-efficiency-absentee complex is the widely recognized subservience of urbanites to modern economic organizations.[17] Furthermore, this dependence is heightened by the intricate interdependence among economic organizations, which leaves little room for personal independence in the economic sphere. Clearly, the extensive corporate structure of urban economics achieves remarkable results, when disturbing conditions are absent. But this organic articulation of the economy accelerates economic chaos in periods of crisis, as the major depressions of the last two generations amply demonstrate.

Corporate efficiency as an ideal points toward an increasingly minute division of labor within the corporation and an accompanying system of bureaucracy to coordinate and regularize proper interrelations.[18] Historically, bureaucracy began in military organizations of emerging empires. In the modern urban region, economic bureaucracies are peculiar mixtures of efficiency and nonrationality, of status concerns and technological objectives. Whatever one's attitude toward bureaucracy, the urban corporation is highly successful from the profit standpoint, despite internal problems of red tape and dissident primary groups. However, the social consequences of economic bureaucracy deserve more attention than they have received.

Together with technological advances, corporate bureaucracy has largely solved problems of production for urban regions. Scientific research, until recently free of bureaucratization,[19] and increasingly bureaucratized development programs have gradually converted bureaucracies from concern for efficient production to a stress on methods of distribution. The changing distribution of employed persons from 1900 to 1953 indirectly confirms this trend.[20]

[16] Leonard I. Pearlin and Morris Rosenberg, "Propaganda Techniques in Institutional Advertising," *Public Opinion Quarterly*, 16 (Spring, 1952), pp. 5–26.

[17] Adolph A. Berle, Jr., and Gardiner C. Means, *The Modern Corporation and Private Property* (New York, Macmillan, 1932); James Burnham, *The Managerial Revolution* (New York, John Day, 1941).

[18] Theodore A. Caplow, *The Sociology of Work* (Minneapolis, University of Minnesota Press, 1954), p. 22.

[19] See for example John Jewkes, David Sawers, and Richard Stillerman, *The Sources of Invention* (London, Macmillan, 1958).

[20] J. Frederic Dewhurst and associates, *America's Needs and Resources*, rev. ed.

The corporate form in urban areas has been adapted to the peculiarities of marketing products and services in a number of ways, which might be considered organizational innovations during the past three generations.

1. independent advertising agencies and marketing divisions of manufacturing corporations

The advertising firm achieved prominence as a type in the twenties and early thirties. It is marked by a very high proportion of professional workers—artists, writers—and the willingness to promote a wide diversity of products for its corporate clients. Until very recently, the advertising role complex was performed by virtually anonymous firms and persons, since the product dominated in the economic sphere. At the present, the advertiser or "huckster" is emerging from the background; his character has been etched in popular novels; several firms have achieved a public identity, such as B.B.D. & O.; and the locale of advertising—Madison Avenue—has acquired a symbolic value akin to that of Wall Street.[21]

2. chain stores

Unlike department stores, which are both older and more varied in merchandise, chain stores try to reach a large segment of the urban population. Their success, dating from the twenties in the United States, rests on perhaps two features: somewhat lowered prices and the attractive freedom of self-service. It is not at all strange that chain stores have concentrated in just half a dozen fields of marketing—drugs, groceries, auto supplies, low-priced variety goods (e.g., Woolworth's), modestly-priced women's clothing (dresses, shoes), and most recently, department stores. These types of products have a wide and continuous demand, and also require relatively few sales clerks.[22]

3. mail order organizations

This form of distribution was first directed at customers remote from retail centers—farmers, small town residents. Both Montgomery Ward and Sears Roebuck, the leaders in this form, have been able to tap a huge market by mail and phone orders through reduced prices and an increasing

---

(New York, Twentieth Century Fund, 1955), p. 731; David Kaplan and M. Claire Casey, *Occupational Trends in the United States, 1900 to 1950*, Bureau of the Census, Working Paper No. 5 (Washington, D.C., 1958), p. 7; Reinhard Bendix, *Work and Authority in Industry* (New York, John Wiley and Sons, 1956), pp. 214, 225.

21 Thomas B. Clark, *The Advertising Smoke Screen* (New York, Harper and Brothers, 1944); Martin Mayer, *Madison Avenue, U.S.A.* (New York, Harper and Brothers, 1958); John Gloag, *Advertising in Modern Life* (London, Heinemann, 1959); Eric Field, *Advertising: The Forgotten Years* (London, E. Benn, 1959).

22 Joseph C. Palamountain, Jr., *The Politics of Distribution* (Cambridge, Mass., Harvard University Press, 1955).

range of merchandise. But mail order houses have also entered the urban retail market with distinct success. By creating, in effect, a double-barrelled chain of department stores and mail order centers (often in the same building), Ward's and Sears have become giants in American urban regions (and in other nations, such as Mexico).[23] Urbanites have the option of buying in person, through catalogues in the stores, or ordering by mail. Though it is difficult to identify those most attracted by the mail order department store, many customers seem to be recent migrants from smaller communities, or mobile urban families, who desire the benefits of nationwide service and repair facilities.

4. sales finance corporations

Perhaps the least recognized innovation in urban economic organization, the sales finance corporation has been instrumental in bridging two forms of consumer credit. During the early part of this century, the major form of credit to individuals was bank loans. Generally, such loans were difficult to obtain and required collateral (property, jewelry, etc.) to protect the lender in case of default. The sales finance corporation, mainly emerging in the twenties, provided credit to the retailer, who was thus able to extend credit to the urban consumer. This innovation helped in the mass sale of automobiles, radios, refrigerators, etc., which have since become the most important items in urban purchases.[24]

Since 1945, with the extension of wartime levels of prosperity, consumer credit has been made more fully available by banks, through department store charge accounts, and mail order accounts—all these combining to form the modern system of consumer credit. However, sales finance companies still play a significant part in facilitating sales of automobiles and major appliances in the United States.

5. labor unions

Unlike the medieval guild,[25] the labor union is a corporate combination of workers; it is intentionally distinct from and antagonistic to employers. The history of effective unionism is relatively short (perhaps from 1850 to the present), though the motivation to form unions can be traced to the eighteenth century in England and the American colonies. Though unions have had political roles, to the urban sociologist their economic significance

[23] A wealth of information is contained in Boris Emmet and John C. Jenck, *Catalogues and Counters: A History of Sears, Roebuck and Company* (Chicago, University of Chicago Press, 1950), especially Chaps. XIX XXI, and XXVI.

[24] Clyde W. Phelps, *The Role of the Sales Finance Companies in the American Economy* (Baltimore, Commercial Credit Corporation, 1952).

[25] See the detailed discussion in Sylvia R. Thrupp, *The Merchant Class of Medieval London, 1300–1500* (Chicago, University of Chicago Press, 1949).

is based on the attempt to affect (if not control) the availability and distribution of workers. The specific motives for this economic role may be varied: material benefits, greater prestige for union leaders, greater share in economic decisions, pursuit of political-ideological goals. In any case, the rise and growing power of unions represent a bureaucratic counterpart to the industrial and commercial corporation.

Though there have been unions of agricultural workers (e.g., the Southern Tenant Farmers' Union), the union is primarily an urban form. Essentially, unions have been virtually the only organizational form suitable for large numbers of otherwise unorganized, ethnically diversified, unskilled and semiskilled urban workers in the United States. White collar workers and professionals, on the other hand, tend to view unions as improper and undignified for themselves, since they regard the white collar and professional roles as both prestigeful and constantly expanding in opportunities. Veteran union men implicitly identify the union as a protector against arbitrary employers and the apparently inexorable process of technological advancement. This dual fear, often grounded in fact, helps to explain the "new" emphasis in union objectives—wages tied to cost of living, fringe benefits (health, retirement), guaranteed annual wages, and the union as a respected participant in industrial planning.[26]

urban consumption patterns (dynamics of the sales base)

Since the character of urban sales depends upon both financial capacity (income) and the value systems (style of life) of urbanites, it is important to locate major trends in these aspects of consumption, as well as the crucial factors in accounting for such trends. Income distribution is of course largely attributable to occupational and educational patterns. But the use of income (and credit) in urban areas seems to be complicated by such factors as age, race, family characteristics, and direction and pace of social mobility.[27]

First, what, if any, are the special features of urban consumption patterns, as compared with rural areas? Clearly, urban families have more disposable income than do rural and small town families. But the distribution of expenditures varies by type of community. Urban families spend proportionately more for housing (including furnishings and upkeep), food, beverages, recreation, and education, but somewhat less for clothing, medical care, and transportation. In general, urban families tend to save less than rural

[26] Philip D. Bradley, ed., *The Public Stake in Union Power* (Charlottesville, University of Virginia Press, 1959); Adolph F. Sturmthal, *Unity and Diversity in European Labor* (New York, The Free Press of Glencoe, 1953); Herbert J. Spiro, *The Politics of German Codetermination* (Cambridge, Mass., Harvard University Press, 1958); Frederick H. Harbison and Robert Dubin, *Patterns of Union-Management Relations* (Chicago, Science Research Associates, 1947).

[27] Lincoln Clark, ed., *Consumer Behavior* (New York, Harper and Row, 1958); George Katona, *The Powerful Consumer* (New York, McGraw-Hill, 1960); Margaret G. Reid, *Housing and Income* (Chicago, University of Chicago Press, 1962).

families at many comparable income levels (particularly in higher income categories). In gross terms, these patterns suggest that urbanites support both the expensive, intangible services and also the manufacturing or processing of continually replaceable items (foods, appliances).

However, urban consumers differ considerably among themselves in patterns of purchasing.

1. Obviously, income differences affect expenditure patterns. For example, there is a positive relation between clothing expenditures and income. Similarly, the higher the income level, the higher the proportionate expenses on recreation, and to a lesser extent, on ownership of automobiles. In addition, installment debt (largely for automobiles and major appliances) appears to have a curvilinear relation to income: 25 percent of families with under $2000 annual income are in debt, rising to 60 percent of families in the $5000–7000 category, and then dropping to 46 percent of those with $10,000 and over.[28]

2. Holding income constant, Negro consumption patterns differ somewhat from those of white families. Negro families tend to spend more than white families of comparable income and size on recreation as a whole. This is particularly true of small families (one or no children). More specifically, Negro families spend more than comparable whites on liquor and perhaps theaters and films, but less on reading materials. In other respects, Negro and white patterns of expenditures are quite similar. On the other hand, if income is not controlled, the effects of significantly lower incomes among Negro families are visible in greater proportionate expenditures on food, housing, and clothing, lesser expenditures on recreation, education, and medical care.

It has been suggested[29] that Negro families spend proportionately more on recreation than their white counterparts in the attempt to compensate for well-known cultural and social deprivations encountered by Negroes in the United States. As income rises, according to this interpretation, Negroes try to "make up for lost time" in the amenities enjoyed by middle income whites. Consequently, recreational activities receive special attention. The exception is expenditures for reading, which may be partly explained by formal education limitations. Indeed, a special correlation between race and expenditures for reading indicates that the effect of education on expenditures is much more pronounced among Negro families.

3. Unfortunately, we have no data on total distribution of expenditures for each family type or phase, or even for each age category of household heads. Instead, we must be content with variations in family characteristics for each type of expenditure. For example, purchases of furniture and appli-

[28] George Fisk, *Leisure Spending-Behavior* (Philadelphia, University of Pennsylvania Press, 1963), pp. 93–94; Gabriel Kolko, *Wealth and Power in America* (New York, Praeger, 1962), p. 105.

[29] Fisk, *op. cit.*, pp. 144–148.

ances are more frequent in young families without children, least frequent in older, childless families. Similarly, these purchases decline in frequency with age of the head of household. For recreational items, however, family phase provides rather weak predictions of differences. Normally, family phase is roughly correlated with income level. But, controlling for income, few significant differences in expenditures can be found. Of these, most seem to occur in medium income groups ($6,000–10,000 in 1950), with the largest differences between childless families and those with young adolescents.

When age of head is considered, somewhat greater differences in recreational expenditures have been found. At almost all income levels, proportionate expenditures tend to decline with increasing age. In most income categories, the highest expenditures occur when the major breadwinner is under 35.

A closely related pattern appears in the distribution of installment credit, a substantial portion of which (about 26 percent) is for new automobiles. Generally, amount of debt decreases with age, with the period of greatest indebtedness when the head is between 35 and 44 years of age. This pattern is largely applicable to large appliances and furniture; for automobiles, debt does not began to decline appreciably until age 55. By family type, installment debt is most prominent in young families with children, least in older families (head 45 years or over) without children. Not unexpectedly, debt is more prevalent in the suburban areas of the largest metropolitan regions, where young families with children are most likely to reside.[30]

4. We would expect expenditures to reflect major differences in value systems or styles of life. Since consumption data usually deal with such accessible marks of status as income, occupation, education, and residential location, it is only possible to infer the existence of style of life differences and their impact on purchasing patterns.

The evidence is uneven and difficult to organize in adequately meaningful ways. However, if educational level can be viewed as an aspect of style of life, then installment debt shows a modest degree of patterning. Those with little education (under eight years) have the least debt (whether this is by choice or by failure to obtain credit is not known). Moderate formal education (high school through some college) is associated with the greatest prevalence of indebtedness. Thereafter (college degree or better) a moderately lesser debt level is found, which seems to be only partly related to the superior income levels associated with higher education.[31]

Style of life can be inferred, alternatively, from broad occupational categories, when income is controlled. On recreational expenditures, for example, unskilled workers spend less than white collar workers and professionals of

[30] George Katona et al., 1964 Survey of Consumer Finances (Ann Arbor, Survey Research Center, University of Michigan, 1963), Monograph #32, p. 78.

[31] Ibid., pp. 47, 61, 78.

the same income level. This patterned difference is particularly clear for reading expenditures, while the reverse pattern is found for purchase of alcoholic beverages.[32] Unfortunately, these kinds of controlled comparisons are possible primarily at low and moderate income levels. It is quite probable that high income—and consistent earning at higher income levels—dilutes previous differences in consumption objectives.

5. While we have several studies on occupational mobility (largely comparing generations), the relation between the process of social mobility (and its important dimensions) and behavior is not well understood (see discussion in Chapter 11 on stratification). Yet scattered clues indicate that upwardly mobile urbanites develop objectives and behavioral patterns that distinguish them from nonmobile persons in similar occupational and income categories. Therefore, we can reasonably expect mobility to affect consumption patterns. But for lack of an unequivocal, generally useful indicator of degree of mobility (or relative desire for mobility), let us tentatively borrow the premise that mobile people tend to save for specific purchases or future services, while nonmobile people tend to spend their income for immediate use. Let us also hypothesize that upward mobility entails special (or greater than average) expenditures on education, certain types of recreation and entertainment, selected kinds of home furnishings, and unusual foods. It follows that such expenditures usually strain current levels of income; consequently, mobility should be accompanied by (and perhaps be indicated by) the specialized use of installment credit.

Available information on these points is simply not detailed enough for our purposes. However, it is reasonably clear that families who have savings also tend to incur debts in inverse relation to amount of savings.[33] Thus, those with little or no savings are more likely to use installment credit than those with savings of $500 or over. The amount of debt, however, is also negatively related to amount of savings, which refutes our earlier prediction. But it is interesting to note that these debt patterns are largely due to automobiles and large appliances, rather than items connected with mobility.

Our focus should be on families with moderate and increasing incomes, with some savings and average amounts of credit, as compared with poor, over-extended families and well-to-do families with comparatively low debts and substantial financial reserves. But the data allow us to make relatively few and rather shaky conclusions: (1) mobile families tend to use credit less in higher income categories; (2) mobile families with recent increases in income tend to use credit more than those with no income rise; (3) savings in our core group are more often intended for children's education than among families with lesser income and savings; (4) the importance of saving for children's education is greatest among families with children over

    [32] Fisk, *op. cit.*, pp. 122–131.
    [33] Katona, *The Powerful Consumer*, p. 91; Katona *et al.*, *1964 Survey of Consumer Finances*, pp. 68–69, 77–78.

six and with a head under 45 years of age [34]—the stereotype of the upwardly mobile family. We do not have direct information on expenditure patterns of mobile families, except that they are more likely than nonmobile counterparts to purchase furniture and appliances and to acquire and maintain life insurance.

Perhaps the major import of these patterns—admittedly the factual base is not yet adequate—is the implicit dependence of urban economic systems on a few key characteristics of resident populations. If cities are to develop in complexity—a perennial thrust of urbanism—they require adequate proportions of relatively young, successfully mobile families, with above average incomes and future-oriented styles of life. These categories seem to be the primary patrons of recreational and leisure services, of expensive durables (furniture, appliances), of continually varied kinds of clothing, and of nonbusiness banking and credit facilities. With the exception of clothing and furniture, all of these services and products encourage employment in white collar, professional and administrative skills—which in turn recruit and/or produce young, successfully mobile families. The employment base, in short, establishes lines of development for the sales base of urban areas.

Both in theoretical and practical terms, then, the occupational structure of urban areas may be considered the sociological trigger for many cultural and organizational phenomena that accompany the normal operation of urban and metropolitan entities. But if the temptation to convert this into economic determinism seems compelling, we should remember that (*a*) occupations and jobs are resultants of decisions to locate firms, businesses, etc. in given areas; and (*b*) these decisions are stimulated or hindered by political acts (conscious or unconscious) in such public sectors as government, formal education, and transportation. We shall return to this problem in a later section.

the taxation base

The routine availability of public services for urbanites is no longer a dull or insignificant matter. As urban populations grow and diversify, and as economic growth proceeds, the demand for such services becomes more insistent and more comprehensive in scope. Indeed, to some extent, urban families move in search of more adequate public services, often leaving behind those families whose problems place great burdens on key services (e.g., welfare) and yet are unable to seek better circumstances.

In general, urban areas serve to develop expenditure patterns largely in relation to population density, rather than to population size. As expected, metropolitan centers spend considerably more (on a per capita basis, twice

---

[34] Katona *et al.*, p. 111.

as much) than do nonmetropolitan areas.[35] Likewise, as is well known, public expenditures are largely concentrated in public education and health facilities which correspond to the needs of relatively young social categories and to those with limited financial resources.

The basic financial problem of urban areas is starkly clear: what is the most practical way of maintaining (and expanding) desirable public services in a region which contains sharp differences in ability to pay and is politically and administratively fragmented into autonomous incorporated entities and segments of environing counties?

In the U.S., the evolving solution has been a mixture of revenue sources, which invite sporadic criticism and fascinating political machinations. The traditionally sanctioned property tax is still first in yield, though its relative importance has declined sharply in 20 years. Currently, the next largest source of revenue is a variety of service charges (school tax, garbage and refuse service, public utilities taxes) followed by grants from state and federal governments, the sales tax, license and similar fees, and a very distant last, corporate and personal income levies. (See Table 38.)

Perhaps the most crucial question concerning the urban revenue mix is: which social and residential category is most directly tapped by each taxation mechanism? And not to be ignored, which form of taxation either constitutes a special burden to some social category, or permits an unduly low share of responsibility—and even evasion of financial responsibility?

table 38

Local Government Revenue in the United States, by Source, 1962

REVENUE SOURCE	In SMAs		Outside SMAs		U.S.	
	Per Capita	Percent	Per Capita	Percent	Per Capita	Percent
Property taxes	$111.78	50.	$76.30	43.6	$99.09	48.
Other local taxes	18.41	8.2	5.74	3.3	13.08	6.7
State aids	55.35	24.7	64.29	36.7	58.54	28.4
Other general revenues	38.24	17.1	28.73	16.4	34.85	16.9
		100.0		100.0		100.0

SOURCE: Advisory Commission on Intergovernmental Relations, *Metropolitan Social and Economic Disparities: Implications for Intergovernmental Relations in Central Cities and Suburbs* (Washington, D.C., U.S. Government Printing Office, January, 1965), p. 50.

[35] Harvey E. Brazer, *City Expenditures in the United States* (New York, National Bureau of Economic Research, 1959), p. 28; Alan K. Campbell and Seymour Sacks, *Metropolitan America: Fiscal Patterns and Growth Systems* (New York, The Free Press, 1967), p. 96; Robert C. Wood, *1400 Governments* (Garden City, Doubleday, 1964), Chap. 1.

Local taxation in all nations is a subject that generates heated controversy and often offends the sensitivities of otherwise civilized groups. Consequently, accurate information and objective interpretation of available data are rather scarce commodities. But there is some basis for concluding that until recently (if not a continuing pattern) the urban taxation structure has been characterized by inequities in incidence. One analysis demonstrates that greater proportionate shares of local taxes (property, sales and excise types) are borne by lower income categories.[36] If the traditional argument is made that lower economic categories require more public services, then a plausible rationale for this pattern can be attempted. However, it is likewise clear that these families are least capable of coping with the impact of taxation, on their limited incomes. Instead, it might well be argued that the attempt to charge low-income recipients of public services for a significant portion of their costs serves to mire these families more deeply in dependence on welfare and related services.

Another frequently cited inequity in urban taxation is the imputed insulation of suburban and fringe residents from "adequate" contributions to operating costs of the central city. This is a particularly difficult charge to validate. Clearly, nonresidents of the central city do not pay city property and general taxes, but they do support city services to the extent that they patronize city firms (sales tax). As we have already noted in Chapter 6, however, suburban shopping centers (often with branches of city-owned retailers) are increasingly infringing on the sales volume (or normal increases in sales volume) of center city stores. In addition, the migration of above-average income families to peripheral locations (a phenomenon of the forties and early fifties in the U.S.) may have caused some decline in city property values, though this has not been firmly established. In recent years, suburban growth (apart from natural increase) in some metropolitan areas is more likely to be due to migration from other suburban areas rather than the central city. In Atlanta, for example, the net loss of the central city to other parts of the region in 1955–60 was 36,000 persons. Significantly, migrants to the Atlanta area during that period were largely in suburban and fringe areas (61 percent). On the other hand, a very substantial portion of important jobs in the central city are manned by suburban residents. To the extent that such skills are not available among city residents, the economic vitality of cities may be said to derive from suburban categories.

But several tenable conclusions about metropolitan taxation can be drawn.[37]

[36] Ruth L. Mace, *Municipal Cost-Revenue Research in the United States* (Chapel Hill, Institute of Government, University of North Carolina, 1961).

[37] Robert A. Sigafoos, *The Municipal Income Tax* (Chicago, Public Administration Service, 1955), pp. 145–146; Robert H. Connery, ed., *Municipal Income Taxes* (New York, Academy of Political Science Proceedings Vol. 28, #4, 1968), p. 12; Advisory

1. The general property tax is neither fairly levied nor an adequate source for swelling municipal expenditures. In many areas, assessments are unrealistic, usually undervaluing (and undertaxing) the more expensive homes and buildings. Changing or updating property assessments is often not politically feasible. Consequently, while the national income (largely metropolitan income) has risen dramatically in recent decades, property tax yields have declined as a proportion of urban revenues. Ability to pay as a principle of taxation is no longer served by the property tax.

2. Sales taxes, while their yield has grown substantially since the thirties, still do not tap adequate sums at present rates (3–5 percent) or by means of the flat rates that are currently applied. The latter aspect, as has been frequently asserted, places the taxation burden on lower income consumers and likewise conflicts to some degree with the "ability to pay" principle. Expansion of the yield of local sales taxes is possible only through (a) increased purchasing; (b) higher basic rates, or (c) progressively increasing rates on more expensive sales (e.g., over $500). The first possibility assumes availability of greater purchasing power, which normally means some inflation in wages and prices, and therefore increased municipal expenditures. The second alternative represents increasing hardship for families with modest incomes; it is not very probable from a political standpoint. Finally, graduated rates for sales taxes would clearly be fought by manufacturers and retailers of high cost items (e.g., automobiles, jewelry).

3. The rise of a municipal income tax as a significant source of revenue has been largely confined to Ohio, Pennsylvania, and scattered cities in the mid-continent (such as St. Louis, Kansas City, Louisville, and Detroit). In these areas, a very low rate (around 1 percent) produces somewhere between 15 and 30 percent of general revenues. Philadelphia, for example, received 28 percent of its revenues from the income tax, almost as much as from its property tax (32 percent). Detroit, Cincinnati, and Pittsburgh, on the other hand, seem to have relatively low yields (12–15 percent), depending more heavily on property taxes. But the interesting aspect of the local income tax is its impact on suburban and fringe contributions to central city revenues. Despite prevailing low rates, income tax revenues derive 10–20 percent of their annual yield from noncity residents. St. Louis, however, receives 25 percent of its income tax receipts from suburbanites.[38]

As matters now stand, the revenue-producing potentialities of the municipal income tax are great, except where peripheral incorporated areas

Commission on Intergovermental Relations, *Metropolitan Social and Economic Disparities: Implications for Intergovernmental Relations in Central Cities and Suburbs* (Washington, D.C., U.S. Government Printing Office, January, 1965), p. 50.

[38] Sigafoos, *op. cit.*, pp. 69, 87–106; Robert C. Wood, *Metropolis Against Itself* (New York, Committee for Economic Development, 1959), p. 27.

have legally monopolized this form of taxation. Where income taxes are used, the effect is, apparently, to shift the burden from the property tax. Yet resistance remains extremely powerful. Incomes are already taxed by federal and (in many cases) state levels and to many "triple jeopardy" seems a close approximation to confiscation or governmental exploitation. But the generally low rates at the municipal level appear to refute such an argument—at least as long as rates remain near current levels. It seems likely that the income tax will be the only practical alternative to state and/or federal grants to urban regions.

4. In recent years in the U.S.—and for long periods in other nations— a substantial share of urban funds (perhaps 20 percent or more) has been contributed by Congress and state legislatures through intermediary agencies (e.g., HUD, Office of Education). As local programs reach more specifically into complex areas of service (preventive health services, special education projects, housing), the costs of providing these services already exceed reasonable local capacities. Ideology aside, federal and state funds seem to be the most probable form of additional financing for urban areas. Since federal revenues largely come from taxes on urban populations, we can expect this fact to be increasingly employed to justify not only ear-marked grants, but lump sum allocations to urban or metropolitan regions.

the political-administrative framework of urban political economy

Perhaps the major feature of urban political organization is its relatively slower pace of adaptation to the complexities of the modern urban region. As we have already seen, urban economic structures have been comparatively renovated, or marked by innovation. It may well be that urban leadership and the general population more clearly recognize the economic functions of urban areas. On the other hand, it is perhaps easier to persuade urban groups of the necessity for changes in the more rational sphere of the economy, where the benefits can be demonstrated, than in political organization, which must coordinate a wider diversity of essentially nonrational interests. In any case, both political scientists and urban sociologists agree that urban political institutions are now generally unequal to their tasks.

Clearly, the universal trend has been toward expanded services provided by governmental agencies. This expansion is both in range of services and in annual expenditures for specific types. In American cities, for example, governments have assumed some responsibility for virtually every physical and social need of their constituents—protection, health, education, welfare, recreation, art, housing, utilities, and transportation. During the period

1900–1942, public expenditures rose principally in well-established functions, such as health, public welfare, and public works. Since World War II, further increases (excluding those due to inflated costs) [39] indicate the intensified demand of urbanites for public services.

However, if the content of public services has grown more complex, the organizational forms tend to remain faithful to tradition. This is particularly true in those urban areas that are politically subservient to national governments [40]—Washington, D.C., Rio de Janeiro, Buenos Aires, Bombay, and Calcutta. In these urban regions, political control is to a large extent exercised by national officials responsible to a federal authority (e.g., Minister of Internal Affairs, a committee from the national legislature, or the President), not to the residents. Consequently, changes in political institutions and programs are possible only by effecting prior changes in the officials or broad policies of the national government.

On the other hand, several significant political innovations have been introduced—or seriously considered—in relatively autonomous urban regions. One trend is a growing emphasis on efficiency and specialization in political-administrative roles. As Gulick, a well-known authority on public administration has rightly concluded, "large scale [in cities] does not allow dependence on simple, inherited, amateur, informal, and voluntary approaches to government." [41] Urban political organization has gone through dynastic control of leading families, to the dominance of political machines, and gradually toward professionalization and bureaucratization. This is reflected in widening use of civil service and merit systems, and the demand for experts in public health, crime control, city planning, public education, and industrial development. [42]

In accord with professionalization in urban government, there has been some experimentation in administrative forms. The traditional form consists of a city council or board of aldermen and a chief executive (mayor), all elected for definite terms. In some instances, the council members elect one of themselves as mayor. But the complexities of urban problems are normally beyond the capabilities of elected officials, no matter how dedicated to government efficiency. During the past 50 years, American cities have tried to improve their urban government in one of two ways.

[39] Solomon Fabricant, *The Trend of Government Activity in the United States Since 1900* (New York, National Bureau of Economic Research, 1952), pp. 77–78, 83; Robert C. Wood, *Metropolis Against Itself* (New York, Committee for Economic Development, 1959), pp. 20–21.

[40] See William A. Robson, ed., *Great Cities of the World* (London, Allen and Unwin, 1954), Introduction.

[41] Luther Gulick, "Metropolitan Organization," in Meyerson, *op. cit.*, p. 57.

[42] Orin F. Nolting and David S. Arnold, eds., *The Municipal Year Book 1958* (Chicago, International City Managers' Association, 1958), pp. 129–132, 141, 146–165, 228–231.

1. the commission form

Unlike the council-mayor type, the commission form divides administrative authority among three, five, or seven elected commissioners, each of whom is responsible for a special group of municipal services. Both legislative and executive powers are combined in each commissioner, thus in practice dispensing with a central executive, and inviting specialized efficiency at the expense of coordination.[43] In general, the system is now quite rare. Even Galveston, Texas, where this innovation first appeared in 1900, has abandoned it.

2. the council-manager form

Earlier examples of this form may be found as far back as fifteenth century Italy, when cities such as Venice hired a *podesta*, or foreign noble, at a high salary to run city services for a city council divided by family feuds.[44] In the modern period, the city manager is an administrative expert (with training in either public administration, engineering, or accounting) appointed by the city council to assume complete executive responsibility for all city services.[45] The manager, ideally, is nonpartisan and immune to the appeals of special interest groups, since he is presumed to be a professional rather than a politician. It is interesting to note that city managers rarely remain in one community until retirement age; part of this is due to the shortage of city managers, and perhaps another factor is an inevitable loss of impartiality, which interferes with his professional role. Nevertheless, the council-manager type enjoys growing popularity, particularly in middle-sized American cities.

political coordination problems

Despite experiments with political form and increasing professionalization, the major problem in urban government is the lack of political coordination between the central city and the myriad communities in urban regions. This has been particularly acute in the last 30 years, as population growth has been most rapid in the suburban and fringe areas (see Chapters 4 and 7). Significantly, most of this fringe growth is in substantial commu-

[43] A brief survey of this form is in Stuart A. Queen and David B. Carpenter, *The American City* (New York, McGraw-Hill, 1953), pp. 312–313.

[44] Max Weber, *The City*, trans. by Don Martindale and Gertrud Neuwirth (New York, The Free Press of Glencoe, 1958), p. 131.

[45] *Municipal Yearbook, 1958*, pp. 241–245.

figure 15

Map of Seattle, Washington, Showing 17 Types of Governmental Jurisdiction

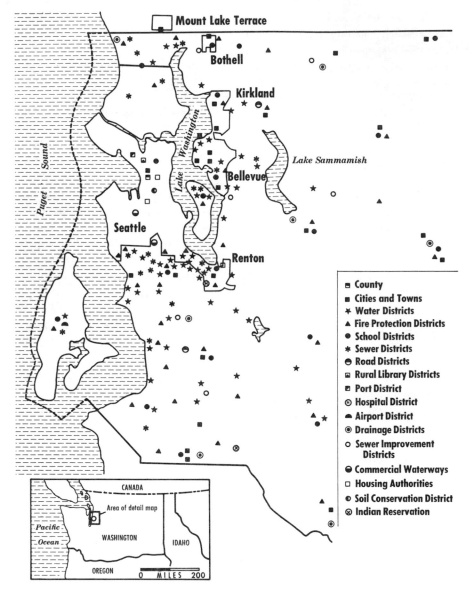

A CHALLENGE· This map of the Seattle area, showing 17 types of governmental jurisdiction, illustrates how complex municipal functions and services are in expanding cities
today. A bill was recently introduced in state legislature to enable Seattle and its environs
to establish a metropolitan government to operate on an areawide basis.

SOURCE: *The New York Times,* Feb. 3, 1957.

nities or municipalities of 10,000 to 50,000 population. These are precisely the kinds of communities that demand a full range of urban services and facilities—and yet are too small (and therefore financially unable) to provide these services independently. However, many such communities try "to go it alone," with a resultant inefficiency and confusion that belie the presumed "rationality" of urban civilization.

For example, there is the well-known anomaly of Detroit, which includes within its municipal boundaries the independent island communities of Hamtramck and Highland Park, each with its own government. Less spectacular but more widespread is the existence of hundreds of separate governmental units within the same metropolitan region in the United States and Great Britain. According to one authority, Chicago had 954 local units, Los Angeles had 319, Philadelphia had 705, Dallas had 63, Boston 112, Madison (Wisconsin) 229, and New York City—1074.[46] As Figure 15 graphically demonstrates, Seattle, a moderate-sized city, is enveloped in a bewildering array of overlapping jurisdictions: counties, water districts, school districts, sewer districts, library districts, housing authorities, etc. In England, the situation is much the same. Within a six-mile radius of Manchester there are 67 different local councils. And in the six largest urban regions (conurbations) there is a stupendous total of 232 separate housing authorities, many of them directly competing with one another for housing sites.[47]

The widespread recognition of the urban region as a new political entity is on the horizon. In the United States, a few cities are engaged in serious attempts to coordinate government services between central cities and surrounding communities. One such experiment is the urban county system, which centralizes authority for providing one or more services for all communities in the area (e.g., water, airport, sewage disposal, planning) in an organ of the county in which the central city is located. Los Angeles, St. Louis, and London are among the leaders in this movement. A second trend, which is often hotly contested, is political annexation of neighboring communities. Los Angeles is largely a history of successive annexations, but many American cities of substantial size have also found it more expedient to coordinate services and responsibility by annexation than by specific agreements. Some cities have had frequent annexations: San Jose, California, leading with 95 and Decatur, Illinois, with 52.[48]

The newest, the most direct, and the most controversial experiment is a genuine metropolitan government. At present, only Toronto has been given the legal basis for this political form (in 1954), though Miami is in process of developing a similar system. In the case of Toronto, the metropolitan

[46] *Municipal Yearbook, 1958,* pp. 41–44; Victor Jones, *Metropolitan Government* (Chicago, University of Chicago Press, 1942), pp. 126–129.

[47] Peter Self, *Cities in Flood* (London, Faber and Faber, 1959), pp. 55–56.

[48] *Municipal Yearbook, 1958,* pp. 53–55.

government is responsible for services to 245 square miles of the Toronto area, including what were previously 13 local governments. The latter at present provide only local services: water, street maintenance, sewerage, police and fire protection (to be transferred to the metropolitan government), and licensing. Significantly, the metropolitan government has area-wide jurisdiction over public transportation systems, highways, health services, housing, taxation and financing, justice, and correctional programs, regional planning, and to an increasing extent, public education.[49] It is much too early to assess the achievements of metropolitan government, but many American cities are following Toronto's experiences with great interest, and are engaged in studies that seem to anticipate some future imitation of this form.

special districts

During the past few decades, in the absence of metropolitan government in the U.S., specific forms of functional coordination have been established through special districts and area-wide public authorities. These urban administrative bodies have specialized in transportation (airports, bridges and tunnels, highways, rapid transit systems), parks, water supply, sanitation, and fire protection. In California urban areas, the so-called Lakewood Plan has enabled urban counties to provide service by contract to many small communities within the urban region. However, these various forms of "fluid federalism"—or fractionated metropolitanism—have been severely criticized by public administration experts, who argue that these arrangements impede such needed developments as incorporation, annexation, and intelligent coordination of regional resources.[50]

---

[49] *Ibid.*, pp. 45–49; Robson, *op. cit.*, pp. 376–377; James B. Milner, "The Metropolitan Toronto Plan," *University of Pennsylvania Law Review*, 105 (February, 1957), pp. 570–587; Frank Smallwood, *Metro Toronto: A Decade Later* (Toronto, Bureau of Municipal Research, 1963); Harold Kaplan, *Urban Political Systems: A Functional Analysis of Metro Toronto* (New York, Columbia University Press, 1967); Edward Sofen, *The Miami Metropolitan Experiment* (Bloomington, Indiana University Press, 1963).

[50] See Roscoe C. Martin, *Metropolis in Transition: Local Government Adaptation to Changing Urban Needs* (Washington, D.C., Housing and Home Finance Agency, September, 1963); Michael N. Danielson, ed., *Metropolitan Politics* (Boston, Little, Brown, 1966), Part 5; Robert G. Smith, *Public Authorities, Special Districts, and Local Government* (Washington, D.C., National Association of Counties Research Foundation, 1964); John C. Bollens, *Special District Government in the United States* (Berkeley, University of California Press, 1957); Robert O. Warren, *Government in Metropolitan Regions* (Davis, Calif., Institute of Governmental Affairs, 1966); Winston W. Crouch and Beatrice Dinerman, *Southern California Metropolis* (Berkeley, University of California Press, 1963).

political participation in urban regions

The formal structure of urban metropolitan government is variably responsive to urban problems. Perhaps the major clue to any marked lack of responsiveness is variability and inconsistency of political interest (and demands) among urban citizens, who are largely engaged in other affairs. Undoubtedly, the small town–New England image of citizen participation is grossly misplaced in the metropolitan setting, though it is likewise inaccurate to view urbanites as uniformly apathetic denizens of the urban polity. Political participation involves several kinds of activity, each of which entails its own characteristic interests, information base, and formal organization.

Most of the recent research in urban political behavior seems to support the use of three rough categories of participants. First, there is a substantial segment of *actives*, who are serious and continual members of the electorate, as evidenced by sustained interest, sophisticated knowledge of local political mechanics, regularity of voting, and membership in one or more politically resonant groups (such as a political party or League of Women Voters). Second, and probably the most typical category, is the *political casuals*, a somewhat heterogeneous category of persons who share great variability in political interest, irregular voting habits, inadequate information, and variably rationalized immunity to political organizations. Finally, a sizeable number of urbanites may be designated as *politically nonengaged* or *isolates*, because they appear to be both unable and unwilling to take part in any aspect of civic or political concerns.[51]

It would be quite a feat if we could specify the major factors that account for these differences in urban political participation. However, the necessary factual base is not yet available; instead, we have scattered vignettes for given urban areas on selected kinds of politically relevant matters such as: (1) knowledge about current officials and leaders; (2) knowledge about current local issues; (3) regularity in voting; (4) participation in organized politically active groups; (5) financial and/or personal contributions to local candidates or parties; and (6) willingness and opportunity to run for office. But perhaps the basic contours of urban political behavior can be sketched from the following kinds of clues.

1. *Knowledge and identification of local leaders.* Several studies show moderate to poor ability to identify more than one or two local leaders among representative samples of voters. In general, central city voters seem more knowledgeable than suburban voters, though differences are not sharp

51 Scott Greer, "The Social Structure and Political Process of Suburbia: An Empirical Test," *Rural Sociology*, 27 (December, 1962), pp. 438–459; Metropolitan Community Studies, *Metropolitan Challenge* (Dayton, 1959), pp. 232–238.

or consistent. As expected, actives surpass both casuals and isolates in identifying local officials. Likewise, those who belong to voluntary associations
(political or civic) tend to be more acquainted with the names and activities of their officials.[52]

2. *Interest in local issues.* Clearly, about four of five eligible metropolitan voters are less than passionately or actively interested in local governmental problems—apart from the voting phase, to which we shall return
soon. Slightly more interest is sustained among central city residents than
suburban categories; and again this interest is more nearly a monopoly of
the actives. Greer suggests that suburban politics is perceived as rather bor-
ing.[53] Perhaps this is only temporarily true, since as suburbs become more
complex, suburbanites show much more interest in such problems as schools,
garbage collection, and zoning. While there is some relation between formal
education and level of interest, education by itself is not a reliable predictor
of political interest.[54] Very recently, in metropolitan areas of the United
States, racial status is becoming a crucial factor in political participation—
particularly on such matters as housing, zoning, educational policy, and
police work.[55] Such class factors as education and occupation thus tend to
lose their earlier significance; age, neighborhood location, and length of
residence seem increasingly crucial for political interest of urban Negroes.

3. *Voting.* It is well known that, on the whole, urbanites are more interested in candidates (positively or negatively) than in referenda, but turnout rates (percent of eligible voters who actually vote in given elections)
vary by a few social and personal characteristics of the electorate. Generally,
the following seem to vote more regularly than their opposites or contrasted
categories:

> males
> those between 35 and 60 years of age
> homeowners
> long-term residents of neighborhood and county
> at least some college education
> city residence
> those with organizational memberships

The character of the urban vote (approval or disapproval rates) is
quite complex; it seems to vary with the kinds of issues and with local political cultures. For example, bond issue elections (schools, public improvements) and referenda on substantial administrative changes tend to polarize

[52] *Metropolitan Challenge*, pp. 150, 238; Greer, *op. cit.*, p. 445; R. H. Smuckler and
G. M. Belknap, *Leadership and Participation in Urban Political Affairs* (E. Lansing,
Government Research Bureau, Michigan State University, 1956), p. 12.

[53] *Metropolitan Challenge*, pp. 234–235.

[54] Alvin Boskoff and Harmon Zeigler, *Voting Patterns in a Local Election* (Philadelphia, Lippincott, 1964), Chap. 3; John C. Bollens, ed., *Exploring the Metropolitan
Community* (Berkeley, University of California Press, 1961), p. 233.

[55] Donald R. Matthews and James W. Prothro, *Negroes and the New Southern
Politics* (New York, Harcourt, Brace and World, 1966).

electorates into two segments: one seems to be imbued with notions of progress and a willingness to provide material support for desired services (civic responsibility); the other fears changes and suspects costs of such changes will be unduly placed on them (the insulated and alienated). In the first group, we tend to find younger persons with above average education and income, suburbanites, and those with more definite party affiliations. However, there is also some tendency for this category to be so optimistic about election outcome that their turnout rate is less than adequate.

The second category of urban voters is older, poorly educated, and in predominantly blue collar or small proprietor occupations, and often involves locally unassimilated ethnic categories (e.g., Poles, Czechs) either in the central city or in fringe areas.

Despite the wistful quest for nonpartisan elections, it is reasonably clear that the dominant party labels (local and national) form part of urban political cultures—though this is more evident when candidates are at issue. Metropolitan areas certainly differ on party preference for state and national candidates. Equally important, these preferences change somewhat as a consequence of (a) the relative attractiveness of competing candidates and (b) demographic and economic changes in specific metropolitan areas.

In general, metropolitan areas have favored the Democratic Party, particularly during periods of crisis (depression and war). While Eisenhower swept many urban areas in 1952 and 1956, urban congressional districts remained dominantly Democratic. It is likely that class—rather than location in the metropolitan region—accounts for a good deal of the party vote on the state and national level. Thus, for such areas as New Orleans, New York City, Philadelphia, and Detroit, lower status categories voted for the Democratic presidential candidate in 1952 and 1960, while middle and upper levels were solidly Republican in 1952 and 1956, but were more strongly attracted to Kennedy in 1960.[56] However, population mobility and considerable changes in voting choice for the same voters in successive elections (the so-called floating voters) prevent us from drawing firm conclusions about class and party vote. Indeed, in a comparison of the 1952 and 1956 presidential vote, almost a third (31 percent) of the votes represented a switch from the preceding election.[57] Furthermore, the evidence for switching was almost equally distributed among the various status categories.

Few studies have focused on a sufficiently extended time span of elections for specific urban areas—an obvious necessity for appraising the possible effects of migration patterns on voting behavior. Yet scattered clues indicate

[56] William C. Havard et al., The Louisiana Elections of 1960 (Baton Rouge, Louisiana University Press, 1963), p. 109; Edward H. Litchfield, Voting Behavior in a Metropolitan Area (Ann Arbor, University of Michigan Press, 1941), Government Studies #7 pp. 7, 15; Hugh A. Bone and Austin Ranney, Politics and Voters (New York, McGraw-Hill, 1963), p. 49.

[57] H. Daudt, Floating Voters and the Floating Vote (Leiden, H. E. Stenfert Kroese, 1961), p. 77.

that, for given social categories, relative stability in political orientation and preference is the rule. There is a strong tendency for given economic and social categories (e.g., skilled workers, white collar workers, managers) to retain former political preferences after moves from central city to periphery, from small towns to cities or suburbs, or from city to city.[58]

Occupational mobility may be a significant aspect of migration in our attempt to understand political shifts among urbanites. Campbell's study of the 1956 presidential election [59] incidentally showed that people who were occupationally mobile (either upward or downward) had changed their party identification since 1952. While the number of cases was too small for a reliable pattern, the major movement in party preference was toward Independent. There was no particular relation between direction of mobility and change in party preference, though the upwardly mobile were somewhat more attracted to the Republican label.

Since one of the most visible demographic changes has been the suburban expansion of the last two decades, the possible political effects of this redistribution have been much discussed. The evidence, however, is quite mixed—perhaps because writers have failed to distinguish different kinds of suburbs and different migrant streams to suburban locations. But two general conclusions seem to be warranted at this point in our knowledge. First, based on presidential elections alone, since 1952 suburban areas as a whole have tended to favor Republican candidates, but with comparatively little gain (as against city trends) in Republican strength in 1952 and possibly 1956. In fact, the suburban vote for Nixon in 1960 was generally less than for Eisenhower in 1956, except in Kansas City suburbs. Furthermore, as Lazerwitz has shown, the largest Democratic gains in congressional seats (1952–1956) were concentrated in suburban areas.[60]

Second, suburban voters tend to express the characteristics of their presuburban residence and status features. Thus, Berger found blue collar migrants to a California suburb were continuing their former Democratic sympathies. Wallace likewise concluded that suburban dwellers in the Westport (Conn.) area were as Republican as their parents in urban settings.[61] It has also been suggested that many suburban areas—not the stereotyped Park Forests and Crestwood Heights—have attracted large numbers from small

58 Bone and Ranney, op. cit., pp. 47–48.

59 Angus Campbell et al., The American Voter (New York, Wiley, 1960), pp. 458–459.

60 Bernard Lazerwitz, "Suburban Voting Trends: 1948 to 1956," Social Forces, 39 (October, 1960), pp. 29–36; Frederick M. Wirt, "The Political Sociology of American Suburbia: A Reinterpretation," Journal of Politics, 27 (August, 1965), pp. 647–666; David Wallace, "Some Functional Aspects of Stability and Change in Voting," American Journal of Sociology, 69 (September, 1963), pp. 161–170.

61 Wallace, op. cit., pp. 163–164; Bennett Berger, Working Class Suburb (Berkeley, University of California Press, 1960), Chap. 3; Kevin R. Cox, "Suburbia and Voting Behavior in the London Metropolitan Area," Annals of the Association of American Geographers, 58 (March, 1968), pp. 111–127.

town, rural, and fringe areas, which typically favor the Republican Party.[62]

In the last few years, suburban voting behavior has been tentatively linked with type of family orientation. Interviews in a suburban zone northeast of Atlanta found several patterns of voting shift and continuity. For example, upwardly mobile families showed decided shifts from Democratic to Republican votes, while well-to-do, continuous participants in local affairs tend to remain Democrats. Significantly, families who moved to the suburbs as an escape from the burdens of city life, or who have marked internal dissension about goals, either tended to remain nonvoters or shifted from nonvoting to the Republicans.[63]

But party preference does not exhaust the picture of political participation among suburban dwellers. During the early years of the suburban resurgence in the United States (1946–1955), one of the dominant emphases was escape from congestion, taxes, and city politics. Consequently, the young suburban migrants tended to focus on family and job. However, more recent migrant streams have included families with more experience and more dedication to local problems in suburban and county settings. Though the evidence for this change is still only suggestive, the clues from county bond issue elections seem to point to markedly increased responsibility among residents in the more settled suburbs. For example, school bond elections in the East Lansing and Syracuse areas were most strongly supported by suburbanites. This pattern is even more sharply revealed in a crucial ten-part county bond issue election near Atlanta in 1961. Suburban districts provided highest levels of voter support on most of the bond items. But even more important, low income suburbanites were almost as decisive in their vote as their higher status counterparts.[64] This suggests that, in the recent political situation, suburban areas attract families with either a transplanted or a new sense of civic responsibility. Interviews with a sample of voters confirm the notion of suburban involvement and civic responsibility in two complementary forms. First, suburbanites—as compared with fringe or rural voters—more often gave specific, positive reasons for their votes (e.g., "this is needed for progress in the county"; "we have needed this improvement for years"). Second, we found greater interest and exposure to county papers (which provided extensive discussion of projected improvements) among suburban voters than any other voting segment of the county.[65]

[62] Campbell, op. cit., p. 465; Herbert J. Gans, The Levittowners (New York, Pantheon Books, 1967), p. 266.

[63] Alvin Boskoff, "Social and Cultural Patterns in a Suburban Area: Their Significance for Social Change in the South," Journal of Social Issues, 22 (January, 1966), pp. 91–92.

[64] Warner Bloomberg et al., Suburban Power Structures and Public Education (Syracuse, Syracuse University Press, 1963), pp. 24, 131, 155; Gary King et al., Conflict Over Schools (E. Lansing, Institute for Community Development and Services, Michigan State University, 1963), p. 17; Boskoff and Zeigler, op. cit., Chap. 3 and pp. 136–137.

[65] Boskoff and Zeigler, op. cit., pp. 59–60, 81–83.

implications

As urban areas evolve—or accelerate processes of development—their political economies require constant adaptations and more rapid meshing of political and economic components. In a sense, urbanism involves a built-in dynamic for creating changes (improvements, novelties, expansions, etc.) that challenge previous solutions and also stimulate greater opportunities for decision making (and not incidentally, errors in judgment). In the past, the economic sector provided the major source of such changes. But we are beginning to see with more clarity that political structures (and mundane government decisions) can greatly affect the location and implementation of economic opportunities in specific urban settings.

The current thrust of urban economic activities and organizations emphasizes variety, youth, expansiveness—both as ideals and achievements. This entails subtle forms of stress on urbanites: variety can mean too many options for behavior; youth requires constant learning (or simulation) of new skills and tastes; expansiveness may demand greater effort in selling and servicing urban goods and services. Further mechanization (the presumed effects of automation) may partially contain these stresses, though it is also likely that increasingly rationalized production will contribute an indeterminate addition to stress by facilitating further quantity, variety, and availability of consumable items. Control and coordination therefore become increasingly important problems for urban entities.

Yet the political framework of urban areas is reaching a critical point in its checkered development of the past hundred years. During the past few decades, the formal structure has gained in complexity and professionalization, but the decisions that flow from this structure are far from cumulative or intelligible in terms of any positive conception of future need-clusters. At the same time, the overall level of citizen participation creates a persistent problem. There is considerable evidence of polarization between a small category of active (but not necessarily united) participants and a relatively large set of passive, disinterested, and even alienated residents in metropolitan regions. Migration, of course, changes the local geographic distribution of these types, but the overall structure of responsibility does not seem to vary significantly.

In practice, then, the political economy of urban regions is becoming subject to the patterned or unpatterned policies of key officials—either as facilitators of local economic processes (through zoning, taxation and taxation relief) or as mediators of economic and social programs derived from the national level (Congress, federal agencies, or private national organizations and foundations). Ultimately, as Galbraith has recently argued,[66] the tech-

---

[66] John Kenneth Galbraith, *The New Industrial State* (Boston, Houghton Mifflin, 1967), Chap. 6.

nology of urban industrialism may not be the prime factor in metropolitan difficulties, as a generation of critics have written. Instead, technology may become the tool of determined politicos who are dedicated to orderly processes of urban growth. In short, if the intermittent chaos of the immediate does not blind us to urban potentials, the political economy of future urbanism may once again represent the dominance of the political principle, through the medium of metropolitan planning. The elements of such an innovative structure are already apparent in variably timid and bold attempts to encourage educational facilities, artistic experiences for wider audiences, and the superior availability of varied recreational activities for participants in the contemporary urban wave.

selected references

BOLLENS, John C. and SCHMANDT, Henry J., *The Metropolis* (New York, Harper and Row, 1965).

BOSKOFF, Alvin and ZEIGLER, Harmon, *Voting Patterns in a Local Election* (Philadelphia, J. B. Lippincott, 1964).

COULTER, Philip B., ed., *Politics of Metropolitan Areas* (New York, Thomas Y. Crowell, 1967).

DIMOCK, Marshall E., *The New American Political Economy* (New York, Harper and Row, 1962).

JANOWITZ, Morris, ed., *Community Political Systems* (New York, The Free Press, 1960).

MILBRATH, Lester W., *Political Participation* (Chicago, Rand McNally, 1965).

WOOD, Robert C., *1400 Governments* (Cambridge, Harvard University Press, 1961).

14

major urban institutions: religion, education, and welfare

religious organization in urban regions

Religion as a field of human interest and activity is, of course, preurban. On the other hand, many of the currently established religious organizations can be traced to the social conditions of earlier urban waves. Apparently, religious interest is universal, but religious organization is subject to considerable change over time. What, then, are the effects of modern urbanism on religion as an institutional activity?

The vitality of urban religions remains remarkably high, despite apocalyptic visions of religious decay. However, the expression and organization of urban religion are marked by experimentation, great diversity, uncertainty, and sometimes conflict. This should not be surprising, if the nature of modern urban regions is recalled. Institutionalized religion, in varying degrees in different nations, is enmeshed in two typically urban problems: specialization (or perhaps overspecialization), and competition from informal or incidental sources of religious interest.

diversity, specialization, and bureaucratization

Throughout the modern world, urbanization is accompanied by some separation of institutionalized religion from other spheres of activity. This trend is particularly clear in American urban regions, where traditional religion is highly compartmentalized as a result of an unparalleled division of labor in the community. Four important consequences have generally followed, though in different degrees in various societies. These are a growing variety of religious organizations, the assumption of nonreligious functions by religious groups, bureaucratization of religious organization, and a variably visible stratification in religious affiliation.

Once the prevailing established forms of religion become distinct from kinship organization (as in the urbanization of formerly preliterate groups) or the government structure (as in the United States, Canada, and to some extent in Germany and England), urbanites acquire a measure of freedom in their religious affiliations. Any real or imagined dissatisfactions on theological matters, morality, authority, or the personality of clergymen may find an outlet in reduced participation and diluted religious beliefs or formation of new religious organizations. The first alternative has been more prevalent perhaps in nations where one church (Catholic, Mohammedan) holds a continuing monopoly; the second appears in urbanized nations that have no "established" church, as in the United States.

In American urban regions, the number of separate religious groups is staggering—almost 300 denominations and cults.[1] The yellow pages of the telephone directory in most large cities normally list a bewildering alphabetical array of churches, many of which are only vaguely recognizable to nonmembers. Apparently, two major kinds of religious groups account for the greater part of this diversity. The more numerous type is a series of cults and sects, usually of an emotional, highly fundamentalist faith, which seek to break away from the staid, complacent, established churches (mainly Protestant). With few exceptions, these schismatic groups attract lower status urbanites, particularly those who have recently migrated from rural areas. In this latter category are a considerable number of Negroes. Religious organization tends to be personal and nonbureaucratic. Often each group is distinguished by its name, rather than a special theology. Some examples are:[2] The Seventh-Day Adventists, Jehovah's Witnesses, Church of the Nazarene, New Thoughts, Theosophy, the I Am Movement, Spiritualist, Church of God, Holiness Sects.

The other type consists of relatively few well organized denominations (from a historical standpoint, these are successful survivals of an earlier schismatic movement): e.g., Episcopalian, Congregational, Methodist, Lutheran, Baptist, and Presbyterian. In recent years, both in the United States and England, the Oxford Group Movement (and Moral Rearmament) seems to be developing away from its cultish form toward a less emotionalized organiza-

[1] Robin M. Williams, Jr., *American Society*, 2nd ed. (New York, Alfred A. Knopf, 1960), pp. 341–344. For descriptions of the variety in religion, see Elmer T. Clark, *The Small Sects in America* (Nashville, Tenn., Cokesbury Press, 1937) and Charles S. Braden, *These Also Believe* (New York, Macmillan, 1949).

[2] W. B. Selbie, *English Sects: A History of Nonconformity* (New York, Holt, Rinehart, and Winston, 1925); Braden, *op. cit.*; Arthur H. Fauset, *Black Gods of the Metropolis: Negro Religious Cults of the Urban North* (Philadelphia, University of Pennsylvania Press, 1944). For the medieval counterpart of this trend, see also Norman Cohn, *The Pursuit of the Millennium* (London, Secker and Warburg, 1957).

tion.[3] In general, the denominational form represents groups with more stable adjustments to urban living than that of cult and sect members.

competition of religious forms

Religious diversity in the free situation of American urban regions has meant competition for potential adherents. Often, since theological differences are slight or virtually immune to examination, many additional services have been assumed by religious groups with the hope of attracting and holding members. The weekly sermon comes to be engulfed in pastoral counseling on family matters, recreational programs, social gatherings (teas, suppers, picnics), babysitting services, the newsletter, welfare activities, fund raising, public relations, representation in civic affairs, and sometimes political action. In short, competitive religious groups have tried to provide a vital, attractive religious organization.

Urban religion, embarking on such a quest, has been forced to follow the well-worn path to increasing bureaucratization. The minister (or rabbi)—and often his wife—is a religious executive, supplemented by assistant or associate ministers, secretaries, governing boards, directors of religious education and music, laymen's committees, and a variety of intradenominational organizations (local, state, regional, and national). Consequently, urban religion in its institutionalized forms is to many urban residents a poor substitute for traditional forms of religion. One typical reaction is passive participation; [4] another is a gradual assumption of a secular attitude that blurs any previously meaningful distinction between the routine and the extraordinary. Still another reaction is the segregation of dissidents into factions jockeying for power. Most important, however, is a tendency toward stratification, which is understandable on historical and theological grounds as well.

Several studies clearly demonstrate that urban social classes (in terms of occupational and income differences) are unequally represented in the prevailing variety of religious groups. Table 39, based on the composition of major religious bodies in 1945-1946 for the United States,[5] indicates a rather significant tendency for middle class persons to be adherents of Methodist, Episcopal, Congregational, and Jewish faiths, while lower class families seem to be more prevalent in Catholic and Baptist groups It is tempting to exaggerate the meaning of the differences summarized in this table. But several cautions must be observed. Unfortunately, we have few figures on historical

---

[3] Allan W. Eister, *Drawing-Room Conversion: A Sociological Account of the Oxford Group Movement* (Durham, Duke University Press, 1950).

[4] John Wicklein, "Lack of Religion Found in Church," *The New York Times*, January 8, 1961.

[5] See Bernard Barber, *Social Stratification* (New York, Harcourt, Brace, and World, 1957), p. 157. A similar connection between status and religion is demonstrated in Walter Goldschmidt, *As You Sow* (New York, Harcourt, Brace, and World, 1947).

table 39

Social Class Composition of Major Religious Groups in the U.S., 1945–1946
(in percent)

RELIGIOUS GROUPS	UPPER CLASS	MIDDLE CLASS	LOWER CLASS
National Sample	*13.1*	*30.7*	*56.2*
Episcopal	24.1	33.7	42.2
Congregational	23.9	42.6	33.5
Presbyterian	21.9	40.0	38.1
Jewish	21.8	32.0	46.2
No preference	13.3	26.0	60.7
Methodist	12.7	35.6	51.7
Protestant (unspecified)	12.4	24.1	63.5
Lutheran	10.9	36.1	53.0
Christian (unspecified or Disciples of Christ)	10.0	35.4	54.6
Protestant (various smaller bodies)	10.0	27.3	62.7
Catholic	8.7	24.7	66.6
Baptist	8.0	24.0	68.0

SOURCE: Bernard Barber, *Social Stratification* (New York, Harcourt, Brace and World, 1957), p. 157.

trends or changes in the class composition of religious bodies. Furthermore, we cannot interpret this table very satisfactorily until we know that class status strongly influences religious affiliation, that religious affiliation provides opportunities for achieving specific status levels, or that both religious membership and class status are related to some third factor—perhaps income. In addition, membership figures do not tell us about degrees of participation, personal involvement, and satisfaction in urban religious groups.

However, a few tentative conclusions may be drawn. Established religions in urban areas fail to provide satisfying religious services to a substantial number of lower class families, both white and Negro. As a result, cities are breeding-grounds of religious experiments by migratory or unadjusted lower class persons. The "store front" church, the "tent revival," are symbols of a search for a "traditional" religion in the urban setting. Some denominations, notably the Methodist, recognize the consequences of this trend; they find that as they discourage (implicitly or explicitly) lower class whites and virtually all Negroes, these denominations are slowly shifting from the core to the periphery of American urban regions (e.g., in Boston, Detroit, Pittsburgh, and Chicago). However, while the proliferation of suburban churches is well documented, there is some evidence that this trend is no longer at the expense of inner city churches. Myers' study of Seattle in 1958 is notable for the discovery that the prior location of suburban churches was more often in outer residential areas of the city than in central areas. In addition, there has been a determined effort on the part of several Protestant denominations to revitalize (or simply initiate) religious and related services in poverty areas of large cities. The "inner city ministry" is still in the experimental state and it is difficult to know whether its impact is mainly in the area of religion or welfare.[6]

If these recent attempts to halt religious trends do not succeed, the social segregation of religion may counteract the functional interdependence of the components of the urban region with a renewed emphasis on class divisions— not, as Marx predicted, from the contradictions of the capitalist market, but from the subtle monopolies of the religious market.

During the past two decades, the notion of an urban religious "revival" has been countered by some searching self-analyses by major denominations. Methodists, Lutherans, and Congregationalists report declining membership in cities, while suburban rolls show steady expansion. Jews likewise show impressive suburban gains, but with smaller declines (if any) in established city neighborhoods. On the other hand, the significance of religious membership figures is clouded by the apparently widespread practice (largely among Protestants) of shifting affiliation for reasons of convenience, rather than theological commitment. And it is well known that belated (or renewed) religious affiliation is often either a reflection of sociability or a gesture for the religious exposure of one's children.[7]

the fragmentation of religion

Religion in modern urban regions seem to be slowly adjusting to its setting by trial-and-error: by separation and by addition of new services; by general appeals and by narrowed, class-like emphases. But institutionalized religion must also face the fact that there are strong competitors in the urban religious sphere that have no church or temple or bible, that competitors are normal consequences of urban communities and cultures.

Perhaps this situation can be understood by analyzing religion in terms of four distinctive aspects or parts.[8] (a) Religious beliefs (or theology) con-

6 George C. Myers, "Patterns of Church Distribution and Movement," Social Forces, 40 (May, 1962), pp. 354–363; Truman B. Douglass, "Ecological Changes and the Church," Annals of the American Academy of Political and Social Science (November, 1960), pp. 80–88.

7 Douglass, op. cit.; The New York Times, April 5, 1959, and January 8, 1961.

8 Cf. Emile Durkheim, The Elementary Forms of the Religious Life, tr. by Joseph Ward Swain (New York, The Free Press, 1947), Books 2 and 3; Charles Y. Glock and Rodney Stark, Religion and Society in Tension (Chicago, Rand McNally, 1965), Chap. 2; Anthony F. C. Wallace, Religion: An Anthropological View (New York, Random House, 1966), Chaps. 2, 3.

sist of a series of cultural norms that define the nature of a supernatural (or supernaturals), its powers and their expression. (*b*) *Religious rites* or *ceremonies* refer to occasions in which religious beliefs are reinforced by proper use of religious objects—material items that symbolically represent specific religious beliefs. (*c*) *Religious experience* is the individual's feelings of exaltation, spiritual satisfaction, or excitement, which derive from his contact (direct or indirect) with some supernatural. In this sense, Joan of Arc had religious experiences when she heard the "voices" that encouraged her entrance into the political arena. Similarly, the decision to follow a specific vocation (literally a "calling") may be based on an assumed "message" from God or other supernatural agents. (*d*) Finally, for our purposes, religion may develop *religious social organization*, a specialized group dedicated to regularizing contacts with the supernatural by providing expert leadership, properly indoctrinating adherents, and furnishing material and social bases for religious experience.

Traditionally, all four components of religion have been fused into unities known as institutionalized religions. In modern urban regions, however, this fusion is yielding to fragmentation. Of particular significance is a growing autonomy of the first three components from religious social organization—which has the consequence of permitting a greater variety of religious beliefs and supernaturals, and also of expanding the range of situations capable of providing religious experience for urbanites. This process is one aspect of the often noted "secularization of religion," which some believe is the end of religion. But secularization may also be interpreted as "experimentation in religion," in this case by more direct contact with the cultural and psychological components of religion.

For example, urbanites seem to be seeking new or supplementary supernaturals in such varied guises as Science, Education, political idols (Roosevelt, Churchill, Eisenhower, Adenauer, De Gaulle, etc.) and even in legendary sports figures. To the urbanite, these "supernaturals" possess the advantage of being widely known and yet retaining the sacred aura of distance so necessary for reverence.[9]

The fragmentation of urban religion is exemplified in the development of so-called religious styles, or differential focus on basic religious components. There is, of course, the traditional distinction between religious involvement (emphasizing beliefs) and formal church attendance (emphasizing the organizational aspects). But a study of the United Church of Christ (Congregational Christian, Evangelical and Reformed Church merger) identified five styles:

1. *The unquestioning believer*—religious beliefs and other components highly regarded as interlocking and indispensable facets.[10]

[9] Durkheim, *op. cit.*, Chap. 1.

[10] *The New York Times*, January 8, 1961; Erich Good, "Class Styles of Religious Sociation," *British Journal of Sociology*, 19 (March, 1968), pp. 1–16.

2. *The religiously knowledgeable*—characterized by "liberal" interpretation of beliefs and rituals.

3. *The organizational member*—primarily responsive to organizational aspects, attendance, and voluntary contributions.

4. *The inward-experiencing devotional member*—emphasis on religious experience of a direct, personal kind.

5. *The nominal*—members with no marked attachment to any of the components.

As might be expected, social rank is somewhat correlated with the kinds of religious fragmentation just noted. In general, formal participation and nominal types tend to be middle and upper socioeconomic persons, while the devotional and unquestioning believer types predominate in lower status categories. Even the meaning of religious participation seems to vary with social rank, according to Glock and his associates. Upper class women, they found, devote themselves to church activities as part of a larger concern for community issues; they view religion as meeting the challenge of social difficulties. On the other hand, lower class women seem to seek church involvement as a substitute for participation in groups and organizations to which they have little access (political, civic, and educational groups).[11]

Religious experience, or its psychological equivalent, is increasingly available in nontraditional forms as a normal aspect of the urban milieu. One important variety is the relentlessly captivating appeal and sensation of the mass media of communication. Urbanites receive a basically nonrational satisfaction or thrill from news stories, picture magazines, favorite television fare, and to some extent from films (but note the attempt to play up the element of sensation by wide screens, color, third-dimensional techniques, and even the use of special odors). As a classic survey demonstrated,[12] missing the newspaper as a result of a strike meant an interruption to many of a ritualistic, semicompulsive, security-giving experience.

Another major form of urban religious experience is gambling. Here the "supernatural" is the very ancient one of luck or chance. Excepting the professional gamblers, who follow gambling as a vocation, urbanites seem to be extremely vulnerable to the unsophisticated lure of games of chance—cards, bingo, horse racing, various sports contests, commercial contests, and even

[11] Good, *op. cit.*, pp. 2–9; Charles Y. Glock, Benjamin B. Ringer, and Earl R. Babbie, *To Comfort and to Challenge* (Berkeley, University of California Press, 1967), pp. 91, 106–108. See also Peter L. Berger, *The Sacred Canopy* (Garden City, Doubleday, 1967); *Journal for the Scientific Study of Religion*, 2 (Fall, 1962). Symposium—The Problem of Attempting to Define Religion (esp. the papers by Stanley, Lazerwitz, and Salisbury).

[12] Bernard Berelson, "What 'Missing the Newspaper' Means," in Paul Lazarsfeld and Frank Stanton, eds., *Communications Research, 1948–1949* (Urbana, Ill., University of Illinois Press, 1949), pp. 111–128.

betting on the choice of a number (the notorious "policy game" of New York City, Chicago, and other urban centers).[13]

These subtle and largely neglected sources of religious participation in urban regions are clearly unlike our usual conceptions of organized religion. Moreover, these newer forms seem to reflect some of the characteristic features of urbanization. Almost all of the religious substitutes emphasize the primacy of individual participation (rather than family or other groups), as well as the anonymity of the individual. Furthermore, they require little or no preparation, or deep levels of involvement, for any extended time period. In fact, the diffuseness and lack of visible formalization tend to minimize both the effectiveness of community controls and the ability of religious groups to compete for the allegiance of urbanites. Urban religion, therefore, is a study in contrasts; more slowly than the economic and political spheres, it is involved in readjusting once dominant values and organizations to the complex cultural and ecological changes of modern urban regions.

urban education

Education, the process of relaying cultural experience from one generation to another, is a universal necessity, but urban communities are by their very nature both unusually dependent on education and faced with special difficulties in insuring adequate performance of this function. The reasons are fairly obvious. There is, first, the relatively larger number of persons involved in urban education. Perhaps more important is the heterogeneous nature of populations in urban regions: long-term residents and migrants; differences in status levels, occupation, income, religion, nationality, and race. Third, the sheer weight and complexity of culture to be transmitted presents practical problems that are still unsolved in the most advanced urban areas. Education, for example, must develop skills in reading, writing, calculation, in vocational pursuits, as well as some general technical and scientific knowledge.

But these technical difficulties are magnified by the extraordinary reliance of urban regions on pervasive and efficient educational processes. Because of its great accessibility and its continually expanding contacts with other communities and societies, the urban region requires the best available information about its own operation and about regions with which it maintains political and economic relationships. More important, this information must be gathered, analyzed, and applied by competent persons as residents and as agents of urban regions. This is probably the core of the social importance of urban education. Indeed, the world's underdeveloped nations, striv-

[13] See Walter C. Reckless, *The Crime Problem* (New York, Appleton-Century-Crofts, 1950), Chap. XIII.

ing for industrialization and urbanization, recognize the crucial function of education with greater pungency than do "advanced" societies, because the former are trying to achieve rapidly improved education with limited resources and personnel.[14] Specifically, educational processes are crucial for the maintenance of the urban region in at least five respects.

1. The most obvious, which was briefly mentioned above, is the necessity for quick, efficient, and meaningful communication among urban groups. In one sense, the urban complex is a network of decision-making processes—decisions on location, production, control, distribution, and exchange of goods and services. As members of formal groups and as individuals, urbanites strive to make intelligent, rational decisions, though emotion and tradition are not completely absent. Urban education provides the necessary tools of communication—ideas, techniques, and acquired interests.

2. Urbanization and the urban way of life largely depend on a vast network of occupations and vocations, each with its own skills, experiences, and problems. With the separation of home and job, the traditional preparation for vocations or trades through the medium of the family is no longer feasible. Indeed, the diversity of needed skills, and the comparative freedom in selecting one's occupation, hinder the role of the family as a direct transmitter of occupational skills. Consequently, a specialized educational system is necessary to transmit vocationally relevant skills. In the urban region, clerical and trades skills are acquired through secondary schools and vocational schools or business and secretarial colleges, while professional and administrative skills seem to require higher educational programs in college and universities.

3. It is not sufficiently recognized that the urban economy, which is fundamentally dependent on diversified and expanding demand for urban products, is thereby inevitably affected by the character and distribution of educational programs. Consumer demand (within or between urban regions) reflects not only available income, but the cultivation of tastes and desires for goods and services. In general, the greatest expansion in urban consumer demand has been in products that symbolize status ascent or the widening of personal experience. Larger and better equipped homes, unusual foods, more varied and better styled clothing, the use of professional services (physicians, dentists, attorneys, architects, etc.), automobiles, and the steady flow of new appliances—all these are familiar examples of such products.

Essentially, the increasing trend toward consumer interest in these acquired needs has been accompanied by the extension of urban educational processes to a growing proportion of urbanites. Advertising, a crucial urban invention, is an obvious and variably effective part of urban education, but the importance of formal public education in conditioning consumer habits

[14] Lyle W. Shannon, ed., *Underdeveloped Areas* (New York, Harper and Brothers, 1957), Chaps. IV, IX, X; Edward H. Spicer, ed., *Human Problems in Technological Change* (New York, Russell Sage Foundation, 1952).

should not be neglected.[15] Indeed, teachers and other students often un-wittingly create preferences and valuations about food, recreation, clothing, etc.

4. The urban region is simultaneously an economic entity and a frame-work for meeting the noneconomic needs of its residents. It is sometimes for-gotten that the latter functions soon come to have as much importance to urban residents as the former. In fact, urban Americans seem to give extraor-dinary attention to such community services as public utilities, schools, library facilities, parks and other recreational areas, etc. in job changes and decisions to move.[16] These increasingly desired services, however, depend on revenues from various kinds of local and regional taxes, as some suburbanites belatedly discover. However, the ultimate source of taxation is current income (not land, as the outmoded real property tax has assumed). Urban income, in turn, is rather directly related to the concentration of highly skilled, profes-sional, and managerial workers. We have already noted that expansion of the higher paid, higher status occupations results from the extension of formal educational opportunities to more and more urbanites. In short, formal educa-tion and its immediate consequences are indispensable to the maintenance and enhancement of urban amenities, which give character to the urban region and motivate urbanites to supply needed manpower.

5. Finally, the hallmarks of urbanism—creativity and change in many spheres—can be traced to a developed, specialized educational system. Inno-vations, which are normally contributed by a small segment of the population (though not necessarily an elite in intelligence or responsibility), stem from disciplined dissatisfaction, independence from traditional restraints, some form of specialized knowledge, and often an unverbalized respect for the value of curiosity, comparison, objectivity, and progress.[17] Though some urbanites undoubtedly develop these characteristics without much exposure to formal education, most of the widely accepted urban creations have been the rare fruit of education in schools, colleges, and institutes. Increasingly, business-men, professionals of all kinds, and experts in public and private service—our primary sources of invention—are recruited from those with formal edu-cation. By contrast, the innovators in urban areas of 2000 to 5000 years ago

[15] See Lincoln H. Clark, ed., *Consumer Behavior: Research on Consumer Reactions* (New York, Harper and Brothers, 1958), pp. 13–37, 93–219; David Riesman, *The Lonely Crowd* (Garden City, Doubleday Anchor Books, 1953), Chaps. III, IV.

[16] Richard Dewey, "Peripheral Expansion in Milwaukee County," *American Journal of Sociology*, 54 (September, 1948), pp. 118–125; Peter Rossi, *Why Families Move* (New York, The Free Press of Glencoe, 1955); Walter T. Martin, *The Rural-Urban Fringe: A Study of Adjustment to Residence Location* (Eugene, Ore., University of Oregon Press, 1953).

[17] See Joseph Rossman, *The Psychology of the Inventor* (Washington, D.C., The Inventors Publishing Company, 1931); John Jewkes *et al.*, *The Sources of Invention* (London, Macmillan & Co., 1958); H. G. Barnett, *Innovation* (New York, McGraw-Hill, 1953), Chaps. VI, X.

were not blessed with formal education; they wrought their contributions out of the practical problems of warfare and religion.[18]

Public education, rarely more than one hundred years old, is a vast, expensive urban experiment in preparing urbanites for the responsibilities and opportunities of urban living. Previously, education was largely informal and intermittent; formal education was limited to a favored minority of professionals (ministers, lawyers, physicians) and merchants, who received their training under private auspices (family or church).[19] With few exceptions, such education was considered inappropriate for females, who needed only the simple domestic skills and a steady devotion to household labor.

The institution of free (i.e., supported by general taxation), public, universal, formalized education has placed a large "finis" to preexisting forms of education, at least at the lower level. It has become a symbol and a goal for those nations and regions striving to become urbanized or to emulate the fruits of urbanism (literacy, secularism, technical advancements). To the sociologist, public education is marked by a number of specially urban features, which help in understanding the accomplishments and the gnawing problems of modern education throughout the world.

1. extensiveness

Public education, by law and by custom, is available to all residents of a given age range, regardless of sex, religion, color, and financial status of parents. Though public schools do not achieve full coverage—some families prefer private schools, and some urban youngsters maintain a startling immunity to any formal education—they normally serve such a vast proportion of young people that public education is necessarily a mass enterprise.

2. internal specialization

Despite the large numbers served, urban public education has tended to decry uniformity as an inevitable educational feature. In general, uniformity is greatest at the primary level, with increasing concern for variety and individual needs in secondary and college programs. However, classes for retarded and "exceptional" children, schools for the blind and the deaf, for serious behavior problems (the famous "600" schools in New York City) are increasingly evident in American urban regions. On the secondary level, many cities provide general programs, college preparatory courses, vocational or

18 See Lewis Mumford, *Technics and Civilization* (New York, Harcourt, Brace and World, 1934); and Herbert Spencer, *The Principles of Sociology* (New York, D. Appleton and Co., 1897), Vol. 3.

19 N. Freeman Butts, *A Cultural History of Western Education*, 2nd ed. (New York, McGraw-Hill, 1955); Abraham Flexner, *Universities: American, English, German* (New York, Oxford University Press, 1930).

trade schools, commercial programs, plus adult education courses in English for foreigners to world politics. Comparatively few cities boast municipally owned colleges, but the number is gradually increasing as the pressure for college education comes to exceed the capacities of private colleges and bulging state university centers.

3. bureaucratization

The scope and variety of educational programs, the rapidly expanding student bodies, and emphasis on improved teaching create problems of organization that help to explain the complex networks of educational bureaucracy. Education has become a community responsibility of intense interest and astronomical expense. Public education is by far the largest expenditure in the municipal budget—about 32 percent.[20] Consequently, urban education must be planned and reviewed; it must give due attention to hiring and retaining qualified teachers, administrators, and maintenance personnel; it must prepare and house records of its students and their achievements; finally, it must maintain contacts with local government, civic organizations, business firms, and parents. Tests, assignments, awards, meetings, reports become components in the educational establishment; sometimes (the extent is a deliciously moot question) they compete with the learning process.

Educational bureaucracy is understandably concerned with educational techniques and experimentation. Urban education is so extensive and so visibly important to urbanites that criticism may (and does) arise from all quarters. Consequently, to forestall and to answer these criticisms, a recurrent need for novelty and experiment in educational methods is a major theme in urban education. In this respect, the educational bureaucracy is somewhat unique, for bureaucratic systems are normally antagonistic to change, however necessary. Perhaps the dilemma of modern urban education lies in the conflict between bureaucratic forms and the essential dynamics of urban education. In any case, suggested procedures and programs are almost constantly on trial: television classes, teachers' aids, foreign languages in the early grades, the two or three track system, easy or rigid promotion, instruction by ability groups, enrichment programs, teaching machines and "programmed learning," etc.[21]

4. development of regional segments in public education

As urban regions develop, their component areas tend to become more specialized in function, population features, and social class. In the United

[20] Bureau of the Census figures, cited by James A. Quinn, *Urban Sociology* (New York, American Book Company, 1955), p. 310.

[21] For a good summary see C. Winfield Scott and Clyde M. Hill, eds., *Public Education Under Criticism* (Englewood Cliffs, N.J., Prentice-Hall, 1954), Parts II, III, and VII.

States, urban education also reflects in some degree this basic sociographic division. While most educational personnel are drawn from middle status groups, schools in the fringe and in many parts of the central city largely serve lower status children. Since these areas generally have limited interest in formal education, and since few of these students aspire to college levels, educational leadership has not been encouraged to experiment with programs or techniques. The school systems in such areas tend to be grudgingly content with keeping discipline (if they can) and transmitting minimal skills.

By contrast, suburban school systems are oriented to the needs of students from rising middle class families. In these areas, educational experiment is so prevalent that they are often easily caricatured by critics.[22] Suburban school systems in the United States, it is important to note, have been the stronghold of "progressive education."

crises in urban education

The great importance of education to urban areas is countered by the emerging solidification of crisis and disillusionment in public educational systems in the United States. While urban education in Europe likewise faces the familiar problems of adequate curricula, dropouts, recruitment of teachers, and subtle discrimination against low-income youngsters, the major arena of educational ferment is clearly the United States. But to regard it as primarily derived from the Negro situation is a partial and essentially short-sighted view of public education.

Since the end of World War II, if not before, urban school systems have been variably criticized for failing to modernize curricula, for inadequate performance in teaching basic skills (reading, arithmetic, spelling), and for bureaucratic pursuit of convenient uniformities. In general, the response of educational administrators was either defensive or composed of ineffective verbal attempts at change. Some concerned parents transferred their children to private or parochial schools; others tried to contend with school boards, superintendents, and principals. In the early fifties, a silent national scandal in education was visible, and then the impact of Sputnik provided the first public, national jolt.[23] Science and mathematics were a new focus of innovation, but it is now clear in retrospect that the overall quality and efficiency of urban education had not been altered.

[22] See, for example, John Keats, *Schools Without Scholars* (Boston, Houghton Mifflin, 1958); Albert Lynd, *Quackery in the Public Schools* (Boston, Little, Brown and Co., 1953).

[23] James B. Conant, *The American High School Today* (New York, McGraw-Hill, 1959), and *Slums and Suburbs* (New York, McGraw-Hill, 1961); James D. Koerner, *The Miseducation of American Teachers* (Boston, Houghton Mifflin, 1963); Hyman G. Rickover, *Education and Freedom* (New York, Dutton, 1959), and *American Education, A National Failure* (New York, Dutton, 1963).

Negroes, Puerto Ricans, and other minorities did not suddenly erupt in the late fifties, but their role in the educational complex was perhaps to crystallize and exacerbate a central difficulty. For the schools had not learned the basic lesson of merchandising: either develop an improved or superior product or develop adequate, competent service or "repair" facilities. Since public education cannot follow its products in the latter respect, it had no choice but to seek significant improvement. It did not, or could not, do so.[24] As desegregation rules became clarified, as minorities became more vocal and better equipped with leadership, and as school systems became seared with numerous conflicts, the nation learned that public education was simply unsuited for, and uncomfortable with, lower class children to whom upward mobility was not a prime objective.[25] And again, with very few exceptions, the educational systems could not fashion adjustments.

During the sixties, almost all the relevant innovations in urban education derived from groups outside the school system, though some were adopted or included in some form of collaborative effort (e.g., Vista Volunteers, Headstart, Mobilization for Youth). But belated "solutions" have limited effects. Discipline problems become unbearable; teacher morale is often questionable; teachers' strikes—for salaries and program improvements—indicate sharp disaffection from educational administrators and school boards (e.g., in New York City, Pittsburgh, and Florida cities).[26] There is a poignant but misplaced reliance on crash programs or faddish remedies—such as preschool enrichment, team teaching, programs for dropouts, or parent involvement. However, deep-seated changes, at substantial increases in cost, are in the wings, awaiting crucial decisions that cannot be long postponed. For example, the Ford Foundation has suggested extensive administrative reorganization and decentralization for New York City.

social welfare, social work, and urbanism

Charity, philanthropy, social work, relief, social welfare—these are much abused epithets and poorly understood processes in modern communities.

[24] Marilyn Gittell ed., *Educating an Urban Population* (Beverly Hills, Sage Publications, 1967), pp. 205–239; David Street, *The Public Schools and Metropolitan Change* (New York, Russell Sage Foundation, 1968).

[25] Martin Trow, "Two Problems in American Public Education," in Howard S. Becker, ed., *Social Problems: A Modern Approach* (New York, Wiley, 1966), pp. 76–116; C. W. Hunnicutt, ed., *Urban Education and Cultural Deprivation* (Syracuse, Syracuse University School of Education, 1964); Harry A. Passow, ed., *Education in Depressed Areas* (New York, Teachers College, Columbia University, 1963); Harry A. Passow et al., eds., *Education of the Disadvantaged* (New York, Holt, Rinehart and Winston, 1963).

[26] Robert A. Dentler et al., eds., *The Urban R's* (New York, Praeger, 1967); Abraham Bernstein, *The Education of Urban Populations* (New York, Random House, 1967); Charles Winick, "When Teachers Strike," in James Raths and Jean D. Grambs, eds., *Society and Education: Readings* (Englewood Cliffs, N.J., Prentice-Hall, 1965), pp. 225–241.

Most of the difficulty with these terms can be traced to fixed political ideologies, to acknowledged errors in carrying out these activities, and most significantly, to a failure to understand the historical relation between social welfare and the urban region. Perhaps a first step in clarification is recognizing that charity, philanthropy, relief, and social welfare all refer to a particular set of functions or services provided by specialized agencies of the community. Social work, on the other hand, comprises the professional techniques and skills with which services are performed through responsible organizations designed to regularize and coordinate competent performance. For example, one might drop a coin in the tin cup of a blind man at a busy downtown corner. This is charity or philanthropy, but not social work. It is perhaps altruistically motivated; yet this act tends to be impulsive and soon forgotten. A social work agency may also provide financial aid to the blind man, but this assistance is ideally a result of careful investigation, personal interviews, and a professional interest in the future of the person or client.

Social welfare in its various forms has a long history. However, this type of community service was for a long time sporadically provided by groups with other dominant functions (family, church, government). Toward the end of the second urban wave—in the seventeenth century in England and the Low Countries—welfare activities began to exhibit some specialization, innovation, and some independent status.[27]

Understandably, social welfare has consistently been an urban function. From the eleventh century to the present, urban communities have been characterized by a number of social conditions and problems that to some degree produce community incapacities. Most visible are the continuing processes of urbanward migration and consequent pressure of population on available space and services. Second, generally rapid economic and social changes—which are otherwise desired in urban areas—have tended to require personal and family adjustments for which some persons have been unprepared. Particular mention should be made here of the growth of industrial production, the importance of a steady job, the emphasis on more and more acquired skills, the tendency toward increased opportunity for status change and status inconsistency, and the growing variety of consumer products and services.

Third, during the period of greatest urbanization (eighteenth through twentieth centuries in the Western World; the twentieth century in Asia and Africa) the prevailing social organizations were in process of transition to newer, more complex forms. The enormous social consequences of religious deviations and denominations during the Reformation and afterward can perhaps be summarized by reference to the uncertainties and controversies experienced by urban populations in the Ages of Reason and Individuation.[28]

[27] See Walter Friedlander, *An Introduction to Social Welfare*, rev. ed. (Englewood Cliffs, N.J., Prentice-Hall, 1955).

[28] Preserved Smith, *The Age of the Reformation* (New York, Henry Holt, 1920).

A similar picture of transition and crisis can be found among native peoples who have been weaned from tribal religions and obligations after migration to urban centers in Africa, the Pacific, and the United States.[29] Likewise, government structures still tended to be attuned to limited populations and the old municipal problems of physical safety and commercial facilitation. As a result, essentially part-time and volunteer government officials could not easily recognize, much less manage, the problems of continual migration and congestion.

These transitional urban features did not immediately stimulate the search for appropriate solutions. From the sixteenth century till the middle of the nineteenth, with few exceptions, two attitudes effectively hindered any sustained, realistic concern for the deleterious by-products of urbanization (dependency, illness, overcrowding, etc.). One such attitude stressed man's personal responsibility for his troubles; consequently, the community sought to protect itself from assuming the growing burden of unemployment and destitution among urban migrants. The usual consequence was repressive legislation, symbolized in the English Poor Laws. A related attitude during much of the nineteenth century considered "social problems" a natural, inevitable part of social development. The dominant approach was therefore one of laissez faire or a refusal to tinker with social processes; in particular, public programs were regarded as impertinent and ineffectual, as persuasively argued by Herbert Spencer in England, by William Graham Sumner in the United States.[30]

Yet by the middle of the nineteenth century, these attitudes were increasingly challenged by humanitarian movements sparked by vigorous leadership and more experienced organization. Based on an obvious but deferred application of Christian ethics, humanitarianism launched a devastating critique of urban problems on specific fronts—penal reform, the blind, the mentally ill, the destitute, and the orphaned. But a cardinal shift in attitudes must be noted; humanitarianism viewed migrants and their problems not as outsiders and bothersome intruders, but as part of the community and its responsibility.[31] For some decades, this revised evaluation was expressed largely through private organizations and programs (e.g., the Charity Organization Society in England and the United States, the YMCA, the Children's Aid Society, and Hull House in Chicago). Gradually, urban communities came to supplement private welfare functions with new publicly financed and admin-

[29] Laura Thompson, *Culture in Crisis* (New York, Harper and Brothers, 1950); I. Schapera, *Migrant Labour and Tribal Life* (London, Oxford University Press, 1947); Margaret Mead, *Cultural Patterns and Technical Change* (New York, Columbia University Press, 1953).

[30] Stuart A. Queen, *Social Work in the Light of History* (Philadelphia, J. B. Lippincott Company, 1922), Part III; Herbert Spencer, *Social Statics*, 3rd ed. (New York, D. Appleton and Co., 1890); W. G. Sumner, *The Forgotten Man and Other Essays* (New Haven, Yale University Press, 1919).

[31] Queen, *op. cit.*, pp. 319–320.

istered programs, principally after World War I in the United States, but considerably earlier in England and Germany.[32]

There is much confusion and disagreement about the essential functions that give some identity to social welfare in the urban region. Historically, the services of urban welfare agencies began as supplements to, or substitutes for, established institutions—such as kinship, public government, medicine, and education. Under this conception, welfare services were primarily designed for lower status families and individuals. Specific services most often provided, therefore, were financial assistance, occupational advice, child care and child placement, and treatment of the indigent, disabled, and the sick. As viewed by social workers, social welfare was a means of serving other institutions by helping individuals who had difficulties in using older institutional arrangements. This has been called the residual approach to social welfare.[33]

Perhaps it is useful to relate the residual conception of social welfare to earlier stages in the development of modern urban regions. In these earlier stages, cities were marked by rapid and uncontrolled growth, by precarious economic periods, and by many families unaccustomed to urban conditions. Since 1940 or thereabout, the essentially negative, emergency character of social welfare has lost its former prominence in the thinking and programs of welfare agencies. The trend is now toward consideration of welfare as a normal, specialized institution for a broader range of urbanites. Several new features seem to accompany this modern conception. Perhaps the central innovation is the emergence of responsibility for providing welfare services to the whole community (and region). As this broader service area has developed, more services have been demanded and made available to middle status groups (e.g., vocational counseling and job placement, marital counseling, psychiatric services, etc.). As a consequence, while financial aid is still provided, it is generally receding in importance, in contrast to noneconomic services, for which the client is increasingly expected to pay. In such a shift of attention, wherever possible urban welfare agencies also stress preventative programs designed to reduce the financial and psychological disabilities of urbanites.[34] Thus far, however, this ideal has not been successfully translated into well-designed and properly financed programs. Finally, modern social welfare has necessarily devoted extraordinary attention to coordination of many specialized services and agencies in the community.

As a genuine product of urban development in the last 80 years, so-

[32] Mary P. Hall, *The Social Services of Modern England* (London, Routledge and Kegan Paul, 1953) ; Madeline Rooff, *Voluntary Societies and Social Policy* (London, Routledge and Kegan Paul, 1957).

[33] Helen L. Witmer, *Social Work: An Analysis of a Social Institution* (New York, Holt, Rinehart and Winston, 1942), pp. 24–27, 87–121; Harold L. Wilensky and Charles N. Lebeaux, *Industrial Society and Social Welfare* (New York, Russell Sage Foundation, 1958), pp. 138–140.

[34] Wilensky and Lebeaux, *op. cit.*, pp. 14–15, 147, 171; George R. Nelson, ed., *Freedom and Welfare* (Copenhagen, Ministries of Social Affairs of Denmark, Finland, Iceland, Norway, and Sweden, 1953), pp. 498–499.

table 40

Forms of Specialization in Social Welfare in Modern Urban Regions

BASIS OF SPECIALIZATION	ILLUSTRATIVE TYPES
Purpose (or program)	Public assistance, corrections, recreation, vocational rehabilitation
Skill category	Social casework, group work, vocational counseling, psychiatry, community organization
Clientele	Children, adults, the aged, veterans, income category
Auspices and control	Government (federal, state, local, state-local), voluntary (sectarian, non-sectarian, joint-financed)
Geographic location	Geographic limits and boundaries of service

SOURCE: Adapted from Harold L. Wilensky and Charles N. Lebeaux, *Industrial Society and Social Welfare*, p. 248.

cial welfare is marked by the familiar qualities of specialization, bureaucratization, and professionalization. Table 40 summarizes the major subdivisions, which are found in virtually every large urban region in the Western world. But this intensive specialization has not been achieved without two uniquely urban trends. First and more obvious is the development of public and private bureaucracies in social welfare. Lady Bountiful and the dedicated volunteers of the past have little place in modern urban welfare work. Instead we have administrative agencies,[35] increasingly staffed with graded ranks of certified specialists—case workers (junior and senior), supervisors, executive director, home economists, physicians, psychiatrists, stenographers, dictaphone operators, receptionists, and often interns in casework. In addition, both private and public agencies operate with that telltale mark of bureaucracies—definite salary scales for each position or rank, and some timetable for salary increments.

A second trend deserves special attention from the urban sociologist and urbanites in general. Urban welfare groups have been compelled to design innovations in organization and coordination of services. As early as the 1880s in England and the United States, the operation of private and public agencies, religious and secular groups, and often of unwittingly competing agencies clearly pointed to the need for liaison and regularized cooperation among urban welfare groups. One of the earliest devices, which had come

[35] As one student has summarized this trend: "America is the land of the free and the home of the committee." See Edward C. Jenkins, *Philanthropy in America* (New York, Association Press, 1950), p. 33.

to be basic to welfare organization, was the social service exchange.[36] The exchange functioned as a clearing-house for all cooperating agencies; it provided a continuous, up-to-date listing of the names of agency clients. This insured in most instances avoidance of duplication, but also enabled specific agencies to obtain a broader picture of their client's needs by knowing past (or concurrent) contacts with community agencies. However, in recent years the exchange has been increasingly derided as a cumbersome policing device. The "discovery" of multi-problem or hard-core families stimulated a philosophical change which encouraged case workers to emphasize services rather than agencies or jurisdictions. Consequently, the exchange has largely faded away.

An extremely important innovation, consciously aimed at coordination, is the council of social agencies. First used in such areas as Liverpool, Denver, New York, London, Chicago, and Pittsburgh, the council form provides centralized administration and often some planning for member agencies. The exact functions of the council vary somewhat from urban region to urban region. But the most common services are; revamping or combining existing agencies; facilitation of interagency conferences; a source of community and extraregional information for member agencies; advice and coordination of public relations; and a concern for professional standards in skills and salaries.[37] In the United States, since most of the member agencies are under private auspicies, the council tends to be dominated by the private agencies. By contrast, in Great Britain, each county has its own public assistance committee, which has legal responsibility for overseeing local services in health, assistance, and education.

It is difficult to evaluate the contribution of the council of social agencies. While some coordination of services has been accomplished, many agencies tend to be concerned with maintaining their identity; and it is more than probable that the larger agencies carry unusual weight in council deliberations. Consequently, most councils have not been able to achieve the consensus necessary for genuine long-range planning. But the recent confrontation of urban poverty, racial disorders, and the jarring contrasts of traditional programs and newly articulated demands have compelled leaders to entertain self-critical examination of the structure and operation of such councils. Generally, three kinds of issues have dominated these discussions: (a) the appropriate interrelation between private agencies and public (largely federally financed) welfare programs; (b) some revision (if not a much needed clarification) of priorities in the kinds of welfare services provided (e.g., recreation, family stability, vocational counseling, teenage adjustments); and (c) the improvement and extension of services to low-income nonwhites in the "impenetrable" ghettos. It is too early to detect clear trends, but initial

---

36 Wilensky and Lebeaux, op. cit., Chap. 10.
37 Frank J. Bruno, Trends in Social Work, 1874–1956 (New York, Columbia University Press, 1957), pp. 192–198.

tendencies seem to be toward erratic modification of councils, with more two-way collaboration between member agencies and council executives and professionals.

In Atlanta, for example, the council–community chest has developed two hopefully major innovations. First, in 1960 a full-time research and planning agency was formed, largely to identify and document primary gaps in services for the metropolitan area. In the last four years, this has become a key facility—called upon by a variety of private and public agencies for authoritative data, particularly related to poverty areas. Since 1967, it has been primarily financed by the United Appeal, though the lines of formal responsibility are still under discussion.

Second, in 1968 the traditional, somewhat perfunctory budget panel system for determining allocation to member agencies was discarded. In its place now is the Agency Relations and Allocation Division, which (a) groups agencies in functionally related categories—e.g., family and children's services, (b) encourages year-round consultation between panel and agency; (c) makes recommendations in terms of functional rather than merely agency needs for the coming year; and (d) selects panel members for their professional knowledge of matters related to specific agencies. It is hoped that this system will be more flexible and will allow more careful comparative evaluation of social welfare functions.

Fund raising for the numerous private welfare services was in the past a very onerous task. Contributors were plagued by numerous appeals, which tended to be both inconvenient and undignified. Furthermore, contributors could not easily allocate their donations according to the needs of competing fund drives. The community chest both simplifies and dignifies fund raising by one combined appeal, normally in the fall. But another coordinating function of the chest is equally important. In arriving at reasonable, workable financial goals, the chest must act as a goad to each agency to prepare justifiable budgets. Indeed, the needs of each agency must be considered in the light of other agencies' programs, as well as in terms of the financial capacity of the community and region. The success of this budgetary coordination depends on close association with the council of social agencies, and also on the relatively autonomous position of the chest, which is usually staffed with professional fund raisers and people with business experience.

some recent alterations

Urban social welfare is self-consciously (but perhaps not always willingly) engaged in change. The key ingredients may be summarized provisionally in the following simplified manner.

1. Considerably more emphasis is being given to hard-core poverty areas, largely with the encouragement and financing of federal agencies and

private foundations. This entails a shift from the office appointment to the home and the street.[38]

2. New programs (with old foci) are constantly devised, so that an encyclopedic memory for funds, groups, and federal laws (and their specific titles) is increasingly necessary. Essentially, these programs center on the neighborhood rather than the individual or family—recalling the classic objectives of Hull House, Toynbee Hall, and the settlement movement that matured before World War I. However, unlike the traditional welfare services, these new programs tend to be staffed with more volunteers, non-social work professionals, and local neighborhood leaders.[39]

3. Because of a continuing shortage of professionally certified case workers, and also because of recent evaluations of case work practice, there is much experimentation in group counseling and services to entire families.

4. Closely related to the preceding point, social services are increasingly probing the possibilities of preventative work, to supplement the necessary concern with treatment of advanced cases of personal need. This emphasis, often called family life education, assumes that urban families normally face critical periods for which clear solutions cannot be obtained without early professional counsel. Some examples are: rearing retarded children; the adopted child; teen-age problems of autonomy; pre-marital problems; early marriage; coping with severe or disabling illness; extended unemployment; retirement problems.

5. Social work training seems to be on the threshold of immense re-orientation, though the imprint of dynamic psychology (psychoanalytic varieties ranging from Freud to H. S. Sullivan) remains relatively strong. There is some evidence of increased attention to skills in group settings and in community activation and to the relevance of such skills for disadvantaged minorities.

Religion, education, and welfare share the same discomfort in modern urban regions: an implicit, long-term neglect of the immobile lower status enclaves. Their recognition that this deficiency is critical constitutes one of the genuinely radical trends in the twentieth century. But the flurry of programs and projects is marked by haste, inconsistency, staffing problems, and uncertainties in finance. Adequate coordination seems to be well beyond reach. Perhaps entirely novel organizational forms (cf. the later discussions of planning, pp. 324–336) are required to perform these crucial functions for urbanites in the near future.

[38] Irving Spergel, *Street Gang Work: Theory and Practice* (Reading, Mass., Addison-Wesley, 1966) ; Nathan S. Caplan *et al.*, "The Nature, Variety, and Patterning of Street Club Work in an Urban Setting," in Malcolm W. Klein and Barbara G. Meyerhoff, eds., *Juvenile Gangs in Context* (Englewood Cliffs, N.J., Prentice-Hall, 1967), pp. 194–203.

[39] Wilensky and Lebeaux, *op. cit.* (1965 ed.), pp. xxxii–xliv.

selected references

COHEN, Nathan E., *Social Work in the American Tradition* (New York, Holt, Rinehart and Winston, 1958).

GITTELL, Marilyn, ed., *Educating an Urban Population* (Beverly Hills, Sage Publications, 1968).

GLOCK, Charles Y. and STARK, Rodney, *Religion and Society in Tension* (Chicago, Rand McNally, 1965).

STREET, David, *The Public School and Metropolitan Change* (New York, Russell Sage Foundation, 1968).

WILENSKY, Harold L. and LEBEAUX, Charles N., *Industrial Society and Social Welfare* (New York, Russell Sage Foundation, 1958; also The Free Press, 1965).

ZALD, Mayer N., ed., *Organizing for Community Welfare* (Chicago, Quadrangle Books, 1967).

15

mass communications and urban leisure: a new urban ethic

The major organizational forms—primary groups, established institutional groups, and the stratification system—of the urban region have created a new and still emerging type of human community, dedicated to the ends of variety, complexity, and productive efficiency. However, these important forms of social organization have had to serve and guide relatively large and mobile populations, as well as continue the normal pursuit of these modern urban goals. Essentially, the underlying problems of urbanization have been to produce "proper" motivation, effective conditions of learning, and a fundamental, meaningful coordination of roles and ideals in urban populations. Consciously or unconsciously, developments in mass communications and leisure have operated as significant supplements (perhaps as necessary accompaniments) to urban social organization. The major task of this chapter is to outline the special structure and operation of modern mass communication systems and their social and cultural consequences for the urban region.

Mass communication systems are almost wholly urban innovations, principally of the last 50 years. Despite their recency, mass communications have become an integral part of urban living; they are—in one form or another —highly acceptable, even difficult to avoid, and most significant, they are taken for granted by most urbanites. To the sociologist, however, mass communications reveal a special cluster of characteristics in the complexities of urban regions.

1. scope or coverage

The range of persons reached by the major mass media today is without precedent. A speaker or performer may be heard by two or three thousand people at best—without the aid of some mass medium. But the daily audience of a local radio station or newspaper may easily be several hundred thousand, or many millions if connected with a radio network or newspaper syndicate. Competitive program ratings for television broadcasts also indicate that considerable proportions of the fifty million television receivers are regularly tuned to specific programs.

2. uniformity

Although there are obvious variations in exposure, attention, and interpretation of media content, the scope of mass media inevitably raises the level of uniformity of stimuli or reactions among urban consumers. Indeed, marketing and audience research is often devoted to the problem of adjusting media content (e.g., commercials, film stories) to increase the probability of uniform impact on audiences. Motivation research, which has been a much discussed field recently,[1] is essentially a scientific quest for greater uniformity by discovering and playing on unconscious common motives or themes in audiences.

3. rapidity

The daily newspaper (and news broadcasts on radio and television) is probably the best, continuous demonstration of speed in collecting stimuli (news), editing and coordinating media content, and finally dissemination. Few urbanites care for delayed reporting of news ("there's nothing deader than yesterday's newspaper"), repeats of recent television programs, or even many old movies. Probably few would show any interest in a return to the weekly newspaper. Improved communications and mass production techniques enable the purveyors of mass media to contract space and time in reaching and satisfying their respective consumers. This technical rapidity is an implicit fascination to many urbanites; it inspires confidence and dependence, which in turn engender desires for regular communication among devotees of each medium.

4. regularity

From the viewpoint of both disseminators and their audiences, mass communication must be available in a predictable, periodic fashion.[2] Indeed, one useful way of classifying media (or a segment of one medium, such as

1 George H. Smith, *Motivation Research in Advertising and Marketing* (New York, McGraw-Hill, 1954) ; Ernest Dichter, *Handbook of Consumer Motivations* (New York, McGraw-Hill, 1964) ; James M. Carman, *The Application of Social Class in Market Segmentation* (Berkeley, Institute of Business and Economic Research, University of California, 1965).

2 Bernard Berelson, "What 'Missing the Newspaper' Means," in Paul F. Lazarsfeld and Frank N. Stanton, eds., *Communications Research, 1948–1949* (New York, Harper and Brothers, 1949), pp. 111–128.

a specific type of column) is by degree of regularity: hourly (news high-lights on radio); daily (newspapers, soap operas); weekly (some magazines, television programs; monthly (magazines); periodically but not with clearly predictable regularity (new films).

5. exposure during leisure time

In general, mass communications achieve their coverage and effectiveness by aiming mass media to coincide with the largest segments of leisure time. Newspaper circulation and delivery reach their height before and after regular working hours (from 6:30 to 8:30 A.M. and 4:30 to 6:00 P.M.). Choice television and radio hours, recognized by both audiences and sponsors, are daily from 8:00 to 10:00 P.M. and Sunday evenings. Weekly magazines are likewise on newstands and in mail boxes by Friday, so that readers may find time to scan them before they disappear under tables, in magazine racks, or in junior's junk-pile. Furthermore, the expansion of leisure time has been a necessary precondition of the successful multiplication of mass media, despite some competition between media—e.g., films and television.

6. influence

Perhaps the key feature of modern mass media is the basic technique employed to direct various aspects of behavior among urbanites. Older, more direct techniques of control—violence, threats, intimidation, bribery—are both difficult to impose (unless some form of despotic government is involved) and highly immoral to most urbanites. Instead, mass communications typically attempt to influence the opinions, ideas, and behavior of audiences and publics. The techniques of persuasion, gentle or indirect argument (the "relaxed" or "soft" sell), the subtle appeal to semiconscious motives, even the brash repetitiousness of some commercials, are all designed to appear as reasonable and acceptable as possible. In short, as the well-known publicist Edward L. Bernays has phrased it, "the engineering of consent" is the goal not only of public relations in particular, but—in some degree—of all mass communications.[3]

7. diversity of influences

While there is considerable diversity in types of mass media (film, radio, television, magazines, telephones, books, pamphlets, newspapers), mass

[3] Paul F. Lazarsfeld, "Foreword," in Leo A. Handel, *Hollywood Looks at Its Audience* (Urbana, Ill., University of Illinois Press, 1950), p. xi; Edward L. Bernays, ed., *The Engineering of Consent* (Norman, Okla., University of Oklahoma Press, 1955); Nicholas Samstag, *Persuasion for Profit* (Norman, Okla., University of Oklahoma Press, 1957); Thomas Whiteside, *The Relaxed Sell* (New York, Oxford University Press, 1954).

communications as an adjunct to urban social organization likewise consists of several forms or contexts of influence.

1. *Advertising.* The most ubiquitous is advertising, which attempts to influence the process of selection among competing commodities, as well as to develop new needs and tastes for status items.[4] In general, advertising is more or less skillfully grafted on other forms of mass communication, such as entertainment (the commercial). There is some controversy among economists and social analysts about the actual effectiveness of advertising in influencing, diverting, or increasing sales of particular products, compared with the role of personal influence.

2. *Public relations and institutional advertising.* These constitute a second subcategory of mass communications influence. Instead of direct attempts to focus choices on specific products, public relations functions as a relatively subtle, indirect attempt to create an acceptable, respectable image of an individual, an organization, or a complex role-cluster (e.g., higher education, private enterprise, or the labor movement). Characteristically, public relations has the task of removing or countering previously hostile images or opinions by emphasizing the positive aspects of its sponsors and by avoiding controversial or inflammatory statements.[5] The classic instance of this process is the adept manner in which John D. Rockefeller, Sr. was "transformed" from a "robber baron" into a respectable—if eccentric— philanthropist by Ivy Lee, a publicist with shrewd appreciation of the nature of his audience. Since good will, reputation, etc. are highly subjective and difficult to measure—as compared with variations in sales of products—the impact of public relations cannot be easily evaluated. However, personnel and expenditures in this area have increased substantially since Rockefeller's "sanctification by public relations" and we must assume that those who pay the bills receive (or expect) positive results.

3. *Press agentry,* another form of urban mass communications, should be distinguished from advertising, and especially from public relations, with which it is sometimes identified. Essentially, the press agent is interested in publicity—literally "keeping before the public"—for his client. Unlike advertising, press agentry does not seek to influence specific purchases directly; instead, it tries to make its clients dramatically interesting by stressing their individuality and eccentricities, under the assumption that the unusual will

[4] Good discussions of advertising's role and effects are available in William H. Whyte, *Is Anybody Listening?* (New York, Simon and Schuster, 1952); Elihu Katz and Paul F. Lazarsfeld, *Personal Influence* (New York, The Free Press of Glencoe, 1955); Neil Borden, *The Economic Effects of Advertising* (Chicago, Richard D. Irwin, 1942); B. W. Schyberger, *Methods of Readership Research* (Lund, C. W. K. Gleerup, 1965), Chaps. 2, 8.

[5] Bernays, *op. cit.,* Chaps. XIV–XVI; Leonard I. Pearlin and Morris Rosenberg, "Propaganda Techniques in Institutional Advertising," *Public Opinion Quarterly,* 16 (Spring, 1952), pp. 5–26; Leila A. Sussman, "The Personnel and Ideology of Public Relations," *ibid.,* 12 (Winter, 1948–49), pp. 697–708; S. H. Walker and Paul Sklar, *Business Finds Its Voice* (New York, Harper and Brothers, 1938).

be remembered longer and more vividly. If necessary, the press agent can create arresting distinctiveness by such expedients as a catchy stage name, manufactured biographical items, public brawls, and clients' appearances at elite ceremonial occasions.

4. *Political campaigns.* The organization and operation of mass communications in political campaigns shows some resemblance to both advertising and public relations. However, there are several important differences which merit some analysis. In the dominant type of political campaign, mass communications channels are employed for relatively short periods preceding an election, after which mass media return to their normal commercial and entertainment functions.[6] This concentration in time is accompanied by attempts to obtain coverage in all or most media. Campaigns for political office seek to create acceptable images, as in public relations, but media content stress the necessity of a definite act ("vote for . . ."), unlike public relations. Similar to advertising, political campaigns offer their audiences the possibility of exchange, an urban revival of barter. For choosing a particular brand or candidate, the consumer or voter is promised a desirable effect in return. But while advertising proffers immediate, definite rewards ("brighter teeth") and often some guarantee ("your money back if you are not satisfied that . . ."), political campaigns are notably and predictably vague about their proposals. We have the Federal Trade Commission and the Federal Communications Commission to prevent misrepresentation in advertising. Few people expect political campaigns to observe comparable limitations; indeed, a request for safeguards against the semitruths, fabrications, and broken promises of campaigners would hardly prompt more than a snicker.

Unlike other forms of mass communications, political campaigning is normally marked by controversy, argument, attack, and imputation of ulterior motives. But rarely are political opponents permitted to debate their differences in the same medium at the same time (the Nixon-Kennedy debates were quite exceptional). Consequently, political mass communications tend to be a confusing mixture of positive assertions and critical observations, with pressures for equal time to "set the record straight." Fortunately, political audiences do not expose themselves to the blatant inconsistencies of political appeals. Several recent studies show a tendency to select media content congenial to preconceived political choices.[7]

[6] Studies of mass communications in political campaigns are rather rare, but are on the increase. See Stanley Kelley, *Professional Public Relations and Political Power* (Baltimore, Johns Hopkins University Press, 1956); Department of Marketing, Miami University, *The Influence of Television on the Election of 1952* (Oxford, Ohio, Oxford Associates, December, 1954); Paul F. Lazarsfeld *et al., The People's Choice* (New York, Columbia University Press, 1948).

[7] Lazarsfeld, *The People's Choice*, Chaps. XV, XVI; Bernard Berelson *et al., Voting* (Chicago, University of Chicago Press, 1954), Chaps. VI, VII; Heinz Eulau, "Identification with Class and Political Role Behavior," *Public Opinion Quarterly*, 20 (Spring, 1956), pp. 515–529. But cf. Joseph Trenaman and Dennis McQuail, *Television and the*

5. *Mass entertainment.* A very substantial part of modern mass communications is in the form of amusement, entertainment, or recreation for its audiences or publics. Necessarily, the entertainment aspect of mass media is superimposed on a commercial advertising base. While the two go hand in hand, they should not be confused. Essentially, mass entertainment media present a contrast to the serious intent of advertising and public relations; they strive to create and maintain a state of mind desired (or thought to be desired) by their audiences. Mass media entertain by providing "intangible necessities" of urban life—humor in various forms (radio, films, television, newspaper comics), information and news, human interest, drama, sensation, and vicarious participation in sports.

6. *Public education.* A little reflection is sometimes necessary to remind us that public education (from kindergarten to graduate school) is an increasingly important locus of mass communications. In the urban setting, population size and concentration, diversity of backgrounds, and the complexity of urban culture inevitably remove education from the dominantly personal relationship of traditional education as typified in the country school. The classic pedagogical formula of education—Horace Mann and a boy at opposite ends of a log—is attractive, but quite obsolete. Urban education, with its relatively large classes and variety of courses, depends on mass-produced textbooks, on films and filmstrips, and in the near future, on closed television circuits. These media supplement the role of the teacher, but may subtly place the teacher in a position of subservience to media content. One of the key problems in public education has always been the limits of desirable control over teachers by school boards and organized interests in the community—in selection of textbooks, for example. The increasing use of mass media, which are both expensive and centralized, tends to simplify and impersonalize formal education, to convert the teacher into a mediator between standardized stimuli and students. The teacher as opinion leader, as disseminator of the content and values in selected mass media, has already been identified.[8] We can only guess at the prevalence of this type.

It should be obvious that public education—particularly with the addition of modern mass media—constitutes a special system of mass influence. Formal education transmits basic cultural skills, but also values, attitudes, and aspirations. Sociologists generally agree that public schools (explicitly or implicitly) sustain or develop middle class values.[9] Since urban regions take

Political Image: A Study of the Impact of Television in the 1959 General Election (London, Methuen, 1961), pp. 194–200.

[8] David Riesman, *The Lonely Crowd* (Garden City, N.Y., Doubleday and Company, 1953), p. 83.

[9] See particularly Robert J. Havighurst and Hilda Taba, *Adolescent Character and Personality* (New York, John Wiley and Sons, 1948); A. B. Hollingshead, *Elmtown's Youth* (New York, John Wiley and Sons, 1949); W. Lloyd Warner *et al.*, *Who Shall Be Educated?* (New York, Harper and Brothers, 1944).

their character from the middle status categories, public education performs an essential service in reaching the largest number of children. Whatever the deficiencies of public education, it cannot be even temporarily replaced by private education. Those who would close public schools to preserve racial segregation are primarily rural in character; they believe middle class values can be properly inculcated by small, almost personal private educational groups. The facts, however distasteful, are otherwise.

Mass communications in modern urban regions operate as relatively private (i.e., not controlled by governmental agencies) systems. Their importance—the effects they produce, the problems they create—depends on the nature of the urban community and the evolving structure of the mass communications sphere. The latter is especially pertinent at this point because it has developed an intricate network of preexisting and newly created organizations and interaction chains which provide clues to the special position of modern mass communications in urban behavior.

Figure 16 is a simplified outline of the major components in mass communications processes. This schematized summary explicitly disregards vari-

figure 16

Basic Structure of Urban Mass Communication Systems

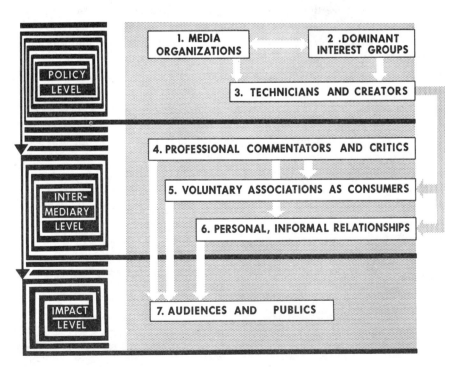

ations found in specific forms and media of communications. Basically, mass communications is conceived here as organized in terms of three levels and seven substructures or role-clusters. In general, the key to the entire process —in terms of kinds and degree of influence (not in technical processes) —is the intermediary level, which may be relatively dependent or independent of the policy level, and which is differentially developed in specific communities and in specific forms and media of communication.

1. media organizations

Normally, privately owned corporations apply technological developments in communications for business purposes. Theoretically, these groups merely furnish facilities for access to audiences and publics. However, a purely objective attitude toward the influence process is not maintained by all media organizations—particularly among the printed media (newspapers, magazines, books). For example, definite political and economic viewpoints may be found in such media as *U.S. News and World Report, The Reporter,* the *New Republic,* the Chicago *Tribune,* and the *Reader's Digest.* With the increasing trend toward concentration of media ownership (newspaper chains, interlocking ownership of newspapers, radio, and television), it is likely that the commercial objective will be supplemented by more or less conscious attempts to inspire opinions congenial to those of media owners.

2. dominant interest groups

As suggested in the preceding paragraph, influence patterns may be determined to some extent by media organizations. More often, dominant interest groups (industry, labor, agriculture, political parties) in the nation or in specific urban regions tend to control media content by (a) directly buying time or space in mass media—as advertisers or sponsors, or (b) indirectly influencing media owners to favor or reject given types of media content (e.g., salacious stories, crime as adventure, etc.). The latter type of control is covert and informal, and therefore difficult to investigate. But, with such exceptions as "personal journalism" (Harry Golden, for example), media organizations depend on interest groups of some kind for financial support. It is no secret that, in maintaining such support, it often becomes desirable to anticipate (rather than follow) the basic orientation of dominant interests. The day of the independent crusader, beholden to no one, is no longer evident, when mass communications are so technically complex and so expensive.

3. implements: technicians and creators

Those who convert policy orientations into the continuous flow of radio and television programs, magazines, newspapers, lectures, billboard ads, and

books—the mass producers of influence—play a difficult role in urban regions. This is especially true of the creators and their coordinators (editors,
etc.), who develop or direct creativity so that it can be suitably adjusted
to the demands of mass communication and mass impact. Surprisingly little
is known about this category of persons—despite their importance—apart
from such fictional sources as *The Hucksters, What Makes Sammy Run?*,
etc. Two exceptions must be mentioned, however. A study of public relations
men in the late forties indicated that a large proportion had internalized
an ideology that effectively resolved any possible conflicts between creativeness and standardization. Specifically, these men conceived themselves as
"crusaders" in achieving good will for their clients (usually large business
organizations). Consequently, their own skills were regarded as subordinate
to the need for persistently functioning channels of mass communication.[10]
By contrast, as Spectorsky has delightfully reported on the world of the
exurbanites, many writers, illustrators, and advertising men feel uncom-
fortably cramped by the insatiable demands of media organizations and their
sponsors. The exurbanites aspire to artistic creations of a high but unmar-
ketable quality, but they cannot or will not escape from the "treadmill," the
"rat race," of wider and wider mass communications.[11]

4. professional commentators, reviewers, and critics

The conscience or watchdog of mass media reposes in the activities of
a small grouping of specialized observers—radio and television film critics,
book reviewers, and unofficial censors. Because of the staggering output of
modern mass media, some form of evaluative sieve, some selector, is needed
by the urbanite who tries to be both up-to-date and reasonably sane. This
need is the usual justification for the media critics and reviewers. However,
it must be noted that critics do not function in the same manner in all mass
media, nor do they seem to exercise the same degree of influence on consumers of the various media. For example, it is doubtful that either newspapers or magazines are evaluated by their readers with the assistance of
professional critics, as is often the case in selecting movies, current books,
and perhaps television programs. We can only guess at the relative success
of specific reviewers in promoting or panning books, shows, and programs.

In general, the role of the critic-reviewer in the mass communications
process has been limited to a rather small portion of media consumers, most
of whom apply standards of discrimination and careful screening of the
available mass media. To this special public, the judgments of a Walter
Kerr on drama, a John Crosby on television, a Bosley Crowther on films,
and a Clifton Fadiman on books have carried considerable weight. For other
urbanites with different or vaguer standards, the critic-reviewer is perhaps

[10] Sussman, *loc. cit.*
[11] A. C. Spectorsky, *The Exurbanites* (Philadelphia, J. B. Lippincott, 1955).

less necessary, or merely less apparent. For example, the largest of the book clubs dispense several million books each month to their members. Technically, book selections are in the form of "recommendations" which can be rejected. Actually, book clubs thrive only on the acquiescence of their members. Do book clubs serve primarily as evaluators of current books, or as distributors? Are decisions about club choices dictated by intrinsic qualities of the books or by shrewd guesses as to what club members will accept?

Two current trends suggest that the critic-reviewer role is being usurped or by-passed by organizations which ordinarily function on the policy level in mass communications. Something which has long been suspected in the popular record-radio complex has finally been publicly exposed: the widespread but covert practice among record manufacturers of paying disk jockeys to play and otherwise promote their products—payola. Apart from the moral aspect, this reflects an attempt to streamline the mass communications system by dispensing with an independent critical phase. In fact, there is some evidence that some record companies have also fabricated to their own satisfaction lists of popularity and sales of current records, and then furnished such lists to disk jockeys as the results of "objective" surveys. To the extent that such practices exist, portions of the record-buying public are inadequately equipped to maintain personal independence of a mass medium.

If the situation in mass recordings seems trivial or peripheral, a related trend in urban mass communications merits close attention. A recent report on history textbooks used in public school systems found that publishers and text writers have produced texts in American history that clearly refuse to present interpretations of events or periods. Instead, the texts are written in such a way that "issues are artificially balanced in order to please partisans on every side of each controversy." The result is a "bland uniformity" which leaves little effective choice among competing texts by responsible school officials and teachers.[12] Of course, it is difficult to predict how texts might be selected if a genuine variety were available. But this situation likewise demonstrates that the critic-reviewer role has been implicitly constricted in segments of public education.

5. voluntary associations as intermediaries

In some instances, the urbanite either receives mass communications through affiliation with one or more specialized associations or discusses and evaluates mass communications (independently received) by participating in such associations. For example, professional people often receive technical and other periodicals through membership in professional organizations. Some of these periodicals are published by the organizations themselves; others are not. Voluntary associations are perhaps more significant as for-

[12] Fred M. Hechinger, "Education in Review," *The New York Times*, February 14, 1960.

ums for digesting, debating, and interpreting specific items from the mass media. Various types of fan clubs, civic groups such as the League of Women Voters, business and fraternal groups, and library or musical clubs often function in this manner. But this substructure in mass communications is primarily available in segments of the urban middle classes.

6. informal contacts and personal influence

The myth of urbanites as a mass cruelly exposed to the direct impact of impersonal mass communications still lingers in modern folklore, perhaps because it is to a very limited extent true. For most residents of the urban region, however, personal and informal contacts or pressures serve as intermediaries or supplements to media content.[13] According to several studies, urban children show a marked tendency to watch television or attend movies with family members or friends.[14] Comic books seem to be read in periods of social seclusion. However, the exchange and discussion of comic books among neighborhood youngsters must constitute a very effective form of personal influence in selecting and evaluating this medium.

Turning to the adult setting, there is a growing fund of studies that suggest that personal influence often plays a decisive role in affecting reactions to mass media. Lazarsfeld and his associates have shown that family and friends are specially important in determining voting behavior of undecided or semiapathetic persons during a political campaign. Indeed, Lazarsfeld concludes that mass media in elections merely activate dormant political interests; that socioeconomic factors and personal influences largely explain consistency and change in urban voting. On the other hand, Janowitz found that primary group pressures on voters generally reinforced the mass media in producing higher levels of voting. Furthermore, conflicting primary group pressures served to reduce voting in social categories affected in this manner.[15] (See Table 41.)

[13] Katz and Lazarsfeld, op. cit., Part II, Chaps. X, XI, XIII, XIV; Joseph T. Klapper, The Effects of Mass Communication (New York, The Free Press of Glencoe, 1960), Chaps. IV, V; Robert K. Merton, "Patterns of Influence: A Study of a Local Community," in Lazarsfeld and Stanton, op. cit., pp. 180–219; E. Jackson Baur, "Public Opinion and the Primary Group," American Sociological Review, 25 (April, 1960), pp. 208–219; Daniel Lerner and Wilbur Schramm, eds., Communication and Change in the Developing Countries (Honolulu, East-West Center Press, 1967), Chap. 4.

[14] Matilda W. Riley and John W. Riley, Jr., "A Sociological Approach to Communications Research," Public Opinion Quarterly, 15 (Fall, 1951), pp. 445–460; Eleanor E. Maccoby, "Television: Its Impact on School Children," ibid., pp. 421–444; Eliot Friedson, "The Relation of the Social Situation of Contact to the Media in Mass Communication," ibid., 17 (Summer, 1953), pp. 230–238; Robert V. Hamilton and Richard H. Lawless, "Television Within the Social Matrix," ibid., 20 (Summer, 1956), pp. 394–403.

[15] Lazarsfeld, The People's Choice, pp. 74–82; Morris Janowitz and Dwaine Marvick, Competitive Pressure and Democratic Consent (Ann Arbor, Mich., Institute of Public Administration, University of Michigan, 1956), pp. 92–94.

table 41

Effects of Primary Group Pressures on the Voting Behavior
of Different Categories of Voters

PARTISAN PREDISPOSITION AND PRIMARY GROUP PRESSURES	VOTING BEHAVIOR, 1948–52		
	Pro-Republican vote	*Pro-Democratic vote*	*Persistent nonvoters*
Republican partisans under concerted pro-Ike primary group pressures	95.4	2.6	2.0
Non-Republican partisans under concerted pro-Ike primary group pressures	83.6	9.6	6.8
Republican partisans under conflicting primary group pressures	68.8	11.0	20.2
Uncommitted electors under conflicting primary group pressures	36.2	27.1	36.7
Democratic partisans under conflicting primary group pressures	27.2	50.0	22.8
Non-Democratic partisans under concerted pro-Stevenson primary group pressures	12.8	72.3	14.9
Democratic partisans under concerted pro-Stevenson primary group pressures	6.9	80.1	13.0

SOURCE: Janowitz and Marvick, *op. cit.*, p. 94.

But since mass media are more pervasive in economic contexts, how do primary and informal pressures operate in the related processes of merchandising and advertising? The few investigations of this problem involve urbanites in status-conscious, middle class areas. In this segment of the population, according to several independent surveys, specific families informally function as opinion leaders or pacesetters for a given circle of acquaintances. Despite the wide and expensive coverage provided by newspapers, radio, and television advertising, Whyte found that such major appliances as home freezers, hi-fi equipment, and air conditioners were concentrated in a few blocks in Philadelphia. Furthermore, few of these purchasers were influenced by salesmen or advertisements. The key to consumer decisions was word-of-mouth networks, which operate by local standards of appropriate possessions.[16] This principle is sometimes applied by shrewd salesmen (e.g., in selling encyclopedias). But a particularly successful in-

[16] William H. Whyte, Jr., *The Organization Man* (Garden City, N.Y., Doubleday and Company, 1956), Chap. XXIV.

stance was the sales campaign of the gas company in New York in increasing gas consumption among its customers. A concentrated and highly attractive promotional effort sought out informally influential families who were persuaded to buy gas appliances of various kinds. The informal networks were apparently effective, since gas consumption in the test areas rose appreciably.[17]

meaning and effects of mass communications

A good deal of controversy in recent years centers on the meaning and effects of mass communications. Manipulators of mass media vigorously interpret their function as agents of progress, civilization, and practical democracy. On the other hand, intellectuals of many stripes condemn mass communications for their poor taste, the apparent premium placed on non-rationality, and the development of drab uniformities of experience. These claims and counterclaims are difficult to evaluate. It may well be that too much attention to the content of mass media and to their intended effects tends to obscure the unintended but extremely important functions of mass media for the vast urban audiences and publics.

A few suggestive studies cast considerable doubt on the efficiency of mass media as molders of opinions and tastes.[18] Paradoxically, urbanites often seem to be more interested in the medium than its content. Thus, political campaigns in newspapers, radio, and television excite public attention, but influence few votes. Sponsors of television programs are beginning to recognize the disconcerting fact that viewers of the most popular shows are often oblivious to the commercials, and cannot identify the product or brand. The only conclusion to be drawn from these items is that urban publics are somehow converting mass communications for their own conscious or unconscious purposes.

It should not be surprising that, from the consumers' standpoint, mass communications are primarily instruments of leisure, rather than sober, serious problems for careful resolution. Apparently, urbanites take the simple viewpoint that experiences bearing the label of "leisure" should be treated accordingly. But if mass communications are not clearly instruments of persuasion—as their sponsors hope—what are some of the specific leisure functions served by the mass media? Though there are some variations by status level, the following themes seem to recur.

17 The New York Times, September 25, 1955.
18 See in particular Whyte, Is Anybody Listening?; Lazarsfeld, The People's Choice; Klapper, op. cit.; Robert Alden, "Advertising: Suckers' Birthrate Declines," The New York Times, February 21, 1960. A contrary view is taken by Packard, op. cit. Lee Adler and Irving Crespi, eds., Attitude Research at Sea (American Marketing Association, 1966).

1. information

With much of his time still committed to the routines of work, voluntary groups, and informal contacts, the urbanite depends on the mass media for easily accessible information on a variety of topics or interests (news, sports, commercial recreation, weather, etc.). The educational role of the newspaper and magazine is particularly important; consequently, many urbanites rely on regular deliveries or subscriptions to replace outmoded facts with newer ones.[19] Note that in most instances this information is not worldshaking or related to one's occupation. It is more often superficial, transitory, even frivolous.

2. desire for meaningful, minor changes

Fads, fashions, vogues, and crazes are part of the acquired needs of urbanites, though many decry the irrationalities of particular fashions. Apparently, both adolescents and adults participate in an informal status game [20] (sometimes reaching serious proportions) which provides excitement, anxiety, and some escape from sober responsibilities. The essence of fashion is the anticipation of change without much predictability of the content of change.[21] Fashions therefore provide the illusion of movement and an accompanying excitement. Most fashion changes are comparatively gradual, perhaps because a greater number of small changes is more congenial to urbanites than a small number of drastic changes.

In any case, the attractive superficiality of fashion is a substantial segment of urban leisure and recreation—in clothing, appliances, and vacations. Perhaps a major service of mass communications is the opportunity to obtain quick and extensive coverage of minor and major variations in fashion. This is not only true of the fashion magazines (e.g., *Vogue, Harper's Bazaar, Mademoiselle*) but of newspapers and magazines generally. Advertisements are, over time, newsworthy in showing changes in style while apparently offering a specific branded article. Incidentally, the primary mass media of fashion are inevitably the written, rather than the visual or aural type, because the former give more time for leisurely appreciation and study.

[19] Berelson, "What 'Missing the Newspaper' Means," *loc. cit.*
[20] The "status game" is discussed by C. Wright Mills, *White Collar* (New York, Oxford University Press, 1953), Chap. XI; and by Paul F. Lazarsfeld and Robert K. Merton, "Mass Communication, Popular Taste, and Organized Social Action," in Wilbur Schramm, ed., *Mass Communications, 1949* (Urbana, Ill., University of Illinois Press, 1949), pp. 459–480.
[21] A. L. Kroeber and Jane Richardson, "Three Centuries of Women's Dress Fashions: A Quantitative Analysis," *Anthropological Records*, 5 (1940).

3. contact with wider ranges of experience

Mass media content is, by the nature of its creation and dissemination, largely nonlocal or concerned with activities and events outside the normal routine. While urbanites show some interest in purely local items as presented in newspapers and on television (e.g., the local weather report), they seem to prefer mass communications that transcend the immediate and the personal. Often this preference is called escapism, but such a label assumes special frustrations and dissatisfactions. Whether or not the label is justified, the essential specialization and segregation of urban living do present limitations in experience which belie the insistent urban values of variety, expanded scope, and cosmopolitanism.

The role of the mass media as intermediary to the unusual or the dramatic has been directly suggested in studies of the attractiveness of daytime soap operas to housewives in recent years.[22] Indeed, the great popularity in urban regions of news magazines and picture magazines can be understood in this way. In the advertising field, special use is made of inaccessible but attractive personages and places—such as the Tetley Tea Taster, the testimonials of society matrons and film stars, the Rolls Royce in whiskey ads— and also of the bizarre, exotic, and unusual—as in ads for Maidenform Bras and Hathaway Shirts. Following this clue, it is not surprising that the most popular programs on television are the Westerns, the crime and private eye category, and the panel show featuring assorted celebrities.

4. attractive advocacy of middle class values

Despite constant criticism of its uniformity, lapses from good taste, and so on, mass communications as a whole are clearly and openly approved by urbanites. Within each medium, however, there are substantial differences in appeal to existing status levels (e.g., readers of *Harper's* are not likely to read *True Story*, and vice versa). Yet this general acceptance persists, and it probably rests not only on the themes or functions previously discussed, but on the implicit or explicit ways in which mass media promote and justify the basic values of middle status groups,[23] and those seeking to simulate those values. Only a few studies have thus far dealt with this aspect of mass communications, but the facts are so familiar that they need only be noted at this point.

Without much exception, the mass media emphasize optimism, adjustment, and a basic acceptance of modern society. There is an underlying

---

[22] W. Lloyd Warner and William Henry, "The Radio Daytime Serial: A Symbolic Analysis," *Genetic Psychology Monographs*, 37 (1948), pp. 7–69.

[23] This is persuasively presented in John W. Bennett and Melvin M. Tumin, *Social Life* (New York, Alfred A. Knopf, 1948), Chap. XXXI.

philosophy, expressed in both serious and humorous form, that modern social problems are difficult, but amenable to treatment through education, money, research, and the "good sense of most people." While social criticism is by no means absent from mass media, it tends to be scattered, aimed at specific persons or specialized organizations rather than major institutions, and therefore it tends to be superficial and unexciting to audiences and publics. Crusades, campaigns, and exposés in newspapers and magazines often serve a recreational purpose rather than stimulate desire for fundamental social or cultural change.

Advertising and mass fiction (found in most media) retain their appeal for urbanites as a constant reminder of the need for (and techniques of) personal striving for success, mobility, and progress. Indeed, the mass media have essentially converted the search for status from a hit-or-miss, amateur interlude to a strategic avocation.[24] It is not too extreme to suggest that modern mass communications constitute a wondrous education for "middle-classness," from the inspirations of a Norman Vincent Peale and a Dale Carnegie, to the innumerable tips from advertisers.

Intimately related to the preceding is the widespread concern with such highly regarded middle class values as possession, size, speed—in short, the stress on quantity. As delineated in the mass media, these values form a morality of status. At the same time, these values are easily measurable, thus providing for the urbanite a continuing picture of his relative status. Part of the fascination of the mass media probably lies in their use as a status measuring rod.

5. content for personal relationships

It has sometimes been suggested that the urbanite uses mass communications as a substitute for personal contacts, that mass media serve to limit the desire for social participation. This is probably true of a number of deviant personalities or confirmed isolates. But the available evidence gives little support to this notion among urbanites in general. With the possible exception of television,[25] exposure to mass media does not seem to replace personal contacts. Indeed, the social categories most involved in social interaction (suburbanites, middle class families, and blue collar families)—see Chapter 9—make considerable use of the mass media.

Perhaps this connection rests on the fact that in the urban milieu in-

[24] Patricke Johns-Heine and Hans H. Gerth, "Values in Mass Periodical Fiction, 1921–1940," *Public Opinion Quarterly*, 13 (Spring, 1949), pp. 105–116; Leo Lowenthal, "Biographies in Popular Magazines," in William Petersen, ed., *American Social Patterns* (Garden City, N.Y., Doubleday and Company, 1956), pp. 63–117; Ralph Glasser, *The New High Priesthood* (London, Macmillan, 1967), esp. Chap. 3.

[25] Bennett and Tumin, *op. cit.*, pp. 635–640; Hamilton and Lawless, *loc. cit.*; Frank L. Sweetser, "Home Television and Behavior: Some Tentative Conclusions," *Public Opinion Quarterly*, 19 (Spring, 1955), pp. 79–84.

formal interaction largely depends on items and events beyond the direct experience of the urbanite. Most conversations would sputter into a merited silence if they dealt only with one's aches and pains, what one did recently, and the state of one's children. Instead, social interaction abounds in matters of indirect or vicarious experience—world news, professional sports, weather reports, and notable or notorious events in favorite media. The urbanite, in effect, must keep abreast of the mass media in order to participate on an equal basis in informal conversation with relatives, friends, and acquaintances.

Mass communications, it is alleged, have combined with mass leisure to produce mass culture, an urban lowest common denominator of attitudes and values. If mass culture refers to uniformities of values in media content, this interpretation has some merit.[26] But there is little evidence that mass media have created herd-like uniformities in specific responses to media content. Exposure does not insure either attention or acceptance.[27] In this relatively new sphere of urban organization, we can instead suggest a subtle process of interactions between urban populations and the various media. To the manipulator of mass media, the process is predominantly persuasive. To the various publics, mass media present an interesting challenge, combining unequal parts of information and opinion, of sincerity and sensation. The interplay between persuaders and public resembles a semiserious game in which one set of participants "plays to win" and the other "plays for kicks." Out of this bizarre form of contact and interchange a new urban ethic has developed—the ethic of ambiguity.[28]

From the standpoint of both public and mass communicator, the ethic of ambiguity is an ethic of compromise, but each follows its own version of this theme. To the mass communicator, mass media are a shifting amalgam of fact, inference, *non sequitur*, sensation, and special ideology. The game consists of devising mixtures that have audience appeal; the new ethic does not demand total fidelity to fact nor unrestricted falsehood.

The audience or public, on the other hand, practices a reciprocal consumer ethic of ambiguity and ambivalence. As the game is played, resistance and gullibility, the search for fact and the attraction of fantasy, reason,

---

[26] Bennett and Tumin, *op. cit.*, pp. 609–618; Bernard Rosenberg and David M. White, eds., *Mass Culture* (New York, The Free Press, 1957); Philip Olson, ed., *America as a Mass Society* (New York, The Free Press, 1963); Lewis A. Dexter and David M. White, eds., *People, Society, and Mass Communications* (New York, The Free Press, 1964), Parts 2 and 5.

[27] See the interesting discussions of this issue by Herbert Hyman and Paul Sheatsley, "Some Reasons Why Information Campaigns Fail," *Public Opinion Quarterly*, 11 (Fall, 1947), pp. 412–423; Whyte, *Is Anybody Listening?*, Chap. II; Harold L. Wilensky, "Mass Society and Mass Culture: Interdependence or Independence?," *American Sociological Review*, 29 (April, 1964), pp. 173–196.

[28] Cf. William Stephenson, *The Play Theory of Mass Communication* (Chicago, University of Chicago Press, 1967), pp. 64, 194–204.

logic, and faith are major ingredients in audience response to media content. To the urbanite, the challenge lies in exposure to the mixed content of mass communication and in selecting personally satisfying segments of fact and fantasy that can be assimilated without destroying the leisure aspect or suggesting immaturity. The peculiar fascination of the advertisement is the delightful danger of being persuaded even if one "knows better."

An ethic of ambiguity is understandable, though it certainly clashes with the absolutes of traditional morality and the unswerving guidance of the Protestant Ethic. For the urbanite, confronted by variety, change, and the probability of soon being either wrong or out of fashion, the ethic of ambiguity is a form of defense against the basic heterogeneity and dynamism of the urban region. Mass communications—properly or improperly defined as an adjunct of leisure—may be interpreted therefore as an acceptable locus of ambiguities, as a hedge against change.

But the game of mass communications is not always exciting, since creativity is unequal to the demand of repetitive communication. One tires of a favorite program, comic strip, magazine, etc. The ethic of ambiguity is only partly satisfying to urbanites, who are engaged in a search for meaning, order, and consistency. In this quest, it seems, attention is shifting from media content to the formal characteristics of mass media (regularity, wide coverage, etc.). The evolving result is a reinterpretation of leisure as routine, to be planned and organized, rather than a spontaneous activity. It is too early to evaluate the significance of this routinization of leisure for urban regional organization. However, if the meaning of leisure becomes indistinguishable from that of work and responsibility (also routinized), and mass communications tend to be vehicles of such a process, the role of urban regions as creative centers may be transformed into that of super-tranquilizer. While this interpretation is necessarily tentative, it does suggest that an important clue to urbanism and its future lies in the implicit applications of mass media by urban audiences, and in the relation of these new usages to urban organization.

selected references

DEXTER, Lewis A. and WHITE, David M., eds., *People, Society, and Mass Communication* (New York, The Free Press, 1964).

JACOBS, Norman, ed., *Culture for the Millions* (Princeton, Van Nostrand, 1961).

KATZ, Elihu and LAZARSFELD, Paul F., *Personal Influence* (New York, The Free Press, 1955).

KLAPPER, Joseph T., *The Effects of Mass Communication* (New York, The Free Press, 1960).

MEIER, Richard L., *A Communication Theory of Urban Growth* (Cambridge, MIT Press–Harvard University Press, 1962).

SCHRAMM, Wilbur, *Mass Communications* (Urbana, University of Illinois Press, 2nd ed., 1960).

STEPHENSON, William, *The Play Theory of Mass Communication* (Chicago, University of Chicago Press, 1967).

iv

urban planning
and social problems

16

social problems and the urban region

Both laymen and social scientists are concerned by the fact that urban regions continually exhibit contradictory aspects. The catalytic presence of cultural heterogeneity seems to be partially negated by growing uniformities in tastes, consumption, and ideas. Creativity in various fields, a hallmark of urbanism, is accompanied by considerable apathy and a taste for the safely familiar. Despite the variety of activities, the vitality and fascination of city living, there is likewise boredom and countless indecisions about use of leisure time ("What would you like to do?" "I don't know. What would *you* like to do?"). If there is expanded productivity—in comforts and conveniences, as well as necessities—poor or dubious health and physical and mental ills are also quite apparent to the urbanite. Finally, the relatively wide opportunities for personal and vicarious achievement share the urban stage with keen feelings of aimlessness, frustration, and despair (the quiet desperation of Thoreau).

The transitional nature of urban regions, which was discussed in Chapter 8, seems to provide a helpful way of approaching an understanding of these contradictions and the familiar problems that accompany them. Basically, urban regions have reached a transitional phase as a result of three sets of conditions. Most obvious are rapid changes in population, technological capacities, and values. Second, there is the development of relatively autonomous and competing groups in the economic, political, and other spheres. Third, and finally for this brief summary, rather new standards of humanitarianism, progress, welfare, reform, etc. have added powerful pressures for improved functioning in urban systems. Let us call these the structural features of urban transition.

During the greater part of the modern urban wave, the response to these structural features has been a compound of disinterest, ignorance, fitful and hysterical concern, indecisiveness, and narrowly conceived opportunism. The recent history of any major city provides ample evidence of

these responses.[1] As a consequence, despite its material accomplishment:
the urban region has accumulated a formidable repertory of basic, critic
problems, which have in varying degrees disturbed the more thoughtful u
banites throughout the world. These problems of transitional urbanism m
be classified in the following way:

1. Urban congestion and uncontrolled competition for urban space.
2. Personal inadequacy and insecurity.
3. The costs and dilemmas provoked by continual striving for status.
4. The absence of communal cohesion or morality, especially in cri-
periods.
5. The failure to promote orderly physical and social development f
the urban region as a whole.

Other classifications of fundamental problems are of course possi
particularly since the specific aspects of these problems seem to be inter
pendent. But whatever classification is used, these constitute almost the
tire fund of modern social problems. Indeed, in an ever increasing degr
social problems are becoming synonymous with problems of the urb
region.[2]

Social problems may be defined as repeated and relatively widespre
human situations which are in some manner recognized as undesirable a
as requiring drastic modification. In urban regions, several categories of pe
sons may (and do) exhibit awareness of specific social problems: (a) tho
directly affected by difficulties; (b) social scientists, who study such prol
lems as part of their professional pursuits; (c) public officials; (d) publi
cists, journalists, and other mass communicators; and (e) specific public
reached by the media of mass communication. The question often arises:
how many must be aware of the significance of situations before we may
apply the label "social problems?" Such a question is perhaps unavoidable
but it assumes that social problems are both static phenomena and also
numerically decided, as in an election or an "unpopularity" contest.

Serious students of social problems, on the other hand, have made two
things relatively clear. (a) Social problems have histories, courses of devel-

[1] Bessie L. Pierce, *A History of Chicago* (New York, Alfred A. Knopf, 1937–1957),
3 vols.; Blake McKelvey, *Rochester* (Cambridge, Mass., Harvard University Press, 1949–
1956), 3 vols.; T. J. Wertenbaker, *Norfolk* (Durham, N.C., Duke University Press,
1931); William A. Robson, ed., *Great Cities of the World* (London, Allen and Unwin,
1954).
[2] Virtually all textbooks on social problems and social disorganization demonstrate
this connection. See such recent texts as Jessie Bernard, *Social Problems at Midcentur*
(New York, Dryden Press, 1957); Harry C. Bredemeier and Jackson Toby, *Social Pro*
lems in America (New York, John Wiley and Sons, 1960); Robert K. Merton an
Robert A. Nisbet, eds., *Contemporary Social Problems* (New York, Harcourt, Brace,
and World, 1961); Marshall Clinard, *The Sociology of Deviant Behavior*, 2nd ed. (New
York, Holt, Rinehart, and Winston, 1962); Paul B. Horton and Gerald R. Leslie, *The*
Sociology of Social Problems, 2nd ed. (New York, Appleton-Century-Crofts, 1960).

opment—in scope, severity, degree of public awareness, and attempted solutions. (b) As social problems develop, awareness is communicated to broader categories. Often, initial awareness develops among social scientists, certain interest groups, and some mass communicators. Other categories, in varying order, then acquire fleeting or serious concern, hoping and eventually articulating the demand that "something ought to be done."

In general, the existence of urban social problems—or at least the more dramatic and personal manifestations of these problems—is widely recognized. The mass media, the schools, churches, and public agencies have been untiring in attempts to define and illustrate the meaning of crime, juvenile delinquency, gambling, drug addiction, alcoholism, divorce, illegitimacy, labor-management conflicts, racial and religious discrimination, mental disorder, educational deficiencies, inadequate recreation, political corruption, housing problems, slum areas, traffic snarls, the impact of unbalanced local economies and outmoded tax structures, etc. But the causes of such problems, and the factors that explain their persistence, are poorly understood by urbanites. As a matter of fact, social scientists do not yet possess a sufficiently comprehensive explanation of urban social problems, though recent advances in research and theoretical formulations seem promising.[3] Therefore urbanites are understandably confused about appropriate measures or solutions.

From this continuing conflict of concern on the one hand, and bewilderment and honest ignorance on the other, several typical reactions to social problems have emerged.

1. resignation and complacency

Saturated with increasingly banalized accounts of crime, divorce, graft, strikes, etc., some urbanites seem to develop a protective apathy about problems that do not directly and personally impinge on their welfare. Such problems come to be taken for granted, to be noted but no longer worthy of excitement, indignation, or effort. "That's human nature," "politics and honesty don't mix," are some typical statements of this attitude, which approaches social problems as a living folklore, tangible but not completely real.

2. manipulation of personality

For many decades, urbanites have been fascinated by the possibility of fitting personalities to their social environment and thereby reducing those stresses and conflicts which are presumed to cause specific social problems (such as mental disorder or ethnic discrimination). Generally, those who confront social problems primarily through contacts with individual cases

[3] Clinard, op. cit., Chap. I; Merton and Nisbet, op. cit., Chap. XV.

(the clinical setting) assume this approach.[4] The leading proponents of personality manipulation therefore include psychiatrists, physicians, ministers, teachers, and social workers, though there are many in each of these professions who do not accept the validity or the practicality of this sort of solution.

3. institutional change [5]

In contrast to the preceding approach, some urbanites find the source of social problems in imperfect organizational, legal, or administrative arrangements—and in the values that underlie these structures. Consequently, various types of reformers, social engineers, community organization workers, and many social scientists place great reliance on specific alterations in government, economic organization, school and university systems, etc. The essence of this approach is a focus on desired changes in one institutional sector.

4. the planning approach [6]

This is the broadest, the most comprehensive, and possibly the most difficult to apply in practice to urban social problems. It is based on the commonplace observation—a fundamental insight of sociology—that human affairs exhibit intricate interdependence within a complex group, community, or society. In particular, the planning approach stems from the interrelations of human needs and institutions in the organic solidarity of modern urbanized societies. It is exemplified in the attempt to view a social problem in terms of its relation to normal structures in the urban region and its relation to other social problems. Planning, therefore, involves broad knowledge, coordinated programs, and a continuing optimism about the effects of unfamiliar controls.

To achieve some perspective on urban attitudes toward social problems, we might consider a somewhat simplified comparison of community types in terms of a rough continuum of societal complexity [7] (see Table 42). For

[4] E.g., Robert Lindner, *Must You Conform?* (New York, Holt, Rinehart, and Winston, 1956) ; Anna Freud, *The Ego and the Mechanisms of Defence* (London, International Universities Press, 1946) ; William Healy and Augusta Bronner, *Treatment and What Happened Afterward* (Boston, Judge Baker Guidance Center, 1939) ; Rollo May, *The Meaning of Anxiety* (New York, Ronald Press, 1950).

[5] E.g., Robert S. Lynd, *Knowledge for What?* (Princeton, N.J., Princeton University Press, 1945) ; Robert M. MacIver, *The More Perfect Union* (New York, Harper and Brothers, 1948) ; Carle C. Zimmerman, *The Changing Community* (New York, Harper and Brothers, 1938) ; Robert C. Angell, *Free Society and Moral Crisis* (Ann Arbor, Mich., University of Michigan Press, 1958).

[6] The best sociological discussion of planning is Karl Mannheim, *Man and Society in an Age of Reconstruction* (New York, Harcourt, Brace, and World, 1940), especially pp. 155–163, 191–199, 222–236, 374–380.

[7] *Ibid.*, pp. 150–155.

table 42

Types of Societal Complexity and Responses to Problems

SOCIETAL TYPE	DOMINANT COMMUNITY TYPE	DOMINANT SOCIAL MECHANISM
Folk-sacred community	Rural village	Tradition and chance discovery
Transitional society	Urban areas of the 19th and 20th centuries	Discrete or separate invention
Advanced secular or "State civilization"	Large urban regions (stabilized form)	Rationalized planning (authoritarian)

our purposes, the extremes of this continuum should be regarded as reference points for evaluating the structures and probable trends of modern urban regions.

Focusing briefly on the folk-sacred type, in which the dominant community form is normally the agricultural village, the major problems are those of survival, adaptation to the physical environment, and to hostile neighbors. Without a developed division of labor, members of this type of community rely on strong traditional values and on a relatively unpremeditated, trial-and-error approach (chance discovery) to group problems. In our sense of the term, social problems are relatively absent, since tradition provides widely accepted solutions to difficulties in communities untouched by the complex values of rationality and efficiency. Many preliterate societies (until recently) have approximated this general form.[8]

On the other extreme is a type that has perhaps never yet been fully achieved—the advanced principled-secular or "state civilization" form.[9] Modern totalitarian societies (Fascist, Nazi, and Communist) possess several characteristic features (minute division of labor, bureaucratization, centralized authority, emphasis on science and rational procedures, controlled use

[8] Numerous references to studies of preliterate societies can be found in Felix M. Keesing, *Cultural Anthropology* (New York, Holt, Rinehart, and Winston, 1958); and Ralph Linton, *The Study of Man* (New York, Appleton-Century-Crofts, 1936). For a handy collection, consult Elman R. Service, *A Profile of Primitive Culture* (New York, Harper and Brothers, 1958).

[9] Howard W. Odum, *Understanding Society* (New York, Macmillan, 1947), pp. 707–708; Franklin H. Giddings, *Civilization and Society* (New York, Henry Holt, 1932), pp. 280–281; Howard Becker, "Current Sacred-Secular Theory," in Howard Becker and Alvin Boskoff, eds., *Modern Sociological Theory* (New York, Dryden Press, 1957), pp. 155–175; Howard Becker, *Man in Reciprocity* (New York, Frederick A. Praeger, 1956), Chap. XII; Alvin Boskoff, "Structure, Function, and Folk Society," *American Sociological Review*, 14 (December, 1949), pp. 749–758.

of communications media for manipulation of attitudes and values), as well as such related historical instances as the Spartan state and the earlier phases of the Roman Empire. But, to provide a self-consistent and more sharply etched extreme type—and thus perhaps anticipate possible future trends—we might posit a special community form: the stabilized, rationalized urban region.

In such a community, which is an extension of tendencies in modern urban areas, a set of interrelated features might be hypothesized. First and most predictable is the development of the typical urban area as a large land mass, a supercommunity composed of many previously separate communities. Gottmann has already named this "megalopolis" and points to its currently most developed manifestation in the urban sprawl from Boston to Washington and environs.[10]

Second, the rationalized urban regional type operates as a single unified system, with centralized services of many kinds and a related structure of centralized authority. Independent suburbs and adjacent but conflicting tax rates or zoning regulations would therefore be absent.

Third, the dominant institution is the political-legal system, rather than kinship or religion, or a privately operated economic sphere (the market, as in transitional urban communities).

Fourth, while status differences persist—and perhaps become even more evident—the rationalized urban region predominantly operates on principles of impartial service and general public welfare. Such an emphasis may derive partially from humane considerations, but more likely it is based on the desire to protect community functioning from the nonrational, parochial interests of competing groups in the region. This rationalized approach is facilitated by a centralized structure of authority, though it is certainly clear that the latter does not guarantee the former.

Fifth, the dominant method of treating—and anticipating—community problems is planning, a continuous process of controlling, regulating, and coordinating the most significant activities and social processes from key positions of knowledge and authority. It is fruitless, at this point in human experience, to evaluate the efficiency and the full moral implications of planning. In general, the world's experience thus far with community, regional, and societal planning has been disappointing. The major reasons seem to be (a) inadequate use of existing knowledge; (b) poor understanding and faulty cooperation from the majority of citizens; (c) wavering sincerity and arrogance of planning officials; and (d) interference resulting from the policies of other communities and societies. In the extreme type of the rational-

[10] Jean Gottman, *Megalopolis* (New York, Twentieth Century Fund, 1961). This is quite similar to the term "conurbation," as coined by Patrick Geddes in his *Cities in Evolution*, new and rev. ed. (New York, Oxford University Press, 1950), pp. 14–15. See also H. G. Wells, *Anticipations* (New York, Harper, 1902), pp. 53, 67, where the concepts of "megalopolis" and "urban region" are clearly described.

ized urban region, it is hypothesized, conditions (*a*) and (*c*) are considerably improved as a result of scientific advances in data accumulation and analysis, and in selection of planning personnel. But the remaining problems elude rational solution in this type. Consequently, planning is authoritarian rather than democratically conceived or approved.

With these polar types as reference points, let us now return to contemporary, transitional urban regions. In response to rapidity of change and the absence of reliable experience in anticipating or controlling change, urban regions have been experimenting with several methods of meeting social problems.[11] The complacency–laissez faire complex of attitudes is essentially a survival of the chance discovery approach of the village community. However, the dominant approach until the last few decades has been a reliance on single, narrowly conceived solutions to specific immediate problems—what Mannheim has called the stage of inventive thinking. Most of the numerous instances of proposed institutional change and personality manipulation have been of this character. For example, we might refer to political reforms (proportional representation, the referendum, improvements in municipal service, civil service and merit systems, revised taxation systems, new housing projects, mental health programs, etc.). Typically, the essence of these measures has been an attack on limited aspects of a particular problem in isolation from related conditions and a concern for treatment of already affected persons and groups, rather than prevention of future difficulties.

But the inventive is losing its appeal for urbanites as the persistence (and increase) of social problems involves prodigious financial outlays and also serves to threaten the enjoyment of the gracious living so important to the modern urban system of values. In varying degrees, therefore, invention has been challenged by the planning approach. However, since many urban regions share in a political tradition of democracy and long established freedoms, the authoritarian potentialities of planning present further problems. The underlying thread in urban regions as units appears to be the search for a proper blend of planning, invention, and discovery as social techniques—in short, responsible planning, or democratic goals pursued by modern, rational-scientific means.[12]

planning as a process of social change

Planning, and to some extent separate invention, rests on the strategy of mitigating social problems by imposed or controlling processes of change in urban regions. It follows, then, that planning must give careful attention to the general nature of social and cultural change as revealed in modern urban regions and modifications in the normal change process that are con-

[11] Mannheim, *op. cit.*, pp. 150–155.
[12] *Ibid.*, pp. 363–365.

sidered necessary to meet planning goals. Implicitly or explicitly, therefore, the student of urban problems always works with some conception of basic stages or phases in processes of change. The following scheme may provide a simplified means of summarizing these stages.[13]

1. *Dissatisfaction or problem stage.* Recognition of undesirable situations, of inadequate satisfaction of social needs, or of specific strains that seem menacing, produces attitudes of dissatisfaction among a number of appropriately sensitive persons. The source of these feelings may be traced to the impact of other societies or communities, or the development of internal social difficulties. In this early phase, dissatisfaction is not often dramatic, widespread, or organized.

2. *Innovation.* If dissatisfaction is sufficiently strong, one or more persons may seek to remedy the problem by conceiving a new technique, a new principle of organization, a new piece of apparatus, or a new value (goals, morals, etc.).

3. *The trial appraisal stage.* One of the key phases of change occurs at this point—the presentation of innovations to wider categories for their evaluation and trial. Whatever the worth of an innovation, in order to contribute to change, it must be attractively launched toward its prospective public. Debate, advertising, charismatic personality, the lure of novelty are some of the means by which innovations achieve a trial and therefore the crucial stage of appraisal.

4. *Competitive or transitional stage.* If innovations gain some currency and approval, there is yet the necessity of determining their relation to pre-existing practices, values, and forms. Normally, two alternatives appear: (*a*) the eventual replacement of the old by the new; (*b*) the simultaneous acceptance of the innovation and the established form by different categories of persons. In the latter case, the overall process of change may be delayed by group conflicts. The early history of the United States, for example, was marked by conflicting attitudes toward the Constitution and its system of centralized authority, and a consequent formation of separate, contending political parties.

5. *The integrative stage.* Assuming relatively widespread approval of an innovation, there remains the decisive problem of connecting the innovation to traditional forms and values in other spheres of activity. Since human needs and social structures operate as interdependent chains, the process of change inevitably involves either some modification in the accepted innovation or appropriate readjustments in several established forms. In the first case, which is rather rare, the impact of change has resulted in minimal, relatively

---

[13] Alvin Boskoff, "Social Change: Major Problems in the Emergence of Theoretical and Research Foci," in Becker and Boskoff, *op. cit.*, pp. 289–301; Alvin Boskoff, "Functional Analysis as a Source of a Theoretical Repertory and Research Tasks in the Study of Social Change," in George K. Zollschan and Walter Hirsch, eds., *Explorations in Social Change* (Boston, Houghton Mifflin, 1964), pp. 213–243.

insignificant variation. However, genuine and highly significant change occurs in the second instance, as a result of the original innovation, but often from the derivative changes promoted by that innovation.

the strategy of urban planning

We may now explore the interrelations among the three major themes of this chapter: social problems, social change, and planning. The normal progression of social change, as represented by the sequence of five phases, does not operate in a highly rational, consecutive manner in urban regions. Specifically, the process of change seems to reflect difficulties in solving the practical situations connected with phase 4 (the competitive or transitional phase) and phase 5 (the integrative phase). These difficulties largely derive from the numerous innovations in urban life and the rapidity with which they are introduced, the lack of consensus among urban groups and categories about awareness of difficulties, adequate goals, and appropriate means of reducing accumulated stress, and the survival in part of a laissez faire, individualistic philosophy and a consequent hesitation to interfere with the operation of normal groups and their unintended effects on the larger community.[14]

Social problems, then, seem to arise and persist under two sets of conditions: (a) complex and generally rapid processes of change and (b) lack of experience and/or willingness to intervene in an intelligent, systematic manner. Essentially, the rationale of urban planning is its potential role in bridging the gap—as efficiently as possible—between adjacent stages of the urban change process. The theory of planning therefore rests on continuing knowledge of human capabilities and desires, and of altered or improved techniques and facilities for meeting these desires.

Planning also depends on a fundamental strategy or orientation to urban change as a whole. Though this strategy is rarely made explicit, it seems to embody, first, a necessary distinction among demographic, social, and cultural aspects of urban structure and change.[15] But it is the special interrelation of these aspects that is significant for the theory of planning. In simplified form, urban change may be conceived as historically traceable to cultural innovations (see Chapter 2) which encouraged population aggregations in towns and cities. These in turn have been followed by a number of social products (extensive division of labor, bureaucratic structures, specialized publics, etc.).

[14] Alvin Boskoff, "Postponement of Social Decision in Transitional Society," *Social Forces*, 31 (March, 1953), pp. 229–234; Alvin Boskoff, "Social Indecision: A Dysfunctional Focus of Transitional Society," *ibid.*, 37 (May, 1959), pp. 305–311.

[15] A brief but very useful discussion of these aspects of urban structure is Richard Dewey, "The Rural-Urban Continuum: Real But Relatively Unimportant," *American Journal of Sociology*, 66 (July, 1960), pp. 60–66. See also Boskoff, "Social Change," *op. cit.*, pp. 263–265.

However, cultural changes—in the form of mores, laws, tastes, and values—have generally tended to appear less rapidly and with a narrowed scope.

This lag in culture should not be confused with the concept of "cultural lag" introduced into American sociology by Ogburn. Cultural lag refers to different rates of change discovered by comparing developments in value systems and in material technology.[16] In the context of planning theory, a comparison is instead made between value systems and organizational forms. From this standpoint, social problems may be regarded as products of the discrepancy between complex facilities and pressures, on the one hand, and currently inappropriate values and personal motivations on the other. This may be called "achievement lag," following Odum.

Achievement lag is a relatively new phenomenon. It results from greatly expanded capabilities for human achievement derived from complex, impersonal forms of social organization, a concomitant change in motivational demands on the personnel and clientele of these organizations, and a continuing inability to satisfy these demands because of adherence to traditional value orientations. Implicitly, the newer organizational forms seem to express such implied values as size, efficiency, uniformity, centralized power and authority. Whether these are desirable or not is of course important, but temporarily beside the point. Instead, there is considerable emphasis on emotion (love, fear); minor and major prejudices, narrow circles of loyalty, individualism, and fatalism of both the optimistic and pessimistic varieties. Achievement lag, then, is experienced as the tension between traditional values and the need for organizationally (not materially) appropriate values.[17]

Urban planning often takes for granted the desirability of the major social and cultural changes, but in addition seeks to reduce the human costs of achievement lag. Essentially, planning strategy is twofold. The ultimate objective is a gradual reorientation of traditional values (i.e., cultural change) to enable urbanites to reap the objective benefits of social change with minimal disturbance to their security. However, such cultural changes require further experiments in organizational change, since the unplanned social and cultural changes of recent decades clearly have not been accompanied by relevant revisions in values and systems of coordination. The rise of municipal and regional planning organizations since World War I is a material application of this general approach. We shall now turn our attention to planning as a new urban institution and try to evaluate as objectively as possible the degree of consistency between planning theory and practice.

[16] William F. Ogburn, *Social Change*, rev. ed. (New York, Viking Press, 1950), pp. 200–236.

[17] This type of lag has been analyzed under different labels by: Howard Odum, *Notes on the Changing Structure of Contemporary Society* (unpublished memorandum, November 12, 1948); Godfrey Wilson and Monica Wilson, *The Analysis of Social Change* (Cambridge, at the University Press, 1945), pp. 83–116, 125–132; Lowell J. Carr and James E. Stermer, *Willow Run* (New York, Harper and Brothers, 1952), pp. 206–207, 321–322; Boskoff, "Social Indecision," *loc. cit.*

selected references

BECKER, Howard S., ed., *Social Problems: A Modern Approach* (New York, John Wiley, 1966).

BENNIS, Warren *et al.*, eds., *The Planning of Change: Readings in the Applied Behavioral Sciences* (New York, Holt, Rinehart and Winston, 1961).

BERNARD, Jessie, *American Community Behavior* (New York, Holt, Rinehart and Winston, rev. ed., 1962).

BLACK, C. E., *The Dynamics of Modernization: A Study in Comparative History* (New York, Harper and Row, 1966).

BOSKOFF, ALVIN, "Social Change: Major Problems in the Emergence of Theoretical and Research Foci," in Howard Becker and Alvin Boskoff, eds., *Modern Sociological Theory* (New York, Holt, Rinehart and Winston, 1957), Chap. 9.

HOSELITZ, Bert F. and MOORE, Wilbert E., eds., *Industrialization and Society* (Paris, UNESCO, Mouton, 1963).

MANNHEIM, Karl, *Man and Society in an Age of Reconstruction* (New York, Harcourt, Brace and World, 1940).

17

planning as an urban institution

Modern urban planning in practice represents a widespread attempt to pursue the objectives discussed in the last chapter through new organizations. Essentially, then, we have been witnessing the birth and early development of a distinctive social institution, marked by relatively new value systems, technical and social roles, recruitment procedures, and patterns of authority. However, planning as a fledgling institution operates in part as an adjunct to, in part a substitute for, preexisting institutions, particularly, the political and economic institutions. Indeed, it is this amalgam of competition and collaboration that helps explain the mixed achievements and limitations of urban planning, and the implicit or explicit resistances it inevitably faces in its formative stages.

Table 43 summarizes what seem to be the basic value similarities and differences among planning, political organization, and economic structures in Western society. In general, the orientation of planning is more congenial to that of modern economic institutions than to political institutions—especially at local levels. Increasingly, economic units have recognized the need for intelligent planning in their respective operations to maximize profits, as well as their competitive position in local, regional, and national markets.[1] On the other hand, political institutions (in the form of charters, constitutions, and traditional offices) tend to represent the political conditions of bygone eras. In practice, some economic groups (businessmen, unions) have tried to alter the orientation of government operations in the direction of a quasi-planning approach, through such innovations as budgeting, forecasting of capital expenditures, estimates of revenue sources, development of relevant

---

[1] Several readable discussions of economic planning in modern society are specially recommended: Kenneth E. Boulding, *The Organizational Revolution* (New York, Harper and Brothers, 1953); Robert A. Dahl and Charles E. Lindblom, *Politics, Economics, and Welfare* (New York, Harper and Brothers, 1953); Carl Landauer, *Theory of National Economic Planning* (Berkeley, University of California Press, 1947); Karl Mannheim, *Freedom, Power, and Democratic Planning* (New York, Oxford University Press, 1950); and W. Arthur Lewis, *The Principles of Economic Planning* (London, Allen and Unwin, 1950).

table 43

A Comparison of Dominant Values in Planning, Political, and
Economic Institutions of the Modern World

PLANNING INSTITUTIONS	POLITICAL INSTITUTIONS	ECONOMIC INSTITUTIONS
Nonpartisan	Party emphasis	Politically "opportunistic"
Experts	Laymen	Experts
Continuity of program	Discontinuity	Continuity of program
Future orientation	Immediate present	Present and future orientation
General welfare, tangible and intangible	Power	Tangible profits
Increase of effective radius of co-ordination	Narrow radius	Relatively wide radius

funds of data, the use of expert assistance in analyzing and making recommendations about local problems. These conditions—the conservatism of the political sphere, the development of a narrowed thrust toward economic planning, the influence of economic on political institutions—provide a fundamental backdrop to planning as an emerging institution.

It is important to remember that the necessity of adapting new institutions to previously dominant ones is a recurrent theme in Western civilization. This process involves changes in preexisting institutions, as well as in the newly developing institutions. A particularly clear case is the rise of modern capitalism (sixteenth to nineteenth centuries) as a challenge to the political-economic complex of feudalism. The newer institutional components (the corporate form, commercial law, credit instruments, nominally free labor) were in competition with manorialism, the system of independent principalities, and with the dominant church. As capitalism developed, its adherents both influenced and were influenced by the rise of national, centralized governments, and likewise the emergence of various Protestant denominations. A similar process may be found in the rise of science (especially in the nineteenth century), in its conflict and accommodation with religion, and its more recent interaction with government and education.[2]

[2] R. H. Tawney, *Religion and the Rise of Capitalism* (New York, Penguin Books, 1947) ; Amintore Fanfani, *Catholicism, Protestantism, and Capitalism* (New York, Sheed and Ward, 1955) ; Henri See, *Modern Capitalism* (London, N. Douglas, 1928) ; Norman

Returning to urban planning as a "new" institution, its major problems (and therefore specific forms of experimentation and adjustment) seem to vary in emphasis from society to society. In the United States, for example, the development of planning is hampered by a continuing lack of consensus on the desirability or necessity of regional planning and its goals. By contrast, Scandinavian countries have long accepted the need for urban planning as a means of insuring the welfare of large segments of their populations. Great Britain has achieved substantial consensus about broad planning goals during the past 25 years, though specific programs have sometimes created intense dissatisfactions.[3]

Still another issue confronting the creators of a new instituiton is the choice and coordination of satisfactory techniques for carrying out institutional goals. This is an especially difficult problem for planners because urban planning has arisen in an era of very rapid changes, planners must rely on impressionist evaluations of scattered experiences rather than organized funds of knowledge, and to this very day there is a critical dearth of professional planners, whose role must be filled instead by otherwise capable people from engineering, public administration, architecture, or business. In the past 50 years, therefore, a large number of specific proposals—ranging from a purely physical orientation to dramatic, Utopian social schemes—have been debated, attempted, and partially evaluated by urban planners.[4] This search for appropriate planning techniques, with its accompanying successes and

---

Jacobs, *The Origin of Modern Capitalism and Eastern Asia* (Hong Kong, University of Hong Kong Press, 1958).

[3] For useful summaries of the planning movement in Great Britain, see M. P. Fogarty, *Town and Country Planning* (London, Hutchinson's University Library, 1948); William Ashworth, *The Genesis of Modern British Town Planning* (London, Routledge and Kegan Paul, 1954); J. H. Nicholson, *New Communities in Britain* (London, National Council of Social Services, 1961); John Tetlow and Anthony Goss, *Homes, Towns, and Traffic* (London, Faber and Faber, 1965). A detailed account of resistance to planning is in Harold Orlans, *Stevenage* (London, Routledge and Kegan Paul, 1952).

[4] See Ebenezer Howard, *Garden Cities of Tomorrow*, rev. ed. (London, Faber and Faber, 1945); Jose Luis Sert, *Can Our Cities Survive?* (Cambridge, Harvard University Press, 1942); Lewis Mumford, *From the Ground Up* (New York, Harcourt, Brace and World, 1956); Louis Justement, *New Cities for Old* (New York, McGraw-Hill, 1946); J. Tyrwhit *et al.*, eds., *The Heart of the City* (London, Lund Humphries, 1952); Harvey S. Perloff, ed., *Planning and the Urban Community* (Pittsburgh, University of Pittsburgh Press, 1961); Hans Blumenfeld, *The Modern Metropolis* (Cambridge, MIT Press, 1967); Edmund N. Bacon, *The Design of Cities* (New York, Viking Press, 1967); Richard L. Meier, *Developmental Planning* (New York, McGraw-Hill, 1965), Chap. 21; Christopher Tunnard and Boris Pushkarev, *Man-Made America: Chaos or Control?* (New Haven, Yale University Press, 1963), Part I; Constantinos A. Doxiadis, *Between Dystopia and Utopia* (Hartford, Trinity College Press, 1966); Camillo Sitte, *City Planning According to Artistic Principles,* tr. by George R. Collins and Christine C. Collins (London, Phaedon Press, 1965)—also called *The Art of Building Cities,* tr. by Charles T. Stewart (New York, Reinhold, 1945); Leonardo Benevolo, *The Origins of Modern Town Planning* (Cambridge, MIT Press, 1967).

failures, is an enlightening illustration of the problems connected with trying to translate the knowledge and insights of social science into practical situations. We shall consider urban planning programs more fully in Chapter 18 and 19.

Intimately related to the problems of consensus on values and planning techniques is the problem of appropriate planning organization and authority. Since planning represents a relatively new set of objectives and a new combination of skills and talents, many of the preexisting groups in urban government, business, and welfare have not been able to assume responsibility for planning without carrying over values and techniques that are implicitly antagonistic to planning. Consequently, a key step in the rise of planning as a social institution has been the formation of specialized groups designed to facilitate planning as an ongoing function, and also to sustain (and develop) an embryonic "culture" of planning.

Once again, experimentation has been a cardinal feature in two important respects. First, the developing organization of planning has been marked by the emergence of new roles (or new applications of older roles), both official and unofficial. Specifically, urban planning may be analyzed in terms of *administrative, professional, technical, lay,* and *public relations* roles. In recent decades, experimentation has consisted of attempts to operate a planning structure with greater and greater emphasis on the whole spectrum of relevant roles, as we shall see below and in Chapters 18 and 19.

The second aspect of this groping toward a successsful institutionalization of urban planning concerns the practical problem of coordinating various roles in the planning process—and especially the crucial one of discovering workable relations between neighboring planning areas and between local and national planning bodies. In short, urban planning—as in the case in any social institution—requires patterns of authority and regulation that are consistent with general planning objectives and the special characteristics of given urban regions. Early efforts in this direction seemed to reflect the survival of two extreme and mutually antagonistic approaches. In such nations as Great Britain and the United States, urban planning was a chaotic mosaic of localisms, without coordination within metropolitan areas and virtually innocent of the need for responsible integration between areas. The opposing orientation, found in some degree in France and in several Latin American nations, placed major responsibility for specific planning programs in a department of the national government.

Since about 1930, the urbanized nations of the world have recognized the limitations of both approaches to the regulative aspects of urban planning. Currently, three partly overlapping systems of authority may be identified, though changes in organization and functioning occur quite frequently. We may conveniently call these the British System, the American System, and the Continental or Traditional System.

the British system

Urban planning in Great Britain, the Netherlands, New Zealand, and Scandinavia [5] has achieved an organizational structure that seeks to combine a faith in democratic values and processes, a concern for the planning needs of relatively small nations, and a solution to the problems of integrating various local programs. For example, in the Netherlands, the initiative for urban planning comes from municipalities and provinces (states), which are responsible for regional planning. At the same time, national responsibility is lodged in the Ministry of Housing and Physical Development and a cabinet-level Physical Planning Council—which approve regional planning proposals and also can stimulate broad policy developments at lower planning levels. This two-way flow of responsibility is also becoming more visible in France, where regional planning (in line with a national program of decentralization) is slowly developing in a reversal of traditional rigidities. But since this general orientation has been highly developed in Great Britain, we may profitably review British experience since World War II.

One key to the British system is the creation of several planning levels. Beginning at the local level, there are five segments of the total urban planning institution.

1. The local council—borough, district, and small county councils.

2. The large metropolitan council, such as the London County Council (L.C.C.)—now called the Greater London Council.

3. Joint planning executive committees, made up of various local authorities.

4. Regional offices of the Ministry of Housing and Local Government (formerly called the Ministry of Town and Country Planning).

5. The Ministry of Housing and Local Government in London.

[5] Fogarty, *op. cit.*, pp. 19–24, 61–71, 173–203; J. B. Cullingworth, *Town and Country Planning in England and Wales* (Toronto, University of Toronto Press, 1964), especially Chaps. 3–6 and *Housing and Local Government in England and Wales* (London, Allen and Unwin, 1966); Beverley J. Pooley, *The Evolution of British Planning Legislation* (Ann Arbor, Legislative Research Center, University of Michigan Law School, 1960); Daniel R. Mandelker, *Green Belts and Urban Growth* (Madison, University of Wisconsin Press, 1962); J. Brian McLoughlin, "The Changing State of British Practice," *Journal of the American Institute of Planners*, 32 (November, 1966), pp. 350–355; R. J. Polaschek, ed., *Local Government in New Zealand* (London, Oxford University Press, 1956); United Nations, *Planning of Metropolitan Areas and New Towns* (New York, Department of Economic and Social Affairs, United Nations, 1967), pp. 93–105; United Nations, *Regional Planning: Housing, Building, and Planning* (New York, Department of Economic and Social Affairs, United Nations, 1959), pp. 170–179; Cornelius De Cler, "Dutch National Land Use Planning," in H. Wentworth Eldredge, ed., *Taming Metropolis* (Garden City, Doubleday, 1967), Vol. 2, pp. 1143–1157.

In addition, the British system includes the auxiliary services of:

1. Development councils, usually organized by business groups.
2. University consultants and research organizations.
3. Special commissions appointed by Parliament.
4. Private development corporations operating under charters of official planning bodies.

Since 1947, when the important Town and Country Planning Act reaffirmed and clarified a systematic approach to urban planning, the British system has experimented in allocating specific responsibilities among local, regional, and national levels. Through this law (and subsequent revisions), the national level imposes an obligation on all local planning authorities to study their respective needs in housing, transportation, industry, etc., and to conceive a detailed, comprehensive plan for meeting these needs. County councils, which often represent larger cities, and had been granted planning powers since 1929, are now required to exercise these functions in consultation with smaller local authorities within their regions. Where county councils do not exist, or where the need for coordination of adjacent community development is clearly recognized, a functional equivalent of the county council is the Joint Planning Committee. In the Birmingham area, for example, 23 local authorities have grouped themselves into six joint planning authorities.[6]

Significantly, the national government does not initiate specific urban planning programs, with one exception to be noted later. A local authority normally secures the services of professional planners in drawing up a set of planning proposals. In many cases, there is consultation with the ministry during the formative stages of a planning program. When a given plan is approved by the local authority, it is evaluated either by the ministry in London, or by regional offices of the ministry. In the latter case, the various national bureaus are represented by two coordinating commissions, to which local authorities may apply for information and provisional approval. One such commission, the Distribution of Industry Panel, provides aid and encouragement in matters of economic development. Regional Physical Planning Committees, on the other hand, are concerned with problems of physical planning, such as housing, roads, parks, and greenbelt areas.

If it seems necessary, the Minister of Housing and Local Government may legitimately establish joint planning boards for urban regions marked either by a maze of conflicting authorities or simply inertia with respect to local problems. The members of these boards are appointed by the local authorities concerned, so that planning functions remain faithful to local needs and resources. However, the joint board automatically supersedes the author-

---

[6] West Midland Group, *Conurbation: A Planning Survey of Birmingham and the Black Country* (London, The Architectural Press, 1948), p. 57.

ity of component local councils; it possesses full powers to make appropriate investigations, to devise comprehensive programs, and to implement these programs when the ministry bestows its official blessing.

The design of urban planning programs is therefore a local or regional responsibility, with the assistance of the national government. However, the ultimate planning authority is by law the Ministry of Housing and Local Government, which must approve any plan before it can be transferred from paper to practice. In general, the ministry's consultative role in early stages of a plan's preparation eases the problem of securing final approval without protracted conflicts between levels of authority. According to one close observer of British local government,[7] the administration of urban planning processes has been relatively smooth and remarkably lacking in controversy.

the case of London

A major exception to this system of local initiation, national consultation, and national supervision is the London region. As Robson has pointed out, the chaos of local authorities and the traditionally unsympathetic attitude of Parliament had made planning extremely necessary but virtually impossible. Consequently, the Town and Country Planning Act of 1947 specifically singled out the London region for extraordinary treatment. The L.C.C. was designated as the key planning authority for the London area, though the small downtown City of London was allowed to retain its medieval autonomy on such matters. On the other hand, the ministry has discretionary powers of initiating surveys and plans, in all probability for the special case of London rather than to impose general controls over British urban planning as a whole. The ministry has therefore sponsored the famous Greater London Plan by Patrick Abercrombie, which spelled out recommendations for decentralizing London's population and industries through the development of 12 (now 15) New Towns. It should be noted also that somewhat similar recommendations were presented by Abercrombie in a plan sponsored by the L.C.C.[8]

The British system, in short, emphasizes areal and regional responsibility for urban planning, with legal (though not always practicable) coordination provided by a national authority.

---

[7] Richards, *op. cit.*, p. 115.

[8] William A. Robson, *The Government and Misgovernment of London* (London, Allen and Unwin, 1939); Cullingworth, *Housing Needs and Planning Policy*, Chap. 8; Ministry of Housing and Local Government, *The South East Study 1961–81* (London, H.M.S.O., 1964); Peter Hall, *London 2000* (London, Faber and Faber, 1963); Frank Smallwood, *Greater London: The Politics of Metropolitan Reform* (Indianapolis, Bobbs-Merrill, 1965); Edward Carter, *The Future of London* (Harmondsworth, Penguin Books, 1962); Donald L. Foley, *Controlling London's Growth* (Berkeley, University of California Press, 1963); J. T. Cappock and Hugh C. Prince, eds., *Greater London* (London, Faber and Faber, 1964).

the American system

Unlike the recent British approach, urban planning in the United States has been largely a local responsibility. Cities are incorporated through charters granted by the various states. In general, state governments have not been sympathetic to urban problems within their borders, nor have they encouraged any comprehensive approach to city and regional planning—either morally or financially. Until recently, the federal government likewise reserved its energies for interstate and international issues. No national agency devoted specifically to urban affairs existed until the recent Department of Housing and Urban Development. Since 1949, however, as a consequence of housing and slum clearance legislation, the federal government has come to demonstrate some interest and control of city planning programs, principally through the power to withhold federal funds for local redevelopment programs.[9]

Consequently, urban planning is almost exclusively local in origin and in responsibility. But this system of local autonomy also reflects a basically cautious orientation to planning and a hesitancy to develop efficient lines of authority. Within the typical local (city) planning structure, therefore, three separable segments operate with variable degrees of cohesion with one another.

1. *The municipal executive*—including the mayor, the city manager, and the city council.

2. *The planning department or bureau*—a group of professionals who are full-time employees of the municipal government.

3. *The planning commission*—a group of appointed, unpaid laymen with legal powers to participate in the planning process.

Formally, the central, legally recognized authority for city planning is the mayor and his council. Both the planning bureau and the planning commission have been set up to operate as specialized advisory bodies. The planning bureau has the responsibility of gathering data, developing a Master Plan (to be discussed in Chapter 18), relating numerous requests to the Master Plan, and presenting proposals for planning projects. In many instances, particularly in cities under 50,000 population, private planning consultants are hired to supplement the bureau. Normally, the mayor and council are

[9] Robert A. Walker, *The Planning Function in Urban Government*, 2nd ed. (Chicago, University of Chicago Press, 1950); Roy Lubove, *The Urban Community: Housing and Planning in the Progressive Era* (Englewood Cliffs, N.J., Prentice-Hall, 1967); John W. Reps, *The Making of Urban America: A History of City Planning in the United States* (Princeton, Princeton University Press, 1965); John B. Willmann, *The Department of Housing and Urban Development* (New York, Praeger, 1967); Robert M. Fisher, *Twenty Years of Public Housing* (New York, Harper and Row, 1959).

authorized to secure these services, with the advice of the director of the planning bureau. The planning commission, on the other hand, is both an advisory and a policy-making agency. It makes recommendations to the executive and the legislative arms for their approval and financial support. However, such recommendations originate as proposals by the planning bureau (or special consulting groups) to the planning commission, which usually has the authority to accept or reject plans, and thus determines what is available to the ultimate planning authority (mayor and city council). Under these conditions urban planning is in reality an inherently competitive process, a system of checks and balances. Neither the elected officials nor the professional staff of planners play a decisive role in planning.

Since the planning commission seems to exercise veto power, it has become the key component of local planning and therefore merits closer examination. As a leading student of planning organization has pointed out,[10] the planning commission is a survival of a period in which professional planning was nonexistent and in which the need for planning was ignored by most urban residents. Leading citizens therefore organized themselves to prod city governments to provide a planning orientation and to develop specifically needed programs (e.g., zoning). Indeed, most municipal functions (including police and fire protection, health and welfare services) began in this manner.

However, as city planning became a regular function of local governments, the commission of leading citizens lost its initial and very important role as a public relations arm of planning. As provided by law, the planning commission remains a policy-making body. But this role, as it is widely recognized by students of city planning, is an inherently difficult one for the members of planning commissions, for three reasons.

1. By custom, the members are predominantly laymen and representative of the middle and upper status levels—particularly local businessmen. While commission members are conscientious and well meaning, they understandably follow perspectives that reflect their limited (though often highly regarded) experience.[11] Urban planning, however, requires concern for broader viewpoints and experience, especially those of lower status groups and urban minorities.

2. Again, by virtue of their background as laymen and businessmen, commission members rarely possess the interest or the general training that can inculcate a genuine understanding of the nature and scope of urban planning. Normally, therefore, they emphasize the more tangible, discrete aspects of planning. They interpret their function as limited to consideration of physical planning, to practical (immediate) problems—such as zoning regulations or a matter of traffic rerouting.

3. Finally, the planning commission as a unit normally operates with some ambiguity in status and responsibility. Although armed with substantial

---

10 Walker, *op. cit.*, p. 133. See also Webster, *op. cit.*, pp. 102–109.
11 Walker, *op. cit.*, pp. 153–163.

powers (developing comprehensive plans, reviewing petitions for variations from plans, hiring the planning staff), the commission tends to be somewhat apart from the regular administrative system and therefore not clearly subject to public control. Commission members are appointed by the mayor or city council, but thereafter they are notably independent; their dismissal or removal can only be on the difficult grounds of incompetence and malfeasance. Furthermore, the laws establishing planning commissions seem to mix advisory and policy-making functions without awareness of the practical difficulties this confusion entails. As a consequence, there are numerous opportunities for frictions and misunderstandings with the mayor and council, and with the professional planning staff.

With this general division of authority, the institutionalization of urban planning often seems like an exercise in futility. In short, the planning structure is self-defeating. The planning staff has its elaborate, long-range blueprints that may seem daring to the cautious layman. The mayor or the city council are busy with the routine affairs of government, and the prospect of reelection; they often view planning as necessary, but the responsibility of other agencies. The typical planning commission is made up of part-time, unpaid lawyers, realtors, and businessmen who regard themselves as guardians of thrift, sanity, and other civic virtues, and who prefer the pace of hesitation to the leaps of bold creativity. A built-in deadlock in urban planning thus prevails until one or more strong personalities comes to sit in the mayor's chair, on the city council, in the office of the planning bureau director, or at the table of commissioners. Sociologists have generally discarded the "great man" theory of history, but the dedicated, highly competent and persuasive personality seems to be the crucial element in converting institutional inertia into a process of achievement. In New York City, for example, city planning was largely stimulated by Mayor La Guardia and the many-titled commissioner, Robert Moses. In Philadelphia, the planning successes of the last decade can be attributed to the indefatigable director of city planning and a dynamic mayor. Similar cases of individual catalysts in planning can be found in many cities, among them Los Angeles, Milwaukee, Cincinnati, and Pittsburgh.

the continental system

In line with their respective national histories, the Soviet Union, Spain, and several Eastern European countries (Poland, Rumania, and to some extent, Czechoslovakia and Yugoslavia) can be taken as illustrations of the Continental approach to urban planning, which is a survival of nineteenth century forms of administrative centralization. The essence of this planning structure may be found in a highly bureaucratized system of agencies in which initiation of planning is primarily a national responsibility, the desires of local populations are not consulted at most stages of the planning process, and the execution and financing of plans are principally (if not completely) in the hands of a national authority.[12]

Urban planning in the Soviet Union has passed through several phases of experimental centralization. Between 1921 and 1940, planning was formally centralized in the State Planning Commission (Gosplan) and the Central Executive Committee of the Communist Party. In practice, however, local

figure 17

The Formal Structure of Urban Planning Organization in the Soviet Union

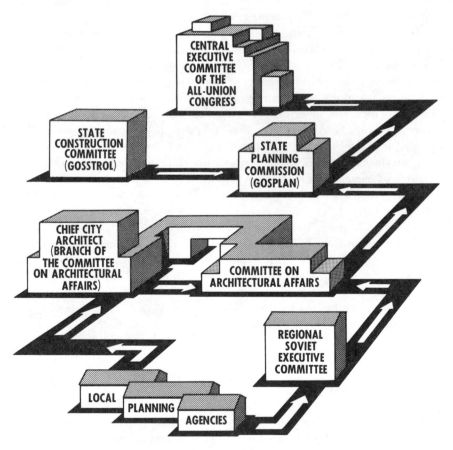

SOURCE: Maurice F. Parkins, *City Planning in Soviet Russia*, pp. 87–88, 98.

[12] Leo Grebler, *Europe's Reborn Cities*, Urban Land Institute, Technical Bulletin No. 28 (Washington, D.C., March, 1956), pp. 71, 87–88.

city planning was a jumble of uncoordinated programs, of general plans that were executed with unanticipated freedom of interpretation. The pressure for economic achievement and an ambitious program of rebuilding or creating hundreds of cities explain the enormous gap between formal structure and practice. The second phase, roughly corresponding to the forties, reflected three basic innovations in organization: more careful consultation between the State Planning Commission and the local planning authorities; creation of an Administrator of Architectural Affairs to inspect planning activities of city planning bodies; the reduction of competitive participation in the planning process by hundreds of local government and party groups (a decree of 1948). Despite such measures, Russian city planning did not achieve its current stage of tight, bureaucratic centralization until the early fifties.[13] A simplified framework of control is presented in Figure 17.

As a developing urban institution, planning is undergoing experimentation not only in organizational structure and patterns of authority, but in planning mores and distinctive techniques. Unfortunately, the overall goals of urban planning—rational control of urban regional development and anticipation of future needs—contain no inherent strategies of implementation. Planners and planning groups may be inspired by visions of seductive possibilities in urban living, but they must often face the fact that the planning function has been grafted on to communities with long histories and insistent practical problems. Under these conditions, urban planning has developed and variably emphasized a set of somewhat competitive practical mores and related methods of planning procedure.

types of planning orientation

The broadest and yet the most important issue in urban planning is the relative attention devoted to the physical and social aspects of the planning function.[14] Theoretically, both are intimately interrelated in any community; the location, use, and significance of physical structures act upon and reflect the values of organized groups in a given area over a definite time period. As a practical matter, however, urban planners must choose some degree of

[13] Maurice F. Parkins, *City Planning in Soviet Russia* (Chicago, University of Chicago Press, 1953); Jack C. Fisher, "Urban Planning in the Soviet Union and Eastern Europe," in Eldredge, *op. cit.*, Vol. 2, pp. 1069–1087; Jack C. Fisher, ed., *City and Regional Planning in Poland* (Ithaca, Cornell University Press, 1965), Chaps. 2, 3; Peter Hall, *The World Cities* (New York, McGraw-Hill, 1966), pp. 166–181; United Nations, *Planning of Metropolitan Areas and New Towns* (New York, Department of Economic and Social Affairs, United Nations, 1967), pp. 201–208.

[14] Lewis Mumford, *The Culture of Cities* (New York, Harcourt, Brace, and World, 1938), Chap. VII; William H. Form, "The Place of Social Structure in the Determination of Land Use: Some Implications for A Theory of Urban Ecology," *Social Forces*, 32 (May, 1954), pp. 317–323.

focus on either the physical or social for a definite segment of the planning process. Though this is a difficult choice, a decision must be made. Consequently, we can identify a basic distinction between physical planning and social planning in the urban region.

Essentially, physical planning serves to emphasize the design, allocation, construction, and interrelation of necessary facilities or means of urban living. Physical planning largely takes for granted the definition of necessary means, the ways in which physical facilities will be used, and the social consequences of their use. Social planning, on the other hand, is predominantly concerned with the creation, maintenance, or alteration of desired influences on the behavior, values, satisfactions, and interaction patterns of an urban population.

Inevitably, another critical choice confronts the urban planner, regardless of his varying decisions about physical and social aspects. Again, the pressure of specific, continuing urban problems (e.g., traffic, slum areas, overcrowded schools) demands a selection between tactics: the corrective approach and the creative approach.

In terms of our distinction in the last chapter (pp. 316–319), the corrective approach is normally on the level of discrete invention; it aims to repair or patch up existing cases of difficulty. Since transitional urban communities represent many such cases, it is obvious that they cannot be ignored. But how much effort should be given to treating symptoms as contrasted to attempts to search out conditions that can be appropriately altered? The former, while it is necessary, is peripheral to planning; the latter is more difficult, but represents the essence of planning as an urban institution.

The actual combinations of decisions on these issues can be presented in a simplified tabular form as the basic strategic-tactical kit of the urban planning institution (Table 44). In the following chapters, we shall review a number of programs that illustrate this variety of planning orientations. We

table 44

Classification of Urban Planning Orientations

Planning Orientation Types	Applications in Urban Regions
Corrective physical orientation	Routine medical and hospital facilities, street repairs, traffic, zoning, downtown redevelopment
Creative physical orientation	Public health programs, subdivision controls, provision of adequate greenbelts
Corrective social orientation	Case work programs (public and private)
Creative social orientation	Well-designed new communities or areas, neighborhood unit approach

shall also try to evaluate the consequences of the planning institution for the structure of urban regions.

selected references

ALTSHULER, Alan, *The City Planning Process: A Political Analysis* (Ithaca, Cornell University Press, 1965).

ASHWORTH, William, *The Genesis of Modern British Town Planning* (London, Routledge and Kegan Paul, 1954).

BERNARD, Philippe J., *Planning in the Soviet Union* (New York, Pergamon, 1966).

FRIEDMANN, John and ALONSO, William, eds., *Regional Development and Planning* (Cambridge, MIT Press, 1964).

GALLION, Arthur B. and EISNER, Simon, *The Urban Pattern: City Planning and Design* (Princeton, Van Nostrand, 2nd ed., 1963).

MANNHEIM, Karl, *Freedom, Power, and Democratic Planning* (New York, Oxford University Press, 1950).

MEYERSON, Martin *et al.*, *Face of the Metropolis* (New York, Random House, 1963).

MUMFORD, Lewis, *The Culture of Cities* (New York, Harcourt, Brace and World, 1938), Chaps. 6, 7.

SPREIREGEN, Paul D., *Urban Design: The Architecture of Towns and Cities* (New York, McGraw-Hill, 1965).

WALKER, Robert, *The Planning Function in Urban Government* (Chicago, University of Chicago Press, 2nd ed., 1950).

WEBSTER, Donald, *Urban Planning and Municipal Public Policy* (New York, Harper and Row, 1958).

18

corrective planning

It should come as no surprise that an overwhelming proportion of urban planning has been corrective rather than creative in nature. The reasons are fairly clear and are important in understanding the development of planning and its role in the urban region. First and foremost, the rapid and uncoordinated growth of urban agglomerations has produced a vast Pandora's Box of problems, which must be seriously confined to manageable limits before new vistas of urban living can be soberly approached. Indeed, the failure to achieve a measure of success with such urban problems as congestion, traffic snarls, crime, etc. has, in the second place, drained urban finances that might otherwise be allocated to genuinely creative programs. Thirdly, in the formative stage of urban planning administration (roughly 1900–1950), most of the members of planning bodies and commissions were implicitly committed to tangible, immediate programs whose results could be visibly determined by the layman. Fourthly—and perhaps not so clearly—a corrective approach reflects the persistence of traditionalistic, nonrational attitudes among urbanites, instead of the amusingly false picture of the typical urban emphasis on rationality, the attraction of new ideas, and action.

As a consequence of these conditions, we may note an interesting division of labor in the overall planning function of urban regions—at least in the United States. Public and semipublic planning agencies have assumed (or been given) responsibility for corrective physical planning and aspects of creative physical planning. The major responsibility for corrective social planning— e.g., welfare, rehabilitation, education, and interpersonal relations—remains in the preexistent mosaic of school boards and social work agencies. Creative social planning, which has a long and uneven history as a property of monarchs, politicians, legislatures, and utopian writers, is still not a routine concern of any established, reputable organization. It is largely a reflection of the critical role of individual philosophers, architects, political idealists, educators, and some social scientists. As we shall see in the next chapter, public planning agencies have attempted occasional entries into the difficult area of creative social planning. However, thus far this extension of normal planning functions can be found mainly in European urban planning.

the master plan

Corrective urban planning, particularly in the U.S., is a phase in a larger, idealized process of planning, in which creative planning is an ultimate objective. If the immediate problems of urban planning seem to predominate, planners have invented a link between corrective and creative programs in the concept and practical implementation of the Master Plan, or the "comprehensive city plan." [1] Fundamentally, the Master Plan is a graphic summary of present and projected patterns of land use, transportation, community facilities, and financing for an urban region. It represents an attempt to evaluate and select desirable current trends in the physical development of the region, and design changes in specific physical trends for a given period in the future (e.g., 20 years). Consequently, the Master Plan serves as a measuring rod for evaluating the significance of any category of community information (birth rates, tax revenues, school population, etc.), any existent public program, or any proposed revisions in community policies. It is important to understand that the Master Plan emphasizes trends and goals, orientations rather than detailed blueprints for specific means. Consequently, planning agencies possess a somewhat flexible instrument that provides links and constant guides to thinking and acting, rather than a definitive, eternal, sacred commitment. As information and experience accumulate, the Master Plan can be (planners assert it *must* be) altered to take account of changing events and new conceptions of desirable goals.

In a sense, corrective planning is a preliminary to the planner's fundamental objective—the creation of an urban region that provides the maximum in physical services and social amenities for its residents, as these are interpreted by a continuing interchange of ideas between urbanites and planners.[2] The role of corrective planning measures, therefore, is to clear up outstanding urban "debts" (unprofitable costs, social and personal wastage, chaotic development) so that newer and more promising responsibilities can be assumed. In other words, before deep-seated changes can be seriously attempted, the possibility of appreciating, financing, and absorbing such changes must be adequately increased by more immediate and somewhat prosaic correctives. The basic sociological problem in corrective urban planning therefore becomes: to what extent do specific corrective measures actually prepare the urban region for the more difficult process of guiding urban development in

[1] Mary McLean, ed., *Local Planning Administration*, 3rd ed. (Chicago, International City Managers Association, 1959), pp. 34–35; T. J. Kent, Jr., *The Urban General Plan* (San Francisco, Chandler, 1964).

[2] Herbert Simon, "Decision Making and Planning," in Harvey S. Perloff, ed., *Planning and the Urban Community* (Pittsburgh, University of Pittsburgh Press, 1961), pp. 189–191; Wolf Von Eckardt, "Zoning Fails in Suburbs, Proves Invitation to Bribes," *The Washington Post*, October 12, 1966.

terms of orderly, comprehensive, and yet practicable images of the future?

We shall review and evaluate in this chapter a representative selection of current forms of corrective urban planning—principally in the area of physical planning. Perhaps we can begin with one of the oldest and most controversial forms: urban zoning.

zoning and its contributions

Though European cities have long established controls over land use within their municipal borders, the younger and more dynamic cities of the United States were, until recently, so enamoured of sheer growth that considerations of the costs of rapid and uncoordinated growth were ignored. Recognition of the persistent problems of blight, decay, congestion, and wasted or unused land areas finally led to a national conversion to the zoning ordinance as a belated first step toward civic stabilization. Citizens groups, businessmen, architects, and planners were particularly vocal and persuasive in the twenties and thirties, after the pioneer zoning efforts of such cities as New York City and Boston.[3]

As a primary type of corrective physical planning, zoning normally has several basic objectives. First is the necessity of arresting the long-term trend toward purely individualistic, undesirably heterogeneous use of the city's dwindling supply of land. Prior to effective zoning, city lots and parcels were available to either the first or the highest bidder, without regard for the welfare, safety, or economic effect on neighboring areas.

Second, zoning has often been designed to control or limit the growth of population. This is accomplished by zoning laws that specify maximum densities of population or maximum number of dwelling units per acre.

Third, zoning laws reflect the planner's desire to salvage a reasonable balance among residential, commercial, industrial, and public needs for land in the urban region. Without the guidance of informed zoning, many American cities have an understandable tendency to overestimate commercial land needs—a survival of the widespread economic optimism of 1909 to 1929.[4]

the limitations of zoning

Theoretically, these crucial objectives make zoning an extraordinarily promising mechanism—almost the fundamental mechanism—of corrective physical planning. In practice, however, zoning has often achieved little to

[3] Theodore Caplow, "Urban Structure in France," *American Sociological Review*, 17 (October, 1952), pp. 544–549; Charles M. Haar, *Land Planning Law in a Free Society* (Cambridge, Mass., Harvard University Press, 1951), pp. 180–195; *Local Planning Administration*, Chap. XI.

[4] See Philip H. Cornick, *On the Problems Created by Premature Subdivision of Urban Lands in Selected Metropolitan Districts* (Albany, N.Y., Division of State Planning, 1938); Haar, *op. cit.*, p. 180.

warm the hearts of genuine planning groups. Several persistent difficulties help to account for this lack of achievement.

One brutal fact inevitably reduces the theoretical potential of zoning: decades of uncontrolled growth present planners with a virtually completed physical pattern that cannot easily (or inexpensively) be changed. Street patterns, location of buildings, etc. are of course not eternal, but they constitute a complex mold for large portions of the central city. Zoning therefore inherits a set of limits that only the irresponsible and the impractical can ignore.

A second important difficulty is the failure to integrate zoning regulations with a comprehensive urban plan. While this situation now receives more attention by planning bodies than in the past, it is often the case that the time-consuming process of developing a long-term plan based on careful analyses is deferred for the more immediate, more tangible, and less difficult process of drawing up zoning ordinances and maps.[5]

Zoning laws, in the majority of cases, are limited to municipal boundaries of central cities, or at best, enabling acts permit city zoning authorities to control land use within a narrow band outside the city line (1.5 to 5 miles). Since the greater part of urban population increase has occurred in peripheral areas (in the 5–20 mile band beyond the city proper), this kind of limitation encourages the very difficulties that zoning is supposed to correct. Indeed, one of the consequences of this situation is the development of competing zoning groups, often with divergent objectives. For example, in the New York City metropolitan region, outer suburban areas (such as Norwalk and New Canaan in Connecticut) have designed their zoning regulations to restrict population increase and exclude lower and middle income groups from their areas by requiring four-acre sites. This so-called snob zoning—regardless of its intrinsic merits or shortcomings—intensifies the already formidable problems of achieving orderly development in modern urban regions.[6]

A fourth difficulty common to zoning, in the United States and to some extent in Great Britain, is the desire to maintain property values. While this is a legitimate objective, in practice it leads to decisions that invariably delay or even contradict the normal aims of zoning. One of the widespread zoning problems is nonconforming uses or variances—in short, official permission to continue activities that clearly violate legal specifications for given types of zones (residential, commercial, or industrial). Permitted continuation of nonconforming uses is based on the laudable desire to avoid economic hardships for property owners who invested their resources in buildings before the development of zoning regulations. However, the removal of nonconforming

[5] "Facelifting Cities: Renewal Programs Show New Signs of Life, But Progress Still is Slow," *The Wall Street Journal*, May 7, 1958; Donald Webster, *Urban Planning and Municipal Public Policy* (New York, Harper and Brothers, 1958); Coleman T. Woodbury, *The Future of Cities and Urban Redevelopment* (Chicago, University of Chicago Press, 1953), pp. 641–642.

[6] Webster, *op. cit.*, p. 370; *The New York Times*, November 11, 1956; December 16, 1956; March 13, 1960.

uses is generally recognized as an exceedingly slow process. One of the leading planning consultants in the United States (Harland Bartholomew) asserts in addition that failure to reduce nonconforming uses is a major condition in the persistence and spread of blight in areas of transition.[7]

Perhaps another consequence of this concern for protecting existing property values is the practice of spot or piecemeal zoning, which consists of zoning decisions based on current locations of activities and uses, rather than a comprehensive, relatively independent scheme for determining proper patterns of land use.[8] Spot zoning can be identified in instances where an otherwise homogeneous area (e.g., a predominantly residential area) contains a totally different variety of land use (e.g., a gas station or a bottling plant) that is approved by the local zoning body. Significantly, spot zoning stems from acquiescence to requests from both existing or prospective owners of nonconforming property. To the student of planning, spot zoning not only invites further requests for a patchwork of variant uses; it also serves to interfere with the corrective function of zoning, and likewise creates additional obstacles to creative planning.

Still another aspect of the difficulties of zoning is the ever present danger of overzoning. Whether it can be traced to inadequate surveys of crucial information or special pressures on zoning bodies, the practice of overzoning— or allocating too large a proportion of urban land for a specific type of use— inherently encourages speculation, narrowly conceived interests, and blight. For example, in American cities, zoning officials have tended to reserve unrealistically large areas for business purposes, thus restricting opportunities for residential expansion. It has been estimated, to take an extreme case, that an earlier zoning ordinance for New York City would permit working space for 340 million people in business and industrial zones. The same ordinance, parenthetically, designated residential areas and densities that would have housed 77 million people.[9]

housing programs

The city's dual status as a productive area and a residential entity has often been forgotten. While major efforts have been directed toward more efficient manufacture, processing, and commercial enterprises, the prosaic task of housing urbanites has—until recently—been left to chance and the

---

[7] Webster, op. cit. p. 404; Haar, op. cit., p. 195; Sidney M. Willhelm, Urban Zoning and Land-Use Theory (New York, The Free Press, 1962); S. J. Makielski, Jr., The Politics of Zoning (New York, Columbia University Press, 1966); Richard F. Babcock, The Zoning Game (Madison, University of Wisconsin Press, 1966); John W. Reps, "Requiem for Zoning" and Dennis O'Harrow, "Zoning: What's the Good of It?" in H. Wentworth Eldredge, ed., Taming Megalopolis (Garden City, Anchor Books, 1967), Vol. 2, pp. 746–763.

[8] Local Planning Administration, pp. 321–322.

[9] Haar, op. cit., p. 180.

well-known inadequacies of the private housing market. With few exceptions, the net result in the world's cities has been congestion, greatly deteriorated housing facilities, and the popular "escape to the suburbs." Recognition of the deficiencies of urban housing is almost universal; more than 50 nations have organized national agencies designed to improve the availability and the quality of housing.[10] In addition, numerous local, state, and regional organizations are currently engaged in mitigating the long-term effects of slums and borderline deterioration.

Surveying the range of urban housing programs, we can fairly conclude that there are several types (or aspects) of housing problems, rather than the oversimplified notion of slums and slum clearance as *the* problem. There is, in accord with this complexity, a formidable network (perhaps "maze" is more correct) of public and private, local and national, professional and lay groups concerned with urban housing.[11] Paradoxically, in a period that presumably emphasizes planning as a comprehensive, coordinated function, the responsibility for planning housing (at least in the United States) is not primarily lodged in the city or metropolitan planning department. Instead, there is a progressive division of responsibility (with attempts at articulation) and a bewildering variety of specific programs. In fact, anyone interested in modern housing must acquire a bulging glossary of terms that define somewhat distinctive objectives and agencies: urban renewal, urban development and redevelopment, rehabilitation, conservation, and relocation. At this point, however, we shall focus our discussion on the corrective physical aspects of housing planning.

planning housing for growing populations

As a result of population increase in cities, and also of changes in urban social strata, the housing supply has been inadequate quantitatively and qualitatively unsuitable as well. In Paris, the general absence of new building is indicated by the fact that the average age of its dwellings is more than one hundred years. The French Minister of Construction estimates that the Paris

[10] *Ibid.*, p. 170; Timothy Sosnovy, *The Housing Problem in the Soviet Union* (New York, Research Program in the U.S.S.R., 1954); Edward C. Banfield and Morton Grodzins, *Government and Housing in Metropolitan Areas* (New York, McGraw-Hill, 1958); George S. Duggar, ed., *Renewal of Town and Village, II: Ten Special Reports from Five Continents* (The Hague, Nijhoff, 1965).

[11] Mabel L. Walker, *Urban Blight and Slums* (Cambridge, Harvard University Press, 1938); Robert M. Fisher, *Twenty Years of Public Housing* (New York, Harper and Row, 1959), pp. 17–33; J. B. Cullingworth, *Housing Needs and Planning Policy* (London, Routledge and Kegan Paul, 1960); Charles Abrams, *Man's Struggle for Shelter in an Urbanizing World* (Cambridge, MIT Press, 1964); Paul F. Wendt, *Housing Policy: The Search for Solutions* (Berkeley, University of California Press, 1963); Richard O. Davies, *Housing Reform During the Truman Administration* (Columbia, University of Missouri Press, 1966).

region needs a minimum of 75,000 new dwellings each year to replace unsafe units and accommodate an expanding population. Prior to a planning program, less than 10,000 units a year were built (between 1945 and 1954), though this was increased to 50,000–68,000 more recently.[12] The French program now consists of three parts: government loans to stimulate building, the chartering of special companies to build reasonably priced rental units, and government control of speculation in housing sales.

In the United States the urban housing supply has likewise been unequal to demand, especially since 1945. With few exceptions during the late forties and early fifties, the demand for houses and apartments was primarily met by private developers and contractors in fringe or suburban locations. For various reasons, the first waves of postwar housing bypassed considerations of quality and coordination with other community needs and programs. This was the period of "projects," new subdivisions, and rapidly constructed, artfully advertised "developments." [13]

In general, American cities have not been able to keep pace with the increasing demand for additional (rather than replacement) housing. Local planning bodies in many instances have adequately surveyed housing needs for their respective regions, but appropriate land is either unavailable or is too expensive for local budgets. State and federal subsidies for housing are largely for replacement housing—and this is in most cases for lower income groups.

Somewhere in the border zone between replacement housing and expanded housing is the continuing problem of providing rental housing for middle income urban families. In several metropolitan areas, the major alternative to crowded facilities has been a flight to the suburbs, where, incidentally, rental housing is overshadowed by homeowner property and cooperative apartments. Less than ten years ago in the New York City region, there was an estimated shortage of about 105,000 dwelling units, most of which were needed in the city proper. At the same time, about 20,000 "excess" dwelling units (mainly houses) were available in the suburbs. During the past ten years, planning for middle income housing within the city limits has been obstructed by impossible financial obstacles. However, New York City took a faltering first step in 1958 by constructing a nineteen-story apartment house in Brooklyn for 205 families in the $5,990 to $7,490 income range. This is adjacent to a low-income housing project of about 1,000 units. Four more combined (middle and low-income) projects in other boroughs are still in the blueprint stage.[14]

[12] The New York Times, October 22, 1959.

[13] Compare the discussions in Glenn H. Beyer, Housing: A Factual Analysis (New York, Macmillan, 1958) and his Housing and Society (New York, Macmillan, 1965); John Keats, The Crack in the Picture Window (New York, Ballantine Books, 1957); Albert Mayer, The Urgent Future: People, Housing, City, Region (New York, McGraw-Hill, 1967), pp. 30–65.

[14] The New York Times, May 11, 1952; March 23, 1958.

slums, housing, and variably deficient experiments

Whether considered from a moral, esthetic, economic, or administrative standpoint, a key problem in corrective physical planning is slum housing—the deteriorated residential nuclei around the city's core or the suburban agglomerations of shacks and lean-tos for impoverished migrants. The latter slum location is now a world phenomenon, with culturally distinct names: favela in Brazil, rancho in Venezuela, jacalo in Mexico, barriada in Peru, tegurio in Colombia, villa miseria in Argentina, poblaciones callampas in Chile, bidonvilles in Africa. All over the world, urban planners have devoted much thought to congested, inadequate housing, though perhaps European planners have generally been permitted to implement plans earlier and with somewhat more effectiveness. This is at least partly explainable by the tradition—virtually unknown in American cities—of public purchase of large tracts of land (both within the city and at the fringes) for future housing needs. But, to understand the prevalence of slums and the continuing gap between need and performance, we should briefly review some fundamental conditions in contemporary urbanism on this score.

First, while slum areas have been evident in some degree since the sixteenth century, the multiplication and expansion of slums in the twentieth century are in part consequents of languishing rural economies and/or economic opportunities in cities. Dense migrant streams from rural or village areas in short time periods normally expand the demand for housing well beyond the supply.[15]

Second, and still relatively unchanged, owners of slum housing (primarily in the urban core) enjoy a financial advantage from maintaining deteriorated housing, without much effective criticism from urban residents or official control from local authorities.

Third, the restricted incomes of slum dwellers severely limit the unaided search for alternative housing locations. Consequently, the expectation that slum dwellers can gradually improve their housing by moving to quarters vacated by upwardly mobile families ("filtering") is unduly optimistic. In addition, as Cullingworth points out, filtering is necessarily limited by the enormous numbers in slums, as well as by local patterns of ethnic or racial discrimination.[16]

[15] Charles Abrams, *Man's Struggle for Shelter in an Urbanizing World* (Cambridge, MIT Press, 1964), pp. 50–53; Jewel Bellush and Murray Hausknecht, "Public Housing: The Contexts of Failure," in Jewel Bellush and Murray Hausknecht, eds., *Urban Renewal: People, Politics, and Planning* (Garden City, Doubleday Anchor Books, 1967), pp. 451–461.

[16] J. B. Cullingworth, *Housing and Local Government in England and Wales* (London, Allen and Unwin, 1966), p. 266; Martin Meyerson *et al.*, *Housing, People, and Cities* (New York, McGraw-Hill, 1962), pp. 38–42; Alvin L. Schorr, "Housing the Poor," in Warner Bloomberg and Henry J. Schmandt, eds., *Power, Poverty, and Urban Policy* (Beverly Hills, Sage Publications, 1968), Chap. 4.

public housing

Historically, the first serious attempt to provide an alternative to (not the removal of) slum housing was the public housing project, either financed by federal governments directly or through guarantee of appropriate private ventures. Largely a product of the depression period, and still a widespread though controversial device, public housing attempts to create low-cost housing by intensive use of land (i.e., high-rise apartments or other concentrated sets of multi-dwelling units). Often, public housing is constructed in or near central slum areas, as in the United States. British housing estates and the more recent *grands ensembles* in France, however, economize on land costs by peripheral locations.

Numerous criticisms have greeted the efforts of urban housing planners. In general, European achievements—particularly in England, Sweden, and the Netherlands—have been somewhat more pronounced; they have involved relatively more units built, more care in design, and somewhat more concern with the relation between housing and such matters as jobs and transportation. In the U.S., however, after 30 years, only about 600,000 units have been produced, due to excessive land costs in inner areas, administrative delays, the opposition of private real estate interests, and the problems of shifting slum families from old to new facilities on the same acreage. But public housing has also been castigated for its drabness, its failure to provide related physical facilities (recreation, shopping), its continuation of existing racial segregation patterns, and the unwitting encouragement of crimes against the person in halls, corridors, and elevators. And some critics find that the process of rehousing shatters former personal linkages in slum neighborhoods.[17]

Traditional public housing in the U.S. was recognized as inadequate, at least in principle, by the housing acts of 1949 and 1954. These laws asserted (1) that public housing was part of urban planning and (2) that slum clearance must be accompanied by concern for displaced families. Consequently, a number of adjuncts or alternative mechanisms were developed, including the following.

1. A requirement that slum clearance programs be geared to larger, more comprehensive urban plans produced a moderate-sized crusade for Master Plans in many cities—since few cities had little more than variably out-of-date

[17] Alvin Schorr, "Slums and Social Security," Herbert J. Gans, "The Failure of Urban Renewal: A Critique and Some Proposals," in Bellush and Hausknecht, *op. cit.*, pp. 415–424, 465–484; Daniel M. Wilner *et al.*, *The Housing Environment and Family Life* (Baltimore, Johns Hopkins Press, 1962); Herbert J. Gans, "Effects of the Move from City to Suburb," in Leonard J. Duhl, ed., *The Urban Condition* (New York, Basic Books, 1963), pp. 184–197.

land use maps in their planning offices. These hastily devised plans did not appear to alter the process of creating public housing, however. Indeed, technical details and local unpreparedness resulted in long delays, both in obtaining federal approval and in local implementation.

2. Federal and local housing authorities and agencies created relocation divisions, whose primary purpose has been to aid displaced slum families in finding other quarters while public housing is being built. While official reports indicate considerable success, several analysts conclude that such reports generate misplaced gratification, that careful study of specific community programs demonstrates that 20–60 percent of displaced families are either unaided or are "helped" to substandard housing.[18]

3. Since 1954, federal financing has made available loans for home or apartment purchase by displaced families.

urban renewal

Urban renewal, which officially dates from 1954, is an explosive planning cocktail with two ingredients: slum clearance and urban redevelopment (i.e., nonresidential improvements in previously unsightly or uneconomic areas of the central city). But unlike an expertly concocted drink, urban renewal contains competing ingredients—and, according to a highly verbal set of critics, the formula for mixture varies considerably.

The strategy of urban renewal on the level of legislation seems to be one of regarding deteriorated areas as an urban resource whose manipulation should be determined by local perceptions of physical needs (housing, etc.). But the economic competition between housing and commercial needs on the local level is far from a contest of equals. As a result, an increasing proportion of previous slum areas is being converted to nonresidential use. The original act permitted 10 percent of these areas for nonresidential purposes, but succeeding revisions have raised the legal limit to 40 percent. Urban renewal land, therefore, is dotted with motels, hotels, luxury apartment buildings, expressways, commercial buildings, industrial firms, and civic structures—all worthy, needed, or sources of urban tax revenue, but no solution to the housing needs of slum residents.[19] In addition, it has been found

[18] Chester W. Hartman, "The Housing of Relocated Families," in Bellush and Hausknecht, *op. cit.*, pp. 315–353; Nathan Glazer, "The Renewal of Cities," *Scientific American*, 213 (September, 1965), pp. 199–200.

[19] James Q. Wilson, ed., *Urban Renewal: The Record and the Controversy* (Cambridge, MIT Press, 1966); Martin Anderson, *The Federal Bulldozer: A Critical Analysis of Urban Renewal, 1949–1962* (Cambridge, MIT Press, 1964); Jewel Bellush and Murray Hausknecht, "Relocation and Managed Mobility," in Bellush and Hausknecht, *op. cit.*, pp. 366–377; Werner Z. Hirsch, ed., *Regional Accounts for Policy Decisions* (Baltimore, Johns Hopkins Press, 1966), p. 7.

that much of the new housing (up to 90 percent, it is claimed) in renewal areas is significantly more expensive than slum rents (which are relatively high for the facilities). Certainly, better physical facilities involve higher costs. But such costs automatically exclude an overwhelming proportion of the slum residents for whom the new housing was presumably constructed.[20]

model cities

In November, 1966, the Congress implicitly recognized the limitations of urban renewal as a viable mechanism for significant improvement of slum population. The Demonstration Cities and Metropolitan Development Act of that date instead seeks a total attack by encouraging local planning of Model Neighborhoods (now generally called Model Cities Programs) with the following projected features:

1. Substantial increase in new, low-cost, standard housing (public or private) in designated blighted areas within a short period.
2. Rehabilitation of existing housing, where feasible, to minimize problems of relocation.
3. Development of comprehensive, local facilities for health services, shopping, education, welfare, recreation, and jobs—to supplement housing improvements.
4. Local citizen participation in the planning of facilities and services.

About 70 areas have been granted federal funds for initial planning of Model Cities. These include such large cities as Chicago, New York City, Atlanta, Philadelphia, Baltimore, Washington, D.C., Detroit, Boston, St. Louis, Pittsburgh, and Minneapolis—and also fairly small cities (e.g., Pikesville, Ky., Winooski, Vt., Eagle Pass, Tex.).[21] It is too early to appraise this new approach, since specific planning proposals were due in Washington in November of 1968. However, it is feared that many cities will continue former practices, that citizen participation has either been ignored or is less practical than desired, and that lack of experience in coordinated programs will prove to be a formidable barrier to significant change. In Atlanta, where there have already been experimental neighborhood programs in slum sections of the Model City area, the provisional plan calls for five distinct neighborhood units (some Negro, some with mixed population, and one white area), each with a different combination of physical and social services for their residents.

[20] Anderson, op. cit., p. 93.
[21] The Washington Post, November 17, 1967.

rehabilitation and reconditioning

Another approach to housing problems is rehabilitation and reconditioning, which are less dramatic than slum clearance, but yet are extremely important and much less expensive.[22] Essentially, these programs apply to residential areas that have become shabby through neglect and lack of local pride, yet not to the point of presenting immediate slum problems. Rehabilitation attempts to prevent advanced stages of deterioration by moderate repairs and remodeling by affected property owners. Several such programs have had the support and technical assistance of local planning departments, but often the major initiative and financing stem from individuals and private civic organizations (such as ACTION and Fight Blight, Inc.). Occasionally, public officials and planning bodies are less than enthusiastic about the possibilities of rehabilitating marginal areas. In Washington, D.C., remodeling of the quaintly named Foggy Bottom area (the near northwest side) was accomplished without official encouragement or financial aid. However, in such cities as Baltimore, Chicago, New Orleans, and Miami, the method of rehabilitation has demonstrated that inner areas of the city can be salvaged without enormous cost for lower and lower middle class families.

urban conservation programs

A final type of program is an adjunct to planning: urban conservation. Though linked with rehabilitation, either in aims or specific practices, conservation involves a renewed emphasis on enforcement of existing housing code regulations. In many cities over the last decade, revised housing codes have been designed to encourage or require minimum standards of upkeep (e.g., adequate toilets, window screens, hot water, tubs or showers). However, as time elapses and other municipal problems require attention, enforcement of codes often becomes spotty. Legal controls and their proper application are surrounded by an ominous silence—until a crusade arises. Conservation begins when the staff of inspectors is either invigorated or expanded, when code violators are actively sought out, and violators are pressed for compliance; when, finally, the residents of substandard housing really hope for and demand facilities of which they can be proud enough to maintain in good condition.

[22] Nash, *op. cit.,*; Martin Millspaugh and Gurney Breckenfield, *The Human Side of Urban Renewal* (Baltimore, Fight-Blight, Inc., 1958) ; Chester Rapkin and William G. Grigsby, *Residential Renewal in the Urban Core* (Philadelphia, University of Pennsylvania Press, 1960).

traffic and transportation

The street pattern of cities is one of the most permanent of man's creations—and normally the most outmoded. If urban regions are inherently dynamic, their street and road networks are embedded in concrete and asphalt molds. But the problem of urban transportation is magnified by the fact that almost one third of the city's land area is invested in a grid of thoroughfares. Consequently, any major change in usage demands corrective measures of staggering proportions.

During the past thirty years, the crucial change in usage has been the double-edged adoption of the automobile and the truck. This made possible the modern reclustering of residential and industrial facilities in suburban and fringe areas, the increasing separation of services from their clienteles, an infinitely greater dependence on transportation, and thus a continually burdensome competition for space in the flow of traffic.[23]

Having accepted the automobile as indispensable though troublesome to a high degree, urban planners and their publics in American cities, Paris, London, Rome, Honolulu, and other metropolitan areas are forced to be ingenious within narrow limits. With one or two exceptions they cannot (or will not) control the use of cars; certainly, they are unable to stabilize the supply or the demand for cars. Traffic and transportation planning, therefore, has become a desperate attempt to stave off the inevitable strangulation by auto until some new and creative approach to urban transportation can be devised.

Perhaps four major types of corrective planning can be noted.

1. increased efficiency of present thoroughfare systems

Since the investment in existing streets and roads is enormous, a good deal of planning is devoted to maximizing and speeding traffic flow. This is

[23] The best general discussion is Robert B. Mitchell and Chester Rapkin, *Urban Traffic: A Function of Land Use* (New York, Columbia University Press, 1954). See also George C. Hemmens, *The Structure of Urban Activity Linkages* (Chapel Hill, Center for Urban and Regional Studies, University of North Carolina, September, 1966), pp. 20 ff.; John W. Dyckman, "Transportation in Cities," *Scientific American*, 213 (September, 1965), pp. 163–174; Lewis Mumford, *From the Ground Up* (New York, Harvest Books, 1956), selections 23–25 and *The Highway and the City* (New York, Harcourt, Brace and World, 1963); Lowdon Wingo, Jr., *Transportation and Urban Land* (Washington, D.C., Resources for the Future, 1961); Wilfred Owen, *The Metropolitan Transportation Problem* (Washington, D.C., Brookings Institution, 1956); George M. Smerk, *Urban Transportation: The Federal Role* (Bloomington, Ind., University of Indiana Press, 1965); Lyle C. Fitch and associates, *Urban Transportation and Public Policy* (San Francisco, Chandler, 1964).

accomplished by: widening streets (a time-consuming process); the use of one-way streets in congested downtown areas; restriction or elimination of on-street parking; the development and improvement of traffic light systems on major thoroughfares, so that the timing of lights is electronically adjusted to changing patterns of traffic density.[24]

2. rerouting of traffic

Increasingly, city planners are turning to the construction of new thoroughfares as alternative routes for auto traffic. These are the so-called belt or circumferential parkways, bypasses, expressways, freeways, and interstates, which skirt the most congested areas and connect with major arteries. In the U.S. federal funds have financed most of these routes as part of a national interstate network, ostensibly for military transportation. European nations have similar highway networks, particularly in France, Britain, and Germany. But because of exceedingly high construction costs (about $4 million per mile, plus incalculable costs to displaced groups and the extra expenditures for traffic control systems and policing), expressways cannot be constructed at a pace that is remotely appropriate to the production and use of cars, trucks, and trailers. Few cities, incidentally, possess enough land for an expressway system as consuming as that in the Los Angeles area.[25] City planners and many urbanites are therefore entertaining the notion of rapid transit.

3. solutions to parking problems

The dual use of thoroughfares for transportation and parking inevitably interferes with the primary purpose—maximum movement. Consequently, planners have tried to separate these needs as much as possible in the downtown areas. A drastic and, therefore, largely unimitated solution has been attempted in Philadelphia, over considerable protest in the beginning. The city imposed a "no parking" regulation in a square-mile area of the downtown district, with the result that downtown traffic was visibly smoother and the accident rate was almost halved. Another and more popular solution is the provision of public or privately owned parking lots at the fringe of the

[24] *The New York Times*, March 4, 1956; Leo Grebler, *Urban Renewal in European Countries* (Philadelphia, University of Pennsylvania Press, 1964), pp. 23–26.

[25] Dyckman, *op. cit.*, pp. 165–169; *The New York Times*, January 28, 1966; Urban Land Institute, *The New Highways: Challenge to the Metropolitan Region* (Washington, D.C., Urban Land Institute, Technical Bulletin No. 31, 1957); James H. Lemly, *Expressway Influence on Land Use and Value: Atlanta 1941–1956* (Atlanta, Georgia State College, 1958); William L. Garrison and Marion E. Marts, *Influence of Highway Improvements on Urban Land* (Seattle, Highway Economic Studies, University of Washington Press, 1958), pp. 53–55; Mark Reinsberg, "Growth and Change in Metropolitan Areas and Their Relation to Metropolitan Transportation: A Research Summary," in Sylvia F. Fava, ed., *Urbanism in World Perspective* (New York, Crowell, 1968), pp. 502–511.

business district. However, there is some concern that the solution is ultimately as undesirable as the problem. In Chicago's downtown area (and in other cities, too), many blocks are gigantic parking lots, with 60–100 percent of their land used for cars rather than businesses.[26] Yet in the realm of parking problems, success is highly deceptive. According to one leading traffic analyst, Wilfred Owen:

> . . . the more space and the lower the rates (for parking), the greater the inducement to drive into the city despite the inadequacy of its street capacity. . . . Most of America's car owners would rather abandon the city than the car.[27]

Still another device is a rather widespread requirement that new structures (office buildings and commercial establishments) include provision for off-street parking—either in lower or upper parking garages, or by reserving adjacent areas for parking. In outer areas, where the parking problem is less crucial, adequate space is usually available. But in heavily built up areas, the scarcity of space means added costs to the developer or builder, which are inevitably passed on in the form of higher rents or purchase prices.[28]

4. mass transit and rapid transit

In the age of the auto, that symbol of apparent individualism, previous forms of urban transportation have tended to wither from neglect and scorn. Yet the suburban trek makes commuting by auto or mass transit (bus, rail, or some variation of these) the only alternatives. A study of New York City's 370,000 suburban commuters indicates that over half depend on railroad lines, while 100,000 come by car, and 63,000 by bus. From an economic standpoint, interurban rail lines are suffering from insufficient business; they can neither maintain nor improve commuter service. But from the standpoint of efficiency, rail lines have been found to be superior to any existing mode of transportation. About 48,000 persons can be transported per hour on one rail line, while only 6,700 per hour can be moved by bus per expressway lane, and a mere 2,250 per hour per car for each expressway lane.[29]

Many of the world's large cities developed mass transit systems (subways) before World War II—notably London, Paris, Moscow, New York

---

[26] The New York Times, December 16, 1952; "Facelifting Cities," loc. cit.

[27] Wilfred Owen, "Shortage in Curbs," The New York Times, March 9, 1952.

[28] The New York Times, December 16, 1952; April 23, 1961; October 8, 1961; November 13, 1966; Fitch, op. cit., Chaps. 1, 2.

[29] Local Planning Administration, pp. 200–203, 219–222; The New York Times, February 22, 1959. See also John F. Kain, "The Commuting and Residential Decisions of Central Business District Workers," in National Bureau of Economic Research, Transportation Economics (New York, Columbia University Press, 1965), pp. 245–275; John B. Lansing et al., Residential Location and Urban Mobility (Ann Arbor, Mich., Survey Research Center, University of Michigan, June, 1965); Michael N. Danielson, Federal-Metropolitan Politics and the Commuter Crisis (New York, Columbia University Press, 1965).

City, Berlin, Chicago, and Boston. Recently, but on a somewhat smaller scale, subways are becoming important parts of urban transit in Montreal, Rotterdam, Tokyo, Stockholm, Milan, Helsinki, and Oslo.[30] Construction costs are quite high and considerable space is required for such lines. Surface rail systems—principally for commuting from suburban and fringe areas—were popular, efficient, and relatively inexpensive before World War II (i.e., before the vast expansion of urban populations). In the fifties, however, both use and service on such lines declined sharply in American urban regions —a process which is epitomized by the experience of commuters on the much criticized Long Island Railroad. Yet, planners have occasionally tried to regenerate this form of mass transit. Philadelphia, for example, has inaugurated a program of encouraging suburbanites to use interurban rail lines by subsidizing reductions in fares and by simplifying and reducing the expense of transfers to city bus and train lines.

Where subways are not feasible, and where local rail facilities are as yet undeveloped, the current focus of interest is on regional rapid transit systems. Rapid transit is mass transit with two additional ingredients: higher average speeds (80 miles per hour or so) and a planned radial network that integrates four or more crucial population sectors in a defined region. Several German cities (e.g., Essen, Dusseldorf) have considered the use of a monorail, while others (Frankfurt, Stuttgart, Cologne) appear to favor a less sensational combination of depressed rail beds in the inner areas and surface rails in fringe and suburban areas. In the U.S., San Francisco has been planning the first rapid transit system in the nation since about 1956. After much opposition and delay, a four-pronged system of computer-controlled trains is scheduled for operation in 1971, with both elevated and subway lines providing attractively high speed commuting.[31] Other cities have studied needs and cost of regional transportation systems (including Philadelphia, Minneapolis, St. Louis, and Washington, D.C.), but only Atlanta seems to have advanced to the serious planning stage. Its rapid transit scheme envisages serving five counties (San Francisco now plans to serve three, though five counties may ultimately be involved) in approximately the same manner as San Francisco's Bay Area Rapid Transit. The latest estimate is that operation will begin in 1975, though this is perhaps buoyed by more hope than hard cash.

Urban transportation provides means for circulation; its effectiveness depends not only on technical and engineering criteria, but on the location and relocation of urban facilities. Both expressways and rapid transit systems currently feed congestion (or promise to), simply because old patterns of central location (of office buildings, for example) inevitably tax the capacity of such systems. Adding more expressways and/or enormously expensive

---

[30] Grebler, *op. cit.*, pp. 27–29.
[31] Dyckman, *op. cit.*, pp. 168–174.

rapid transit provides only temporary solutions,[32] unless (1) the permissible range of cars is drastically altered in central cities or (2) substantial decentralizing of job opportunities is seriously pursued. Failure to acknowledge this difficult conclusion—especially in the U.S.—can only perpetuate ritualistic remedies and the illusion of achievement by extravagant action.

redevelopment in the central business district

It is no surprise that the central or downtown area, the oldest part of the city, should be currently scrutinized and diagnosed as requiring extensive physical alterations. Virtually all the major problems of the modern city —traffic congestion, parking facilities, deteriorated or unsightly buildings, housing and community services for minority groups—coexist and intensify one another in the central zone. The result is often an ugliness that repels customers of downtown services and likewise discourages the maintenance of stable neighborhoods near the city's core. Businessmen realize that the downtown district will always be needed, but they cannot ignore the eloquence of comparative sales figures. In several large cities, downtown sales in the last decade of population expansion and enormous spending have tended to decline 5–10 percent, while suburban sales rose by 20–35 percent.[33]

Downtown redevelopment faces many problems, however. Some merchants assume a defeatist attitude: "everything's going to the suburbs anyway." Tradition, particularly in the older cities, can delay attempts to revitalize business districts. In Cambridge, England, a modest plan for modernizing a seven-acre tract near the center—notorious for its congestion—has been vigorously opposed in order to preserve the "historical and architectural value of an ancient street (Petty Curl)." City planners propose to provide underground parking, three new ten-story buildings, and a shopping zone reserved for pedestrians.[34] For similar reasons, local plans for modernization of the business center of Venice—including a set of new commercial buildings and more adequate parking facilities—were vetoed by the Italian government.

In the United States, where tradition is somewhat weaker, downtown innovations have met disapproval by taxpayers, who resent the initial costs. But where local planners receive necessary cooperation from business groups, plus financial encouragement from the federal government, revivified and striking business districts have been planned and at least partially rebuilt.[35] Cincinnati is in process of redeveloping 170 acres of a master-planned central

[32] James Q. Wilson, "The War on Cities," in Robert A. Goldwin, ed., *A Nation of Cities* (Chicago, Rand McNally, 1968), p. 27; Donn Fichter, *Individualized Automatic Transit and the City* (Providence, R.I., Donn Fichter, 1964).

[33] "Facelifting Cities," *loc. cit.*

[34] *The New York Times*, November 22, 1959; April 30, 1961.

[35] *Ibid.*, May 3, 1953; Charles M. Brown, "'Downtown' Enters a New Era," *The*

industrial district in which former slums adjacent to the core are to be replaced by light industrial super-blocks (with adequate parking and trucking
facilities), convenient apartment buildings, office buildings, and a new convention center. On a smaller scale, Lowell, Massachusetts, is rebuilding its
central business district by constructing three large parking areas, a new
civic center, and, eventually, a modern shopping area free from traffic.
Philadelphia and its much publicized Penn Center represent a particularly
interesting attempt to spruce up a previously ugly complex of railroad walls
and outmoded buildings by creating a unified business, shopping, and hotel
center around a graceful plaza, in the manner of the older Rockefeller Plaza
in New York City. Pittsburgh, with support from local industrial corporations, has cleared large segments of its Golden Triangle for more than 50
new office buildings since 1945. New York City is engaged in a complicated
series of projects for the bewildering mosaic known as lower Manhattan.
The basic redevelopment plan calls for several housing projects near the
waterfront, large commercial buildings to replace a patchwork of other buildings, and improvement of pier and docking facilities.

To name just a few more examples, Baltimore's Charles Center, Rochester's Midtown Plaza, Dallas' Main Place (privately financed) are often
discussed among downtown renovation attempts in the U.S. In other nations,
mention might be made of similar programs in Coventry, Newcastle, Helsinki,
Nagoya, and Stockholm.[36]

After 15 or 20 years of planning, numerous difficulties, and actual construction in many cities, it is now possible to identify a common set of
features in downtown redevelopment. The cardinal trait is continuation of
major functions in the city's core, but with improved accessibility and
efficient segregation of cars from commercial and recreational space. Of particular interest is an emphasis on large office buildings (as in Stockholm,
Charles Center in Baltimore, and Pittsburgh) adjacent to (or including)
varied retail establishments. A second common tendency is separation of
pedestrian from vehicular traffic—by means of shopping malls, ramps, escala-
tors, and underground parking. In many instances, plans call for focal
restaurants or cafes, theaters, and open spaces in the form of parks and
squares. But while the esthetic effect may be more attractive than the ugly,
congested downtown of the past, the overall impact may be little genuine
change. Many of the planning mechanisms unwittingly encourage congestion,
however beautiful the physical setting. The next few years will reveal whether

New York Times Magazine, January 31, 1960; Special Supplement to The New York
Times, November 13, 1960; Mumford, op. cit., Selections 11–14, 18; Victor Gruen, The
Heart of Our Cities (New York, Simon and Schuster, 1964).

  [36] Martin Millspaugh, ed., Baltimore's Charles Center (Washington, D.C., Urban
Land Institute, November, 1964, Technical Bulletin #51); Goran Sidenbladh, "Stockholm: A Planned City," Scientific American, 213 (September, 1965), pp. 109–110;
John Tetlow and Anthony Goss, Homes, Towns and Traffic (London, Faber and Faber,
1965), pp. 170–182.

or not such planning merits the dedication and the expenditures of the past decade.

an evaluation of corrective physical planning

Corrective physical planning is so prevalent and varied in detail that the preceding discussion was necessarily limited to a sampling of efforts of this type. A tremendous amount of money, materials, discussions, and practical compromises has been devoted to the basic problem of arresting blight, congestion, and the deepening ugliness of the urban environment. And yet those who pause to survey the fruits of these programs—urban sociologists, political scientists, city officials, and the professional planners themselves—cannot conclude that these extensive efforts have yielded dominantly positive results.

Three or four underlying criticisms are crucial not only to the student of urban planning, but to the thoughtful urbanite as well.

1. lack of integration

Despite the growth of interest in Master Plans and comprehensive plans, in practice much physical planning has been compartmentalized. There has been little serious effort to coordinate the prevailing variety of corrective programs—either with one another, or with a Master Plan. For example, housing developments and highway planning normally are mutually isolated. In general, the lack of coordination may be traced to specialization of authority at the local level and the multiplication of planning agencies on the state and federal levels. It should be recalled that an overwhelming share of funds for corrective physical planning is appropriated by the Congress. Yet neither the Congress nor specially designated federal agencies (e.g., the Bureau of Public Roads, the Housing and Home Authority, the Urban Renewal Administration) has provided any machinery for insuring cooperation and coordination among agencies serving urban planning needs or requiring that federal funds for various programs be sensibly used by local coordination of specific planning programs.[37] With the increasing role of the federal government in urban planning, the alternatives of local or federal coordination are quite obvious, if physical planning is to avoid defeating its avowed purposes.

2. city vs. regional orientation

Because of traditional political barriers, and despite the suburbanization of urban populations, a great deal of urban physical planning treats the

[37] Connery and Leach, *op. cit.*, pp. 54–55, 59.

corporate city as the major unit of planning, rather than the urban region. This is particularly apparent and disturbing in the case of highway plans and housing developments in outer areas. Rarely do the designers of highway routes concern themselves with the larger consequences of new roads for an entire metropolitan area: the attraction of residential and industrial developments near highways in fringe areas and a resultant relocation of demand for urban services. Indeed, any planning program that involves change of land use or movement of population and services inevitably has regional implications.[38]

3. unintended consequences

The preceding criticisms are important in understanding a third critical judgment: that, with some exceptions, the tendency of existing physical planning programs is toward intensifying the very problems they are designed to ameliorate. Many cities in the United States are beginning to recognize that the modern traffic jam is not yielding to the frenzied construction of more, wider, better designed highways. In fact, these improved facilities seem to encourage the same (or even greater) concentration of cars in central areas of the city. Continuing delays in improving and extending mass transit facilities likewise aggravate traffic congestion.

Furthermore, many public housing and downtown redevelopment programs also contribute in some degree to urban congestion. As long as housing remains relatively scarce—as has been the case since the early forties—public housing and the prerequisite clearance projects require considerable relocation of displaced families—in most cases, probably by doubling up with relatives or in other inadequate accommodations. But another spur to congestion is the persistent location of public housing in central (or closely situated) areas. Since land is expensive in such areas, large apartment buildings are most economical, but nevertheless preserve congestion. It is significant to note that neither local nor national agencies have encouraged public or private construction of multiple-dwelling units where there is considerably more space—at the fringes of cities. Consequently, and this is the paradox of modern urban regions, while congestion persists near the core, many urbanites in the United States remain attracted to the fringes for single family dwellings and unrealistic quantities of space, thus extending the scope of urban sprawl and devouring land that might be used more judiciously and economically in the future.[39]

As far as downtown planning is concerned, there has been a growing tendency to convert beautification and opening of central areas into opportunities to increase the number of large office buildings. Some of these buildings

---

[38] *Ibid.*, p. 53; Mitchell and Rapkin, *op. cit.*, pp. 178–180.
[39] Connery and Leach, *op. cit.*, p. 15; Nash, *op. cit.*, p. 197.

are particularly well designed and interesting additions to the urban land-scape. But in such cities as New York, Denver, Chicago, and San Francisco, the construction of additional buildings may overburden the facilities of the central district and also increase the already bursting traffic load of metropol-itan regions. If, on the other hand, the amount of added space for offices out-distances foreseeable needs (as has been suggested is the case in Denver),[40] the new buildings serve to interfere with the satisfaction of other legitimate downtown uses (e.g., hotel space, off-street parking, park areas, or necessary public structures).

4. symptoms, not causes

By its very nature, corrective physical planning is largely restricted to concern with the concrete, surface aspects of urban problems—symptoms rather than basic causes. In line with this orientation, therefore, existing values are accepted as "givens" by corrective planners, instead of being ex-amined and critically assessed as components in urban problems. The unre-stricted use of the auto, for example, is one such value that merits close scrutiny, though it is certainly imbued with a sacredness that many would not care to challenge.[41] Yet there is also an implicit acceptance of the worth of size and growth in urban affairs, without adequate attention to the diffi-culties these expansive goals entail. In short, corrective physical planning tends to accentuate urban trends; its contribution to control of urban change and development is therefore quite limited.

Perhaps the most telling aspect of corrective physical planning, as we have seen it in the United States, is an unwitting emphasis on physical pro-grams for upper and upper middle business and commercial groups, on the one hand, and lower status and minority groups on the other. Highways and downtown renewal bring primary benefits to the former; public housing projects are largely beneficial to the latter. The astonishing fact is that com-paratively little corrective planning serves the needs of middle status families, who constitute not only a large segment of the urban region, but also seem to be the most typical carriers of urban culture and social organization. A con-tinuous failure to develop the city as an attractive, desirable locale for middle status families helps to explain not only the vast exodus to the suburbs, but the apparently stubborn desire to remain in suburban zones despite incon-veniences and high costs.

[40] "Facelifting Cities," *loc. cit.*
[41] A recent exception is John Keats, *The Brazen Chariots* (Boston, Houghton Mifflin, 1959).

selected references

BEYER, Glenn H., *Housing: A Factual Analysis* (New York, Macmillan, 1958).

BREESE, Gerald and WHITEMAN, Dorothy E., eds., *An Approach to Urban Planning* (Princeton, Princeton University Press, 1953).

BRENNAN, T., *Reshaping a City* (Glasgow, The House of Grant, 1959).

CULLINGWORTH, J. B. *Housing Needs and Planning Policy* (London, Routledge and Kegan Paul, 1960).

FISHER, Ernest M. and FISHER, Robert M., *Urban Real Estate* (New York, Holt, Rinehart and Winston, 1954).

FISHER, Robert M., *Twenty Years of Public Housing* (New York, Harper and Brothers, 1959).

GREBLER, Leo, *Europe's Reborn Cities*, Urban Land Institute, Technical Bulletin No. 28, (Washington, D.C., March, 1956).

McLEAN, Mary, ed., *Local Planning Administration* (Chicago, International City Managers' Association, 1959).

RAPKIN, Chester and GRIGSBY, William G., *Residential Renewal in the Urban Core* (Philadelphia, University of Pennsylvania Press, 1960).

SELF, Peter, *Cities in Flood* (London, Faber and Faber, 1969).

WOODBURY, Coleman, ed., *The Future of Cities and Urban Redevelopment* (Chicago, University of Chicago Press, 1953).

19

creative planning:
an application
of urban sociology?

If corrective planning with its limited objectives has confronted obstacles and opposition, creative planning is understandably more controversial and beset with difficulties. Instead of accepting current modes of social and cultural change, and devising remedies for the problems engendered by these changes, creative urban planning seeks to construct urban regions in which changes can be consciously selected and articulated with one another so as to achieve the highest level of experience and opportunity from the urban potential. This is of course an ideal, a projected image, a Utopian perspective in the meaning suggested by Mannheim.[1] We have yet to explore the degree to which the distinctive objectives of creative planning have been realized.

But it is first important to recognize that creative planning rests on a cluster of three contributory elements, all of which are necessary for the analysis and appraisal of creative planning.

the essential nature of urban regions

Implicitly or explicitly, creative planning depends on understanding the basic structure of urban regions in this third urban wave, as analyzed by urban sociology and related disciplines.[2] Reviewing the discussion in previous chapters, certain constants or themes seem to emerge from sociological studies of urban regions. Since these have been discussed at length, let us briefly re-state them at this point.

1. Cities and their regions constitute relatively organized, interdependent

[1] Karl Mannheim, *Ideology and Utopia* (New York, Harcourt, Brace and World, 1936), Chap. IV.
[2] See Ernest Manheim, "Theoretical Prospects of Urban Sociology in an Urbanized Society," *American Journal of Sociology*, 66 (November, 1960), pp. 226–229.

networks of population, cultural activities, and land areas—not accidentally juxtaposed fragments.

2. Urban regions, while more highly specialized in function than typically rural communities, nevertheless exhibit considerable diversification. This is evidenced in a typical range of economic specialties (light and heavy industry, finance, wholesale and retail activities, transportation, and communication), and also in the demand for the entire range of cultural services men require or come to expect. These services include religion, art, education, recreation, social welfare, health, and public sanitation. In short, the urban region is an enlarged community, not a series of islands connected by roads and bridges.

3. Closely related to the preceding is the complementary relation between residence and family on the one hand, and occupation and place of work, on the other. The sharp separation of the two—the journey to work— may be a transitional phenomenon due to rapid urbanization and lack of planning, rather than an inherent urban antagonism between home and plant or office. Consequently, a characteristic differentiation between economic and family functions does not require that they be widely separated physically for a substantial part of residents in the urban region.

4. While status distinctions are not rigid in urban regions, they do exist as a consequence of division of labor and differential opportunity to achieve desired styles of urban living. In fact, class differences (however fluid) represent one aspect of the cultural diversity that is so typical of the urban region. Therefore, the organization and services provided by urban regions inevitably develop sensitivity to the needs and desires of specific status categories. Because of the vocal and symbolic preponderance of middle status categories, the urban region appears to emphasize facilities and services for this segment. But there is a relatively large proportion of lower status families, which are likewise part of the urban order, and therefore contribute to the operation and the problems of urban regions.

5. The urban region is neither comparable to the village nor a highly rationalized, mechanized superplant. It is instead a peculiar composite which draws from these extreme forms of organization, but typically reinterprets these forms in the urban context. More concretely, the urban region represents a complex amalgam of formal, bureaucratized organizations and informal structures. Apparently, urbanites need and support both forms. Indeed, both forms have been built in to most urban organizations studied by social scientists.

6. Perhaps another aspect of the preceding feature is the urban mixture of needs and facilities for both public and private activities. The widespread (and amazingly contradictory) notions of the urbanite as an extroverted, wise-cracking busybody who is always "on stage" or a withdrawn, isolated, lonesome island of quiet desperation probably refer to extreme deviants, or persons in the earliest stages of adjustment to urban living. As suggested in

Chapters 9 and 10, urbanites seem to desire privacy *and* involvement in various aspects of public affairs.

This appears to mean that urban organization tends to expand opportunities for both specific, individualized activities, and relatively common, generalized motives and affiliations. It is not difficult for us to grasp the need for privacy—as a reaction to rural and small town "grapevines," and the desire for self-expression and creativity. But privacy is complemented by a new and uniquely urban orientation to the public aspect of living, which has two important facets. For the urbanite, the public aspect is apparent in generally available facilities and services, which sustain similarities of interest and basic information despite the diversity of social and cultural milieux. Some examples are police and fire protection, water supply, public education, and such privately operated services as media of communication, department and retail stores, and major transportation lines.

In addition to "publicness" of use and availability, there is the increasing sense of responsibility as a public phenomenon. This likewise has two aspects: organizational responsibility for providing and improving services (through government agencies, planning bodies, and civic organizations) and personal responsibility to support public organizations by active participation and financial aid. There are of course wide variations among urban regions of the world in the strength of these forms of responsibility. Yet the era of apathy and uncontrolled splinter groups is clearly yielding (though not without reversions) to an emerging urban concept of complex community cohesiveness.

7. Urban regions have rediscovered and perhaps reinterpreted the importance of leisure and the esthetic component as ends in themselves. The desire for pleasant, attractive surroundings as a necessity rather than a luxury is increasingly emphasized—not as a vagrant dream of a distant future, but as a realizable goal in a visible present. This rather new urban focus is a measure of the material achievements of urban technology, of the shift from production to consumption as the crucial aspect of economic organization, and of the accompanying opportunity to become concerned with the amenities of life instead of its harsher aspects.[3] City beautification, the interest in design as an instrument of esthetics as well as utility, and the greater concern for urban space for living and recreation all reflect a growing conception of previously neglected values in urbanization.

8. A final theme drawn from sociological analysis of urban regions is the recognition that the physical and ecological structure of specific regions is not inevitable or eternal. Good or bad, orderly or chaotic, the location of

[3] Edward L. Ullman, "Amenities as a Factor in Regional Growth," *Geographical Review*, 44, (January, 1954), pp. 119–132; Christopher Tunnard and Henry H. Reed, *American Skyline* (New York, The New American Library, 1956), especially Parts VI–VIII; Kevin Lynch, *The Image of the City* (Cambridge, Mass., Harvard University Press, 1960); Charles M. Haar, *Land-Use Planning: A Casebook on the Use, Misuse, and Re-use of Urban Land* (Boston, Little, Brown, 1959), pp. 314–315.

groups, facilities, and services in space is an application of prevailing values —not of immutable laws of natural human motivations. Since these values are not identical in contemporary urban regions, since urban values have changed, are changing, and can be changed, the ecological structure of modern urban regions cannot be accepted as a rigid, unyielding framework for urbanites. In short, urban studies demonstrate that the physical and the sociocultural aspects are inseparable and inherently dynamic in their reciprocal consequences for one another.

pockets of inconsistency and disorder

While urban regions seem to possess an underlying pattern, it is equally evident that urbanization is still a transitional process marked by continuing deviations from, or exceptions to, the evolving urban order. These are survivals from earlier social attitudes, and social techniques, that may be interpreted as pockets of inconsistency in an otherwise regular movement toward rational organization and coordination. To the urban planner, these constitute underlying problems whose resolution is imperative to creative planning and the future outline of urban organization.

The most obvious and most frequently cited inconsistency is the jumble of competing (or hardly cooperative) formal political authorities in urban regions. Economic and social relations have outgrown traditional administrative limits much as a normal six-year old bursts through recently bought shoes, dresses, shirts, and coats. But it is infinitely easier to buy larger and more comfortable clothes than to obtain expanded and more realistic political units for urban regions.

A particularly crucial element in urban disorder is the inordinate pursuit of technical and social efficiency through specialization, social segregation, and division of labor, without sufficient concern for urban coordination and synthesis. To the extent that this general orientation continues, such phenomena as suburban movement inevitably result in slums, traffic problems, increased costs of public services, and lack of understanding between racial and other status divisions in urban regions.

One of the most fundamental aspects of urban difficulties, at least in most of the Western nations, is a continuing individualistic approach to land use and ownership. As a reaction to feudal restrictions and as a means of establishing a necessary variety of land uses in early stages of modern urbanization, this attitude is quite understandable and (in its earlier expression) useful. But if permitted to develop unchecked for very long—as was the case in American cities—the practical consequences are often uneconomical and unnecessary development of urban land. This "gold rush" psychology over several generations produces a hardened pattern of land use that is unsuitable for social and economic changes of later periods and, for any immediate period, an acute shortage of land throughout the urban region. Essentially, the limitations in land use impose comparable restrictions on city planners; indeed, the overwhelming proportion of planning under these circumstances is usually corrective physical—with all the shortcomings described in the last chapter.

Though others might be mentioned, a final type of inconsistency stems from a simple fact: a substantial but not easily measured proportion of residents is not clearly urban except in the matter of location. Relatively few urbanites (city or suburban) can trace urban residence in their families more than two generations. This is particularly evident in the heavy currents of rural-urban migration since World World I and in the movement of Negroes and Puerto Ricans to major cities of the U.S.[4]

Consequently, many families in cities and fringe areas carry over values that are inconsistent (though not always antagonistic) with the opportunities and responsibilities of urban living. This is dramatically reflected in the case of persons maladjusted to urbanism—the criminals, a large proportion of the mentally disturbed and disordered, the compulsive gamblers and alcoholics, the chronically unemployed, and those with continually unstable home life. But it is easy to forget that many others are prosaically uncomfortable with or unaccustomed to the peculiar freedom and diversity of the urban region. Statistics on this point are difficult to obtain, yet we can point to such relevant phenomena as disinterest in the facts and issues of community affairs, non-voting, and the relative disregard of such community resources as museums and libraries. Some will undoubtedly suggest that this is a matter of taste, about which argument is fruitless. However, the important point here is that the insulation of tastes from wider and more diversified forms nullifies the presumed advantages of urban living. It is similar to the incongruous situation of a man entering a restaurant noted for exquisite food and calmly attacking a stale sandwich of peanut butter and jelly, which he has brought for the occasion.

planning visions and ultimate values

The third component of creative urban planning is abstract, visionary, but nonetheless of decisive importance: a guiding conception of an ideal yet ultimately realizable urban region. At this point, planning largely departs from the realm of facts and investigations for an immersion in the less

---

[4] C. Wright Mills et al., *The Puerto Rican Journey* (New York, Harper and Brothers, 1950) ; Christopher Rand, *The Puerto Ricans* (New York, Oxford University Press, 1958) ; Oscar Handlin, *The Newcomers: Negroes and Puerto Ricans in a Changing Metropolis* (Cambridge, Mass., Harvard University Press, 1959).

definite provinces of philosophy and art. Creative planners try to serve as critics of the contemporary, and as links to the future development of urban regions. Both roles apply a set of ultimate objectives or values that draw on the achievements and failures of urban experience, and also provide stimuli for effort toward positive goals. Since creative planning partakes of broad ideals and social interpretation, it bristles with judgments, evaluations, and assertions: it is therefore typically exposed to debate and controversy, to opinion and fashion, and the scorn of those with myopic vision. What are the goals of creative planning in our era? We shall merely list representative goals with brief descriptions.

1. orderly development and responsibility

Mumford and others [5] stress the importance of creating plans that insure smoother incorporation of the physical, economic, and social changes in given regions. In addition, there is a growing concern for designing urban regions to achieve greater articulation and reciprocal relations with other urban regions. This conception disposes of the earlier role of cities as insurgent, highly competitive entities for a more mature contribution to the larger society. In short, creative planning seeks to "socialize" the urban region by developing internal responsibilities for stability and external responsibilities for national service.

2. renewal of internal responsibility

The consensus among urban planners is that the urban region of the future should encourage a consistent and widespread desire to participate actively in neighborhood, community, and regional affairs of various kinds.[6] This goal is based on the prior development of identification and affiliation, rather than withdrawal and alienation. Creative planning seeks to provide the physical setting that restores or expands social participation and community involvement.

[5] Lewis Mumford, *The Culture of Cities* (New York, Harcourt, Brace and World, 1938), pp. 6, 371, 441; Lewis Mumford, "Introduction," in Ebenezer Howard, *Garden Cities of Tomorrow,* enlarged edition (London, Faber and Faber, 1945), p. 38; José Luis Sert, *Can Our Cities Survive?* (Cambridge, Mass., Harvard University Press, 1952); Percival Goodman and Paul Goodman, *Communitas* (Chicago, University of Chicago Press, 1947).

[6] Mumford, *The Culture of Cities,* pp. 483–484; Goodman and Goodman, *op. cit.,* pp. 75–76, 125–126. Cf. Herbert J. Gans, "Urban Poverty and Social Planning," in Paul F. Lazarsfeld *et al.,* eds., *The Uses of Sociology* (New York, Basic Books, 1967), pp. 442–443.

3. livability and general practicality

According to these planning goals, the emphasis is on providing urban regions designed for comfort and convenience for most urbanites, rather than a favored few. The ideal is to create cities in which to enjoy the fruits of modern technology, not their troublesome by-products.[7] In this view, urban areas should become increasingly desirable places to live, as well as work.

4. flexibility

Contrary to some popular apprehensions, creative planners give great prominence to the need for developing flexible designs and plans. The essence of urbanism, they assert, lies in constant development and the quest for new experiences and solutions to the needs of human association. Since future needs cannot be anticipated in great detail, urban planning should reserve space, facilities, and resources so that changes desired by future generations can be achieved without prohibitive cost and needless frustrations.[8] The urban region is conceived not as a monument or museum, but as a continuing frontier in human achievements and satisfactions.

Creative planning, then, is a difficult and evolving combination of basic knowledge of urban trends, a critical survey of urban problems, and a vision of hitherto untapped urban potentialities. In theory and in practice, this type of planning treats the physical and social aspects as inevitably intertwined, a viewpoint that is supported by the social sciences and the arts (both fine and applied). Furthermore, creative planning explicitly approaches the urban region not only as a product of its society and civilization, but as a model for change, as a leader in the development of modern societies. This ambitious role is often greeted with reserve, suspicion, or the ambivalence of lip service. Consequently, few experiments in creative urban planning have reached beyond the discussion or blueprint stage.

But the limited number of such cases—literally "essays in creative urban planning"—deserves some appraisal. In particular, we should attempt to find in each instance the extent to which plans actually apply social science, and the practical obstacles in transferring goals into working models. Significantly, creative planning has almost wholly focused on previously undeveloped areas; either establishing new communities, or inserting new, planned areas in the vacant pockets of established communities. Is creative planning necessarily limited to such situations, or may wider applications be feasible in the future?

[7] Henry S. Churchill, "Trends," in Paul K. Hatt and Albert J. Reiss, Jr., eds., *Reader in Urban Sociology* (New York, The Free Press of Glencoe, 1951), p. 680; Clarence S. Stein, *Toward New Towns for America* (Liverpool, University Press of Liverpool, 1951), p. 206.
[8] Mumford, *The Culture of Cities*, p. 441; Stein, *op. cit.*, p. 205.

selected examples of creative urban planning

Radburn, N.J.: a study in pioneering and frustration

It is quite understandable that the first attempt to plan a permanent community in the creative manner should be located in the New York metropolitan area, about 16 miles from New York City.[9] Radburn was an ambitious gesture, designed to demonstrate the feasibility of establishing a relatively self-contained and orderly island in the urban sprawl. Essentially, its planners envisioned an area with a maximum of 25,000 population, with built-in amenities, and with physical features geared to a conception of a balanced, wholesome community.

Under private financing, without government subsidy or loans, Radburn was opened for occupancy in May, 1929. Its residential area was in the form of two superblocks (three in the original plan), each with well-placed clusters of one-family homes (and later some two-family homes), internal park areas available to every family, a separation of pedestrian and automobile routes, and dead end lanes for beauty and isolation from through traffic.

As originally conceived, Radburn was to be a community, rather than a suburban appendage. Three elementary schools were planned, one for each superblock, as well as a combined junior and senior high school, and an accessible commercial center. There was even provision for an industrial section at the southwest edge of the super-blocks and yet close to a railroad line and a major highway.

But several available facts were ignored, while the imminence of the Great Depression merely intensified the difficulties of rearing a totally new kind of community. First, the planners had located their community in an area of generally inadequate transportation facilities, either for access to New York City or to other cities in New Jersey. Thus, potential residents with jobs in New York City were not greatly attracted. Only 400 families took residence there before the war. The painfully slow growth of Radburn was a tremendous financial burden. Furthermore, the old vision of locating employment opportunities nearby was quickly blurred by the unwillingness of industry to move into the area. Looking backward, this is quite understandable: the adjacent rail line was not on a main route; there were no financial inducements; and there was simply no provision in the plan for attracting employers. Finally, because of virtually nonexistent local employment and the costs of residence, Radburn could not develop a balanced status structure. It became—and remains—a homogeneous enclave of middle class commuters.

Despite the defects of its conception and implementation, Radburn pro-

[9] Stein, *op. cit.*, Chap. II.

vided an early illustration of the potentialities of imaginative urban planning and some necessary cautions to further explorations of the "Radburn idea." Perhaps the most important contribution was the awakening of community participation through the superblock and the civic associations encouraged by tastefully planned proximity. A measure of the value attributed to this style of living is the return of former residents after World War II, and the number of Radburn children who decided to rear their own families in the setting they themselves had enjoyed in the thirties. Also important is Radburn's demonstration that suitable, orderly neighborhoods could be achieved without the drab uniformity of "packaged" suburbs, and yet with adequate provision for future growth. It is no surprise, then, that the essentials of Radburn are already classic and that several European cities have adopted these features in constructing extensive additions to established communities.[10]

The Radburn experience likewise offers very instructive lessons to the creative planner. First, urban plans must give serious attention to the larger region and particularly to the nature of transportation facilities. If the new area is to develop desired social and cultural features, the probable impact of existing facilities must be carefully appraised, and if necessary, an appropriately planned transportation system shoud be an integral part of a practical scheme. The Radburn experiment demonstrates, in the second place, that such imperative considerations as transportation and a favorable economic base require a congenial framework of cooperation with relevant governmental bodies—for information, coordination of activities, and, where necessary, adequate financing. As Stein bluntly remarks in his account of Radburn: ". . . a private corporation has only a gambling chance to carry through to completion the building of a city . . . there must be a certain amount of government cooperation." [11] Finally, to insure a proper range of community services, a creatively planned area must be a politically independent unit, not an appendage of a neighboring and perhaps jealous community. Radburn's residents discovered this essential fact of community living when their plan for a new high school was decisively voted down by their "neighbors" in 1935.

Greenbelt, Md.: variations on the Radburn theme

If Radburn was an outgrowth of private vision in the last gasp of American prosperity, Greenbelt and its sister communities (Greendale, Wis. and Greenhills, Ohio) were attempts at creative urban planning by the federal government in the mid-depression years (1935–1938).[12] Unlike Radburn,

10 *Ibid.*, pp. 67–68; Leo Grebler, *Europe's Reborn Cities*, Urban Land Institute, Technical Bulletin No. 28 (Washington, D.C., March, 1956), pp. 58–59.
11 Stein, *op. cit.*, p. 67.
12 *Ibid.*, Chap. VIII.

Greenbelt has continued to grow and to exhibit its potentialities, despite a radical change in ownership. Greenbelt must be viewed as the leading peace-time candidate for successful creative planning in the United States, though it, too, retains questionable aspects found in Radburn.

Located about 13 miles northeast of an increasingly congested Washington, D.C., Greenbelt was planned as a relatively complete community of 875 residential units arranged in a pleasing arc set in a green belt of Maryland. Its original population of about 2,800 was provided with a modest approximation of Radburn principles: the superblock of attached housing units; the separation of pedestrian walks from automobile routes; the use of dead end lanes and service courts; and consistent provision of small play areas near each set of units, as well as larger recreational areas at various points. Because of its closeness to Washington, and as a matter of policy, Greenbelt was at first a community of lower level government employees (about 70 percent of the community), most of whom were high school graduates. But when an additional 1,000 units were put up in 1941–1942, the typical resident was of higher status in income, formal education, and level of employment in government agencies. By the early fifties, the total population reached almost 7,000 (approximately the projected size of each neighborhood unit in Radburn), many of whom were rather long-term residents in Greenbelt.

However, the nature of the physical setting and a more detailed plan combined to make Greenbelt an improvement over Radburn in several respects. Perhaps the most striking advance was a centrally located community and shopping center, consisting of police and fire departments, the town hall, a large cooperative supermarket, auto repair service, post office, bank, theater, swimming pool, several other stores, and a youth center—all within a half-mile from most units, and just under a mile from the most distant houses. A second feature was the creation of Greenbelt as a political entity with its own government, first under the control of the federal government, and more recently, as a municipality. Consequently, Greenbelt's residents have had considerable direct experience in active government on a number of local problems.[13]

Third, Greenbelt had the important advantage of federal financing, research, and professional planning during the difficult first years of any creative planning venture. In 1951, Greenbelt was sold to a private cooperative of its residents, who operate the community through a city council, mayor, and a city manager.[14]

Fourth, there is the incomparable, long-term benefit of the surrounding greenbelt, which is both a buffer to unwanted urban expansion and an invaluable recreation area for adults and children.

Finally, by mere accident, Greenbelt is four miles from the campus of

[13] Ibid., pp. 147–151.
[14] Christian L. Larsen and Richard D. Andrews, The Government of Greenbelt (College Park, Md., Bureau of Public Administration, University of Maryland, 1951).

the University of Maryland, with all the educational and artistic activities a state university normally affords.

Thus, Greenbelt represents the possibilities of an ambitious attempt at initiating an entirely new community with a balanced set of services and facilities. Yet several deficiencies must be noted. Despite the emphasis on the amenities and attractive use of space, Greenbelt's residential units are closely packed together and lacking in the family living space we have come to require since 1945. Perhaps this limitation of indoor family space is a reflection of the depression period, of the small family of that time. Furthermore, in comparison with Radburn, there is greater uniformity of unit design, which contributes to a "project" look and detracts from the creative planner's quest for beauty.

Once again, no provision for industrial or commercial development was made by Greenbelt's planners. It is, consequently, an area of commuters, adding to the continually troublesome traffic problems of the capital. But a further consequence of its basic dormitory character is a homogenized, one class (middle, white collar), one occupation (federal employee) community—only slightly distinguishable from scores of unplanned residential suburbs that are the objects of so much derision.

the new towns of Britain: creative decentralization on a large scale

Without doubt, the most extensive program of creative urban planning is the New Towns network that has been transforming the urban regions of Great Britain in the short space of 20 years. The problems of the seven large metropolitan regions (or conurbations), marked by congestion and sprawl, have finally provoked organized attempts at decentralization, and yet the retention of community life. British planners and political leaders, willing to experiment, devised three types of solutions. Housing estates (large public housing projects) located in urban fringe areas merely shifted congestion to newer quarters and disrupted local community ties. A second expedient, satellite towns built and owned by large cities within an hour's travel time, became suburban appendages and caused little change in either the residential or transportation situation of such conurbations as London. The New Towns, however, 18 in number to date, give promise of providing solutions that urban regions of the world cannot ignore.[15]

[15] Peter Self, *Cities in Flood* (London, Faber and Faber, 1959), pp. 88–90; Frederic J. Osborn and Arnold Whittick, *The New Towns: The Answer to Megalopolis* (London, Leonard Hall, 1963), Chaps. 1–6; John Tetlow and Anthony Goss, *Homes, Towns, and Traffic* (London, Faber and Faber, 1965), Chap. 5; Lloyd Rodwin, *The British New Towns Policy* (Cambridge, Harvard University Press, 1956), Chaps. 4, 7; Peter Hall, *The World Cities* (New York, McGraw-Hill, 1966), pp. 31–58 and *London 2000* (London, Faber and Faber, 1963), Chap. 6.

Since eight of the New Towns are in the London region, let us focus on these, recognizing, however, that they are not equally developed or uniformly planned. All but one, Stevenage, is approximately 30 miles from downtown London, beyond congested rings of suburbs and at the borders of a permanent greenbelt of woods, farm land, and parks. Each of the towns was designed by a team of planners under the supervision of a Development Corporation, which is responsible to the Ministry of Housing and Local Government and to Parliament.

In view of our previous discussion, a cardinal feature of the New Towns is the attraction of industrial firms (mainly from London) to provide a local employment base. Crawley, for example, had 79 factories by 1962 (for a population of about 40,000). In Hemel Hempstead, 85–90 percent of the residents work locally, rather than commute to London. It has been estimated that only about 15 percent of the gainfully employed in the New Towns around London now work in London's conurbation (i.e., the built up area 12–15 miles from Charing Cross).[16]

Other features of the New Towns are reminiscent of Radburn and Greenbelt: neighborhood units of superblocks, a greenbelt, neighborhood shops, a centrally located community and shopping zone, and the general separation of pedestrian and motor traffic. But the nature of housing facilities constitutes another step forward in creative planning. Despite the obvious bias toward lower income housing, planners have been able to provide a wider range of facilities than is available in most suburbs. In addition to subsidized housing for working and lower middle groups, there is a growing encouragement of housing for middle and upper income families, developed by private construction firms. Furthermore, some towns undertook to build a fair number of more expensive and attractive houses (either for sale or lease) at the very beginning of town development.[17] To this extent, the New Towns have provided a basis for social variety, even to the point of building special one-story houses expressly for older persons, judiciously dispersed among units for younger families.

In general, the New Towns have been successful in establishing solid roots and in satisfying the social and psychological wants of the loyal and highly traditionalistic Londoner. By contrast with the rapid turnover in the housing estates, where lower status Londoners continue to grumble about the "strangers" who are their neighbors and the lost ties of East End areas, less than 4 percent of Crawley's families have to date moved away. Part of this stability, which has been achieved in a remarkably short time, is due to the provision of garden plots, to the rapid development of a variety of religious, athletic, and educational associations, to the community Common Rooms for

[16] Self, op. cit., pp. 59–60; Osborn and Whittick, op. cit., p. 180; Albert Mayer, The Urgent Future (New York, McGraw-Hill, 1967), p. 81.

[17] Self, op. cit., p. 88; B. J. Heraud, "Social Class and the New Towns," Urban Studies, 5 (February, 1966), pp. 33–58.

many social functions, and to the closeness of work and home. Adequate community facilities are understandably a problem of new communities; there are yet shortages in playing fields, movie theaters, and meeting rooms. But planned towns like Harlow, Crawley, and Hemel Hempstead clearly demonstrate the general direction in which urban planning may fruitfully point.

But the New Towns in Great Britain are not a monopoly of the London region. Liverpool has begun two towns (Skelmersdale and Runcorn—each planned to be about 50,000 population) since 1962. Glasgow established its New Town (Cumbernauld, 15 miles away) in 1958, with distinct industrial districts and an unconventional abandonment of the neighborhood unit pattern. Indeed, Cumbernauld has a linear form, which is now reviving interest among city planners after many years. In Wales, Cardiff has its Cwmbran. In the north and midlands, Newcastle has Peterlee and Newton Aycliffe; Birmingham has Dawley and Corby. And several more New Towns are being discussed.[18]

Ciudad Guayana, Venezuela

As a recent example of attempts to plan an industrial metropolis in the hinterlands, Ciudad Guayana is of great interest to city planners, because it is a case study of achievement and limitations when planners "start from scratch." [19] The ingredients for a major city were: adjacent sources of mineral wealth; location on the Orinoco, which gives access to the ocean; the presence of iron ore plants and a steel plant; increasing streams of workers for local industries; and federal funds for urban and further industrial development. With the help of planners from the Massachusetts Institute of Technology, a city of functional nuclei was projected: (1) in the center, a business, commercial, and civic area, with nearby undeveloped land suitable for residential use; (2) east of the center, a cultural complex is envisaged, containing a technical college, a museum, a library, botanical and zoological gardens, a hotel, and a public park; (3) farther east, a medical center, and an outer core of light industry, commercial establishments, and warehousing facilities; (4) south of the business area, two or three residential areas, plus an amorphous residential area near the cultural center; (5) a heavy industrial sector on the west side.

The connective key, necessitated by the general linear (west to east) location of urban nuclei, is a major highway—the carrying capacity of which is problematical. Since the current population is about 100,000, transportation

18 Osborn and Whittick, op. cit., pp. 294–329; Derek Senior, ed., The Regional City (London, Longmans, 1966), pp. 103–104; International Council on Social Welfare, Urban Development: Its Implications for Social Welfare (New York, Columbia University Press, 1967), pp. 41–42.

19 Lloyd Rodwin, "Ciudad Guayana: A New City," Scientific American, 213 (September, 1965), pp. 122–132.

is not yet a crucial problem. But projected population estimates for 1975 are 400,000–500,000, which would require more arteries and possibly some mass transit.

The lineal city in this case is an adaptation to geography and reflects the attempt to link preexisting industrial nodes. However, Cuidad Guayana is still being planned; and there is the advantage, from the planner's standpoint, of public ownership of undeveloped land in the region. At this point, Ciudad Guayana is still a partial physical entity, an urban embryo, whose population is dependent upon decisions made by outsiders. The development of an urban region essentially different from—or superior to—the unplanned metropolis of North America and Europe is a question for another generation.

new towns in the fringe: Reston and Columbia

In partial emulation of the British New Towns, two private developments in the Washington, D.C.—Baltimore area merit close attention. Reston, Virginia (west of Washington in suburban Fairfax County) is a physically planned community that consciously mixes housing types and costs in a set of villages, which will ultimately contain a population of 75,000. With an initial loan from the Gulf Oil Company, the planning team has begun the first village (about 1964) with a range of recreational facilities (lake, golf courses) and housing (high-rise apartments, town houses, and single family homes). Currently, several nearby light industries provide employment for 10–15 percent of the residents. However, plans call for considerable local employment in industry and government agencies (which are expected to relocate from inner Washington). School sites for each village have been reserved, as well as village centers for shopping, churches, and civic activities.[20]

Some 60–70 miles to the northeast, Columbia, Maryland, is a planning twin of Reston—with similar auspices, aims, and facilities. However, Columbia will be larger (about 125,000) and will ultimately consist of nine "towns." The housing mix is aimed at a diversified population (in terms of occupation, income, and race); houses will sell for as little as $10,000 and as much as $100,000. As in Reston, towns will have centers with schools, churches, shopping, and some offices, but Columbia will also have a bus system, with frequent runs throughout the area.[21] At present, local employment is limited (a few research laboratories are close by), but plans include the attraction of distribution firms, and perhaps more research organizations.

[20] The New York Times, December 5, 1965; Edward P. Eichler and Marshall Kaplan, The Community Builders (Berkeley, University of California Press, 1967), pp. 79–86; Derek Senior, ed., The Regional City (London, Longmans, 1966), pp. 113–119.
[21] Eichler and Kaplan, op. cit., pp. 54–79; J. W. Anderson, "A Brand New City for Maryland," Harper's Magazine (November, 1964), pp. 100–106.

Brasilia: the grandeur of a new capital

A magnificent opportunity to plan a completely new community, literally from the ground up, has recently been taken by the Brazilian government in its decision to construct a new capital 600 miles inland from Rio de Janeiro. Clearly, the design of capital cities presents certain problems, and allows a certain latitude, simply because they differ in function from the more prevalent commercial and industrial cities. In Canberra, constructed in 1918, for example, it was decided to create a capital with an uncluttered central area, one strangely planned for golf links and a race track. Completely excluding any industrial development, the plan sharply separated commercial, governmental, and residential clusters to the point of formal beauty and structured inconvenience. The inevitable price has been a considerable traffic problem in a community of about 54,000.[22] To what extent has Brasilia profited by the experience of its Austrialian counterpart?

After eight years of construction, Brasilia is still somewhat unfinished. It consists of a core and several unplanned peripheral satellites (Gama, Taguatinga, Sobradinho), which have a combined population of over 100,000. In 1962, about 4,000 lived in Brasilia proper, but estimated growth is now up to 150,000—with an expected maximum for the area of 500,000. Completed building is primarily for government offices, a hotel, the airport, several housing complexes, in addition to several broad highways and a huge artificial lake.

The basic quality of Brasilia lies not in its very modernistic architecture, but in a radical deviation from the familiar urban pattern, composed of a core commercial area and a series of rough zones, sectors, and clusters arrayed in amoebic fashion around the core. Brasilia consists of three major parts, which form a unique cross (or in the description of the *New York Times* art critic, "a giant dragonfly").[23] The major "spine" of the city contains a variety of business, civic, and recreational buildings. Crossing the spine in the shape of arched wings is a set of residential superblocks, with accessible shopping, schools, and churches. Then at the head of the major axis is a triangular arrangement of the capital's administrative offices. Because of this monu-

[22] Homer Bigart, "Once Bleak Canberra Emerging as Modern Capital for Australia," *The New York Times*, February 12, 1961; Tillman Durdin, "Canberra Begins to Fulfill Dream," *ibid.*, January 24, 1965; Herbert W. H. King, "The Canberra-Queanbeyan Symbiosis, A Study of Urban Mutualism," *Geographical Review* 44 (January, 1954), pp. 101–118.

[23] Aline Saarinen, "Brasilia Rises," *The New York Times*, October 18, 1959; Armin K. Ludwig, "The Planning and Creation of Brasilia: Toward a New and Unique Regional Environment?" in Eric N. Baklanoff, ed., *New Perspectives of Brazil* (Nashville, Vanderbilt University Press, 1966), pp. 179–204; Edmund N. Bacon, *Design of Cities* (New York, Viking Press, 1967), pp. 220–227.

mental design, transportation links are especially important. The plan, therefore, calls for a network of highways, cloverleafs, multilevel roads, special
pedestrian lanes, and boulevards 400 feet broad.

The boldness of the plan and the obvious attempt to provide a city of
dazzling vistas and abundant space mark Brasilia as a city of glamor and
persistent interest. It seems to be a huge outdoor museum, a city dedicated to
the public aspect. But it remains to be seen what the residential clusters,
composed of towering apartment buildings, contribute to the essentials of
privacy, family life, and personal involvement in local affairs. We can only
guess, secondly, at the ultimate success or failure of constructing a city
dependent on auto transportation for its operation. Finally, the purposeful
lack of industrial or commercial development may reduce congestion, but it
also denies Brasilia a certain balance that urban regions seem to need. Very
probably, national capitals constitute a separate type of city. Yet if one com-
pares the specialized with the more balanced world capitals, which type provides better living and more varied experiences? To be more specific, how do
Washington, D.C., Canberra, Tel Aviv, and Brasilia compare with London,
Paris, Berlin, Stockholm, and Tokyo? In other words, to what extent does the
governmental function create the basis for community living?

regional planning

The creation of new towns and new cities (as capitals or industrial
centers) is one of the unheralded but expanding trends of our time. In fact,
Osborn and Whittick required eight pages of small type to list the planned
towns since 1900 all over the world.[24] However, many of these creations involve small populations and do not directly deal with the need for more
creative direction of growth and development in the more densely populated
centers. But there is now some evidence of attempts to anticipate and control
urbanization on a regional and national basis.

One type of illustration of this emerging pattern is the conception of the
"finger metropolis"—the planned spacing of complete towns or corridor cities
along each major radial of such cities as Copenhagen, Stockholm, and Washington, D.C., and with some variations, Paris.[25] The underlying principles in
these projections seem to be (1) the inevitable growth of fringe areas must
be publicly directed throughout a given urban region; (2) planned peripheral

---

[24] Osborn and Whittick, op. cit., pp. 141–148.

[25] Copenhagen Regional Planning Office, Preliminary Outline Plan for the Copenhagen Metropolitan Region (Copenhagen, August, 1961): Hans Blemenfeld, The Modern
Metropolis (Cambridge, MIT Press, 1967), p. 76; National Capital Regional Planning
Council, The Regional Development Guide, 1966–2000 (Washington, D.C., U.S. Government Printing Office, June 30, 1966); C. F. Ahlberg, "The Regional Plan for the Stockholm Area," in Planning of Metropolitan Areas and New Towns (New York, Department of Economic and Social Affairs, United Nations, 1967), pp. 93–100.

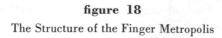

figure 18

The Structure of the Finger Metropolis

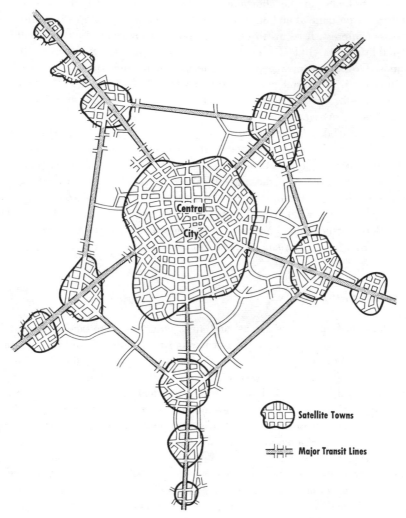

growth should contain a local range of urban facilities and services, and yet utilize current or anticipated transportation lines for integration with the central city.

A second type may be found in the horseshoe-shaped megalopolis of the Netherlands—Randstad Holland or Conurbation Holland (Amsterdam–Haarlem–Utrecht and Rotterdam–The Hague–Leiden). The major problem is intensive suburban growth within the horseshoe, intimating the eventual coalescence of the six major urban areas into one formless sprawl—a Dutch Los Angeles, in Hall's apt phrase. Essentially, regional planning seeks to monitor urban growth by two policies. The first is negative in nature: preventing agricultural use in the inner horseshoe from conversion to industrial or residential use, by routing population and industry into the few existing towns in that area. The second planning objective alters the horseshoe form by directing future growth along radials south of Rotterdam and north and northeast from Amsterdam.[26] Thus, hopefully, neither of the major component cities will lose its identity, nor will the economic and other linkages between cities be sheared.

A third approach is perhaps best illustrated by France, although Great Britain seems to be gradually inclining in the same direction. Briefly, French urban regional planners have come to regard the nation as a network of nine regional units (Paris, Lyons, Nancy, Marseilles, Lille, Bordeaux, Nantes, Strasbourg, and Toulouse), among whom a more workable balance can be reached by 1985.[27] This of course requires rather rigid limitations on Parisian economic growth, and reallocation on a grand scale of such growth to the other regional centers. Thus far, implementation has been microscopic—but another 15 years and more are available to the French planners.

summary

As we review the few serious attempts at creative urban planning, several outstanding features seem to recur. There is, first, the comparative recency of such planning and a consequent incompleteness of execution. Second, creative planners have tended to mix bold visions and questionable retention of past failures. The latter aspect is especially visible in experiments that ignore the need for a balanced economic base, for smoothly flowing transportational and traffic systems, and a setting attractive to a range of status groupings in the urban region. Third, there is a basic quest for restoration of the region as an area of numerous interlocking interests and pursuits, not merely as a place to work and draw income.

Essentially, creative planning has tried to approach the city and its region as an emergent system, in which planning provides crucial connections and strategic additions to effective coordination. Specifically, the essays in creative planning reflect concern for the interrelation of physical, cultural, and social aspects of human groups. In this respect, the planner borrows—or shares—the fundamental orientation of the urban sociologist, who draws from a

[26] Peter Hall, *The World Cities* (New York, McGraw-Hill, 1966), pp. 95–117; Gerald L. Burke, *Greenhart Metropolis* (New York, St. Martin's Press, 1966); Jac P. Thijsse, "Conurbation Holland," in H. Wentworth Eldredge, ed., *Taming Metropolis* (Garden City, Doubleday, 1967), Vol. 1, pp. 320–342.

[27] Hall, *op. cit.*, pp. 81–92; Ambassade de France, *France: Town and Country Environment Planning* (New York, Service de Presse et d'Information, December, 1965), pp. 15–49.

variety of investigations a conception of the city and the urban region as a recognizable but imperfect system, complex though it may be.[28] On the other hand, in the execution of plans, it is often true that the greater emphasis is devoted to the physical and cultural dimensions, with a resultant muting of concern for developing social organizations. The planner hopes to create the proper facilities, not the organizations themselves.

Finally, though a regional viewpoint and philosophy are consistently expressed in the writings and speeches of creative planners, specific planning programs rarely receive the opportunity to treat the urban region as a practical entity. Instead, planners find themselves projecting their insights and ingenuity on a single functional part of the region—a suburb, a satellite, or perhaps an entire but isolated central city (e.g., Brasilia). Thus far, creative planning and the tentative conclusions of urban sociology are closely parallel lines—but they have yet to meet consistently and properly assimilate the unique contributions of one another.

[28] Martin Rein and S. M. Miller, "The Demonstration Project as a Strategy of Change," in Mayer N. Zald, ed., *Organizing for Community Welfare* (Chicago, Quadrangle Books, 1967), pp. 160–191; Homer Hoyt, *The Changing Principles of Land Economics* (Washington, D.C., Urban Land Institute, Technical Bulletin No. 60, 1968); Leo F. Schnore and Henry Fagan, eds., *Urban Research and Policy Planning* (Beverly Hills, Sage Publications, 1967).

selected references

ELDREDGE, H. Wentworth, ed., *Taming Metropolis* (Garden City, Doubleday, 1967), 2 vols.

GOODMAN, Percival and GOODMAN, Paul, *Communitas* (Chicago, University of Chicago Press, 1947).

HOWARD, Ebenezer, *Garden Cities of Tomorrow*, enlarged ed. (London, Faber and Faber, 1955).

KUPER, Leo, ed., *Living in Towns* (London, Gresset Press, 1953).

MUMFORD, Lewis, *The City in History* (New York, Harcourt, Brace and World, 1961), Chaps. XVI–XVII.

STEIN, Clarence, *Toward New Towns for America* (Liverpool, University Press of Liverpool, 1951).

TUNNARD, Christopher and REED, Henry H., *American Skyline* (New York, New American Library, 1956).

VIET, Jean, ed., *New Towns: Selected Annotated Bibliography* (Paris, UNESCO, 1960).

index

Abrams, Charles, 343, 345
Abu-Lughod, Janet, 91
Achievement lag, 322
Adams, Richard N., 183–184
Adams, Robert M., 13, 19
Adler, Lee, 304
Adrian, Charles R., 227, 230
Advertising, 243, 247, 295, 307
Aged persons, 169–170
Ahlberg, C. F., 375
Alden, Robert, 304
Alihan, Milla A., 93
Alonzo, William, 337
Altschuler, Alan, 337
Amory, Cleveland, 114, 165, 203
Anderson, J. W., 373
Anderson, Martin, 348
Anderson, Theodore R., 86
Andrewes, A., 220
Andrews, Richard B., 122
Angell, Robert C., 81, 154, 316
Arnold, David S., 258
Asbury, Herbert, 166
Ashworth, William, 326, 337
Asquith, David, 170
Axelrod, Morris, 160, 161, 163, 178–180

Babbie, Earl R., 276
Babchuk, Nicholas, 179, 183
Babcock, Richard F., 342
Bacon, Edmund N., 326, 374
Bailey, Cyril, 19
Baker, Gordon, 27
Baklanoff, Eric N., 374
Balandier, Georges, 90
Baltzell, E. Digby, 165, 201
Banani, A., 231
Banfield, Edward C., 138, 227–229, 234–235, 343
Banton, Michael, 33, 71, 183–184, 188

Barber, Bernard, 191, 193, 217, 272–273
Barnett, Homer G., 279
Bartholomew, Harland, 93, 236, 342
Bascom, William, 14
Baur, E. Jackson, 302
Bazelon, David T., 217
Bean, Lee L., 86
Becker, Howard, 8, 78, 136, 283, 317, 320, 323
Beegle, J. Allan, 12
Behrman, S. N., 204
Belcher, Wyatt W., 80
Belknap, G. M., 264
Bell, Wendell, 86, 178–179, 181, 187–188
Bellush, Jewel, 345–348
Bendix, Reinhard, 211–213, 217, 247
Benet, Francisco, 12
Benevolo, Leonardo, 326
Bennett, John W., 33, 306–308
Bennett, Ruth, 170
Bennis, Warren, 323
Benoit-Smullyan, Emile, 194
Berelson, Bernard, 276, 293, 296, 305
Beresford, Maurice, 23
Berger, Bennett M., 111, 118, 208, 266
Berger, Peter L., 276
Berle, Adolph A., 246
Bernard, Jessie L., 314, 323
Bernard, Philippe J., 337
Bernays, Edward L., 294–295
Bernstein, Abraham, 283
Berquist, Goodwin F., 110
Berry, Brian J. L., 80
Bettelheim, Bruno, 212
Beyer, Glenn H., 72, 169, 208, 344, 359
Bigart, Homer, 374
Binder, Leonard, 231, 233
Birmingham, Stephen, 201–202
Black, C. E., 323
Black, E. I., 111
Blaisdell, Donald C., 244

Bleton, Pierre, 195
Blumenfeld, Hans, 326, 375
Bloch, Herbert, 167
Bloch, Marc, 222
Blood, Robert O., 157
Bloomberg, Warner, 136, 267, 346
Boak, Arthur E. R., 20
Bogue, Donald J., 57, 68, 71, 76, 97, 99, 123–125, 127–129, 133, 150, 242
Bollens, John C., 138, 241, 262, 264, 269
Bone, Hugh T., 265–266
Bonilla, Frank, 212
Borden, Neil, 295
Boskoff, Alvin, 8, 78, 112, 116, 136, 148, 181, 211, 230, 264, 267, 269, 317, 320–323
Bott, Elizabeth, 171
Boulding, Kenneth E., 324
Braden, Charles S., 271
Bradley, Philip D., 249
Brady Robert A., 244
Braidwood, Robert J., 13
Brasilia, 374–375
Brazer, Harvey E., 121, 254
"Break in transportation" theory, 81
Breckenfield, Gurney, 349
Bredemeier, Harry C., 314
Breed, Warren, 213
Breese, Gerald, 105, 239, 359
Brennan, T., 111, 113, 359
Bridenbaugh, Carl, 8
Briggs, Asa, 9
Bronner, Augusta, 316
Brown, Charles M., 354
Brucker, Gene, 222
Bruno, Frank J., 288
Budge, E. A. Wallis, 19
Burgess, Ernest W., 83, 154–155, 168–169
Burke, Gerald L., 377
Burnham, James, 246
Burt, Nathaniel, 203
Butts, N. Freeman, 280

Cahnman, Werner J., 9, 14
Campbell, Alan K., 254
Campbell, Angus, 266–267
Campbell, Arthur A., 161
Cantor, Mildred, 138
Caplan, Nathan S., 290
Caplow, Theodore A., 91, 246, 340
Cappock, J. T., 330
Carman, J. M., 293
Carpenter, David B., 12, 259
Carr, Lowell J., 322
Carter, Edward, 330
Carter, Harold, 79
Carter, Richard F., 230

Cartwright, Dorwin, 78
Casey, M. Claire, 247
Cauter, T., 208
Cavan, Ruth, 28, 154–155
Centers, Richard, 212
Centralization, 96
Central place theory, 80–81
Chamberlain, Neil, 215
Chapman, Brian, 35
Chase, Stuart, 245
Childe, V. Gordon, 13–15, 27
Chinitz, Benjamin, 241
Christensen, Harold T., 161
Churchill, Henry S., 366
Ciudad Guayana, 372–373
Clark, Colin, 67
Clark, Elmer T., 271
Clark, Lincoln, 249, 279
Clark, S. D., 111, 113
Clark, Terry, 235
Clark, Thomas B., 247
Clarke, Alfred C., 179
Clinard, Marshall B., 138, 148, 208–209, 314–315
Cliques, 164–168
Cloward, Richard A., 168–169, 171
Cohen, Albert K., 168–169, 171
Cohen, Nathan E., 291
Cohn, Norman, 271
Coleman, James S., 166, 208
Collins, Christine, 326
Collins, G. R., 326
Collins, Sidney, 71
Collinson, Peter, 86
Columbia, Maryland, 373
Commercial location, 102–202
Community, 4–6
Conant, James, 282
Concentration, 95–96
Concentric zones, 83
Connery, Robert H., 255, 356–357
Cooke, Edward F., 229
Cooley, Charles H., 81, 154
Coordination as urban process, 141–144
Cornick, Phillip H., 340
Corporations, 245–246
Coughlin, Richard J., 183
Coulter, Philip B., 269
Cowgill, Donald O., 100, 232
Cox, Kevin, 266
Crespi, Irving, 304
Cressey, Paul, 96
Crosby, John, 128
Crouch, Winston W., 262
Cullingworth, J. B., 106, 328, 330, 343, 345–346, 359
Cultural lag, 322

Dahl, Robert A., 225, 227, 235, 324
Danielson, Michael N., 262, 352
Daudt, H., 265
Davies, A. F., 111
Davies, H. Hywel, 91
Davies, Richard O., 343
Davis, Allison, 159, 164, 195
Davis, Don A., 199
Davis, James C., 222
Davis, Kingsley, 42, 48, 50, 64, 71, 76
Decision making. *See also* Power structure
    phases in, 226–229
    variations in, 233–235
De Cler, Cornelius, 328
De Fleur, Melvin, 128
Denis, J., 34
Dentler, Robert A., 283
Deutsch, Karl, 219
Dewey, Richard, 12, 149, 279, 321
Dewhurst, J. Frederic, 246
Dexter, Lewis A., 303–309
Dichter, Ernest, 293
Dickinson, Robert E., 37, 118, 130
Dickson, Lenore, 162
Dickson, W. J., 163
Dill, Samuel, 20
Dimock, Marshall, 238, 269
Dinerman, Beatrice, 262
Dobriner, William, 111, 130, 135
Dopsch, Alfons, 20
Douglas, H. Paul, 108
Douglass, Truman, 274
Downham, J. S., 208
Doxiadis, Constantinos A., 326
Dubin, Robert, 249
Duggar, George S., 343
Duhl, Leonard J., 346
Duncan, Beverly, 86, 96, 100
Duncan, Otis D., 8, 42, 48, 60, 65, 76, 86, 96, 100, 109, 119, 124, 130, 199–200
Dunham, H. Warren, 138
Durant, Ruth, 111
Durdin, Tillman, 374
Durkheim, Emile, 132, 143–144, 274–275
Dyckman, John W., 350–351, 353
Dynes, Russell R., 186, 212
Dyos, H. J., 110

Ecological structure, 77–78, 88–90, 127
    ecological dynamics, 104–105
    ecological mobility, 97
    ecological processes, 95–97
    ecological units, 82–86
    economic dominance, 133
    functional needs and, 87–88
    medieval towns and, 23
    modern cities and, 25

Economic organization: basic structures, 238
    consumption patterns and, 249–253
    employment base and, 239–242
    formal organizations and, 245–247
    political economy and, 236–238
    sales base and, 242–253
    taxation base and, 253–257
    value systems and, 243–245
Education, 277–283, 297–298
Edwards, Hugh, 212
Egeland, Janice, 86
Ehrmann, Henry W., 244–245
Eichler, Edward P., 373
Eisenstadt, S. N., 213
Eisner, Simon, 337
Eister, Allan W., 78, 272
Eldredge, H. Wentworth, 328, 335, 342, 377–378
Elinson, Howard, 215
Emmet, Boris, 248
Enccl, S., 111
Ethic of ambiguity, 147–148, 308–309
Eulau, Heinz, 296
Exurbia, 125–126, 205–206

Fabricant, Solomon, 258
Fagan, Henry, 378
Family structure: changes in, 155–158, 161
    consumption patterns and, 249–253
    friendships and, 163
    parent-child relations, 158–160
    political participation and, 267
    roles of the wife, 156–157
    types of, 159–160
Fanfani, Amintore, 325
Farber, Bernard, 171
Faris, Robert E. L., 138
Farnell, Lewis R., 19
Fauset, Arthur, 271
Fava, Sylvia F., 163, 351
Feldman, Arnold S., 86
Ferman, Louis, 217
Festinger, Leon, 171
Fichter, Donn, 354
Field, Eric, 247
Firey, Walter, 35, 87, 93, 122
Fisher, Ernest M., 359
Fisher, Jack C., 335
Fisher, Robert M., 331, 343, 359
Fisk, George, 250, 252
Fitch, Lyle C., 350, 352
Flexner, Abraham, 280
Fogarty, M. P., 326, 328
Fogelson, Robert M., 93
Foley, Donald L., 107, 330
Folk-sacred type, 317
Folsom, Joseph K., 154

Foote, Nelson, 112
Force, Maryanne T., 178–179, 181
Form, William H., 78, 163–164, 194, 335
Foskett, John, 217
Fowler, Irving A., 232
Francastel, Pierre, 110, 137
Frankenberg, Ronald, 112
Freedman, Ronald, 71–72, 76, 99, 161, 175, 185
Freeman, Howard E., 179, 186–187
Freeman, T. W., 107
Friedlander, Walter, 284
Friedmann, John, 337
Friedson, Eliot, 302
Freud, Anna, 316
Fustel de Coulanges, N. D., 19, 132, 220

Galbraith, J. Kenneth, 26, 243, 268
Gallion, Arthur B., 337
Gangs, 165–169
Gans, Herbert J., 111, 113, 171, 267, 346, 365
Gardner, Burleigh, 165, 194
Gardner, Mary, 165, 194
Garrison, William L., 88, 351
Geddes, Patrick, 32, 130, 318
Geis, Gilbert, 169
Generalization as urban process, 139
George, Pierre, 79
Germani, Gino, 184
Gerth, Hans H., 307
Gibb, H. A. R., 19
Gibbard, Harold A., 86
Giddings, Franklin H., 317
Gillen, Paul, 30–31
Gilchrist, David, 105
Gilmore, Harlan W., 31, 91–92, 101
Gist, Noel P., 87, 90, 98, 129
Gittell, Marilyn, 283, 291
Glass, David V., 211–212, 217
Glasser, Ralph, 307
Glazer, Nathan, 347
Gloag, John, 247
Glock, Charles Y., 274, 276, 291
Goldman, Eric, 9
Goldschmidt, Walter, 272
Goldstein, Sidney, 76, 113
Goldwin, Robert A., 354
Gomberg, William, 218
Good, Erich, 275–276
Goode, William J., 158, 162
Goodman, Paul, 365, 378
Goodman, Percival, 365, 378
Gordon, C. Wayne, 179, 183
Goss, Anthony, 326, 355, 370
Gottlieb, David, 166
Gottman, Jean, 318

Grambs, Jean, 283
Gras, N. S. B., 128
Grebler, Leo, 334, 351, 353, 359, 368
Green, Arnold W., 158
Green, James L., 242
Greenbelt, Maryland, 368–371
Greenberg, Joseph T., 50
Greenstein, Fred I., 235
Greer, Scott, 27, 38, 160, 179, 263–264
Grigsby, William G., 349, 359
Grimes, Sandra, 165
Grodzins, Morton, 217, 343
Gruen, Victor, 355
Gulick, Luther, 258
Gurvitch, Georges, 94
Gutkind, E. A., 27

Haar, Charles M., 340, 342, 362
Hagedorn, Robert, 179
Halbert, L. A., 98, 129
Hall, Mary P., 286
Hall, Peter, 107, 130, 330, 335, 370, 376–377
Hamblin, Robert L., 157
Hamilton, C. Horace, 69
Hamilton, Robert V., 302, 307
Hamilton, Walton H., 244
Hammond, S. B., 194
Hamovitch, William, 215
Handel, Leo, 294
Handlin, Oscar, 364
Hansen, P. From, 170
Harbison, Frederick H., 249
Harris, Chauncey D., 84, 108
Hartman, Chester W., 347
Hatt, Paul K., 9, 31, 51, 82, 124, 199, 366
Hauser, Henri, 21
Hauser, Philip, 115, 184
Hausknecht, Murray, 183, 345–348
Havard, William C., 265
Havighurst, Robert J., 159, 297
Hawley, Amos H., 8–9, 45, 76, 86, 105, 121, 128, 184
Healy, William, 316
Heath, Dwight, 183–184
Heberle, Rudolph, 174, 198
Hechinger, Fred, 301
Hemmens, George C., 350
Henderson, David, 9
Henderson, Julia J., 236
Henry, William, 306
Heraud, B. J., 371
Herlihy, David, 22, 222
Herman, Mary W., 200
Herskovits, Melville J., 237
Hertz, Hilda, 42
Hill, Clyde M., 281
Hill, Reuben, 154

Hiller, E. T., 191
Hirsch, Walter, 320
Hirsch, Werner Z., 239, 348
Hoffman, Lois, 157
Holcombe, Arthur N., 134
Hollingshead, August B., 192, 211–212, 217, 297
Homans, George C., 154
Hoover, Edgar H., 130
Horton, Paul, 314
Hoselitz, Bert, 323
Hoskins, W. G., 9, 110
Housing, 342–349
    conservation programs, 349
    public, 346–347
    rehabilitation programs, 349
    slum clearance, 345
Howard, Ebenezer, 326, 365, 378
Hoyt, Homer, 43, 80, 83, 100, 102, 105, 378
Hunnicutt, C. W., 283
Hunter, Floyd, 144, 165, 233, 235
Hutchinson, E. P., 71
Hyman, Herbert H., 178–179, 184–185, 308

Income, 60–63
    consumption patterns and, 250–253
    size of urban area and, 60–62
    voluntary associations and, 179–180
Industrial location, 97–98
Innovation, 139–140
Institutions, 236–237
Invasion and succession, 96
Irelan, Lola, 209

Jacobs, Norman, 309, 325–326
Jacobson, Alvin H., 157
Janowitz, Morris, 129, 212, 269, 302–303
Jenck, John C., 248
Jenkins, Edward C., 287
Jennings, M. Kent, 227
Jewkes, John, 246
Johns-Heine, Patricke, 307
Johnson, Harry M., 7
Johnson, John J., 212
Jones, Emrys, 91
Jones, Victor, 261
Justement, Louis, 326

Kahl, Joseph A., 191, 193, 201, 207–208, 217
Kain, John F., 352
Kammerer, Gladys, 226
Kant, Edgard, 110
Kaplan, David, 247
Kaplan, Harold, 226, 262
Kaplan, Marshall, 373

Karr, Madeline, 166
Katona, George, 249, 251–253
Katz, Daniel, 213
Katz, Elihu, 295, 302, 309
Kaufman, Herbert, 138, 229, 233–234
Kavaler, Lucy, 195, 204
Keats, John, 282, 344, 358
Keesing, Felix, 13, 317
Kelley, Stanley, 296
Kent, T. J., 339
Keyfitz, Nathan, 91
Killian, Lewis, 174
Kimble, George H., 183
King, Gary, 230, 267
King, Herbert W. H., 374
Kirkpatrick, Clifford, 154
Kish, Leslie A., 127
Kitigawa, Evelyn, 97
Klapper, Joseph T., 302, 304, 309
Klein, Malcolm W., 169, 290
Kneedler, Grace, 30–31, 124
Koerner, James D., 282
Kohn, Clyde F., 79, 81, 93, 102, 128
Kohn, Melvin L., 159
Kolko, Gabriel, 250
Komarovsky, Mirra, 154, 158, 178–180
Kornhauser, Arthur, 215
Kraeling, Carl H., 13
Kramer, Dale, 166
Kramer, Stella, 222
Kroeber, A. L., 305
Ktsanes, Thomas, 111
Kuper, Hilda, 183–184
Kuper, Leo, 34, 65, 90, 101, 378
Kweder, B. James, 227

Labor unions, 248
Labovitz, Sanford, 179
Landauer, Carl, 324
Landecker, Werner S., 143
Lander, Bernard, 42
Landis, Paul, 9
Landtman, Gunnar, 191
Lang, Gladys E., 174, 189
Lang, Kurt, 174, 189
Langguth, Jack, 227
Lansing, John B., 155, 352
Lapidus, Ira M., 23
Laski, Harold J., 26
Laumann, Edward O., 213
Lawless, Richard H., 302, 307
Lazarsfeld, Paul, 155, 276, 293–296, 302, 304–305, 309, 365
Lazerwitz, Bernard, 266, 276
Leach, Richard, 356–357
Lebeaux, Charles N., 286–288
Lee, J. M., 231

Lee, Rose Hum, 99
Lemly, James H., 351
Lenski, Gerhard, 194
Lepawsky, Albert, 106
Lerner, Daniel, 302
Leslie, Gerald R., 314
Lestocquoy, J., 21, 222
Leven, Harry, 159
Levy, David, 158
Lewis, W. Arthur, 324
Liebman, Charles S., 113
Liepmann, Kate, 24, 155
Lindblom, Charles E., 324
Lindner, Robert, 316
Linton, Ralph, 317
Lipset, Seymour M., 200, 211–213, 217
Litchfield, Edward H., 265
Little, Kenneth, 183
Litwak, Eugene, 162
Livingston, J. A., 158
Locke, Harvey, 154–155
Loewenstein, Louis K., 155
Loewenthal, Leo, 307
London planning, 232, 330
Loomis, Charles P., 12
Lubove, Roy, 331
Ludwig, Armin K., 374
Lundberg, George A., 162
Lunt, Paul S., 164, 176, 192, 201, 204, 218
Lynch, Kevin, 6, 10, 362
Lynd, Albert, 282
Lynd, Helen M., 164, 192, 217
Lynd, Robert S., 164, 192, 217, 316

Mabry, John, 58
Maccoby, Eleanor E., 159, 302
Mace, Ruth L., 121, 255
McGee, T. G., 91
MacIver, Robert M., 10, 94, 316
McKeever, J. Ross, 102
McKelvey, Blake, 93, 314
McKenzie, Roderick D., 96, 108, 128–130, 133, 150
McKinley, Donald G., 217
McLean, Mary, 339, 359
McLoughlin, J. B., 328
McQuail, Dennis, 296
Mafeji, Archie, 184
Makielski, S. J., 342
Mandelker, Daniel R., 328
Mangiamele, Joseph F., 110
Mangin, William P., 183
Manheim, Ernest, 360
Mannheim, Karl, 316, 319, 323–324, 337, 360
Margolis, Julius, 138
Marsh, Robert M., 200

Marshall, T. H., 136
Martin, Roscoe C., 232, 262
Martin, Walter T., 279
Martindale, Don, 8, 16, 27, 135–136, 220, 259
Marts, Marion E., 351
Marvick, Dwaine, 302–303
Marx, Gary T., 216
Marx, Karl, 134, 193
Mass communications: components, 298–302
    effects, 304–309
    major features, 292–295
    major forms, 295–297
    personal influence and, 302–304
    social class and, 297, 306
Mass society, 133
    mass communications and, 133, 308–309
Master Plan, 339–340, 356
Matthews, Donald R., 264
May, Rollo, 316
Mayer, Albert, 344, 371
Mayer, Harold M., 79, 81, 93, 102, 128
Mayer, Kurt B., 113
Mayer, Martin, 247
Mayer, Philip, 183
Mead, Margaret, 160, 226, 285
Means, Gardiner C., 246
Median location, 88
Meier, Dorothy, 187–188
Meier, Richard L., 140, 310, 326
Melamed, Anshel, 112
Mengelberg, Kaethe, 238
Merchants, 16–18, 21, 221–223
Merton, Robert K., 7, 37, 302, 305, 314–315
Meyerhoff, Barbara G., 169, 290
Meyerson, Martin, 236, 337, 346
Metropolitan area. See Urban community; Region
Migration, 70–73, 96–99, 148–149
    political participation and, 265–267
    stages in, 71–73, 98–99
    suburban types, 71–72, 110–113
    velocity of, 72
    voluntary associations and, 185–186
Milbrath, Lester, 269
Miller, Daniel R., 159, 171
Miller, Delbert C., 78, 163, 232
Miller, Herbert A., 183
Miller, Llewellyn, 163
Miller, S. M., 208, 378
Mills, C. Wright, 108, 196, 207, 217, 233, 305, 364
Millspaugh, Martin, 349, 355
Milner, James B., 262
Miner, Horace, 37, 65
Mitchell, J. Clyde, 33
Mitchell, Robert B., 350, 357
Model Cities, 348. See also Housing

Mogey, John M., 208
Moore, Jane, 72
Moore, Wilbert E., 94, 323
Morgan, Lewis H., 14
Morris, Richard T., 199
Morse, Richard M., 9, 65, 80
Mukerjee, Radhakamal, 79
Mumford, Lewis, 22–23, 32–33, 37, 132, 150, 280, 326, 335, 337, 350, 355, 365–366, 378
Mundy, John H., 21
Murphy, Gardner, 10
Murphy, Raymond J., 199, 215
Murray, Gilbert, 19
Musgrove, F., 166
Myers, George, 274

Nahemow, Lucille, 170
Nam, Charles B., 76
Nash, William W., 349, 357
Natural areas, 82–83
Negroes: residential patterns, 99–102
    consumption patterns, 250–251
Nelson, G. R., 286
Nelson, Lowry, 10
Nesbitt, George D., 100
Neuwirth, Gertrud, 16, 27, 136, 220, 259
New Towns, 370–373
Nicholson, J. H., 326
Niederhoffer, Arthur, 167
Niehaus, Earl, 91
Nimkoff, Meyer F., 155
Nisbet, Robert A., 198, 314–315
Nolting, Orin, 258
Novak, Edwin, 179
Nye, F. Ivan, 157

Occupational distribution, 58–60
    employment base and, 239–242
    voluntary associations and, 180
O'Connor, Edwin, 196
Odum, Howard W., 33, 136, 317, 322
Oeser, O. A., 194
Ogburn, William F., 155, 322
O'Harrow, Dennis, 342
Ohlin, Lloyd, 168–169, 171
Oldman, Oliver, 70
Olmsted, Michael S., 78
Olson, Philip, 308
Olsson, Gunnar, 80
Oppenheimer, Franz, 238
Organic solidarity, 143–144
Orlans, Harold, 326
Ortmeyer, Carl, 193, 196
Osborn, Frederic J., 370, 371, 372, 375
Owen, Wilfred, 350, 352

Packard, Vance, 195, 304
Page, Charles H., 10
Palamountain, J. C., 247
Palisi, Bartolomeo J., 183
Palmer, Gladys L., 200
Park, Robert E., 82–83, 93, 96, 129, 133, 183
Parkins, Maurice F., 334–335
Parkinson, C. Northcote, 176
Parsons, Talcott, 145, 156, 161, 166, 193
Passow, Harry A., 283
Pearlin, Leonard I., 246, 295
Perlman, Mark, 241
Perloff, Harvey S., 326, 339
Pernoud, Régine, 222
Perry, W. J., 16
Petersen, William, 9, 170, 307
Petit-Dutaillis, Charles, 222–223
Phelps, Clyde W., 248
Phelps, Harold A., 9
Pierce, Bessie L., 80, 314
Pinckney, David H., 35
Pirenne, Henri, 9, 20–22, 27, 132, 134, 221–222
Pitts, Forrest R., 80
Pitts, Jesse R., 161
Planhol, Xavier, 91
Planning: controlled social change and, 319–322
    corrective type, 336–358
    creative type, 336, 360–378
    institutional structure of, 324–327
    national variations in, 328–335
    regional, 375–377
    strategy of, 321–322, 364–366
Planning bureaus, 331–332
Planning commissions, 332–333
Polaschek, R. J., 328
Political organization: citizen participation and, 263–268
    coordination problems, 259–263, 268–269
    major trends, 257–258
    new forms, 261–262
Pooley, Beverley, 328
Population: age distribution, 46
    family units, 56–57
    fertility, 67–68
    growth trends, 42–46, 74–75, 127–128
    marital status, 53–58
    minority group composition, 64–66, 99–102
    mortality, 67–68
    replacement of, 66–70, 74–75
    sex ratio, 49–52
Porter, John, 217
Power structure, 144–146
    changes in, 225–226
    earlier historical forms, 220–223
    economic organization and, 244–245, 268–269

Power structure (*continued*)
  operation of, 226–230
  in other nations, 231–233
  types of, 224–225, 233–234
Pred, Allen, 80, 97
Press, Charles, 232, 235
Priestley, Harold, 23
Prince, Hugh C., 330
Principled-secular type of society, 317
Prothro, James W., 264
Pushkarev, Boris, 326
Pye, Lucian W., 233

Queen, Stuart A., 12, 259, 285
Quinn, James A., 8–9, 51, 80, 83, 88, 93, 95,
  105, 129, 281

Radburn, N.J., 367–368, 371
Rainwater, Lee, 158
Ramsey, Charles E., 10, 166
Rand, Christopher, 364
Rank, Katherine H., 154
Ranney, Austin, 265–266
Rapkin, Chester, 349–350, 357, 359
Rashdall, Hastings, 22
Ratcliffe, Richard U., 93
Raths, James, 283
Rationalization as urban process, 139
Reckless, Walter C., 28, 277
Redick, Richard W., 100
Reed, Henry H., 362, 378
Reeder, Leo G., 179
Region, 5–6
  basic processes in, 136–146
  explanations of, 131–136
  inconsistencies in, 146–147, 363–364
  systematic features, 106–108, 126–129,
    143–146, 360–361
Reid, Margaret C., 249
Rein, Martin, 378
Reinsberg, Mark, 351
Reiss, Albert J., 31, 48, 51, 60, 65, 76, 109,
  119, 124, 218, 366
Reissman, Leonard, 111, 179, 187
Religion: components in, 274–275
  early urbanism and, 18–19
  social class and, 272–273, 276
  trends in modern urbanism, 25, 270–277
Reps, John W., 331, 342
Reston, Virginia, 373
Richards, Peter G., 330
Richardson, Jane, 305
Rickover, Hyman G., 282
Ridley, Clarence F., 124
Riesenberg, Peter, 21
Riesman, David, 171, 279, 296

Riessman, Frank, 208
Riley, John W., 302
Riley, Matilda, 302
Ringer, Benjamin B., 188, 276
Robson, William, 37, 81, 149, 258, 262, 314,
  330
Rodehaver, Myles W., 123
Rodwin, Lloyd, 370, 372
Roethlisberger, F. J., 163
Rogoff, Natalie, 211
Rooff, Madeline, 286
Rörig, Fritz, 21
Rose, Arnold M., 170, 173–174, 189, 215
Rosen, Bernard C., 212
Rosenberg, Bernard, 308
Rosenberg, Morris, 246, 295
Rosow, Irving, 169
Rossi, Peter, 149, 227, 279
Rossman, Joseph, 279
Rostovtzeff, Michael, 17–18, 20
Roy, Krishna, 50
Rubinstein, Nicolai, 222

Saarinen, Aline, 204, 374
Sacks, Seymour, 254
Salisbury, Harrison E., 166, 276
Samstag, Nicholas, 294
Sanders, Irwin T., 10
Satellite cities, 123–125
Savard, William G., 230
Sawers, David, 246
Sayre, Wallace, 138, 229, 233–234
Scaff, Alvin, 115, 185
Schachner, Nathan, 22
Schapera, I., 71, 285
Schermerhorn, Richard A., 145
Schmandt, Henry J., 226–227, 241, 269, 346
Schmid, Calvin F., 84
Schmitt, Robert C., 109
Schnore, Leo F., 8, 108, 113, 118–119, 124,
  378
Schorr, Alvin L., 346
Schramm, Wilbur, 302, 305, 310
Schriftgiesser, Karl, 245
Schyberger, B. W., 295
Scott, C. Winfield, 281
Sears, Robert R., 159, 171
Sectors, 83–84
Sée, Henri, 325
Seeley, John R., 115, 209–210
Seeman, Melvin, 212
Selbie, W. B., 271
Self, Peter, 261, 359, 370–371
Senior, Derek, 372–373
Sert, Jose L., 326, 365
Service, Elman, 317
Sewell, William H., 212

Shanas, Ethel, 161–162
Shannon, Lyle W., 278
Sheatsley, Paul, 308
Shevky, Eshref, 51–52, 85–86
Shister, Joseph, 215
Short, Alvin P., 170
Short, James F., 169
Shostak, Arthur B., 218
Shryock, Henry S., 73
Sidenbladh, Goran, 355
Sigafoos, R. A., 255–256
Silberstein, Fred B., 212
Silvert, Kalman H., 231
Simey, F. S., 111
Simmel, Georg, 33, 132, 194
Simon, Herbert A., 339
Sirjamaki, John, 155
Sitte, Camillo, 326
Sjoberg, Gideon, 37, 91
Sklar, Paul, 295
Slum clearance. See Housing
Smallwood, Frank, 226, 232, 262, 330
Smelser, Neil J., 200
Smerk, George M., 350
Smith, George H., 293
Smith, Joel, 164
Smith, Preserved, 284
Smith, Robert G., 262
Smuckler, R. H., 264
Social areas, 85–86
Social change, 320–321
Social class: class consciousness and, 215–216
    consumption patterns and, 250–253
    criteria in urban areas, 193–195
    mass media and, 306–307
    political participation and, 264–266
    rural areas and, 191–192
    social interactions and, 196, 215–217
    social mobility and, 195–196, 211–214
    status and, 190
    styles of life and, 197–210, 251
    taxation and, 255
Social mobility, 211–214, 252, 267
Social problems, 313–319, 321
    responses to, 315–317, 319
    transitional society and, 313
Social welfare, 283–290
Sofen, Edward, 262
Sombart, Werner, 134–135
Sosnovy, Timothy, 343
Southall, Aidan, 183
Specialization, 136–139, 141
Spectorsky, A. C., 125, 205, 300
Spencer, Herbert, 280, 285
Spencer, John, 111
Spengler, Joseph, 42

Spengler, Oswald, 11, 132
Spergel, Irving, 290
Spicer, Edward H., 278
Spiro, Herbert J., 249
Sprague, Theodore W., 215
Spreiregen, Paul D., 337
Stacey, Margaret, 189
Stanton, Frank, 276, 293, 302
Stanton, Richard L., 232
Stark, Rodney, 274, 291
Status phases, 210–212, 214
Stein, Clarence S., 366–368, 378
Stephenson, William, 308, 310
Stermer, James E., 322
Sternlieb, George, 103
Stevens, George P., 155
Stewart, Charles T., 326
Stillerman, Richard, 246
Stone, Gregory P., 164, 194
Stouffer, Samuel A., 154
Strauss, Gerald, 21, 222
Street, David, 283, 291
Streib, Gordon F., 161–162
Strodtbeck, Fred L., 169
Sturmthal, Adolph F., 249
Suburbanization: family types and, 116–118
    political participation and, 266–267
    population aspects of, 45, 48, 119
    role in urban regions, 119–121, 135
    stages of, 111–113
    status differences and, 214–215
    suburbs defined, 109
    types of, 109, 113–119
Sumner, William G., 285
Sussman, Leila, 295, 300
Sussman, Marvin B., 78, 161, 217
Sutherland, Edwin H., 148
Swain, Joseph W., 274
Swanson, Guy E., 159, 171
Sweetser, Frank L., 307

Taba, Hilda, 297
Taeuber, Irene, 47, 51, 71, 76
Tangent, Pierre, 191
Tawney, Richard H., 325
Taxation, 254–257
    income taxes, 256–257
    property taxes, 255–256
    sales taxes, 256
Taylor, George, 230
Taylor, Griffith, 31, 33, 37
Tetlow, John, 326, 355, 370
Theodorson, George A., 93, 105
Thijsse, Jac P., 377
Thometz, Carol E., 227–228
Thompson, James D., 145

Thompson, Laura, 285
Thompson, Ralph V., 183
Thompson, Warren S., 9
Thompson, Wilbur R., 241
Thrasher, Frederic M., 168–169, 171
Thrupp, Sylvia, 21, 248
Tien, H. Y., 213
Tikhomirov, M., 21
Tilly, Charles, 86
Toby, Jackson, 212, 314
Tomars, Adolph S., 187
Tout, Thomas F., 23
Traffic and transportation, 350–354, 357
  mass transit programs, 352–353
Trenaman, Joseph, 296
Trow, Martin, 283
Tumin, Melvin M., 33, 196, 306–308
Tunnard, Christopher, 326, 362, 378
Turner, Ralph, 15, 18, 174
Turner, R. Jay, 213
Tyrwhit, J., 326

Udry, J. Richard, 86
Ullman, Edward L., 26, 29, 79–80, 84, 362
Urban community, 12
  growth of, 29–31, 137
  location, 79–82
  modern types of, 33–37
  prerequisites of, 13–15
  relation to nation-state, 24, 27, 149
  stages of, 31–33, 75, 241–242
  urban waves, 15–25
Urban fringe, 121–123
Urban renewal, 347. See also Housing
  downtown development, 354–357
Useem, John, 191
Useem, Ruth H., 191

Vakie, C. N., 50
Valen, Henry, 213
Vance, James E., 84
Van Cleef, Eugene, 128
Verner, Coolie, 10
Vernon, Raymond, 130, 135
Viet, Jean, 378
Voluntary associations, 172
  family types and, 180–181
  features of, 172–173, 175–177, 187–188
  mass communications and, 301–302
  new nations and, 181–183
  social motivations and, 186–187
  status and, 179–180
  types of, 173–174
Von Eckardt, Wolf, 339
Von Rhode, Carl, 108

Von Stein, Lorenz, 238
Von Vorys, Karl, 233
Voss, J. Ellis, 30

Wade, Richard C., 9
Wagenfeld, Morton O., 213
Walker, Mabel, 102–103, 343
Walker, Robert A., 331–332, 337
Walker, S. H., 295
Walkey, Rosabelle, 169
Wallace, Anthony F. C., 274
Wallace, David, 266
Waller, Willard, W., 168
Wallin, Paul, 168
Walton, John, 224
Ware, Caroline, 9
Warner, Sam B., 110–111
Warner, W. Lloyd, 164, 176, 192, 201, 204,
  218, 297, 306
Warren, Robert O., 262
Weber, Adna, F., 27
Weber, Max, 8, 14, 16–18, 21, 27, 131–132,
  136, 220, 242, 259
Webster, Donald, 332, 337, 341–342
Wehrwin, George S., 122
Weilenmann, Hermann, 219
Weimer, Arthur M., 83
Weinberg, S. Kirson, 10
Wells, H. G., 318
Wendt, Paul F., 343
Wertenbaker, T. J., 314
Werthman, Carl, 111
West, James, 164, 191
Westoff, Charles E., 213
Whelpton, P. J., 161
Whetten, Nathan L., 109
White, David M., 308–309
White, Leslie A., 13–14, 27
Whiteman, Dorothy E., 359
Whiteside, Thomas, 294
Whittick, Arnold, 370–372, 375
Whyte, William F., 163, 168, 171, 215
Whyte, William H., 115, 148, 154, 163, 171,
  195, 205–206, 295, 303–304, 308
Wicklein, John, 271
Wilensky, Harold L., 212–213, 286–288, 290–
  291, 308
Willey, Gordon R., 13
Willhelm, Sidney M., 342
Williams, Gwyn A., 222
Williams, James H., 179
Williams, Marilyn, 51–52, 85–86
Williams, Oliver P., 226–227, 230
Williams, Robin M., 174–175, 188, 271
Williams, W. W., 191
Willmann, John B., 331

Willmott, Peter, 112, 208
Wilner, Daniel M., 346
Wilock, Linda L., 214
Wilson, Godfrey, 322
Wilson, James Q., 138, 348, 354
Wilson, Monica, 183–184, 322
Wingo, Lowdon, 113, 350
Winick, Charles, 283
Wirt, Frederick M., 266
Wirth, Louis, 28, 133–134
Witmer, Helen, 286
Wittfogel, Karl, 17
Wolfenstein, Martha, 160
Wolff, Kurt H., 33, 132
Wood, Robert C., 109, 111, 225, 235, 254, 256, 258, 269
Woodbury, Coleman T., 341, 359
Woytinsky, Emma S., 240
Wright, Charles R., 178–179, 184–185

Wurster, Catherine B., 130

Yablonsky, Lewis, 169
Young, Michael, 111–112, 208
Young, Pauline V., 84
Youngson, A. J., 37
Youth culture, 166–167

Zald, Mayer N., 291, 378
Zander, Alvin, 78
Zeigler, Harmon, 230, 264, 267, 269
Zimmer, Basil, 184, 186
Zimmerman, Carle C., 10, 316
Znaniecki, Florian, 7
Zollschan, George K., 320
Zoning, 340–342
Zorbaugh, Harvey W., 28, 82